FRENCH
CONNECTIONS

FRENCH CONNECTIONS

Hemingway and Fitzgerald Abroad

Edited by
J. Gerald Kennedy
and Jackson R. Bryer

St. Martin's Press
New York

ISBN 0-312-16364-9

Library of Congress Cataloging-in-Publication Data
French Connections : Hemingway and Fitzgerald abroad / edited by J.
Gerald Kennedy and Jackson R. Bryer.
    p. cm.
Includes bibliographical references (p.) and index.
ISBN 0-312-16364-9
    1. Hemingway, Ernest, 1899-1961—Friends and associates.
2. Fitzgerald, F. Scott (Francis Scott), 1896-1940—Homes and
haunts—France—Paris. 3. Fitzgerald, F. Scott (Francis Scott),
1896-1940—Friends and associates. 4. Hemingway, Ernest, 1899-1961-
-Homes and haunts—France—Paris. 5. Paris (France)—Intellectual
life—20th century. 6. Americans—France—Paris—History—20th
century. 7. Authors, American—20th century—Biography.
8. American literature—French influences. 9. Influence (Literary,
artistic, etc.) I. Kennedy, J. Gerald. II. Bryer, Jackson R.
PS3515.E37Z5942 1998
813'.5209—dc21
    [B]   97-49632
                                                             CIP

Design by Acme Art, Inc.
First edition: July, 1998
10 9 8 7 6 5 4 3 2 1

CONTENTS

Preface: Recovering the French Connections
of Hemingway and Fitzgerald vii
J. GERALD KENNEDY AND JACKSON R. BRYER

I. OVERVIEWS: TWO AMERICAN WRITERS IN PARIS

1. The Right Place at the Right Time 3
GEORGE WICKES

2. Fitzgerald's Blue Pencil 15
SCOTT DONALDSON

II. HEMINGWAY AND FRANCE

3. "Very Cheerful and Clean and Sane and Lovely":
Hemingway's "Very Pleasant Land of France" 33
H. R. STONEBACK

4. The Expatriate Predicament in *The Sun Also Rises* 61
ROBERT A. MARTIN

5. City of Brothelly Love: The Influence of Paris
and Prostitution on Hemingway's Fiction 75
CLAUDE CASWELL

6. A Shelter from *The Torrents of Spring* 101
WELFORD DUNAWAY TAYLOR

7. "In the temps de Gertrude": Hemingway, Stein,
and the Scene of Instruction at 27, rue de Fleurus 121
KIRK CURNUTT

8. The Other Paris Years of Ernest Hemingway: 1937 and 1938....141
WILLIAM BRAASCH WATSON

III. FITZGERALD AND FRANCE

9. Fitzgerald, Paris, and the Romantic Imagination 161
RUTH PRIGOZY

10. "France Was a Land": F. Scott Fitzgerald's
    Expatriate Theme in *Tender Is the Night* 173
    JOHN F. CALLAHAN

11. The Figure on the Bed: Difference and American Destiny
    in *Tender Is the Night* 187
    FELIPE SMITH

12. The Influence of France on Nicole Diver's Recovery
    in *Tender Is the Night* 215
    JACQUELINE TAVERNIER-COURBIN

IV. INTERTEXTUAL FRENCH CONNECTIONS

13. Strange Fruits in *The Garden of Eden*: "The Mysticism of Money,"
    The Great Gatsby—and *A Moveable Feast* 235
    JACQUELINE VAUGHT BROGAN

14. *The Sun Also Rises* as "A Greater Gatsby":
    "Isn't it pretty to think so" 257
    JAMES PLATH

15. Madwomen on the Riviera: The Fitzgeralds, Hemingway,
    and the Matter of Modernism 277
    NANCY R. COMLEY

16. The Metamorphosis of Fitzgerald's Dick Diver
    and Its Hemingway Analogs. 297
    ROBERT E. GAJDUSEK

17. Figuring the Damage: Fitzgerald's "Babylon Revisited"
    and Hemingway's "The Snows of Kilimanjaro" 317
    J. GERALD KENNEDY

Notes on Contributors 345

Index 349

PREFACE:

RECOVERING THE FRENCH CONNECTIONS OF HEMINGWAY AND FITZGERALD

J. GERALD KENNEDY AND JACKSON R. BRYER

About two weeks after the publication of *The Great Gatsby* (1925), Ernest Hemingway and F. Scott Fitzgerald met in the Dingo Bar on the rue Delambre in Paris, and from that memorable first encounter they maintained a complicated friendship that endured until Fitzgerald's fatal heart attack in Hollywood fifteen years later. Although they crossed paths on American soil six times from 1928 to 1937, their sustained contact in France—in 1925-1926 and again through much of 1929—determined the sometimes hilarious, sometimes resentful tenor of their relationship. Born of mutual admiration, envy, and implicit rivalry, the bond between them affected their writing for several crucial years. They joked with and parodied each other; they shared drinks and meals; they disclosed their fantasies and anxieties; they read each other's work and discussed it frankly. The younger Hemingway profited in several ways from Fitzgerald's tutelary influence and reached the productive peak of his career during the years bracketing their expatriate association, publishing two great novels and two powerful short-story collections in four years. Hemingway nevertheless proved a reluctant protégé and eventually turned the tables by becoming Fitzgerald's "artistic conscience." Soon after they first traded manuscripts, Fitzgerald began to sense his own failure; he experienced increasing "self-disgust" and worked erratically for eight agonizing years before completing his next novel. Infused with the drama of disintegration, *Tender Is the Night* emerged as Fitzgerald's most compelling novel, the belated fruit of his years of exile. For both Hemingway and Fitzgerald, the personal and literary relationship that grew between them in France and the imaginative attachments they formed with their second country affected their work in lasting ways. These French connections form the focus of this volume, which attempts to unravel the twisted skein of time and circumstance that linked two authors who profoundly influenced the form and substance of modern American fiction.

From their first conversation at the Dingo, Hemingway impressed Fitzgerald as "the real thing," a genuinely talented writer with invaluable personal experience—a man who had proved his courage under fire in the Great War that Fitzgerald himself had missed. Hemingway also got to Paris first: As a recruit for the Norton-Harjes ambulance corps, he spent a few exciting days in June 1918 racing around to the tourist sites while sporadic German shells fell on the city. Fitzgerald got his initial glimpse of Paris only after the war, when he spent a forgettable week there with his pregnant wife, Zelda, in the spring of 1921, ensconced in a fetid hotel room with an uncured goatskin they had purchased. Disappointed by his European tour, Fitzgerald admitted to Edmund Wilson that France made him "sick" and thought it unfortunate that Germany had not conquered continental Europe. From England, he sailed home to the United States in July a confirmed chauvinist.

Conversely, Hemingway's early taste of Paris made him eager to return; encouraged by Sherwood Anderson, he left a job with a trade newspaper in Chicago and, after marrying Hadley Richardson, sailed to France with her in late 1921, arriving in Paris a few days before Christmas. The couple found a tiny Left Bank apartment on the rue du Cardinal Lemoine near the Panthéon, and during the next nineteen months—when he was not traveling as a foreign correspondent for the *Toronto Star*—Hemingway worked to become a serious writer, making crucial literary connections with such expatriates as Gertrude Stein, Ezra Pound, James Joyce, and Sylvia Beach, owner of the Shakespeare and Company bookstore. After a five-month stint in Toronto, where their son was born in late 1923, the Hemingways returned to Paris in January 1924 and resettled in an apartment on the rue Notre-Dame-des-Champs in Montparnasse.

While Hemingway was establishing himself in France as a young writer to be reckoned with, Fitzgerald—sinking in debt and tiring of the Long Island social whirl—followed Wilson's advice to give Europe another chance. Taking advantage of favorable exchange rates, the Fitzgeralds spent the summer of 1924 on the Riviera, where they met the expatriate couple Gerald and Sara Murphy and where Zelda apparently indulged in a brief romance with a French aviator. They moved on to Rome in October, spending the winter there and in Capri, where Scott completed the final revisions of *Gatsby*. When they started north to Paris in April, driving a Renault whose roof had been cut away at Zelda's insistence, rain halted their progress in Lyon. The Fitzgeralds reached the capital by train; attracted by the glamour of the Right Bank, they rented an ostentatious apartment on the rue Tilsitt, close to the Arc de Triomphe.

Since the previous summer, rumors had reached Fitzgerald about the young Hemingway, who was writing for the *transatlantic review* and who was said to have a brilliant future. Shortly after arriving in Paris, the more established Fitzgerald sought out this prodigy at the recently opened Dingo. What transpired during that first conversation and on the subsequent road trip to Lyon to recover the Renault is the stuff of legend and scholarly conjecture. Hemingway constructed his own version of the events many years afterward, principally to contrast his own self-possession and savoir-faire with Fitzgerald's helplessness and imprudence. Although the two writers parted company during the summer months (the Fitzgeralds went to Antibes and the Hemingways to Spain), they were back in Paris together during the fall, with Fitzgerald now self-consciously playing the role of Hemingway's editorial advisor and agent.

The two writers responded to France and to the Parisian milieu in utterly different ways. Hemingway lived on the Left Bank and often walked the city's winding streets. He learned spoken French (and French slang), absorbing as much as he could about the forms and conventions, the phrases and gestures, that defined everyday French life. He appreciated the French reverence for literature and respect for writers; he borrowed books at Shakespeare and Company and read voraciously in nineteenth-century fiction. He also fancied himself a working-class connoisseur of French food and drink. He loved the cafés and liked to analyze the clientele; he quickly learned how to write in a crowded, noisy space. And he enjoyed the sporting scene in Paris, attending horse races, boxing matches, and bicycle races. Fitzgerald, on the other hand, viewed the streets of Paris mostly from the backseat of a taxi and never acquired great interest in the language or literature of France. First an inhabitant of the Right Bank and later of the Left, he liked the cafés and "American bars" that catered to expatriates, and he had a special fondness for the Ritz bar and the jazzy nightclubs of Montmartre. He mainly enjoyed the gaudy social spectacle of the city, although André Le Vot plausibly insists that Fitzgerald's stay in Paris caused him to turn from the literature of the past toward the new, modern idiom, mainly as he encountered it in painting, sculpture, and music. Overcoming an earlier prejudice, Fitzgerald later wrote, "France has the only two things toward which we drift as we grow older: intelligence and good manners." In both subtle and obvious ways, France marked the lives and careers of both writers.

From December 1925 until June 1926, Hemingway and Fitzgerald moved in different directions, the Fitzgeralds decamping to the Pyrenees (where Zelda received treatment for colitis) and then to Juan-les-Pins to be near the Murphys again. Hemingway spent most of the winter skiing in Austria—apart from a quick trip to New York—and returned to Paris, where he negotiated revisions in *The Sun Also Rises* and changes in his domestic life, having entered into a secret liaison with Pauline Pfeiffer. The Fitzgeralds and Hemingways saw each other on the Riviera for a few weeks in June in the company of the Murphys, and Scott gave Ernest shrewd advice about editing the new novel. When Pauline arrived to accompany the Hemingways and the Murphys to Spain for the *feria* at Pamplona in July, the end game in Hemingway's first marriage had begun; stopping by the Murphys' villa after the fiesta, Ernest and Hadley announced plans to separate. They departed for Paris to face the bleakness of a dying marriage, while the Fitzgeralds remained at Juan-les-Pins for several alcoholic months before sailing to America in December.

Aside from a meeting at the Yale-Princeton football game in November 1928 (following Hemingway's remarriage), the two authors did not meet again until 1929, when the Fitzgeralds returned to France and took an apartment in April on the rue Palatine near the Eglise St. Sulpice. They were unaware that Hemingway was living with Pauline in the same *quartier* on the rue Férou, just around the corner. Either to avoid Fitzgerald's pestering or because Pauline disliked Scott and Zelda, Hemingway tried to prevent Fitzgerald from learning his address and swore to secrecy their mutual friend, the editor Maxwell Perkins; but the two writers inevitably met and renewed their friendship. Eager to resume his role as literary advisor, Fitzgerald asked to see the typescript of Hemingway's new novel, *A Farewell to Arms*, and in June 1929 wrote a candid, nine-page letter outlining revisions that would significantly improve the work. Although Hemingway largely followed Fitzgerald's advice, the older writer's solicitude offended him, and in reply he scrawled at the end of the letter, "Kiss my ass EH." The summer of 1929 also witnessed the infamous boxing match between Hemingway and Canadian journalist Morley Callaghan, who flattened his tiring opponent when Fitzgerald, acting as timekeeper, forgot to signal the end of a round. In October both the Hemingways and the Fitzgeralds dined with Gertrude Stein, who goaded Ernest by praising Scott extravagantly. By the fall of 1929, however, Hemingway's new novel was winning great critical acclaim, and Fitzgerald faced an impending crisis in his own marriage. The increasingly unstable Zelda—who had accused Scott and Ernest of a homosexual relationship—pursued a belated career in ballet with a frenzy verging on madness. Then the stock market crashed, and suddenly, almost overnight, "the most expensive orgy in history" (as Fitzgerald called the riotous decade of the 1920s) was over. The Hemingways sold their apartment and left Paris in early 1930, retreating back to Key West; the Fitzgeralds remained in France, caught in a cycle of manic antagonism, until Zelda's mental breakdown and subsequent hospitalization in Switzerland. For both writers, nothing was ever quite the same again.

As their careers diverged, Hemingway and Fitzgerald kept in touch mostly through occasional letters. After the appearance of Fitzgerald's 1935 "Crack-up" pieces in *Esquire*, Hemingway delivered a satirical slap in the same magazine with a reference (in "The Snows of Kilimanjaro") to "poor Scott Fitzgerald" and his delusions about the rich. Stung by public ridicule, Fitzgerald wrote from North Carolina, asking his old crony to "lay off [him] in print." The two met twice, briefly, during the summer of 1937 at gala events in New York and Hollywood, although Fitzgerald wrote after the first encounter: "I don't feel I know you at all." They continued to refer to each other in letters to mutual acquaintances, but direct correspondence appears to have ceased after Fitzgerald's telegram in 1937 praising Ernest's involvement in Joris Ivens's film *The Spanish Earth*. The screening of that film marked their final personal encounter. In 1939 Hemingway asked Max Perkins to convey to Fitzgerald his "great affection," though in the same postscript he made clear enough his own sense of "superiority." He was living in Cuba, reveling in the success of *For Whom the Bell Tolls*, when he learned of Fitzgerald's death in Hollywood. Oddly enough, both writers returned imaginatively to Paris near the end of their lives—Fitzgerald in a cinematic treatment of "Babylon Revisited" shortly before his heart attack and Hemingway in three long works left unfinished at his suicide in 1961: *Islands in the Stream, The Garden of Eden*, and *A Moveable Feast*. The passionate years of their closest association in France marked for each an epoch of lost happiness that had ironically produced some of their most brilliant fiction.

The impetus for this volume and the original source of many of the essays was the Hemingway/Fitzgerald International Conference held in Paris, July 3-8, 1994. The essays by Wickes, Stoneback, Martin, Caswell, Taylor, Curnutt, Watson, Prigozy, Smith, Tavernier-Courbin, Brogan, Plath, and Gajdusek began as papers delivered on that occasion; they appear here substantially expanded for publication. The pieces by Donaldson, Callahan, Comley, and Kennedy were written expressly for this book.

The collection is divided into four sections. The first, "Overviews: Two American Writers in Paris," establishes the background and context for the remainder of the volume. George Wickes, in "The Right Place at the Right Time," provides an authoritative portrait of Paris in the 1920s and indicates what made the city so attractive to American artists and writers of the day. He also suggests how Hemingway and Fitzgerald related to the city in very different ways, how they utilized it in their fiction; and he describes the literary alliances both men—especially Hemingway—formed during their sojourns there. "Fitzgerald's Blue Pencil" by Scott Donaldson focuses more closely on the Fitzgerald-Hemingway relationship in 1925-1926, recounting the editorial assistance Fitzgerald provided Hemingway on *The Sun Also Rises*. Drawing on both published and unpublished sources, Donaldson speculates on the complicated nature of the friendship and describes the different ways in which they remembered the events of the mid-1920s later in their lives.

The second section of the book, "Hemingway and France," begins with H. R. Stoneback's "'Very Cheerful and Clean and Sane and Lovely': Hemingway's 'Very Pleasant Land of France,'" which broadens the usual focus on Hemingway's relationship with France not by looking principally at his associations with and depictions of Paris but rather with the rest of France. Stoneback begins by documenting Hemingway's extensive travels through the France outside of Paris and then examines how he used this familiarity as "symbolic landscape" or "*paysage moralisé*" in his short stories and, especially, in *The Sun Also Rises*. The latter is the primary subject of Robert A. Martin's "The Expatriate Predicament in *The Sun Also Rises*," which deals with the "Americanness" of the three principal American expatriates in the novel—Robert Cohn, Bill Gorton, and Jake Barnes—and how it affects their actions while they are abroad. Seeing them as "representative Americans in Paris during the expatriate period" who demonstrate "the best and worst qualities of Americans abroad," Martin shows how each reacts to the expatriate experience in a different manner. As such, they provide us with "a historical view of the expatriates."

Claude Caswell's "City of Brothelly Love" examines the highly original topic of how the subculture of prostitution in Paris preoccupied Hemingway and ultimately became the basis for his dramatic explorations of the nature of love in a mercenary world. Like Martin, he looks closely at *The Sun Also Rises*; but his attention is directed at one of the novel's minor female characters, the prostitute Georgette Hobin, and at how the "physical and psychological territory of prostitution" is at the heart of the novel, as well as a subject Hemingway explored throughout his writing career.

Turning from what is probably Hemingway's most-studied novel to what is perhaps his least-studied, Welford Dunaway Taylor, in "A Shelter from *The Torrents of Spring*," suggests that Hemingway's voracious reading of Russian masters such as Turgenev—in books obtained from Sylvia Beach's lending library—created an intense "anxiety of influence" that caused him to repudiate his models. In evoking Paris in *Torrents*, Taylor argues, Hemingway showed his contempt for Sherwood Anderson's supposed provincialism and pseudosophistication. This essay presents a plausible new answer to the question of why Hemingway chose to write, in *Torrents*, such a blatantly cruel parody of Anderson, one of his mentors.

Hemingway's most important literary friendship in Paris was with Gertrude Stein, who plays a minor role in Taylor's account. Kirk Curnutt's "'In the temps de Gertrude'" moves beyond the public attacks on Hemingway in Stein's *The Autobiography of Alice B. Toklas* and on Stein in Hemingway's *A Moveable Feast*, using lesser-known essays and unpublished manuscript fragments to shed new light on this volatile relationship. Curnutt argues that memories of this Parisian friendship haunted Hemingway, producing recurrent confrontations with the specter of Stein in his art.

The final essay in the "Hemingway and France" section moves from Hemingway in Paris in the 1920s to the less-studied period he spent there in 1937 and 1938. William Braasch Watson's "The Other Paris Years of Ernest Hemingway" begins by evoking Paris in the late 1930s—a very different Paris from that in the 1920s—and Hemingway in the 1930s—a very different Hemingway from the young ambitious writer of the 1920s. Watson then looks at the eight Spanish Civil War stories Hemingway wrote during his 1937 and 1938 visits to the city, seeing them as critical to his development as a writer in that they provided a transition from his less successful narratives of the 1930s to the very successful *For Whom the Bell Tolls* in 1940.

The third section of the book, "Fitzgerald and France," opens with Ruth Prigozy's "Fitzgerald, Paris, and the Romantic Imagination," which suggests, through a wide-ranging examination of his fictional depictions of Paris, that, for Fitzgerald, the specific, realistic details of place were less meaningful than locale as an imaginative distillation of sources from popular culture and tourism, from romantic poetry, and from his own Emersonian projection into a self-centered "world elsewhere."

John F. Callahan's "'France Was a Land': F. Scott Fitzgerald's Expatriate Theme in *Tender Is the Night*" is the first of three essays on Fitzgerald's only full-length fiction with a French setting. It examines the role played by France in *Tender* and suggests that Fitzgerald's lyrical treatment of the vital ground of that country indicates why America ceases to be a true home or homeland for Dick Diver and for so many other characters in the novel. Similarly, Felipe Smith, in "The Figure on the Bed: Difference and American Destiny in *Tender Is the Night*," deals with Fitzgerald's treatment of Paris in the novel, utilizing a close examination of its manuscript history combined with material drawn from his essays, correspondence, and other writings of the

1930s. Smith attempts to "reconstruct the conceptual evolution of the published novel's intersecting concerns with nationality, race, ethnicity, gender, and sexuality" and sees the murder of Jules Peterson, a black European, in a Paris hotel as a crucial episode and the crux of these concerns. Jacqueline Tavernier-Courbin also is interested in the influence of the French setting in *Tender*; but her focus in "The Influence of France on Nicole Diver's Recovery in *Tender Is the Night*" is, as her title suggests, on the several ways in which France contributes to Nicole's coming to terms with the psychological trauma of incest.

The book's fourth section, "Intertextual French Connections," begins with Jacqueline Vaught Brogan's "Strange Fruits in *The Garden of Eden*," an investigation of Hemingway's ongoing compulsion to top Fitzgerald in writing "the great novel of money," something that the latter had accomplished in *The Great Gatsby*. It takes as its basic text a little-known but important essay, "The Mysticism of Money" (published in a 1922 issue of *Broom*), by Harold Loeb, whom both Fitzgerald and Hemingway knew in Paris. Brogan shows how Fitzgerald (in *Gatsby*) followed Loeb's tenets and how Hemingway (in both *The Garden of Eden* and *A Moveable Feast*) strove to surpass *Gatsby*. James Plath, in "*The Sun Also Rises* as 'A Greater Gatsby,'" also deals with Hemingway's efforts to compete with Fitzgerald; but where Brogan sees Hemingway "rewriting" *Gatsby* in *The Garden of Eden*, Plath suggests that the same process took place in *The Sun Also Rises*. His essay explores the similarities between the two novels, considers the strained friendship between Fitzgerald and Hemingway, and asserts what no previous critic has claimed—that *The Sun Also Rises* may, in fact, have started as a deliberate parody of *Gatsby*.

The next two essays both see similarities between *The Garden of Eden* and *Tender Is the Night*. In "Madwomen on the Riviera," Nancy R. Comley posits an intertextual network between the two novels and Zelda Fitzgerald's *Save Me the Waltz*, in all of which the Riviera functions as a site of origination with an Edenic promise. The three novels, Comley points out, present stories featuring a writer/artist figure and a wife who, while not certifiably insane, is unhappy at being shut out of her husband's creative life and is in search of an outlet for her own energies. Robert E. Gajdusek's "The Metamorphosis of Fitzgerald's Dick Diver and Its Hemingway Analogs" discusses androgyny and sexual role reversals in *The Garden of Eden* and *Tender Is the Night*. Gajdusek sees *Tender* uncovering an important pattern in twentieth-century culture (and one more evident in Paris of the 1920s than elsewhere): the collapse of patriarchal authority and the rise of a matriarchate. Hemingway then used Fitzgerald's novel almost as a model in *Garden*, in which, according to

Gajdusek, he also perceived a sexual/cultural transformation and elaborated his own version of role-switching and metamorphosis.

The final essay in the book, J. Gerald Kennedy's "Figuring the Damage," challenges the conventional view that expatriate literary life was generally "liberating, productive, and transformative" by showing how in two great short stories of the 1930s, Fitzgerald and Hemingway each reassessed the personal damage incurred during their "crazy years" in Paris. Kennedy examines "Babylon Revisited," in which Fitzgerald uses a remarkably precise symbolic geography to expose Charlie Wales's persistent attachment to his alcoholic past, and "The Snows of Kilimanjaro," where Hemingway uses memories of life on the Left Bank to hint at the secret turning point in a writer's self-destruction.

Taken as a whole, these seventeen essays show how, when critics who are conversant with previous scholarship look at Fitzgerald and Hemingway through a French lens, often utilizing little-known or newly discovered manuscripts and letters, the results are pieces that break new ground either by dealing with subjects hitherto unstudied or understudied or by correcting earlier assessments. They also reemphasize the important role France played in the lives and works of these two writers, and they cast further light on the complex and often puzzling personal and creative relationship of two of this country's greatest modern literary artists.

This book would not have been published were it not for the confident enthusiasm for the project and the patience consistently displayed by Michael Flamini of St. Martin's Press. For significant help in the preparation of the manuscript, we wish to thank Marc Singer and Alan Margolies.

For Roger Asselineau

in appreciation of his ground-breaking contributions
to Franco-American literary relations and in gratitude for his many
kindnesses to the editors of this volume

PART I

OVERVIEWS:
TWO AMERICAN WRITERS
IN PARIS

THE RIGHT PLACE AT THE RIGHT TIME

G E O R G E   W I C K E S

"You're an expatriate. You've lost touch with the soil. You get precious.
Fake European standards have ruined you. You drink yourself to death.
You become obsessed with sex. You spend all your time talking, not
working. You are an expatriate, see? You hang around cafés."

T hat's one view of the life being led by the writers who went to Paris in
the 1920s, with its damning conclusion: "Nobody that ever left their own
country ever wrote anything worth printing. Not even in the newspapers"
(Hemingway, *Sun* 115). By the time he wrote this bit of dialogue, Hemingway was in a good position to ridicule the assumptions of the folks back
home, having clearly demonstrated by his own achievements that their
clichés about expatriation were all wrong.

A very different view was expressed by Gertrude Stein when she said,
"Paris was where the twentieth century was"—the great international center
of the creative arts. "So Paris was the place that suited those of us that were
to create the twentieth-century art and literature, naturally enough" (*Paris
France* 11, 12). The trouble with the word "expatriate" is that, like its

common misspelling, it suggests that one has renounced one's native land, whereas the case of Gertrude Stein proves that one could live abroad indefinitely and still remain as American as Ulysses S. Grant or Susan B. Anthony. As she liked to say, "America is my country but Paris is my home town . . ." ("An American and France" 61).

Hemingway made a somewhat similar remark in a letter to Sherwood Anderson: ". . . Americans are always in America—no matter whether they call it Paris or Paname . . ." (*Selected Letters* 218). For more than six years Paris was Hemingway's hometown (even though he was away more often than not), and like many other American writers and would-be writers he found it easy to feel at home there. A recent book, Arlen Hansen's *Expatriate Paris*, the latest of several such studies, takes a survey of the hotels and streets and neighborhoods where they lived, creating the illusion that the city was populated by American writers. And for many who remained within a small orbit, Montparnasse might as well have been an American village. The French waiters and shopkeepers and concierges merely provided a picturesque backdrop, and while a certain number of French phrases were useful, English was the language of most of the people they encountered in "the Quarter." In fact, Hemingway may have intended a swipe at those who affected too much fluency when they called the city by its French nickname, Paname.

It is easy to understand why so many Americans were drawn to Paris in the 1920s. Most obviously in Hemingway's case, it was a better hometown than Oak Park. For young Americans Paris provided an escape from the puritanism and provincialism of postwar America, of which Prohibition was simply the most conspicuous manifestation—the America of Harding and Coolidge, of William Jennings Bryan and Wayne B. Wheeler. Paris was where you could go on a moral holiday without fear of reproach, where the natives did not confuse pleasure with sin.

Fitzgerald, who never felt as completely at home in Paris as Hemingway, nevertheless found it easy to shed his inhibitions there and found Paris a better place in which to carouse than New York. Twice during his first sojourn he summed up his life there as "1000 parties and no work" (*Ledger* 179). Later he immortalized the dissipations of the 1920s in one of his finest stories, "Babylon Revisited." Hemingway may have lived more soberly, but he too put dissipation to literary use in *The Sun Also Rises*. And in his Paris memoirs he celebrated the pleasures of eating and drinking as few American writers have done.

Then too, for Americans the cost of living was amazingly low. Not only did Paris offer food and wine beyond the imagination of Gopher Prairie, but they cost hardly more than a sandwich and a soft drink at the local drugstore. (In "Babylon Revisited," Charlie Wales thinks with regret: "He had never eaten at a really cheap restaurant in Paris. Five-course dinner, four francs fifty, eighteen cents, wine included" [*Stories* 618].) All through the boom time of the 1920s the dollar was worth much more in France than it was at home, and the number of francs to the dollar only increased as the decade advanced. Besides, the trip over on the transatlantic steamers was cheap. No wonder Americans went in unprecedented numbers.

In the 1920s that American colony was the best place for a young writer to be, and no one took fuller advantage of its opportunities than Ernest Hemingway. There he served his literary apprenticeship under the best possible mentors, there he discovered a community of like-minded spirits dedicated to the arts, there he met editors and publishers willing to accept his works when no press or magazine back home would consider them. From the start he had a gift for ingratiating himself with the right people, learning all they had to teach him, then going beyond them after making what he had learned his own. Of course he had talent and discipline as well as the ability to make the most of his opportunities. But nowhere else could he have found such opportunities in such abundance. There is no doubt that Paris played a crucial role in his emergence as a writer. When he arrived, in December 1921, only twenty-two and as yet unpublished (except for journalism), he had nothing to distinguish him from the multitude of aspiring writers who flocked to Paris. By the time he left, in March 1928, he was the famous author of *The Sun Also Rises* and two impressive collections of short stories.

Gertrude Stein was the first of his conquests. Whatever each may have written about the other afterward, there is no doubt that they were very thick during the first few years of their acquaintance and that he learned much about writing from her. Stein had been ensconced in her studio at 27, rue de Fleurus since 1903 and was by this time quite an institution. If nothing else, her painting collection was a revelation to one who had never laid eyes on a Cézanne, much less a Picasso—this at a time when hardly any contemporary painting was accessible to the public. (The Chicago Art Institute, for instance, did not acquire a Cézanne until 1926, and Hemingway could see more Cézannes chez Stein than at the Musée du Luxembourg [Rewald 61].) Just as she had discovered twentieth-century art, so Stein claimed to have invented twentieth-century literature, and certainly her experimental writings were also a revelation. Her famous style was contagious, as Hemingway and a number of other writers found, and though they might scoff and ridicule, they could not dismiss her. Chiefly she was a formidable presence, holding forth with great authority, like a kind of Delphic oracle or latter-day Samuel Johnson. To sit at her feet was an education in itself.

Ezra Pound was another literary dictator Hemingway cultivated. Pound, who had spent a dozen years in England before shifting his operations to Paris, had all sorts of connections in the Anglo-American literary world. The great instigator and patron of the arts, he was tireless in promoting, advising, cajoling, and badgering editors and writers to do what he thought best for them. He knew everyone and introduced everyone to everyone else, especially writers to editors. More than anyone else he discovered new talent and saw that it was published. As Hemingway wrote in *A Moveable Feast*, "Ezra Pound was always a good friend and he was always doing things for people" (107).

Pound was a good friend to have, not only as a sponsor but also as a critic and disciplinarian at a timely moment in Hemingway's writing career. John Peale Bishop, whom Pound introduced to Hemingway in 1922, remembered: "In Paris, Hemingway submitted much of his apprentice work in fiction to Pound. It came back to him blue-penciled, most of the adjectives gone. The comments were unsparing. Writing for a newspaper was not at all the same as writing for a poet." Incidentally, Bishop also quotes Hemingway as saying: "Ezra was right half the time, and when he was wrong, he was so wrong you were never in doubt about it. Gertrude was always right" (40-41). Whatever their respective merits, both Pound and Stein proved to be the best teachers young Hemingway could have found.

It was Pound who persuaded James Joyce to move from Zurich to Paris, and Joyce remained all through the 1920s and 1930s. That awesome presence alone, and of course the publication of *Ulysses* in 1922, made Paris the capital of the literary world for many young writers, Hemingway and Fitzgerald among them. Hemingway may have read only half of *Ulysses* (as the uncut leaves of his copy suggest), but he knew immediately that it was "a most god-damn wonderful book" (*Selected Letters* 62), and for the rest of his life he referred to Joyce with a respect he usually reserved only for dead writers. Similarly, Fitzgerald listed Joyce's *Portrait of the Artist as a Young Man* among the "10 Best Books I Have Read" and characterized *Ulysses* as "the great novel of the future" (Bruccoli 178). Both regarded Joyce with reverence, as did most American writers of their generation.

Not only was Paris the only place where Joyce could find a publisher for *Ulysses*, but it was also the place where *Finnegans Wake* could be published serially under his supervision as it was being written. Credit for both publications belongs to dedicated Americans. Sylvia Beach published *Ulysses* at no profit to herself, willingly making her bookshop Joyce's headquarters and herself his doormat. Similarly, the editors of *transition* made their literary magazine the house organ for Joyce's "Work in Progress" and themselves his "adulators, imitators, editors, translators, and explainers," to quote the irreverent opinion of Joyce's most frequent drinking companion, Robert McAlmon (344).

Another influential elder who liked to consort with young Americans was Ford Madox Ford. Finding France more congenial, Ford left England for good in 1922 and lived in Paris off and on for the rest of his life. (He spent part of each year in Provence, but to the expatriates all of France could be considered an annex to Paris.) Here over a period of four years he wrote the four volumes of his great war novel *Parade's End*. Here he also launched and edited one of the best literary magazines, *transatlantic review*, and while it lasted only a year before running out of funds, it published the writing of many young Americans as well as groundbreaking works by the four most prominent writers then living in Paris: two of Pound's cantos, installments of Gertrude Stein's *The Making of Americans* (at Hemingway's instigation), part of the first volume of Ford's tetralogy, and the first selection from a new work by Joyce to appear in print, christened by Ford "Work in Progress." Joyce was so pleased with the title that he kept the real title a mystery for fifteen years until *Finnegans Wake* finally appeared as a book (Ellmann 563).

Along with Pound and Stein, Ford played an important role in the literary apprenticeship of Ernest Hemingway, one that has generally been underestimated. On Pound's advice Ford engaged Hemingway as subeditor, and while Hemingway soon lost patience with Ford's posturing, he continued to work on the *transatlantic review* and took the opportunity to have the first three Nick Adams stories to appear in print published there. Ford, an incurable mythomaniac, liked to play the role of Tory squire and literary godfather to *les jeunes*, so it is easy to understand Hemingway's irritation. But a young writer could learn much by associating with a literary man of the world who had known Henry James and Stephen Crane, collaborated with Joseph Conrad on three novels, and edited the best literary magazine of prewar London. And there is good reason to suspect that Ford's influence went beyond literary savoir faire, that Hemingway studied Ford's war novel as it was being written and applied the lessons he learned when he wrote his own: The only known typescript of the second volume, *No More Parades*, with many corrections in Ford's hand, ended up in Hemingway's possession (Young and Mann 122).

Of course Ford appears as a character in *The Sun Also Rises* and again in *A Moveable Feast*. And in writing his memoirs Hemingway may well have had Ford's in mind as well as Gertrude Stein's. The preface to *A Moveable Feast* with its much-quoted disclaimer, "If the reader prefers, this book may be regarded as fiction," echoes Ford's preface to his volume of reminiscence covering some of the same ground: "I have tried then to write a novel drawing my material from my own literary age" (6). And if Hemingway intended to announce bluntly, as the manuscripts indicate (Tavernier-Courbin 137), that his book was fiction, then he was even closer to Ford. *It Was the Nightingale* was one of the five books by Ford in Hemingway's library, three of them devoted to literary reminiscence (Reynolds 125-26). Ford, "the great Reminiscer," as Samuel Putnam called him (119), was a notorious fictionalizer of his memories; that was one reason Hemingway resented him. They may have had too much in common.

As the record of the *transatlantic review* and *transition* indicates, Montparnassse was the center of a publishing industry that played an important role in literary history. In addition to these two, half a dozen other literary magazines were published or edited there in the 1920s, and the best place to find the editors was one of the sidewalk cafés on the Boulevard Montparnasse, like the Dôme, which was the favorite hangout of all the Americans who gravitated to the Left Bank. In Hemingway's case the most receptive, besides the *transatlantic review*, were the *Little Review*, edited by Margaret Anderson and Jane Heap, and *This Quarter*, edited by Ernest Walsh. Most of the literary magazines were short-lived or irregular in their appearance or self-congratulatory, displaying the talents of their editors and friends. But a genuine dedication to literature motivated all those who founded and supported the "little magazines," and all of them had as their guiding purpose the discovery of new geniuses. For unknown writers who were rejected by magazine editors back home, the literary magazines offered the best chance of publication with the hope of eventually coming to the attention of New York critics and publishers. Such was Hemingway's case. Until Scribners published *The Sun Also Rises*, his stories were rejected by *Harper's*, the *Saturday Evening Post*, *Vanity Fair*, *Collier's*, the *New Masses*, even by *The Dial* and the *American Mercury*.

In addition to the privately subsidized literary magazines, there were privately subsidized presses in Paris. Of these the most notable were the Three Mountains Press, founded by journalist William Bird when he acquired a hand press and began publishing limited editions under Pound's guidance, and the Contact Publishing Company, launched by writer Robert McAlmon when his wealthy father-in-law gave him £14,000, a fortune in those days (Ford, *Published in Paris* 95, 45). Like the literary magazines, these little presses lasted only a few years, but they rendered invaluable service. There were other private presses in Paris later in the 1920s, but these two did the most to break new ground. Chiefly they are remembered, along with the literary magazines, as Hemingway's first publishers.

The best place to find the literary magazines and publications of the private presses was Sylvia Beach's bookshop, Shakespeare and Company. Along with Pound, Beach was the most generous and selfless in aiding and abetting writers. Though she consented only to publish Joyce, she was more than willing to render all kinds of services for other writers. Shakespeare and Company was their club, where they could meet other writers, receive their mail, cash their checks, even borrow money, and Sylvia Beach was their fairy godmother, always willing to help when they were in trouble. The bookstore was also a lending library, and its library cards provide an interesting record of the borrowers and what they borrowed. And finally, it was a kind of literary shrine with its photographs of writers living and dead and its premises permeated by the odor of sanctity surrounding the presence of James Joyce. Young writers who were too shy to meet him (like Thornton Wilder [Fitch 82] or William Faulkner [Hansen 96]) could go there in hopes of catching a glimpse of the great man, and of course to buy his famous banned book, published by Beach in one edition after another all through the 1920s and into the 1930s. Of all those who helped Hemingway in Paris, Sylvia Beach is the only one to emerge unscathed from the pages of *A Moveable Feast*.

Fitzgerald came to Paris as a successful writer who never had to go through the struggles experienced by Hemingway. As a result he was not much involved in the literary life of Montparnasse with its "cuckoo" literary magazines and "bogus" publishers (as he regarded them [Kuehl and Bryer 131, 135]). But he was aware of what was going on there, for he wrote to Maxwell Perkins recommending Hemingway for his writings published in the *transatlantic review* and lower-case *in our time* six months before he and Hemingway actually met (Kuehl and Bryer 78). Then, when Fitzgerald went up to Paris, they became good friends and saw much of each other. Fitzgerald also made friends with Gertrude Stein and Sylvia Beach at this time (1925), but would have little to do with other Left Bank literary figures. Joyce he venerated from afar but did not meet until three years later.

Fitzgerald made four trips to Europe during the 1920s and spent something like three years in France all told, a bit less than two years of that time in Paris (Le Vot 49)—almost as much time as Hemingway actually spent there (Asselineau 29). But his Paris was the Right Bank of the rich Americans rather than the Left Bank of the bohemians. Though he was willing to drink with Hemingway in Left Bank cafés, his favorite resort was the Ritz, and he liked to spend his nights partying in the cabarets of Montmartre. Bricktop, the black singer and dancer who ran the most famous of these nightclubs, remembers him fondly but recalls especially how he threw money around: "Money burned in his pocket. When he'd go out for an evening, he'd stuff his pockets with bills. . . . He would usually stay out partying until all that money was spent" (95). Bricktop goes on to contribute a few anecdotes to the annals of Fitzgerald's drunken antics in Paris. Fitzgerald himself commemorates a few that may or may not be fictitious in "Babylon Revisited" and *Tender Is the Night.*

As he put it in "Echoes of the Jazz Age," he belonged to that portion of the population that lived "with the insouciance of grand ducs and the casualness of chorus girls" (21). Or as Charlie Wales reflects in "Babylon Revisited," "We were a sort of royalty, almost infallible, with a sort of magic around us," summing up in that statement the privileged status of Americans with money. But he also observes ruefully, "I spoiled this city for myself" (*Stories* 619, 618).

Fitzgerald may have lamented the waste of those years in real life as in his fiction, but they were not entirely wasted. He had gone to Europe in 1924 with the idea of getting away from the hectic life he was leading on Long Island and finding a good place to work. And indeed he succeeded in writing *The Great Gatsby* in one sustained stretch on the Riviera. It was only when he went to Paris that he got caught up in "1000 parties." Yet even then he managed to finish one of his best and longest stories, "The Rich Boy," and began gathering material that eventually went into *Tender Is the Night.*

Thus, in several of his writings the chronicler of the Jazz Age became the chronicler of expatriation in the second half of the 1920s, from the heyday of the summer Riviera, to Lindbergh's heroic flight across the Atlantic, to the ever-increasing invasion of tourists: " . . . by 1928 Paris had grown suffocating. With each new shipment of Americans spewed up by the boom the quality fell off, until toward the end there was something sinister about the crazy boatloads" ("Echoes" 20). In "Babylon Revisited" he takes his reader on a guided tour of Paris nightlife, and in *Tender Is the Night* he conducts another tour, this one of the daytime Paris familiar to affluent Americans—the Right Bank world of first-class hotels, restaurants, and shops, with a visit to one of the American banks. This is the most comprehensive novel about the expatriate life, at least as Fitzgerald lived it, at once a celebration of its best moments and an elegy for its demise, beginning in the magical world created by Gerald and Sara Murphy on the Riviera and trailing off at the end with every expatriate's fate when the time came to return to Batavia, Geneva, Hornell, or even smaller, more godforsaken towns.

During his last and longest sojourn in France—a period extending from 1929 to 1931—the *Saturday Evening Post* published five of his stories about the life of rich Americans in Paris. This was, of course, the time of the stock market crash, not to mention the crumbling of Fitzgerald's personal world, and the stories reflect the end of an era, with characters ending in defeat, disillusionment, and drink.

When Fitzgerald first went to Paris in April 1925 (the month *The Great Gatsby* was published), he was at the very peak of his career, while Hemingway was still awaiting the galleys of his first book to be published in America. Yet Hemingway's star was on the rise while Fitzgerald's was about to begin its decline, and the story of their friendship that began so well was to resume disastrously a few years later during that summer of 1929 in Paris chronicled by Morley Callaghan and was never to be the same again. Paris brought them together, and though they had much in common as fellow writers, they were temperamentally very different and seemed to inhabit entirely different worlds.

In the ideal world of Fitzgerald's fiction one stayed in a grand hotel like the George V, lunched in the Bois de Boulogne, collected mail and cashed checks at the Morgan Bank in the place Vendôme, shopped in the rue de Rivoli and the rue de Castiglione, conveniently located near the Ritz bar. His characters seldom cross the Seine and then only with a sense of adventure. Conversely, Hemingway's characters tend to confine their activities to the other side of the river, frequenting the Dingo Bar and the cafés of the Boulevard du Montparnasse. True, Jake Barnes crosses the river to go to work and as a newspaperman is at home in the Crillon bar, but the Latin Quarter is his natural habitat.

While Fitzgerald dwells on the beauty and glamour of Paris, even in stories dealing with failure, Hemingway often goes out of his way to emphasize its ugliness. Compare a familiar passage from "Babylon Revisited":

> Outside, the fire-red, gas-blue, ghost-green signs shone smokily through the tranquil rain. It was late afternoon and the streets were in movement; the *bistros* gleamed. At the corner of the Boulevard des Capucines he took a taxi. The Place de la Concorde moved by in pink majesty; they crossed the logical Seine, and Charlie felt the sudden provincial quality of the Left Bank. (*Stories* 617)

with this one at the very beginning of *A Moveable Feast*:

> Then there was the bad weather. It would come in one day when the fall was over. We would have to shut the windows in the night against the rain and the cold wind would strip the leaves from the trees in the

Place Contrescarpe. The leaves lay sodden in the rain and the wind drove the rain against the big green autobus at the terminal and the Café des Amateurs was crowded and the windows misted over from the heat and the smoke inside. It was a sad, evilly run café where the drunkards of the quarter crowded together and I kept away from it because of the smell of dirty bodies and the sour smell of drunkenness. (3)

Of course Fitzgerald was catering to the popular expectations of *Saturday Evening Post* readers, while Hemingway was creating a personal legend in describing the squalor of his humble beginnings as a writer. And after all, disillusioned realism was his trademark, just as lyricism was Fitzgerald's. *A Moveable Feast* gives a clear picture of what Paris meant to Hemingway to the end of his life: the scene of his early struggles to master his craft. True, the picture is colored by a nostalgia that romanticizes a bohemian life of poverty, professing that hunger was good discipline, and distorted by a fierce compulsion to denigrate other writers who helped him in those years. Regardless, the book makes it clear that he found Paris "the town best organized for a writer to write in that there is" (182). "Work" is the key word of that book, repeated over and over with an insistence worthy of Gertrude Stein.

Fitzgerald left no such memoirs, no literary last will and testament. His memories of Paris are to be found only in his fiction, and his final summing up could well be something like: "I talk with the authority of failure—Ernest with the authority of success" (Bruccoli 425). His key word could well be taken from "Babylon Revisited": " . . . and he suddenly realized the meaning of the word 'dissipate'—to dissipate into thin air; to make nothing out of something" (*Stories* 620). Yet for all his dissipation, Fitzgerald actually did succeed in making something out of his wasted life in Paris, and the writings that resulted show that he too put his time there to good use; he too was in the right place at the right time.

WORKS CITED

Asselineau, Roger. "Hemingway in Paris." *Fitzgerald/Hemingway Annual 1973*: 11-32.

Bishop, John Peale. *The Collected Essays of John Peale Bishop.* New York: Scribners, 1948.

Bricktop, with James Haskins. *Bricktop.* New York: Atheneum, 1983.

Bruccoli, Matthew J. *Some Sort of Epic Grandeur: The Life of F. Scott Fitzgerald.* New York: Harcourt Brace Jovanovich, 1981.

Callaghan, Morley. *That Summer in Paris: Memoirs of Tangled Friendships with Hemingway, Fitzgerald, and Some Others.* New York: Coward-McCann, 1963.

Ellmann, Richard. *James Joyce.* New York: Oxford UP, 1982.

Fitch, Noel Riley. *Sylvia Beach and the Lost Generation.* New York: Norton, 1983.

Fitzgerald, F. Scott. "Echoes of the Jazz Age." *The Crack-up.* Ed. Edmund Wilson. New York: New Directions, 1945. 13-22.

———. *F. Scott Fitzgerald's Ledger: A Facsimile.* Washington, DC: NCR/Microcard Editions, 1972.

———. *The Short Stories of F. Scott Fitzgerald: A New Collection.* Ed. Matthew J. Bruccoli. New York: Scribners, 1989.

———. *Tender Is the Night.* New York: Scribners, 1934.

Ford, Ford Madox. *It Was the Nightingale.* Philadelphia: Lippincott, 1933.

Ford, Hugh. *Published in Paris: American and British Writers, Printers and Publishers in Paris, 1920-1939.* New York: Macmillan, 1975.

Hansen, Arlen J. *Expatriate Paris: A Cultural and Literary Guide to Paris of the 1920s.* New York: Arcade, 1990.

Hemingway, Ernest. *Ernest Hemingway: Selected Letters, 1917-1961.* Ed. Carlos Baker. New York: Scribners, 1963.

———. *A Moveable Feast.* New York: Scribners, 1964.

———. *The Sun Also Rises.* 1926. New York: Scribners, 1954.

Kuehl, John, and Jackson R. Bryer, eds. *Dear Scott/Dear Max: The Fitzgerald-Perkins Correspondence.* New York: Scribners, 1971.

Le Vot, André. "Fitzgerald in Paris." *Fitzgerald/Hemingway Annual 1973:* 49-68.

McAlmon, Robert, and Kay Boyle. *Being Geniuses Together: 1920-1930.* New York: Doubleday, 1968.

Putnam, Samuel. *Paris Was Our Mistress.* 1947. Carbondale: Southern Illinois UP, 1970.

Rewald, John. *Cézanne and America: Dealers, Collectors, Artists and Critics 1891-1921.* Princeton, NJ: Princeton UP, 1979.

Reynolds, Michael S. *Hemingway's Reading 1910-1940: An Inventory.* Princeton, NJ: Princeton UP, 1981.

Stein, Gertrude. "An American and France." *What Are Masterpieces.* Los Angeles: Conference Press, 1940. 59-70.

———. *Paris France.* New York: Scribners, 1940.

Tavernier-Courbin, Jacqueline. *Ernest Hemingway's "A Moveable Feast": The Making of a Myth.* Boston: Northeastern UP, 1991.

Young, Philip, and Charles W. Mann. *The Hemingway Manuscripts: An Inventory.*
    University Park: Pennsylvania State UP, 1969.

T W O

FITZGERALD'S
BLUE PENCIL

S C O T T D O N A L D S O N

During the first twenty months of their acquaintance—the two men met at the Dingo Bar in Montparnasse late in April 1925—F. Scott Fitzgerald did almost everything in his power to advance the career of Ernest Hemingway. As the older, more established, and more commercially successful writer of the two, he offered Hemingway the benefit of his advice and his sponsorship. He instructed the younger writer in what he had learned about the ways of book and magazine publishers. He loaned him money and offered his support as Hemingway's marriage was coming apart. He trumpeted the virtues of his work to anyone who would listen, and he wrote a laudatory review of *In Our Time*. Acting as intermediary between Hemingway and Maxwell Perkins, he helped to facilitate Ernest's shift from Boni & Liveright to Scribners. Then, with that strategic maneuver completed, Fitzgerald acted as editor at the source both for "Fifty Grand," Hemingway's prizefight story, and *The Sun Also Rises*, the first-novel-in-the-works whose promise induced Scribners to enter into a contract with Hemingway. In essays written thirty years later, and fifteen to twenty years after Fitzgerald's death, Hemingway pointedly minimized the significance of this help, but there can be no question that during the six months between December 1925 and June 1926 Fitzgerald offered Hemingway some extremely valuable editorial advice and that Hemingway very wisely took it.

"Fifty Grand" was part of Fitzgerald's campaign to deliver Hemingway to Maxwell Perkins. As an inducement to persuade Hemingway to sign with the firm, Fitzgerald pointed out that Scribners not only published books but also *Scribner's Magazine,* and so could provide a market for his short stories. Then, taking over as agent, Fitzgerald wrote Perkins on December 1, 1925, inquiring if Robert Bridges, the editor of *Scribner's Magazine,* might be interested in Hemingway's "new short pieces." On the strength of a favorable reply, Fitzgerald sent Bridges "Fifty Grand" for consideration, a story he had already had a hand in amending. As it developed, *Scribner's* did accept "Fifty Grand" for $250, but with the proviso that it would have to be cut by 500 words to fit the requirements of the magazine. This proposal proved unworkable, in good part because Hemingway—acting on Fitzgerald's counsel—already had made important excisions at the beginning of the story (Beegel 13-30; Donaldson 694-97).

The best known of these, because Hemingway commented on it with resentment in his 1959 "The Art of the Short Story," involved the anecdote that originally led off "Fifty Grand":

> "Say, Jack," I said. "How did you happen to beat Leonard?"
>
> "Well," Jack says. "Benny's a pretty smart boxer. All the time he's in there he's thinking and all the time he's thinking I'm hitting him."

Hemingway cut this "lovely revelation of the metaphysics of boxing" when Fitzgerald—who according to Hemingway had heard the story about Jack Britton and Benny Leonard only once before—told him it was an "old chestnut." His "humility" was in ascendance at the time, Hemingway explained, and he made the mistake of trusting Fitzgerald's judgment. "They will all con you, gentlemen," Hemingway went on in the superior tone of that essay. "But sometimes it is not intentional. Sometimes they simply do not know. This is the saddest state of writers and the one you will most frequently encounter" ("Art" 3-5). As it stands, this passage characterizes Fitzgerald as well intentioned but both ignorant and incompetent. It also conceals the fact that Hemingway deleted considerably more than the Britton-Leonard anecdote as a consequence of Fitzgerald's suggestions.

Two documents in the Hemingway collection at the John F. Kennedy Library testify to this fact. One is Hemingway's handwritten comment on a typescript of "Fifty Grand" that reads "1st 3 pages of story mutilated by Scott Fitzgerald with his [undecipherable]." The other, a brief and apparently incomplete critique of the story in Fitzgerald's handwriting, turned up stuffed inside a letter from Sylvia Beach to Hemingway, letting him know that a dozen copies of *In Our Time* had arrived at her Shakespeare and Company bookshop in Paris. The timing makes sense. *In Our Time* was published on October 5, 1925. Hemingway was working on his boxing story during October and November. "Perhaps its conciseness makes it dull," Fitzgerald commented, ". . . the very impossibility of fixing attention for amount of time; the very leaving in only high spots may be why it seemed a slow starter." Following Fitzgerald's guidance, Hemingway deleted about two and a half typewritten pages at the beginning, most of them devoted to establishing the prizefight ambience of the story, with conversations in the gym and in a bar near Madison Square Garden. Half a dozen characters were introduced in this aborted beginning, along with a suggestion—appropriate in a story about fixed bouts and double crosses—that heavyweight champion Gentleman Jim Corbett was a good enough "actor" to throw fights. Without this extraneous background, "Fifty Grand" begins with plot: a reference to the forthcoming fight between champion Brennan and challenger Walcott (Ms., JFK Library 387-88).

"My loyal and devoted friend Fitzgerald, who was truly more interested in my own career at this point than in his own, sent me to Scribner's with the story," Hemingway wrote in "The Art of the Short Story." Though it omits mention of his editorial doctoring, this statement was entirely accurate about Fitzgerald's extraordinary commitment to Hemingway's cause. Hemingway maintained that even before it went to *Scribner's*, "Fifty Grand" had been turned down by *Cosmopolitan* "because it had no love interest." In any case, when the story came back from *Scribner's* with a proposal that it be cut by five hundred words, Hemingway knew how difficult that would be, having already done extensive cutting. In his account, Hemingway does not acknowledge Fitzgerald's involvement and presents himself as his own best editor. "I explained without heat nor hope, seeing the built-in stupidity of the editor of the magazine [Bridges] and his intransigence, that I had already cut the story myself and that the only way it could be shortened by five hundred words and make sense was to amputate the first five hundred. I had often done that myself with stories and it improved them. It would not have improved this story but I thought that was their ass not mine. I would put it back together in a book." Instead, according to Hemingway, Scribners put "a very intelligent young assistant editor" on the job—writer Manuel Komroff undertook the task—and everywhere he cut the story made no sense. "It had been cut for keeps when I wrote it," Hemingway asserted, "and afterwards at Scott's request I'd even cut out the metaphysics" of the Benny Leonard–Jack Britton anecdote ("Art" 4-5).

Hemingway contracted to publish his books with Scribners even though it became clear that "Fifty Grand" would not appear in their magazine, but Maxwell Perkins did not let the matter drop there. Undoubtedly influenced to some degree by Fitzgerald's prodding, he took over as agent for Hemingway's "most excellent" fight story, and shipped it off with his recommendation to other major magazines. It was the first thing Hemingway mentioned to Perkins when he heard that *Collier's* had turned down "Fifty Grand." He was sorry about that, but not surprised, for the story was "quite hard in texture" and not what they wanted at all. It would have "meant very much to me in various ways," he added, for *Scribner's* to print the story. Now he supposed it would come back from the *Saturday Evening Post* and *Liberty*— where Perkins planned to send it next—and so it did (Hemingway, *Selected Letters* 197; Kuehl and Bryer 152). When his initial efforts failed, Perkins involved the Paul Reynolds literary agency, and their "man [Harold] Ober, whom Scott knows about," in attempts to sell "Fifty Grand," but the story was rejected at least half a dozen times before finally appearing, without any further cuts, in the *Atlantic Monthly* for July 1927 (Donaldson 697-701). In the interim Hemingway sent Perkins several stories shorter than "Fifty Grand." He was trying to write "the shortest ones first," he somewhat sarcastically reported on April 1, 1926 (*Selected Letters* 198).

With Hemingway safely delivered to Scribners, Fitzgerald continued to exert himself on his friend's behalf. His most important work as a critic, and arguably the most important thing he ever did for Hemingway, was his editing job on *The Sun Also Rises*. In *A Moveable Feast*, written in the late 1950s, Hemingway gives the impression that Fitzgerald had no influence whatever on that novel:

> That fall of 1925 he was upset because I would not show him the manuscript of the first draft of *The Sun Also Rises*. I explained to him that it would mean nothing until I had gone over it and rewritten it and that I did not want to discuss it or show it to anyone first. . . . Scott did not see it until after the completed rewritten and cut manuscript had been sent to Scribners at the end of April. I remembered joking with him about it and him being worried and anxious to help as always once a thing was done. But I did not want his help while I was rewriting. (184-85)

This passage is accurate but culpably incomplete. The crucial piece of missing information is that once Fitzgerald did see the manuscript of the novel, he made suggestions that led to its radical improvement.

Hemingway did in fact rewrite *The Sun Also Rises* over the fall and winter of 1925-1926 without showing his work-in-progress to Fitzgerald. They had already discussed the novel by that time, however, as early manuscript drafts of the book make clear. "What happened to me is supposed to be funny," Jake Barnes comments in a reference to his war injury. "Scott Fitzgerald told me once it couldn't be treated except as a humorous subject" (Reynolds 308). Moreover, in a discarded foreword to the novel, Hemingway issued a slur against Fitzgerald. The passage recounts the anecdote about Gertrude Stein and the garage owner who told her about "the lost generation," those who had fought in the war. Then it proceeds to differentiate Hemingway's attitude toward that generation from that of Fitzgerald. "This is not a question of what kind of mothers will flappers make or where is bobbed hair leading us," Hemingway wrote (Svoboda 106). Fitzgerald was well known for his *Saturday Evening Post* stories recounting the sometimes frivolous behavior of the Jazz Age generation. It was because of this reputation, Hemingway commented in *A Moveable Feast*, that when he met Fitzgerald he could not think of him as "a serious writer," although reading *The Great Gatsby* changed his mind (155). There also may have been a more immediate occasion for Hemingway's slighting reference. In *McCall's* for October 1925, Fitzgerald published an article entitled "What Became of Our Flappers and Sheiks?" (Hanneman 229).

However he may have characterized the situation in *A Moveable Feast*, letters between the two make it clear that Hemingway was eager to have Fitzgerald's reaction before making final revisions to the novel. Around April 20, 1926, he wrote Fitzgerald that the novel was "all done" and ready to ship to Scribners. He was considering dedicating it

> TO MY SON
> John Hadley Nicanor
> This collection of Instructive Anecdotes

"I'm hoping to hell you'll like it," Hemingway went on. "You'll see it in August. [At that time, the Hemingways planned to spend most of the spring and summer in Spain and to join the Fitzgeralds, Murphys, et al. on the Riviera in August. With the advent of Bumby's whooping cough and his and Hadley's stay at Juan-les-Pins, the timetable for seeing Fitzgerald was moved up to late May–early June.] I think may be it is pretty interesting. Later— you wont [sic] like it." Clearly Hemingway hoped that his work would please Fitzgerald, and clearly he felt uncertain about that. Subsequently in the same letter, Hemingway reiterated the point that he would have a carbon of *Sun* at Antibes "and w'd [*sic*] welcome your advising me or anything about it. Nobody's read any amount of it yet." The letter closed with a set piece designed to kid Fitzgerald both about *Gatsby* and about the novel he had begun dealing with matricide:

> The hero, like Gatsby, is a Lake Superior Salmon Fisherman. (There are no salmon in Lake Superior). The action all takes place in Newport, R.I. and the heroine is a girl named Sophie Irene Loeb who kills her mother. The scene in which Sophie gives birth to twins in the death house at Sing Sing where she is waiting to be electrocuted for the murder of the father and sister of her, as then, unborn children I got from Dreiser but practically everything else in the book is either my own or yours. I know you'll be glad to see it. The Sun Also Rises comes from Sophie's statement as she is strapped into the chair as the current mounts. (*Selected Letters* 199-201)

In reply Fitzgerald took exception to Hemingway's remark about Lake Superior salmon. In *The Great Gatsby* he had described young James Gatz as "a clam-digger and a salmon-fisher" on the shores of Lake Superior (104). Hemingway, an expert fisherman, corrected him on that point, but Fitzgerald argued that the *Encyclopaedia Brittanica* did in fact refer to salmon—or at least "salmon trout"—in the lake. Hemingway wouldn't buy that argument. "There are a hell of a lot more salmon in Encyclopaedia Brit. than in Lake Superior," he wrote Fitzgerald about May 20. By then his wife, Hadley, and son Bumby were in Juan-les-Pins with the Fitzgeralds, where Ernest would be joining them. He would bring along a carbon of *The Sun Also Rises*, and "you can read it" there, he told Fitzgerald. In response to Fitzgerald's recommendation that he drop the part of the dedication about "instructive anecdotes," Hemingway agreed that the book was "obviously *not* a collection of instructive anecdotes and . . . such a hell of a sad story . . . and the only instruction is how people go to hell." It was not a book for a child to read, but he still intended to dedicate it to Bumby "for reasons that will be obvious when you read the book and also for another reason" (*Selected Letters* 204-5). The only "obvious" reason that comes to mind is that Bumby—John Hadley *Nicanor* Hemingway—was named, in part, after a bullfighter. The "other reason" probably had to do with Ernest's desire to make amends for his impending separation and divorce from Bumby's mother.

When he mailed this letter to Fitzgerald, Hemingway still had not heard whether Maxwell Perkins liked his manuscript. By May 28, that word had come through, and it was favorable. Perkins praised the vitality of Hemingway's book. "No one could conceive of a book with more life in it," he commented. The scenes read like actual experience and covered "an extraordinary range of experience and emotion, all brought together in the most skillful manner . . . to form a complete design." He could not express his admiration too strongly, Perkins concluded (Donaldson 704-5). As a matter of fact, though, Perkins did harbor serious reservations about the novel. At the in-house editorial conference, he pushed for the book on the grounds that Scribners would suffer if the word got around among younger writers that they had rejected *The Sun Also Rises*. But "[w]e took it with misgivings," he noted for the record, and he communicated those misgivings to Fitzgerald in a letter of May 29 (Berg 95-98; Donaldson 703). This letter did not reach Juan-les-Pins until after Hemingway arrived there from Madrid, and after Fitzgerald had read the manuscript of *The Sun Also Rises* and suggested substantial changes at the beginning of the novel.

Hemingway was pleased that Perkins liked his manuscript but wanted Fitzgerald's opinion as well. So, the morning after Fitzgerald's drunken misbehavior at a party given by Gerald and Sara Murphy to welcome Hemingway, Ernest delivered the carbon copy of *Sun* to the Villa St. Louis, where the Fitzgeralds were domiciled, and awaited his friend's verdict. Fitzgerald read it at once—as Hemingway's sponsor with Scribners he had a considerable investment in the novel's success—and was appalled at the beginning. As it stood, the first chapter of *Sun* presented biographical data about Lady Brett Ashley and Mike Campbell in a chatty, rather flippant manner:

> This is a novel about a lady. Her name is Lady Ashley and when the story begins she is living in Paris and it is Spring. That should be a good setting for a romantic but highly moral story. As every one knows, Paris is a very romantic place. Spring in Paris is a very happy and romantic time. Autumn in Paris, although very beautiful, might give a note of sadness or melancholy that we shall try to keep out of this story.

So read the first paragraph, followed by information on Brett's two previous marriages, her beauty and her sitting as a subject for portrait painters, her alliance with Mike, his bankruptcy, and their drinking habits.

In the second chapter of the novel as then conceived, Jake Barnes abruptly and self-consciously intervened to introduce himself as narrator:

> So my name is Jacob Barnes and I am writing this story, not as I believe is usual in these cases, from a desire for confession, because being a Roman Catholic I am spared that Protestant urge to literary production, nor to set things all out the way they happened for the good of some future generation, nor any other of the usual highly moral urges, but because I believe it is a good story.

Jake then went on to describe his job with the Continental Press Association and his cynical opinions about Montparnasse and its inhabitants. The latter subject led him to mention Robert Cohn, "one of the non-Nordic heroes of this book" who had spent two years in the Quarter. Next came an extended anecdote about Cohn's friend Braddocks (Ford Madox Ford) supposedly "cutting" Hilaire Belloc and boasting about it, though in fact the man he snubbed was not Belloc at all. (Eventually, this story was resurrected for *A Moveable Feast.*) The chapter ended with Jake's confession that he never felt the same about Braddocks after this incident and that he would avoid putting him into the story entirely "except that he was a great friend of Robert Cohn, and Cohn is the hero" (Svoboda 131-37). After that false lead, the manuscript launched into the passage about Cohn as middleweight boxing champion of Princeton that actually starts the published novel.

Fitzgerald moved cautiously in expressing his objections to this beginning. He was seeing Hemingway daily and before committing anything to writing warned him that he had certain comments to make. Then he wrote a ten-page handwritten letter that spelled out his complaints. This letter alternates sections of severe and quite possibly hurtful criticism with apologies and reassurances designed to soften the blows. Fitzgerald wanted Hemingway to revise his manuscript, but he did not want to lose his friendship into the bargain. "Nowadays when almost everyone is a genius," he began, ". . . the temptation for the bogus to profit is no greater than the temptation for the good man to relax. . . . This should frighten all of us into a lust for anything honest that people have to say about our work" (Svoboda 137-38). In constructing his own books, Fitzgerald added, he had received and acted on excellent advice from a number of people, including Edmund Wilson, Perkins, and his old friend Katherine Tighe who had probably never even read a novel before making important suggestions about *This Side of Paradise.* Fitzgerald as veteran professional was offering the benefit of his experience to Hemingway as neophyte novelist. *I've listened to others with profit; now you should listen to me.*

With that preliminary out of the way, Fitzgerald got to the point: "Anyhow I think parts of *Sun Also* are careless + ineffectual." To some extent the difficulty was the same one he had isolated in "Fifty Grand": a "tendency to envelope [sic] or . . . to *embalm* in mere wordiness an anecdote or joke." To ameliorate the point, Fitzgerald called attention to a somewhat similar fault of his own—his desire to preserve passages of "fine writing" (Svoboda 138). *Don't feel bad: I make mistakes too.*

The first chapter of the *Sun* manuscript gave an impression of "condescending *casuallness* [sic]," Fitzgerald observed. "I think that there are about 24 sneers, superiorities and nose-thumbings-at-nothing that mar the whole narrative . . ." (Svoboda 138). Through the snide commentary of Jake Barnes, Hemingway was writing in much the same wise guy voice that characterized his feature articles for the *Toronto Star Weekly* and *The Torrents of Spring.* "The most obvious mark of the wise-guy," as Delmore Schwartz observed in his essay on Hemingway, "is his sense of humor which expresses his scorn and his sense of independence; he exercises it as one of the best ways of controlling a situation and of demonstrating his superiority to all situations" (71). The tone was all wrong, and did not match that of the more maturely ironic Jake who told the rest of the story as narrator. In particular, Fitzgerald detected snobbishness in the account of Brett's past and the effect of the war on her lovers and husbands. He also disliked the background material on her and on Mike. "That biography from you," he chided Hemingway, "who allways [sic] believed in the superiority (the preferability) of the *imagined* to the *seen not to say to the merely recounted*" (Svoboda 138). In other words, Hemingway had been content to tell without showing, and it didn't matter at all that what he revealed about Lady Brett Ashley was drawn from the actual experience of her real-life model, Lady Duff Twysden.

In his critique, Fitzgerald commingled occasional praise with sharp rebukes. The passage beginning "So my name is Jacob Barnes" was maladroit. The material about Montparnasse and "the Quarter" was in all the guidebooks. The anecdote about Braddocks was "flat as hell." The whole beginning was undermined by Hemingway's "elephantine facetiousness." On the other hand, "remember that this is a new departure for you, and . . . I think your stuff is great." And on the other hand also, "I've decided not to pick at anything else [after the first few chapters] because I wasn't at all inspired to pick when reading it. I was much too excited. Besides . . . This is probably a heavy dose. That novel's damn good" (Svoboda 139). *Take these pills—I know they are hard to swallow but they're good for you, and here's some syrup to wash them down with.*

Fitzgerald made his most telling point near the end of his letter: "Appropos [sic] of your foreward [sic] about the Latin quarter—suppose you had begun your stories with phrases like: 'Spain is a peculiar place—ect' or 'Michigan is interesting to two classes—the fisherman + the drummer'"

(Svoboda 139). In reviewing *In Our Time,* Fitzgerald had marveled at the total absence of exposition ("How to Waste Material" 263). But in writing his novel, Hemingway was guilty of letting merely expository prose take the place of dramatized action. This was true of the introduction of Robert Cohn as well, Fitzgerald thought. In his judgment, the book didn't get going until the start of Chapter III (in the published novel), when Jake picks up Georgette, takes her to the *bal musette,* and Brett appears. But Fitzgerald did not suggest wholesale amputation of the beginning. The section he discussed most thoroughly, up to and including the two brief chapters on Cohn, ran to some 7,500 words, he estimated. He recommended that Hemingway cut them back to about 5,000 words, doing so not "by mere pareing [*sic*]" but by eliminating "the worst of the *scenes*" (*Correspondence* 193-96).

Fitzgerald either walked this letter from the Villa St. Louis to the Villa Paquita where the Hemingways were staying, or Hemingway came to call for it. Reading it over must have been painful, but Hemingway was too intelligent a craftsman to dismiss Fitzgerald's suggestions out of pique. Instead, he took them to heart, talked them over with Fitzgerald, and settled on a drastic remedy. He would not change the opening chapters but go one step further. Instead of paring them down *or* removing the worst scenes in those chapters—the Braddocks episode, for example—he determined to cut them entirely.

This decision he communicated to Perkins in a letter of June 5, accompanied by assurances that Fitzgerald (1) approved of the novel as a whole and (2) concurred with him about lopping off the beginning. Fitzgerald's opinion, he must have understood, would count heavily with Perkins. "I was very glad to get your letter and hear that you liked The Sun a.r.," Hemingway began. "*Scott claims to too*" (emphasis added throughout). Then, after some directions about where to send mail, he revealed his plan:

> I believe that, in the proofs, I will start the book at what is now page 16 in the Mss. ["Robert Cohn was once middleweight boxing champion of Princeton"]. There is nothing in those first sixteen pages [about 3,500 words] that does not come out, or is explained, or re-stated in the rest of the book—or is unnecessary to state. I think it will move much faster from the start that way. *Scott agrees with me.* He suggested various things in it to cut out—in those first chapters—which I have never liked—but I think it is better to just lop that off and he agrees. He will probably write you what he thinks about it—the book in general. He said he was very excited by it. (*Selected Letters* 208)

In this letter to Perkins, Hemingway acknowledges Fitzgerald's assistance while downplaying its importance. He presents himself as having initiated the revision: it is *"Scott agrees with me"* throughout, not *"I agree with Scott."* Yet at the same time he invokes Fitzgerald's authority to help him argue against any further alterations. In his letter praising the manuscript, Perkins made but a single objection. There were other things he was wary about—and which he wrote Fitzgerald about under separate cover—but he did not want to bombard Hemingway with these in a letter of congratulations. The one thing Perkins could not countenance was the passage about "Henry James's bicycle," a reference to a childhood accident that supposedly left James impotent. Though deceased, Henry James had been one of Scribners' most distinguished authors, and there were still people at the publishing firm who knew and admired him. It would be best to eliminate the passage, Perkins wrote Hemingway (Donaldson 704). Characteristically, Hemingway disagreed. James was "as dead as he will ever be," he pointed out, and had left no descendants to be hurt. No insult was intended. Bill Gorton mentioned him as he would any other historical figure. Besides, *"Scott said he saw nothing off-color about it"* (*Selected Letters* 209; emphasis added).

During the next few months, Fitzgerald acted as referee while Perkins and Hemingway sparred over other changes. In his long letter to Fitzgerald of May 29, Perkins paid tribute to Hemingway's skill but confided his reservations both about the subject matter—Jake Barnes's emasculating injury and Brett Ashley's promiscuity—and about the use of "many words seldom if ever used before in print." "When you think of Hemingway's book you recall scenes as if they were memories . . . and you recall people as hard & actual as real ones . . . the mss. wriggles with vitality. The art is marvelously concealed, & yet the whole is composed to the last word. —Yet the book is not an unmixed pleasure because it is almost unpublishable." Perkins regarded the principal characters with a jaundiced eye. They are "such people as I suppose you know in Paris," he rather sniffily wrote. "They belong to 'a lost generation.' Several including the girl are what are now called 'disintegrated personalities,' I suppose." Moreover, the romantic situation between the leading characters was complicated by the shocking fact "that he (who tells the tale) has been so wounded that he can not sexually play the part of a man!" Still, he found the book "never erotic, . . . in a true sense . . . always clean & healthy." The language posed a serious problem, though. The passage about Henry James simply had to come out. Then there were those dirty words (Donaldson 703).

In answering Perkins, Fitzgerald acknowledged that he too had certain qualifications about *The Sun Also Rises*. In particular, he thought Hemingway had bitten off more than he could chew in "the mutilated man." And the lady he didn't like, perhaps because he "didn't like the original," Duff Twysden. Still, he acted as Hemingway's advocate when it came to possible further revision. "Do ask him for the absolute minimum of necessary changes, Max," he counseled their editor. "[H]e's so discouraged about the previous reception of his work by publishers and magazine editors" from whom he'd received a lot of words but "scarcely a single dollar" (*Letters* 228). Some weeks later Fitzgerald came to Hemingway's defense again. The only censorable thing he found in Ernest's book was the conversation about the bulls' balls. He didn't think "the James thing" objectionable but then it seemed to him that James had been dead for fifty years (*Letters* 229-30).

Perkins thanked Fitzgerald for his opinion, which he valued because he thought of him as "rather strict in that regard" (JFK Library: MP to FSF, August 17, 1926). Meanwhile, however, he was waging a campaign to persuade Hemingway to make alterations. By and large, Perkins was a hands-off editor where Fitzgerald and Hemingway were concerned. When Perkins heard about cutting the first 3,500 words, for example, he wrote Hemingway that he rather liked the original beginning himself, for it delivered the kind of information many readers expected of the conventional novel, but he did not insist on the point: ". . . you write like yourself only, and I shall not attempt criticism. I couldn't with confidence." On the other hand, Perkins *was* vigilant about preserving a measure of propriety in his authors' work and about avoiding legal difficulties. In order to win Hemingway over, he warned him about "the danger of trouble from referring to real people in a way to reflect upon them, and the danger of suppression." Libel was a possibility, and so was outright censorship. It would be a shame, Perkins pointed out, if so fine a book "should be disregarded because of the howls of a lot of cheap, prurient, moronic yappers" (Donaldson 706-7). On these grounds Hemingway capitulated. Henry James became Henry, Hilaire Belloc was eliminated, Joseph Hergesheimer's name was changed to Hoffenheimer, and Roger Prescott—too close in sound to the original Glenway Wescott—was altered to Robert Prentiss. In addition, the bulls were unfitted for a reproductive function and the dirty word that rhymed with "Irony and Pity" was deleted.

With that issue resolved, Hemingway wrote Fitzgerald in September offhandedly thanking him for his "sterling attitude on the censorship question. All France is proud of you." Then he signed off on the novel with an implicit recognition of Fitzgerald's editorial advice: "I cut The Sun to start with Cohn—cut all that first part. Made a number of minor cuts and did quite a lot of re-writing and tightening up. Cut and in the proof it read like a good book. Christ knows I want to write them a hell of a lot better but it seemed to move along and to be pretty sound and solid. I hope to hell you'll like it," he concluded, "and I think maybe you will" (*Selected Letters* 216-17).

Even after *The Sun Also Rises* was published on October 22, Perkins proposed that Hemingway write a foreword summarizing some of what had been omitted in the sixteen pages he and Fitzgerald had decided to cut. He realized that this material had not been written in the same "method" as the rest of the novel. But in a brief prologue, Perkins thought, Hemingway "could tell some of the things about Brett which were in the first galleys and did not altogether come out in the narrative." What troubled him, and other readers, was that her scandalous behavior was not adequately prepared for, whereas the discarded beginning created a certain sympathy for her through an account of her troubled past. Hemingway rejected this proposal. Although the "Brett biography" contained "some very good dope" on her, any introduction would break the unity of the book. Besides, Brett was a real person, her story was a real story, and since he'd "protected" James and Belloc and Hergesheimer he might as well protect her too by leaving out the details of her background (*Selected Letters* 223-24).

Late in December, Fitzgerald wrote Hemingway how pleased he was with the good press *The Sun Also Rises* was getting. "By the way," he added, "I liked it in print even better than in manuscript" (*Letters* 325). Neither at that time nor later did he seek any credit for the excision that markedly improved Hemingway's first novel. In a July 1936 letter to John O'Hara, Fitzgerald went so far as to invent a yarn that effectively minimized his role. "[T]he only effect I ever had on Ernest was to get him in a receptive mood and say let's cut everything that goes before this. Then the pieces got mislaid and he could never find the part that I said to cut out. And so he published it without that and later we agreed it was a very wise cut. This is not literally true and I don't want it established as part of the Ernest legend," he concluded, "but it's just about as far as one writer can go in helping another" (*Letters* 559).

By carefully downplaying his influence in this 1936 letter, Fitzgerald illustrated how important it was to him to please Hemingway or at least not to offend him. He understood by then that his days as editor-behind-the-scenes were over. In 1929 he sent Hemingway an extensive and occasionally harsh pre-publication critique of *A Farewell to Arms*, very much in the spirit of the one he provided for *The Sun Also Rises*. This time, however, Hemingway rejected Fitzgerald's advice totally and in correspondence of the early 1950s pointed out how useless it had been. "It is one of the worst damned documents I have ever read," he wrote Arthur Mizener in January 1951. "Not one suggestion made sense or was useful," he wrote Charles Poore in January 1953. In addition, Fitzgerald had recently received a letter from Hemingway cavalierly dismissing his critical commentary on *Green Hills of Africa.* "It was good to hear from you," Hemingway wrote Fitzgerald in December 1935, "but a shame you thought you had to write about the book." Fitzgerald's observations, he went on to say, made it clear that he didn't "know any more when a book is a good book or what makes a book bad than ever" (*Selected Letters* 719, 800, 424-25).

In retrospect, it seems almost as if Hemingway was willing himself to forget the times he had profited from Fitzgerald's ideas about revision. In a draft version of *A Moveable Feast* that was cut for publication, for example, Hemingway submits that he has forgotten whether Fitzgerald read *The Sun Also Rises* in manuscript or in galley proofs. It didn't really matter anyway, he adds, because any decisions about changes were his and his alone (Brenner 534-35). There were several reasons why the close relationship between the two writers in 1925-1926 did not last, but one of them surely was Hemingway's discomfort about obligations he could not repay. Fitzgerald was perfectly willing to write off those debts. No matter what Hemingway said or wrote about him—the damning reference in "The Snows of Kilimanjaro" to "poor Scott Fitzgerald," ruined by his adoration of the rich, appeared in the August 1936 issue of *Esquire*, only weeks after Fitzgerald wrote his letter to O'Hara—he continued to regard Hemingway as his friend and "as an artist . . . a final reference" (*Letters* 286). But in his letters, in *A Moveable Feast,* and in "The Art of the Short Story," all written with Fitzgerald dead for more than a decade and his revival under way, Hemingway demonstrated how difficult it was for him to forgive the crucial editorial assistance Fitzgerald had rendered during the first fine flush of their friendship when he was truly more interested in Hemingway's career than in his own.

WORKS CITED

Beegel, Susan. *Hemingway's Craft of Omission: Four Manuscript Examples.* Ann Arbor, MI: UMI Research P, 1988.

Berg, A. Scott. *Max Perkins: Editor of Genius.* New York: Dutton, 1978.

Brenner, Gerry. "Are We Going to Hemingway's Feast?" *American Literature* 54 (1982): 528-44.

Donaldson, Scott. "The Wooing of Ernest Hemingway." *American Literature* 53 (1982): 691-710.

Fitzgerald, F. Scott. *Correspondence of F. Scott Fitzgerald.* Ed. Matthew J. Bruccoli and Margaret M. Duggan. New York: Random House, 1980.

———. *The Great Gatsby.* 1925. The Authorized Text. New York: Scribners, 1992.

———. "How to Waste Material: A Note on My Generation." *Bookman* 63 (1926): 262-65.

———. *The Letters of F. Scott Fitzgerald.* Ed. Andrew Turnbull. 1963. New York: Dell, 1966.

Hanneman, Audre. *Ernest Hemingway: A Comprehensive Bibliography.* Princeton, NJ: Princeton UP, 1967.

Hemingway, Ernest. "The Art of the Short Story." *New Critical Approaches to the Short Stories of Ernest Hemingway.* Ed. Jackson J. Benson. Durham, NC: Duke UP, 1990. 1-13.

———. *Ernest Hemingway: Selected Letters, 1917-1961.* Ed. Carlos Baker. New York: Scribners, 1981.

———. Manuscripts of the Hemingway Collection, John F. Kennedy Library, Boston.

———. *A Moveable Feast.* New York: Scribners, 1964.

Kuehl, John, and Jackson R. Bryer, eds. *Dear Scott/Dear Max: The Fitzgerald-Perkins Correspondence.* New York: Scribners, 1971.

Reynolds, Michael. *Hemingway: The Paris Years.* Cambridge, MA: Basil Blackwell, 1989.

Schwartz, Delmore. "The Fiction of Ernest Hemingway." *Perspectives U.S.A.* No. 13 (1955): 70-88.

Svoboda, Frederic Joseph. *Hemingway and "The Sun Also Rises": The Crafting of a Style.* Lawrence: UP of Kansas, 1983.

PART II

HEMINGWAY AND FRANCE

"VERY CHEERFUL AND CLEAN AND SANE AND LOVELY"

HEMINGWAY'S "VERY PLEASANT LAND OF FRANCE"

H . R . S T O N E B A C K

There is a magic in the name France. . . . It is a very old magic. France is a broad and lovely country. The loveliest country that I know. It is impossible to write impartially about a country when you love it.

—Ernest Hemingway,
"The Franco-German Situation,"
Toronto Star, April 14, 1923 (*Dateline* 260)

[Clemenceau] stands and looks out at the surf curling along his beach . . . at the red sails of the fishing boats far out on the sea beating up from the coast of Spain toward the very pleasant land of France. . . .

—Ernest Hemingway,
"Talking with the Tiger,"
Toronto Star, March 1, 1992

1.

We all know—at least many of us think we know—all about Hemingway's Paris. Yet few of us know much about, and fewer still have written anything about, Hemingway's France. It is the purpose of this essay to examine the matter of Hemingway's France: Arles, Avignon, Chartres, Hendaye, Menton. To utter such names—as well as those of Aigues Mortes, le-Grau-du-Roi, le Mont-St-Michel, Rambouillet, les Sables-d'Olonne, les Saintes Maries-de-la-Mer, Saint Jean-Pied-de-Port, Villedieu-les-Poêles—and all the other names on the long magical inventory, to chant this litany of French places, is to invoke the most neglected geography of Hemingway's life. It is urgent and most appropriate here to reinscribe the cartography, the geomoral landscape of his life and work, with *France*—not just Paris, but *all* of France—holding the center of the revised new map of Hemingway.

Early and late, for more than forty years, from his first sight of France in 1918 and his early journalistic sketches, to his final visit in 1960 and his most important posthumously published work (*The Garden of Eden*), France profoundly informs Hemingway's life and work. Most Hemingway biographers and critics have been all too content to repeat the usual truisms about Paris, to say little or nothing about the France beyond Paris, and then rush to exclaim the exquisite *O Altitudo!* regarding Hemingway and Spain. All this is freighted with biographical and critical implications for our assessments and reevaluations of Hemingway.

One early piece of journalism that presents striking evidence of Hemingway's engagement with the matter of France is his interview with Clemenceau in September 1922. Rejected for publication, for political reasons, in 1922 and finally published in 1992 by the *Toronto Star,* "Talking with the Tiger" is a little-known but compelling piece that renders the character and presence of Clemenceau, and presents him as the man who "saved France and perhaps the world." Tracking him down in retirement on "the wild coast of the Vendée" at his home in St.-Vincent-sur-Jard,[1] Hemingway talks with Clemenceau on the eve of his departure for an American tour, undertaken to explain the Treaty of Versailles. The twenty-three-year-old Hemingway studies carefully the eighty-year-old Tiger, the "very gracious and charming old man" whose smiling eyes dominate his Ojibway-brown, "healthy Chinese Mandarin's face," whose eyes "get inside of your eyes somehow and fasten claws there," whose eyes grow fierce when "his face [goes] tiger" with passion and then smile again warmly when the Tiger turns charming. The very young but politically very astute Hemingway observes: "It has been said of Clemenceau that *France is his only remaining illusion.* He is going to America now, alone, the only free man in Europe, to defend France" (emphasis added). Clearly, Hemingway sees in Clemenceau the very figure of France, as well as a kind of exemplar-tutor— elsewhere Hemingway called him "one of my great heroes" (*By-Line* 226)— the first in a long line of such wise-and-wounded-old-man figures that would serve his work well.

As Hemingway stresses, and as Clemenceau's biographers have often noted, Clemenceau typifies France. "His character," J. Hampden Jackson writes, "lay at the centre of gravity of France. . . . To understand Clemenceau is to understand France" (xiii). Artists in particular—writers, painters, actors—adored Clemenceau. "Clemenceau is France," Sarah Bernhardt asserted: "I have always loved him, and since this war I devoutly worship him" (Martet 38). It is tempting to say a good deal more about Hemingway's Clemenceau, as touchstone and benchmark for Hemingway's life-long preoccupation with France, yet for our purposes here it must suffice to note that Hemingway wrote more about Clemenceau than just this early sketch and that the development of his views of "one of [his] great heroes" is a neglected subject, rich with implications for deepening our understanding of Hemingway's France.

We should also note Hemingway's engagement here with the French landscape. This sketch shows, as the 1992 *Toronto Star* sidebar declares, "how Hemingway was moving away from ordinary reporting and moving toward a short-story form of writing." I would add that Hemingway's evocation of this little-known far country of France is an important transitional piece of apprenticeship writing in another respect: the uses of *country*, of landscape. Rich in local texture and color, the sketch also demonstrates Hemingway's developing skill with symbolic landscape. Clemenceau's country—"the wild coast of the Vendée"—is one of the least known (especially to foreigners) and perhaps most symbolic landscapes of France. Since the Revolution, the Vendée has been a symbol of resistance and, for much longer, a symbol of determination and endurance in the fierce struggle with a particularly harsh nature. Hemingway catches the essence of this in his brief description of the ride from St. Vincent-sur-Jard to his hotel in les Sables-d'Olonne, "through a scrub-oak, sandy plain where the houses are built close to the ground to avoid the wind and the farmers wage a losing fight against the blowing sand, manuring the ground with kelp hauled from the beach and building windbreaks to keep the encroaching sand out of their gardens." Back at his hotel, Hemingway makes further landscape notes that are not incorporated into the Clemenceau piece: "boats tacking out to sea—wonderful long beach with a thin line of surf crisping in—" ("Clemenceau Interview").

In sum, with his writerly eye sharply focused on actual and symbolic landscape, Hemingway's presentation of Clemenceau's country, his house, garden, and seaview, is precise and compelling. In a few strokes he renders the haunting numinous particularity of place. Moreover, he expresses a key point that Clemenceau's biographers struggle to articulate: the nature of Clemenceau's profound attachment to this landscape, his identity with the Vendée, the ways in which character is suffused with place. (Or how, in the formulation of Lawrence Durrell's axioms concerning the Spirit of Place, character is a function of landscape.) This remarkable sketch concludes with the image of an autochthonous Clemenceau standing in his wind-and-sand-ravaged seaside garden, looking "at his great red fish blowing in the wind at the top of the slim white pole, at the red sails of the fishing boats far out on the sea beating up from the coast of Spain toward the very pleasant land of France and he says—'it is a nice place—this. I was born near here, you know.'" Thus ends one of Hemingway's earliest and most resonant evocations of the France beyond Paris, the strange country of the Vendée and Le Bon Tigre, the Good Old Tiger, the Old Man and the Sea at St. Vincent-sur-Jard.[2]

Other early nonfiction sketches and writing exercises, published and unpublished, yield evidence of Hemingway's deepening engagement with the matter of France. In 1924 he made a trip by himself to Provence, what he called a "pilgrimage" to the "shrines" of the region: Arles, Avignon, Les Baux, Nîmes, and St.-Rémy-de-Provence. In one manuscript fragment entitled "Exercise (Stone)," he carefully describes how "the carvings in the Roman Arch on the plateau above San Remy are worn away by the wind"; with crossouts, deletions, and revisions, he tries to get exactly right the effect of the mistral on the stone at the ancient ruins of Glanum, above St.-Rémy-de-Provence. He seems unconcerned with the sculpture of the Triumphal Arch, depicting chained captives accompanied by women, or with Julius Caesar's subjugation of Massilia (Marseille), of which the arch is a commemoration. Rather, he focuses on the most enduring feature of *place*, the weather, the legendary "scourge of Provence"—the mistral.

In another exercise, carrying the heading "Notes in a bistrot [*sic*] in Avignon," he writes: "The most beautiful things in France are the trees in spring, the women and the horses. The ugliest are the modern furniture, the suburban architecture and the men's clothing. While it was developing the ugliest modern furniture in the world France was producing the most beautiful painting of almost any century." In another series of jottings, he writes: "I saw a drunken workingman sitting in a cafe in Arles who had exactly the same face as Anatole France." And this: "The vue from the garden above the Palace of the Popes in Avignon is really finer than that from the Tour Magne in Nimes"; here it would seem that Hemingway is carefully assessing the accuracy of the guidebooks with regard to one- or two-star views and agreeing with them, since most guidebooks award the Tour Magne view one star, and the Rocher des Doms view two stars. More interestingly, Hemingway makes this observation: "I have not seen one good looking girl in either Nimes or Avignon"; then he sees her, in Arles, of course, under the plane trees at the market: "the girl is letting her bobbed hair grow out." Perhaps these exercises are, as Michael Reynolds has suggested, "seemingly useless" notes (195). Yet each note goes beyond writerly exercise in precise observation; each note reflects Hemingway's continuing education in the matter of France; each in some fashion connects with the spirit of place; each employs some aspect of French or Provençal culture, history, tradition, and placeliness. It is a venerable tradition, proverbially so, that the women of Arles are the most beautiful in Provence. It might also be noted that in this same sequence, which links a beautiful Arlesienne, with bobbed hair growing out, with the Jardin de la Fontaine and the Tour Magne in Nîmes, Hemingway also writes: "beginning for a story. . . . Story is of a girl who always wants to have her hair cut and never does. Finally she does. How she feels. Story of man who always wanted to have long hair." Decades later, in Hemingway's most quintessentially French novel, *The Garden of Eden*, Catherine Bourne would say that she first got her ideas about hair and other changes in the Garden at Nîmes. Thus this 1924 exercise contains the core image, the germ, of *The Garden of Eden*, and it was not Catherine but Hemingway who got the idea in the Garden at Nîmes and wrote it down in a café in Arles.

Clearly, then, Hemingway's apprenticeship sketches and articles manifest his involvement with, his knowledge of, and his love for *la France profonde*, for the France beyond Paris. This is summed up succinctly in his 1923 piece for the *Toronto Star*, "The Franco-German Situation": "There is a magic in the name France. It is a magic like the smell of the sea or the sight of blue hills or of soldiers marching by. It is a very old magic. France is a broad and lovely country. The loveliest country that I know. It is impossible to write impartially about a country when you love it" (*Dateline* 260). I suggest that we hold tight to this rubric as a touchstone that indicates more truly than we have recognized the unvarying signal sent by Hemingway's work, a deep love for "the very old magic" of France that stays with him to the end.

2.

We drove for two hours after it was dark and slept in Mentone that
night. It seemed very cheerful and clean and sane and lovely.
> —"Che Ti Dice La Patria?" *Complete Stories* 230

I hated to leave France. Life was so simple in France. I felt I was a fool
to be going back into Spain.
> —*The Sun Also Rises* 233

How well did Hemingway know the "broad and lovely country" of France,
the "magic" beyond Paris? And how did he use this knowledge in his work?
As I read the prevailing winds of Hemingway studies, one all-too-familiar
set of responses to these questions would be: (1) he lived in *Paris, not* France;
(2) he liked Paris not for its Frenchness but because it was the cosmopolitan
city of writers and artists; (3) when he left Paris, he traveled mainly in other
countries—Austria, Italy, Spain, Switzerland— which he preferred over
France; (4) he was largely indifferent to, and his work generally expressed
disdain for, the France that is not Paris.[3] Of course, all of this is very far from
the truth—as amply demonstrated in his life and work—which is that
Hemingway knew and loved very well *all* of France.

Right from the start, he explored France, not just Paris. In 1922 he
writes to his father that "the country outside of Paris and up into Picardy is
beautiful." He tells of extensive forests, "very wild" and filled with "deer and
wild boar and foxes and rabbits"; and there are "lots of pheasants and
partridges too. I expect to get some good shooting in the fall" (*Selected Letters*
66-67). He and Hadley take forty-mile hikes through the forests of Chantilly
and Compiègne. They make short trips all over the Ile de France and longer
excursions into Normandy, the Loire Valley, Alsace, and the South. In 1924
Hemingway goes alone to Provence. He writes to Ezra Pound: "I wish to
hell I could paint. Jeesus Christ what cypress trees. Down there they do
always with cypresses what Italy does sometimes. I made a pilgrimage to
Van Gogh's whorehouse in Arles and other shrines." He goes to the Corrida
in Nîmes, at the Roman arena, one of the great places in France (and the
world) to witness the *mise à mort* (*Selected Letters* 115).

In 1925 Hemingway spends time alone at Chartres, where he changes
the title of his first novel from "Fiesta," to "The Lost Generation," to *The Sun
Also Rises*, a telling change made in symbolic terrain. He returns again and
again to Chartres, to the numinous ground of the great cathedral and the
mystical Virgin of the Pillar (*pilier, pilar*); he cycles out with Archibald

MacLeish in 1926; a few years later, when he discovers that Morley Callaghan is about to leave France without having visited Chartres, he insists on driving him there (and then criticizes Callaghan for not genuflecting at the high altar of the cathedral). Chartres is indeed one of Hemingway's secret and sacred places; from his pilgrimages there in the 1920s, to his participation in the Liberation of Chartres in 1944, to his visits to the cathedral with his fourth wife, Mary, in the 1950s, it remains one of the most important (and most overlooked) touchstones of *place*, of geomoral landscape, in Hemingway's life. His participation in the Liberation of Chartres, hitherto unnoted, is dealt with in my recent essay concerning Hemingway and the Liberation of France ("Hemingway's 'Happiest Summer'").

In my interviews with Mary Hemingway she said repeatedly that she had been to Chartres with Ernest "many times." Some of these trips are a matter of printed record, some are not. She said that he always lit candles and said prayers, and he would point out to her some detail in the sculpture or the stained glass. When I asked her about the details Ernest pointed out, she was unable to remember precisely whether they were related to the historical and religious "matter of France," or connected with Roland, Saint-Jacques de Compostelle, the Pilgrimages to Chartres, the Virgin of the Pillar, or other details about which I inquired. Some students of Hemingway are aware of his deep engagement with these matters and the related Cult of the Virgin del Pilar in Spain. However, it has not been noted before that another likely (and perhaps primary) source for, among other things, his second wife Pauline's secret nickname (Pilar) and the name of Hemingway's boat may be Notre-Dame du Pilier, Our Lady of the Pillar at Chartres.[4]

The list of French places that signify for Hemingway is so long as to seem nearly inexhaustible. A few more examples must suffice. He honeymoons with Pauline in 1927 in the pilgrimage and crusader country of Saintes-Marie-de-la-Mer, Aigues Mortes, and le Grau-du-Roi, and revisits that highly charged symbolic landscape again in the 1950s. He goes with Pauline repeatedly to Hendaye-Plage, for long stays at that fine beach with excellent swimming and a view of Spain in the near distance, just far enough away across the border. He spends a season on the Côte d'Azur. Throughout the 1930s, 1940s and 1950s, he continues to explore France and revisit old favorite places. In 1938, on what is usually regarded as one of the Spanish Civil War trips, a "Spanish trip" that lasts from August 31 to November 24, Hemingway is in Spain less than two weeks out of the nearly three months. The rest of the time he is in Paris, or hunting in the Sologne, or driving through France. Throughout the summer of 1944, he is deeply invested in the French countryside, from the Normandy Campaign through the liberation of the Cotentin Peninsula, Villedieu-les-Pôeles, le Mont-St-Michel, Chartres, and Rambouillet as well as Paris.

In the late 1940s, giving travel advice to his son Gregory in a letter, Hemingway provides a succinct guidebook to his France (his transcription of French place-names does not improve very much over the years): "If you go down to Provence you can make a circular tour starting from Avignon and see Le Pont du Gard, Nimes, Aigues Mortes, Le Grau de Roi, St. Maries de la Mer, Arles, Les Baux, St. Remy, Tarascon and Beaucaire, taking them in that order." He mentions the corridas at Nîmes, Arles, Béziers, and Bayonne. For another corner of France he gives this advice: "If you go down to the Basque country first you can see St. Jean de Luz, Bayonne, Hendaye, where there is a wonderful beach. . . . It is a very pleasant summer country and beautiful up in the hills by Cambo and St. Jean Pied du Port and Les Aldudes which is the country on the French side opposite Roncesvalles. . . . (the Roncevaux of the Roland)." At least as much for the historical associations and symbolic landscapes as for the country—Roland, for example, had long been an iconic figure in Hemingway's *paysage moralisé*—he especially recommends these two "more or less off the beaten track" itineraries. Not slighting the North and West of France, he adds: "Mont St. Michele is wonderful to see and shouldn't be missed if you can help it. The hotel to stay there if you can is La Mere Poulard which is run by . . . an old friend of mine . . . I practically ran the joint for her at one time." He recommends a bicycle trip along the Brittany coast: "many fine fishing villages and lovely country." Then, after all these detailed suggestions of what to see (and in what order) in France, he makes a brief one-sentence recommendation for Italy (Letter to Gregory Hemingway).

On one of his many trips through the French countryside, Hemingway in 1953 amused himself all down through the Loire Valley "by imagining that he was a medieval knight riding his horse along the riverbank," and the notion "stayed with him all the way south through Dax and St.-Jean-de-Luz to Hendaye" (Baker, *Life Story* 511). This picture presents us with a very revealing image of a Hemingway that few of us know, that we have not sufficiently comprehended; moreover, the notion—*Hemingway's* notion (*and* F. Scott Fitzgerald's notion of Hemingway as Philippe, French knight)—of the writer as a medieval knight of France should stand as a core image for any deliberations on the subject of Hemingway and France. He knew and loved, and profoundly and passionately identified with, French history and French places. On many trips through France, Hemingway displayed this love and this knowledge to his traveling companions, often serving as tour guide, lecturing at such off the beaten track places as Aigues Mortes (on the history of the Crusades), always manifesting his deep response to French history, French placeliness.[5]

Beyond this brief sketch of Hemingway's French places, there are many others, hundreds of routes and ramblings that contribute to Hemingway's French *deus loci*. And one of Hemingway's most important groundings in the French earth, perhaps his most profound baptism (or confirmation) in the French spirit of place—matters far too intricate to deal with here— was his participation in the Battle of Normandy and the Crusade for France.[6] It must suffice to say here that my detailed maps of every region of France indicating the places Hemingway knew, saw, studied, wrote, fought, visited, and revisited are so marked up and crisscrossed with his itineraries that they have become nearly illegible. If we have established that Hemingway truly knew and deeply loved the "broad and lovely" country of France and its "very old magic," then let us assess how he deployed this knowledge and love in his fiction.

One of his earliest stories, "My Old Man," evokes the country just outside Paris and the village of Maisons-Lafitte (some twenty kilometers from the heart of Paris): "Maisons is about the swellest place to live I've ever seen in all my life," Hemingway's boy-narrator asserts. He loves Maisons, with its "swell forest" where, like some French Huck Finn (or Huck Fini?), he "used to go off bumming in all day" (*Complete Stories* 154). It is worth noting another place distinction in the "My Old Man" manuscript that was deleted from the finished story: "Anyway right away I liked Maisons-Lafitte a lot better than I'd ever liked Milan." Aside from the few references to Maisons as a delightful place, "My Old Man" deals primarily with the local texture of Paris and its racetracks.

Another story that employs French settings outside Paris is "A Canary for One," with its account of a train ride along the Côte d'Azur, from Cannes through Marseilles and Avignon, then on to Paris. The French landscape here functions symbolically—the nearly missed train in Cannes, the "switchyards" of Marseilles, the "farmhouse burning in a field" with the bedding and furniture "spread in the field," and the Avignon station (with its resonances of schism, exile, and, in the Petrarchan sense, Babylonian Captivity). All of these place details serve to foreshadow the story's revelation in the final sentence that the American husband and wife are "returning to Paris to set up separate residences" (*Complete Stories* 258-61).

Other stories, largely neglected, have French settings, such as "The Sea Change" (Paris) and "Black Ass at the Cross Roads" (northeast France), with its extensive use of the French language, its evocation of the French countryside in wartime, and its delicate presentation of Claude, the French

Resistance fighter, as one of Hemingway's most compelling exemplars. Yet perhaps more revealing for the reader seeking the core of Hemingway's vision of France are those stories that employ France not as a setting but as subtext, as benchmark of *place* intertwined with *values*, as the countercountry of geomoral landscape. Two of the last three stories of *Winner Take Nothing* (1933) play variations on Hemingway's international theme, with French values significantly contrasted with the American lack of those values. In "Wine of Wyoming" the messy behavior of Americans, the desiccation or spiritual aridity and denial of communion and community in Hemingway's Wyoming, are sharply counterpoised with the clean, well-lighted place of Madame Fontan, an island of transplanted Frenchness in the American Waste Land. "Wine of Wyoming" foregrounds France in order to define America, where there is Prohibition, where there are too many churches and not enough communion, where "it isn't any good to be catholique," where it isn't any good to drink (*Complete Stories* 347). It is a measure of both Hemingway's writerly craft and his love of France that he sets his most insistently French short story in Wyoming and, in one of his comic master-pieces, takes great delight in French language, manners, and tradition.[7]

A similar if less developed use of France as benchmark is found in "Fathers and Sons," the last story of *Winner Take Nothing* and of *The Fifth Column and the First Forty-Nine Stories* (1938), which, in a manner hitherto unnoticed, provides significant closure for both volumes. The boy asks his father why they do not go to pray at the tomb of his grandfather. The reply—"It's a long way from here"—elicits this response from the boy: "In France that wouldn't make any difference. In France we'd go. I think I ought to go to pray at the tomb of my grandfather" (*Complete Stories* 376). In one stroke, then, Hemingway underscores a crucial difference in French and American atti-tudes toward matters of ritual, tradition, and piety. Indeed it is much more than a passing peripheral reference, affirmed by the fact that "Fathers and Sons" was originally entitled "The Tomb of My Grandfather."

The most telling instance of Hemingway's use of France as symbolic landscape, as *paysage moralisé*, in his short stories may be found in "Che Ti Dice La Patria?" This landscape with figures, depicting Fascist Italy, con-cludes at the frontier, with a typically emblematic and charged border-crossing: "We drove for two hours after it was dark and slept in Mentone that night." Back across the border, safe and at home—as always—in France, Hemingway adds: "It seemed very cheerful and clean and sane and lovely" (*Complete Stories* 230). Hemingway arrived at this, one of his most revealing and enduring formulations of his France, through a manuscript process of double superscription. At first he merely noted the arrival in France and that they slept in Menton. Then he added: "It seemed very cheerful and lovely." Finally he inserted "clean and sane." Thus he created his most succinct equation for his France, an image that endures (he repeatedly uses the very words to characterize France elsewhere in his work) and informs his life, his travels, his residences, and his work: "Very cheerful and clean and sane and lovely" equals France.

This is an equation that might help us more truly to understand the several charged border crossings of *The Sun Also Rises*, including the often misread crossing when Jake Barnes says: "I hated to leave France. Life was so simple in France. I felt I was a fool to be going back into Spain" (233). To be sure, France serves Hemingway, in general, and *The Sun Also Rises*, in particular, as anything but a corrupt, sterile, inauthentic, materialistic wasteland or Waste Land (in T. S. Eliot's sense—more a condition of spirit than place). It is anything but the selfish, dull, quotidian, ordinary, pragmatic, mechanistic, capitalistic, false, infertile low country (and so forth ad infinitum) that it has so often been grotesquely depicted as in the Hemingway critical tradition, which, as far as *country* goes—place and placeliness—has been overwhelmingly (and sometimes jejunely) Francophobic and Hispanophilic. Bizarrely *anachronistic* readings of Hemingway's France—especially as it functions in *The Sun Also Rises*—are abundant. Edward Stanton finds the Spanish landscape of the novel sacral and "luminous" and the French landscape a gloomy wasteland; his skewed inversions of the plain facts of the novel would have us believe that the Spaniards are natural, joyful, non-materialistic beings, while the French are artificial, sullen, and grossly materialistic (49, 61-62, 84-88, and passim). Frederic Joseph Svoboda also insists on this France/Spain design, seeing France as "money-centered" and corrupt, finding this ostensible schema particularly important in the border-crossing sequence of Book III (see esp. 80-84).

The notion of Paris—and in the more extreme version of the argument, all France—as a wasteland (or the Waste Land) has been all too common in critical studies of *The Sun Also Rises*, at least since Philip Young's 1952 assertion that "Eliot's London is Hemingway's Paris" (59) and Carlos Baker's 1952 treatment of "The Wastelanders" of *The Sun Also Rises* (*Writer as Artist* 75-93). While Baker and Young treat this matter somewhat moderately, later writers take the argument to such extremes that the Paris/France/Wasteland equation may be said to be one of the truisms and one of the regnant gaucheries of Hemingway studies. Consider Wirt Williams, who belabors the formula of France as the "low country," the "anti-idealistic," "quotidian," "lower reality" contrasted with the "exaltation" of the higher reality of Spain (60-62). Or Svoboda, with his insistence (even while his cited evidence argues to the contrary) on "the novel's France/Spain split in values," on the "easy values" (?) of France contrasted with the "real values" of Spain (82-84). Or Stanton, whose egregious treatment of the matter renders France as a cesspool of "materialism and the reduction of everything to the cash-value principle." For Jake Barnes, Stanton argues (against all the evidence), "life in France is unacceptable"; "France is the nation of the false values in the modern world—materialism, selfishness, a sterile rationalism, mechanization"—that is negatively contrasted with Spain's generosity, luminousness, fertility, and so forth (49, 87-88, and passim). What is there to say to such assertions, completely unsubstantiated, even by misappropriated evidence? Go and see the real France? The France where Hemingway—and Jake—*lived*, and from which they made occasional brief trips to Spain. And reread the actual text of *The Sun Also Rises*, with its luminous French particularity. Above all, avoid the fundamental confusion of reading Life-with/ without-Brett as Life-in-Paris-and-France.

Such readers—indeed all readers who find even faintly alluring these notions of a "France/Spain split in values"—should contemplate with more precision the cumulative force of details as well as the actual polarities that are emphasized in the novel's border crossings. We should reconsider too the image of Paris before dealing with the French countryside. *Jake's* Paris is repeatedly characterized as "nice," "good," "pleasant," "fine," "grand," a place where the locals, the *French* people—if not the Quarter crowd, if not *some* of the expatriates—are civilized, pleasant, loyal, walking (and dancing) incarnations of joie de vivre. There is the accordion-playing proprietor of the bal musette where Jake dances and feels "happy," or that "grand woman" Madame Lecomte who makes such "a great fuss" over seeing Bill and Jake when they eat their fine meal at her establishment (19, 76). Indeed, the first third (84 of 247 pages) of the novel transcribes *Jake's* Paris as the *locus amoenus* of his life, the place where he chooses to live, his cheerful and sane and lovely home, from which he makes brief annual excursions to Spain (and, nota bene, frequent excursions around France). Then we leave this Paris that all too many commentators are pleased to regard as some kind of corrupt, dissolute, gloomy wasteland, a place of "living death" (Stanton 87), a place that, in fact, is carefully and firmly established by Hemingway in Chapters I to VIII as the very touchstone of *place*, the benchmark of *chora*, the ultimate urban manifestation of the *deus loci*. It is, we recall, Robert Cohn who most insistently dislikes Paris; so perhaps it is the critic-as-Cohn who inscribes his or her own Francophobia, urban phobia, or Paname phobia—certainly not Hemingway's, not Jake's.

After we leave this actual and textual Paris, this cheerful and lovely Paris, we move through the French countryside, "beautiful from the start," replete with fertility and memory, the ripening grain and fields of poppies, with green pastureland and "fine trees, and sometimes big rivers and chateaux off in the trees" (84-87). The train moves through the Landes—"all sandy pine country full of heather"—and Jake and Bill "feel the country" (88). The next morning is "bright" and "nice" in Bayonne, which is "like a very clean Spanish town" (that is, it feels/looks somewhat Spanish but is much cleaner). Bayonne has "a cool, fresh, early-morning smell"; the café is "pleasant" and Jake does not want to leave; they have a "good" room at the "nice" and "awfully *clean*" hotel, where the French, "the people at the desk," are "*very cheerful*" (89-91; emphasis added). Outside Bayonne the country is "green and rolling," with "*lovely* gardens"; "the land all looks very rich and green," the villages "look well-off and *clean*" (91; emphasis added). After this sequence of evocations of the French landscape (employing the Menton formula from "Che Ti Dice La Patria?"), Jake describes the border-crossing, the sword-waving, expectorating Spanish border guard who does not like to fish, the "dusty road into Spain," the "gloomy little village" they pass through, and the "brown and baked-looking" and strangely furrowed mountains (92-93).

In fact, as the novel has it, there is much more wasteland-scape in Spain than in France. Examples include the journey north from Pamplona to Burguete: In one stretch, Hemingway writes, "the country was quite barren," "hard-baked," and again "barren," rocky, without grass, and so on (105, 108). As they get farther north toward France, toward Roncevaux, toward Roland country, the land turns green and wooded. The Forest of the Irati, it is to be noted, straddles the border of France and Spain, and the Irati River rises in France (where the Seine also rises). And if rivers figure importantly in any paradigm of wasteland/antiwasteland topography, it should be noted that the Seine, that "nice" river that Jake finds "always pleasant" to cross (41), is described much more than is the Irati. The reader of *The Sun Also Rises*, in fact, never sees the Irati; Jake and Bill do not fish it in the rendered action. They fish the Fabrica, just outside a hamlet known as Fabrica, and Fabrica means factory; the river and the hamlet are named after the ruined munitions factory on the banks at Jake's fishing site.[8] What does all this say about imaginary patterns of Spanish mountain idylls and French wastelands?

And so, of those readers who must see a wasteland in this novel, it is necessary to ask this question: On which side of the border is it? I hasten to add, if it is not yet clear, that I do not see a geographically defined wasteland anywhere in this novel—not Paris, not France, not Pamplona, not Spain. (An Eliotesque "Waste Land" in the hearts and souls of some, a very few, of the expatriate characters is quite another matter.) It is well past time that we recognize certain landscape and place principles as fundamental in Hemingway: (1) he loved country, all country; (2) he loved two countries above all others—France and Spain; (3) he truly and enduringly loved one city in all the world—Paris.

Now then, what about those border crossings and what they tell us about France, about Spain? Consider a few paired scenes and details that involve borders: The chauffeur, the French driver who takes them into Spain, is helpful, apparently quite pleasant (since he "stayed for lunch" with Jake and the others at the Montoya), and, most significantly, he makes no problem over his pay; he makes no attempt to raise the agreed-upon charge (91-94). In contrast, the Spanish driver who takes them back into France after the fiesta is characterized by one detail: When the trip is over, he raises the agreed-upon "fixed" price of 150 pesetas to 200 pesetas. Jake doesn't like it, and he rejects the driver's bargaining and offer to take him to San Sebastian for an extra 50, then 35, pesetas (231-32). That's one paired border scene, and if we must search for the so-called materialism and corruption, it is quite clear from which side of the border they emanate. Other recurrent and contradistinguishing details involve hotels on opposite sides of the border. Jake's only French hotel (he stays there twice, before and after two border crossings), we recall, was "nice" and "clean" and the French proprietors were "very cheerful." In contrast, just across the border at Burguete, the inn is "cold" and overpriced, the innkeeper is "fat" and rather devious, and stingy with her rum (109-10). And at the Hotel Montana in Madrid the maid is "sullen" and dull-faced, the proprietress, a "very fat woman" with "stiffly oiled" hair, is defensive and insistent and "short and commanding" (240-41). Who is materialistic, who is pleasant, who is sullen in these cross-border hotel scenes that resonate with precisely the opposite significance attributed to them in the scheme of the so-called France/Spain split in values? (Of course, there are pleasant and civilized hotels on both sides of Jake's actual borders—for example, the Crillon in Paris and the Palace in Madrid; I repeat, my point here is not the converse of the usual absurd argument regarding France.)

Another vexed critical question involves restaurants and Jake's meals, and the confused and passing references to and obfuscatory readings of Jake's French and Spanish meals, which have also been forced to serve in the design of the supposed cross-border value split.[9] The meal that has received most of the critical attention and radical misreading, as some putative token of French meagerness or avariciousness, is Jake's dinner when he returns to Bayonne after the fiesta. Since so many unfortunate generalizations regarding that meal as representative of all French meals have been carelessly proffered, we should first consider briefly all the meals in the novel to see what pattern, if any, really is present. In France, nine meals are mentioned and five are characterized; dining in the Bois de Boulogne with Brett and the Count, Jake notes that "it was a good dinner" and food has "an excellent place in the Count's values" (as in Jake's). At Madame Lecomte's on the Ile Saint Louis they have "a good meal" and Jake gives the complete menu, the only time in the novel he does so. Other meals in France are characterized as "good" and "pleasant," and at the restaurant in Bayonne, where "one eats very well," Jake has "a big meal for France" (61, 76, 232). This last is the *only* reference to *quantity* in the notation of French meals; all other characterizations have to do with *quality*.

In contrast, seventeen Spanish meals are mentioned and only five are characterized. The meal notations are brief, and they are mostly concerned with *quantity*: "the first meal in Spain was always a shock" (94); at Burguete, they have "a big bowl . . . of soup . . . some sort of a stew and a big bowl" of strawberries (110-11). In Pamplona, at the Hotel Montoya, they have "a big meal . . . the first meal of the prices being doubled for the fiesta" (159); later, they avoid eating there because of the unpleasant maitre d'hôtel, "a continual eavesdropper" with a "dirty little" smile (209). Finally, in Madrid, Brett and Jake leave the Palace Hotel bar, since lunch would be "rotten" there, and go to Botin's. Jake announces that "it is one of the best restaurants in the world," but his only comment on the roast young suckling pig lunch is: "I ate a very *big* meal" (245-46; emphasis added). The pattern, then, such as it is, stresses quantity in Spain, quality in France. Perhaps the main thing that certain Hemingway food critics are really telling us is that, for them, "some sort" of a double Big Mac or Whopper with a shockingly large order of fries is a better meal, more to be valued than, say, *Tournedos Saint-Germain* and *pommes de terre à la Parisienne*. Maybe Hemingway's meal notations are more axiological, even theological, than we have recognized. Gastronomy is a matter of quality, not quantity; gastronomy is founded on taste, which is one of the regnant values of *The Sun Also Rises*. And the deadly sin is gluttony, not gourmandise.

As for Jake's most-discussed meal, after the fiesta, at the modest unnamed café-restaurant in Bayonne where "one eats very well," this may be one of the most frequently misinterpreted scenes in the novel. Typically, Svoboda reads this as a scene that foregrounds the "easy," "money-centered" values of France (in opposition to Spanish values and "the real values that Jake espouses"). For Svoboda, this scene underscores "the French waiter's love of money" (in opposition to some ostensible "real" values that Spanish waiters embody?) and some presumed negativity thought to reside in Jake's inscription of this meal as "carefully apportioned" (81). What really transpires in this scene? Jake eats a "big meal" that *seems*, "after Spain," to be "carefully apportioned." In one sense, this represents no more, no less than the culmination of the France-Spain qualitative-quantitative meal pattern just noted. In another sense, it relates significantly to one of the novel's primary motifs—the arc of experience from the *mesuré* to the *démesuré*, from decorum to excess. To imply, as Svoboda and others have, that *mesure*, that careful apportionment, that moderation or decorum are somehow *negative* qualities associated with France is to miss the point utterly. (Hemingway was not joking when he said that *The Sun Also Rises* was "a tract against promiscuity,"[10] and the category of the promiscuous includes indiscriminate eating.) Indeed, *mesure* is the luminous, profoundly positive essence of France, as it is of Jake's character in its most exemplary sense. It is *mesure*, careful apportionment, properly understood (and in fertile creative tension with passion), that is the foundation of *places* that are "very cheerful and clean and sane and lovely"—people too. It is *mesure* that defines Jake's life year-round in France, with a week of necessary excess, a brief interval of fiesta in Spain. Just as surely as Ash Wednesday follows Fat Tuesday (and one without the other is either mere chaos or mere asceticism), Jake longs for "quiet" and simplicity and *mesure* after the fiesta.

So we are with Jake, in Bayonne, enjoying his "carefully apportioned" meal and a bottle of Château Margaux: "It was pleasant to be drinking slowly and to be tasting the wine" (232). Château Margaux, of course, has for centuries been one of the greatest wines of France (and thus of the world); legendary for its elegance *and* finesse *and* perfect balance, this Margaux is as emblematic of France as any key French fact or symbol in the novel, and it is very much to the point that Jake, in his happiness at reentering France, selects, drinks slowly and tastes deeply his Château Margaux. The point is underlined when the waiter recommends the "Basque liqueur called Izzarra [*sic*]." Izarra is generally regarded, in France, as a dismal and unfortunate counterfeit of the classic French liqueur Chartreuse; for Jake, it is repellent, looks like "hair-oil," smells like "Italian *strega*" (233), and he refuses the offered glass. He orders, most appropriately for his French homecoming, a *vieux marc* (or eau-de-vie de marc), a representative drink of "la France profonde," the deep heart of France. He has a second *marc* after his coffee. At this point, as Svoboda has it, our supposedly avaricious French waiter gets friendly, a ploy "to increase the size of his tip" (81). Nothing of the kind happens, and Svoboda and others get this scene completely wrong, in their familiar and wearisome insistence on the imaginary France-Spain paradigm. What actually happens is this: The waiter seems "a little offended about the flowers of the Pyrenees," Jake's mockingly reiterated epithet for the repellent Izarra, so Jake overtips him. *Then*, not before, the waiter is "happy." We might note also that this waiter is probably *not French*; given the fact that he recommends the Izarra (it is hard to imagine a French waiter doing so) and, moreover, the fact that he is offended by Jake's rejection of the "flowers of the Pyrenees" (233)—given, that is, the *action* of the scene (as well as the setting), the waiter must be Basque.

After Jake tips the waiter, we get the generally miscontrued sequence of observations about France, "the simplest country to live in" because things are on "such a clear financial basis." In France, "No one makes things complicated by becoming your friend for any obscure reason"; as Jake puts it, "I spent a little money and the waiter liked me," and it is "a sincere liking . . . [with] a sound basis." Jake also overtips at the hotel because he "wanted a few good French friends in Bayonne" to make him welcome if he ever comes back: "their friendship would be loyal" (233). Of course, Jake also overtips in Spain; but there, for "obscure" reasons and because "you could not tell about anything" (233) in Spain, he does not always get what he pays for. There is nothing in this scene to suggest that France is any more materialistic or money-centered than Spain, that the French are any more avaricious than the Spanish. What the scene does tell us is that there are certain values that prevail in France—*soundness, sincerity, loyalty,* "simple" (as opposed to "obscure") *friendship*—dictated by a code that is, in part, the same as Jake's stated code: "Just exchange of values. . . . enjoying living was learning to get your money's worth and knowing when you had it" (148). The point is that it is generally preferable, except for maybe two weeks a year (Jake's vacation time in Spain), to get what you pay for; this is surely better than paying for what you don't get, or getting less—or more—than you bargained for, surely better than not being able to "tell about anything."

Jake's "code," of course, has greater amplitude than the exchange-of-values passage suggests; his code or creed includes and is centered on matters of passion—the Church, the Corrida, Fishing, Sport, Art, Pilgrimage—that transcend getting "your money's worth." To be sure, Jake is, in most matters, a rather accomplished axiologist; the clean and cheerful, the sound and sincere, the loyal and simple value patterns of France that he celebrates are very high on the axiological scale of things, as is gastronomy (the quality, not the quantity, of food). Moreover, gastronomy—as one theological commentator recently observed—"is not to be classed among the materialistic 'lower immediacies' at the bottom of the axiological ladder of values . . . but deserves transcendent status!" (Montgomery 25). The deadly sin, it bears repeating, is gluttony, not gourmandise, indulging in quantity, not quality. Early in the novel, Jake entertains a trip to Sainte Odile, the Alsatian pilgrimage site. Perhaps he knows, and surely he would endorse, the ancient invitatory chant of the Confrèrie St.-Etienne, the Alsatian wine guild, regarding food and wine: "'*Primo mirate, deinde gustate, tandem gaudete ad magnam Dei gloriam*' (First look with wonder, then taste, finally give praise to God's great glory)" (Montgomery 25-26). In a well-ordered world, all meals are sacramental. So is Jake's bottle of Château Margaux. *Taste*, as a value, is more than just the opposite of gluttony. It is an index of wonder and glory. Hemingway knows this; Jake Barnes knows this.

For all of these reasons, then, Jake hates "to leave France," feels like "a fool to be going back into Spain" (233). As the French bicycle team manager says to Jake the next night in San Sebastian, "Few people know France" (236). This scene, this meal, has also been read in skewed fashion to force it into the procrustean schema of the France/Spain split in values. Svoboda reads it as the "intrusion" of inauthentic French values into the idyllic San Sebastian setting. The French team manager, Svoboda insists, is "chauvinistic," he "pontificates" on France; the upshot of the scene is "Jake's rejection of bicycle racing" (83-84). If the French manager is so offensively "chauvinistic" and pontifical, why does Jake choose to have coffee with him out on the terrace after the meal? Why does Jake linger and then choose to have a cognac (is that an inauthentic French "intrusion") with him? Because Jake loves bicycle racing. Because Jake agrees with most of what the Frenchman says—the Tour de France has long been and is still widely regarded as "the greatest [and the most demanding] sporting event in the world." And we know Jake agrees with him on another matter, concerning Jake's home: "There is only one Paname."

There is no mockery, *no* irony at the expense of France in this entire scene. The French girls are "good-looking"; all the French are paying "close attention to their meal" and "having a good time." And they are correct—in the 1920s—in saying that the "Spaniards . . . did not know how to pedal" (235-37). Thus Jake deliberately joins the French team manager for coffee and cognac—for an act of communion with one of the "few" who "know France." He does not get up the next morning for the early race departure because he is utterly exhausted from the fiesta, because he has gone to San Sebastian for the quietude, to recuperate, to sleep and to swim. His sleeping late does not imply his "rejection of bicycle-racing" any more than his sleeping late in Pamplona and missing one *encierro* (and barely catching another) implies a rejection of *toreo*. Indeed "few people know France," but Jake does. Perceptive axiologist that he is, Jake properly values sporting France as well as the France that is "very cheerful," "pleasant," "good," "rich," "beautiful," "nice," "very clean," and fertile, green and lovely; and it is his home, where he has made it.

Perhaps such a close reading of the novel will dispel the obfuscatory, jaded notion of a France/Spain axiological crux in *The Sun Also Rises* (or elsewhere in Hemingway's work or life). Perhaps, too, a little informed extratextuality would help, a little more deep geography and geomancy, or place divination, a little more *real* knowledge of *place*. Perhaps it is time for those who truly know and love both France and Spain (as Hemingway did) to remind readers that the Spanish setting of the novel is not *Andalucía*, not deeply Iberian, but Navarre/Navarra, which is, for those who know, the most *French* place in Spain. For centuries it *was* France. The art and the architecture as well as the *deus loci* and the viticulture profoundly manifest this fact. The French influence, of course, streamed copiously south on the roads of "Monsieur Saint Jacques" (Jake's namesake), on the pilgrimage routes of St.-Jacques-de-Compostelle/Santiago de Compostela. Jake and Hemingway know this very well indeed, and the pilgrimage provides the deep structure of the novel.[11]

Even though Hemingway provides more than enough evidence to argue the exact opposite of the usual critical emphases regarding the imaginary France/Spain scheme, such a *reversal* of the topophilic/phobic notion is not at all the point here. Rather, what must be grasped is that the novel—from Paris to Navarre, from St.-Jean-Pied-du-Port to Roncevaux to Pampelune, from Roncesvalles to Pamplona, sacral site of the fiesta of the good San Fermín/St. Firmin (who was a French bishop and has towns named after him all over France)—is centered on the magical numinous intersections of France and Spain, Spain and France.

Maybe, just maybe, if we bury deeply enough the fantasy, the bizarre groundless abstractions concerning the France/Spain "split," then that other master motif that has infected the biocritical tradition for decades—France-as-Wasteland—will also disappear. Even in treatments of Hemingway and France that do not invoke Spain or depend solely on *The Sun Also Rises*, even in discussions that are more nuanced and sophisticated than those just cited, indeed even in such a valuable study as J. Gerald Kennedy's recent *Imagining Paris* (a work that *is* informed by complex notions and theories of *place*), the France-as-Wasteland motif invades the argument. What are we to make of Kennedy's view that Paris caused "the erosion of [Hemingway's] Oak Park values," of his assertion that in a number of ways "life in France undermined [Hemingway's] faith in simple feelings and permanent bonds" (121-22)? What Kennedy seems to mean, given his argument, is that life in *Paris* "undermined" and somehow corrupted Hemingway. What he really says, given his evidence, is that life in the *Quarter* (one small corner of Paris) corrupted Hemingway. Even this notion seems infected with the false

France-as-Wasteland equation and is fundamentally incorrect. The truth is that Hemingway was "undermined" and corrupted—if he ever was truly any more corrupt than he was in the cradle, in Oak Park, in northern Michigan, in Milan, and so on—by association with a bohemian-cosmopolitan group, an international set of expatriates who happened to be in Paris when he lived there. And that has *nothing* to do with *France*. France did not "undermine" Hemingway; Kennedy and many other commentators to the contrary, nearly all the evidence, considered carefully, declares that life in France affirmed and deepened and clarified Hemingway's "faith in simple feelings and permanent bonds."

If we had space here to examine at length what I consider to be Hemingway's three major French narratives—*The Garden of Eden, A Moveable Feast,* and *The Sun Also Rises*—perhaps I could convert most members of the congregation to this liberated vision: there is no French "wasteland," not even a Parisian "Waste Land"—not the generalized "wasteland" of dictionaries or the Eliotesque "Waste Land," not Philip Young's "waste land" (60) or Mark Spilka's "wasteland" (84) or Carlos Baker's "wastelanders" (*Writer As Artist* 75-93)—anywhere in Hemingway's fiction or in his life. Quite to the contrary, *all* France, including Paris, is really "there, in the good place," is "good country," is numinous, is Hemingway's Eden, his Garden, pre- and post- and supralapsarian. If Hemingway falls in France, it is—topologically and theologically—a Fortunate Fall.

Consider briefly his most insistently French novel, his final celebration of France: *The Garden of Eden.* Even the unfortunate published version of the novel (and far more so the manuscript version[s]) amounts to Hemingway's hymn to the numinous country of Provence, to the luminous *deus loci* of the Camargue, from the port and walled city of the good Saint Louis (one of Hemingway's favorite French saints) to the sacral pilgrimage and fiesta beaches of Saintes-Marie-de-la-Mer. In the manuscript, Hemingway writes of the "early morning promise" of the "coast" of Provence; in the published version, with the editorial deletion of the key words ("of that coast"), the matter is detopologized, shorn of the particularity of *place.* For the reader of the published version, it is just another description of another morning, anywhere, and it is not Hemingway's morning in Provence (*Garden* 78). Indeed much of the novel's richly symbolic Provençal landscape, intricately intertwined with French history, with submerged layering, of Catharism, of the Templars and the Crusades, of the pilgrimage of Saintes-Maries, and so forth, disappears from the published text.

Then there is Colonel Boyle, the last of Hemingway's typical wounded-and-wise exemplars, whose true identity is edited out of the published text. When we first encounter Colonel Boyle, in the published version, we read that he is "wearing a dark blue suit" and a black tie (60); in the manuscript, we see that he is also wearing, dramatically foregrounded on his lapel against the dark blue, "the unusual combination of the narrow yellow and green of the *Médaille Militaire* and the rosette of an Officer of the Legion of Honor" ("Garden Manuscript," Bk. 3, Chap. 13, p. 21). Clearly, from the start, it is the *French* identity of Colonel Boyle that signifies. At first glance, it would seem that Hemingway has made an error here, that he is confused about the signification of the Colonel's medals. For, in fact, there is nothing *unusual* about the combination of the two medals Hemingway describes: The *Médaille Militaire* indicates that Colonel Boyle has been at the front, that he has been in combat for France, and the officer's rosette of the Legion indicates that he has served France in some capacity. It is, I repeat, a perfectly usual combination—for a Frenchman, *not* for a *foreigner*, and that is Hemingway's point.[12] Together, the medals signify Colonel Boyle's extraordinary devotion to France. A few pages later (not in the published version but in the manuscript), David explains to Catherine that the colonel is a man who has given his life to France, has fought for her, has lived in service to her like some medieval knight. As with Clemenceau, so it is with Colonel Boyle: His last remaining illusion is France. (We note that when the manuscript version of the Colonel Boyle scene concludes, Hemingway makes a note to himself in the margin to bring the colonel back into the story later, when things get bad ["Garden Manuscript," Bk. 3, Chap. 14, pp. 5-7].) In sum, one of the greatest flaws in the unfortunate editorial process that gave us the published text of *The Garden of Eden* is the deletion of the true identity of Colonel Boyle, Hemingway's Last Exemplar-Knight of France.

After all is said and done, Fitzgerald seems to have understood Hemingway more profoundly than most critics and biographers. Fitzgerald's vision—in some of his last work—of Hemingway as Philippe, Knight of the Middle Ages who fights for France, arrives to us, in this context, with the illuminating force of epiphany. Fitzgerald comprehended Hemingway's French Vision truly, long before the final chapter of Hemingway's knightly passion for France was incarnated in his participation in the Battle for Normandy and the Crusade for France. That is another subject for another essay, but we will recall here Hemingway's repeated assertions that the French campaign "was the wildest, most beautiful, wonderful time ever ever," that August 1944 was "the truly happiest month I've ever had in all my life"; "that summer," he writes in 1946, "from Normandy into Germany was the happiest I ever had in spite of it being war. . . . re-taking France . . . made me feel the best I had ever felt" (*Selected Letters* 574, 566, 591, 608).[13] It seems to me that after his fashion Hemingway believed that he was a knight fighting to redeem France—to save le Mont-St.-Michel, to liberate Chartres, to rescue and reclaim (with wet eyes and "a funny choke" in his throat) the city he loved "best in all the world": Paris. In some strange but very real way, Hemingway was a Knight of France, who, like his early "great hero" Clemenceau, like Colonel Boyle, Officer of the Legion of Honor and proud holder of the *Médaille Militaire*, was fighting for one of his longest-held and last remaining illusions: France.

Throughout Hemingway's life and work, then, the signal does not vary—France holds the center. The message, the signal has been sent repeatedly, through Colonel Boyle, through Jake Barnes and others, through Hemingway's own actions, but it has not often been received and understood. Perhaps we may come to understand, at last, what Jake Barnes *really* means when he celebrates the *simplicitás* of France. Then we might finally understand why Hemingway chose to live more of his life in France than in any other place beyond America. You travel to other countries for fiestas, for safaris, sometimes for wars, but you live—when you truly live—in France. And when you fight your last war—if you are Clemenceau or Colonel Boyle or Hemingway—you fight it for France. Like an old country song, an old French folksong, lilting and measured, Hemingway's haunting refrain reverberates: "Very cheerful and clean and sane and lovely."

NOTES

1. I was reminded at the Hemingway/Fitzgerald International Conference in Paris in 1994, when a conferee asked me about the exact location of Hemingway's interview with Clemenceau, that there is in the record some minor confusion about the exact site. Hemingway by-lines his piece Les Sables-D'Ollone [*sic*]. Actually, les Sables-d'Olonne is where Hemingway spent the night in his hotel. The Maison de Clemenceau is 24 kilometers from les Sables, just outside the village of St.-Vincent-sur-Jard. It is *not in* "St. Vincent du Jard," as Carlos Baker writes in *A Life Story* (101) and Michael Reynolds repeats (71). Since this essay is concerned, in part, with geographical precision, and since there are more than forty St. Vincents in France, it would seem useful to be cartographically and toponymically exact.

2. Clemenceau's popular appellations were numerous: the Tiger, the Old Tiger, the Good Old Tiger, the Old Man, and many others. He was, of course, a favorite subject for cartoonists and caricaturists, and his visage, usually accompanied by a tiger or some tigerish motif, was one of the best-known and most instantly recognizable faces of the early twentieth century. The Musée Clemenceau in Paris has an extensive collection of such depictions, including a number that pair his face and a reclining tiger (Clemenceau usually looking a bit more fierce than the tiger), together with the caption "Le bon Tigre" (sometimes also included in English as "The Good Old Tiger").

3. See, for example, Spilka (84-85), Stanton (26-27 and 49-62), Svoboda (81-84), and Williams (60-62). The specifics of their assumptions and arguments regarding France and Paris are discussed later in the text. It should also be noted that similar assumptions are deeply embedded in much of the biographical writing, in ways too multifarious to be documented here.

4. The Callaghan anecdote is recounted in Baker (*Life Story* 204) and in Callaghan (232-38). For the evidence concerning Hemingway and the Liberation of Chartres, see my "Hemingway's 'Happiest Summer.'" In my "interviews" with Mary Hemingway—more precisely, scores of conversations over the course of a decade—she acknowledged Ernest's interest in these matters, but she could not specify the details of any discussions with him at Chartres. For examination of Hemingway's knowledge of the matter of Saint-Jacques/Santiago, see my "From the rue Saint-Jacques."

5. See Hotchner (passim) and Mary Welsh Hemingway (passim). In my conversations with Mary Hemingway about her travels in Europe with Ernest, she often alluded to his propensity to lecture about the history of the places they visited—*especially* in France. She suggested that he seemed to *know more* about *French places*, seemed, in other words, to know rural France better than rural Italy and Spain. In France, he always wanted to "get off the beaten track" and show her "some place like Aigues Mortes or Les Baux or Carcassonne." Italy, she said, was more about "social life," and Spain was "mostly bullfights and bullfight talk."

6. For a fresh reading of, and new evidence concerning, Hemingway's World War II experiences in France, see my "'I Should Have Kissed Him'" and "Hemingway's 'Happiest Summer.'"

7. For a detailed discussion of "Wine of Wyoming," see my "'Mais Je Reste Catholique.'"

8. For a detailed discussion of this matter, see my "'You Sure This Thing Has Trout In It?'" (115-22).

9. See, for example, Donaldson (30), Stanton (84-89), and Svoboda (40, 81-83). In addition, since the clichés and hackneyed assumptions of any area of scholarly study take root and occur more often in oral than in printed discourse (by their very nature), I note that in scores of lectures and conference papers and discussion sections over the past three decades I have witnessed the misconstruction of Jake's French/ Spanish meals, either as passing reference or as evidence presented in support of some more ambitious France/Spain argument.

10. See Drew (94) and my "From the rue Saint-Jacques" (6-8).

11. See my article "From the rue Saint-Jacques" for close examination of the pilgrimage theme in *The Sun Also Rises* together with details— French and Spanish—concerning the pilgrimage.

12. My interviews with several French officers of the Legion of Honor, with military officers, with Patrice Reboul (one of the leading médaillistes of France), and with the proprietors of "A Marie-Stuart S.A." ("la maison la plus ancienne de France," specializing in medals) in Paris, all confirm that Colonel Boyle's combination of medals is perfectly usual for a Frenchman but highly unusual for a foreigner. It should be noted also that Hemingway's description of the medals is precise and correct: Colonel Boyle is *not* wearing the actual *Médaille Militaire* but the "narrow yellow and green" piece of cloth that indicates that he is such a medalist; the medal itself, tripartite, yellow and green and gold and silver and deep blue, would not be appropriate for wear on such an occasion. As for the rosette of the Legion of Honor, Hemingway is exact in indicating that this means Colonel Boyle is an "Officer": he is not, that is, a *chevalier* of the Legion (the lowest rank), but an *officier* (the next rank, just below *commandeur*).

13. For a detailed examination of Fitzgerald's vision of Hemingway as Philippe, see my forthcoming essay "A Dark Ill-Lighted Place: Fitzgerald and Hemingway, Philippe Count of Darkness and Philip Counter-Espionage Agent." For new information about and interpretation of Hemingway's French experience during World War II, see my "'I Should Have Kissed Him'" and "Hemingway's 'Happiest Summer.'"

WORKS CITED

Baker, Carlos. *Ernest Hemingway: A Life Story.* New York: Scribners, 1969.

———. *Hemingway: The Writer as Artist.* Princeton, NJ: Princeton UP, 1952.

Beegel, Susan F., ed. *Hemingway's Neglected Short Fiction: New Perspectives.* Ann Arbor, MI: UMI Research P, 1989.

Callaghan, Morley. *That Summer in Paris: Memoirs of Tangled Friendships with Hemingway, Fitzgerald, and Some Others.* New York: Coward-McCann, 1963.

Donaldson, Scott. "Humor in *The Sun Also Rises.*" *New Essays on "The Sun Also Rises."* Ed. Linda Wagner-Martin. New York: Cambridge UP, 1987. 19-41.

Drew, Fraser. "April 8, 1955 with Hemingway: Unedited Notes on a Visit to Finca Vigia." *Conversations with Ernest Hemingway.* Ed. Matthew J. Bruccoli. Jackson: UP of Mississippi, 1986. 89-98.

Hemingway, Ernest. *By-Line: Ernest Hemingway. Selected Articles and Dispatches of Four Decades.* Ed. William White. New York: Scribners, 1967.

———. "Che Ti Dice La Patria" manuscript. Unpublished. Hemingway Collection. Item 328a. John F. Kennedy Library, Boston.

———. "Clemenceau Interview: Notes." Unpublished. Hemingway Collection. Item 773b. John F. Kennedy Library, Boston.

———. *The Complete Short Stories of Ernest Hemingway: The Finca Vigia Edition.* New York: Scribners, 1987.

———. *Dateline: Toronto. The Complete "Toronto Star" Dispatches, 1920-1924.* Ed. William White. New York: Scribners, 1985.

———. *Ernest Hemingway: Selected Letters, 1917-1961.* Ed. Carlos Baker. New York: Scribners, 1981.

———. "Exercise (Stone)." Unpublished. Hemingway Collection. Item 719. John F. Kennedy Library, Boston.

———. *The Garden of Eden.* New York: Scribners, 1986.

———. "The Garden of Eden Manuscript." Unpublished. Hemingway Collection. Item 422.1. John F. Kennedy Library, Boston.

———. "I saw a drunken workingman." Unpublished. Hemingway Collection. Item 515. John F. Kennedy Library, Boston.

———. Letter to Gregory Hemingway, July 17, 1949. Unpublished. Hemingway Collection. John F. Kennedy Library, Boston.

———. "My Old Man" manuscript. Unpublished. Hemingway Collection. Item 592. John F. Kennedy Library, Boston.

———. "Notes in a bistrot [sic] in Avignon." Unpublished. Hemingway
        Collection. Item 582. John F. Kennedy Library, Boston.
———. The Sun Also Rises. 1926. New York: Scribners, 1954.
———. "Talking with the Tiger." Toronto Star March 1, 1992: F5.
Hemingway, Mary Welsh. How It Was. New York: Knopf, 1976.
Hotchner, A. E. Papa Hemingway. New York: Random House, 1966.
Jackson, J. Hampden. Clemenceau and the Third Republic. New York: Macmillan,
        1948.
Kennedy, J. Gerald. Imagining Paris: Exile, Writing, and American Identity. New
        Haven, CT: Yale UP, 1993.
Martet, Jean. Georges Clemenceau. London: Longman's, Green, 1930.
Montgomery, John Warwick. "Letter from England." New Oxford Review
        61.10 (1994): 24-25.
Reynolds, Michael. Hemingway: The Paris Years. Cambridge, MA: Blackwell,
        1989.
Spilka, Mark. "The Death of Love in The Sun Also Rises." Hemingway and His
        Critics: An International Anthology. Ed. Carlos Baker. New York: Hill
        and Wang, 1961. 80-92.
Stanton, Edward F. Hemingway and Spain: A Pursuit. Seattle: U of Washington
        P, 1989.
Stoneback, H. R. "A Dark Ill-Lighted Place: Fitzgerald and Hemingway,
        Philippe Count of Darkness and Philip Counter-Espionage Agent."
        F. Scott Fitzgerald: New Perspectives. Ed. Jackson R. Bryer, Alan Mar-
        golies, and Ruth Prigozy. Athens: U of Georgia P, forthcoming.
———. "From the rue Saint-Jacques to the Pass of Roland to the 'Unfinished
        Church of the Edge of the Cliff.'" Hemingway Review 6.1 (1986): 2-29.
———. "Hemingway's 'Happiest Summer'—'The Wildest, Most Beautiful,
        Wonderful Time Ever Ever': Or, the Liberation of France and
        Hemingway." North Dakota Quarterly 64.3 (1997): 184-220.
———. "'I Should Have Kissed Him': Hemingway's Last War—-Ringing
        the Changes." North Dakota Quarterly 63.3 (1996): 99-114.
———. "'Mais Je Reste Catholique': Communion, Betrayal, and Aridity in
        'Wine of Wyoming.'" Hemingway's Neglected Short Fiction: New Perspec-
        tives. Ed. Susan F. Beegel. Ann Arbor, MI: UMI Research P, 1989.
        209-24.
———. "'You Sure This Thing Has Trout in It?': Fishing and Fabrication,
        Omission, and Verification in The Sun Also Rises." Hemingway Repos-
        sessed. Ed. Kenneth Rosen. Westport, CT: Praeger, 1994. 115-28.
Svoboda, Frederic Joseph. Hemingway and "The Sun Also Rises": The Crafting of a
        Style. Lawrence: UP of Kansas, 1983.

Williams, Wirt. *The Tragic Art of Ernest Hemingway*. Baton Rouge: Louisiana State UP, 1981.

Young, Philip. *Ernest Hemingway*. New York: Rinehart, 1952.

THE EXPATRIATE PREDICAMENT IN *THE SUN ALSO RISES*

R O B E R T   A .   M A R T I N

Why is *The Sun Also Rises*, which takes place in Paris and Spain, called an "American" novel, other than the obvious fact of the nationality of its author? How can it be read as "American," and what does this term mean? Can it mean anything in Hemingway's work? "America" is presented in this novel by its conspicuous absence. For how else can it be better understood than by stepping outside of it as a place—a sort of literary displacement? The idea of "American" exists through three characters who have, to varying degrees, left America behind but who do not (or cannot) entirely forsake their internalized American values: Robert Cohn, Bill Gorton, and Jake Barnes.

How they interact and clash with one another, with other Americans in Europe, and as "expatriates" and "foreigners" among the French and Spanish show the limits and the possibilities of American experience and existence. As Gerald Nelson comments in his analysis of Jake Barnes,

> All over the world after the war, one found the disenfranchised and the disenchanted, English, American, French, and German, wandering their different ways, occasionally crossing paths, sharing a common motivation—the world they wanted was a different one from the one

in which they were supposed to live. . . . they were escaping a totally
new type of oppression. They just didn't like where they'd been; they
could have stayed, but they didn't want to. (30)

Among these self-induced exiles were those "who did not wish to go
to Europe as much as they wanted to get out of the United States" (Nelson
30). Robert Cohn is in this category. He is most closely connected with
America through an account of his background there. He appears to have
achieved the American dream: prestigious Jewish family, Princeton graduate, magazine editor and publisher, successful published writer, and European traveler. Yet his seemingly high status is undercut with ironic and pitiful
(to use Bill Gorton's phrase) contradictions: His Jewish background gives
him outsider status. "I never met anyone of his class [at Princeton] who
remembered him," Jake remarks (*Sun* 3). Both his wife and his lover exploit
him (5), and his success in American culture comes, Jake says, through "a
very poor novel" (6) that has been rewarded materialistically by money and
women who "put themselves out to be nice to him" (8).

Cohn's success in America has tantalized him with the sight of new
"horizons": "He's decided he hasn't lived enough. I knew it would happen
when he went to New York," Francis Clyne comments (47). Yet his horizons
are rooted in America, which provides security and identity for him: "[L]ike
many people living in Europe, he would rather have been in America," Jake
remarks (5). He wants to continue to travel, he tells Jake, because he is "sick
of Paris," and "sick of the Quarter" (12). Cohn believes he is adventurously
directing his quest not toward America but toward an exotic image of South
America. In Paris his horizon shifts upon meeting Brett, whom he looks at
as if looking at "the promised land. . . . he had that look of eager, deserving
expectation" (22). Brett is Cohn's Daisy Buchanan; she has become the
repository of his Romantic illusions of true love, fidelity, and chivalric honor,
which have been stimulated by his success in American culture. She provides
a reason for Cohn to assert himself at last, to defend something he believes
has value and meaning: "until he fell in love with Brett, I never heard him
make one remark that would, in any way, detach him from other people,"
Jake comments (45).

Amused, Harvey Stone refers to Cohn as "a case of arrested development" (44). As we see later, Cohn is unable to play by the rules of the game,
to "behave himself" among Jake, Brett, Bill, and Mike. His hopeless pursuit
of Brett and his Gatsby-like naïveté do not suit him for survival in this new
world of the lost generation in Europe, especially among the Paris expatriates. He belongs to an earlier generation that represents the ideals of the old

America, an America whose development is perhaps also "arrested" in its need for an impossible happy ending. Jake mocks, "He was so sure that Brett loved him. He was going to stay and true love would conquer all" (199). Nelson describes American expatriates such as Cohn:

> . . . they brought with them their own versions of the peculiar Puritan American vitality to a world where it just wouldn't work. They had left home and said, sincerely, that they never wanted to go back. But they missed it. . . . The American ego is quite different from that of any other nation. It is one American product that is not exportable. The American hopes to hell he's right and even if he isn't he will triumph. (32)

Cohn's conceit, vanity, and naïveté go hand in hand with his inability to appreciate the sense of beauty in Paris and in Spain and the passion and camaraderie of the fiesta at Pamplona. While driving through the Spanish countryside, he is asleep (93); while drinking with the Basques, Cohn has passed out and is left in the dark (158); he does not speak Spanish and, thus, makes no attempt to communicate with the Spanish people[1]; at the bullfight he is "afraid [he] may be bored" (162). Cohn is a classic outsider whose horizon is limited to the position of "the Other," here labeled "American." Cohn is so entrapped within his perspective that he is unconscious of it and thus does not attempt to overcome it. When he asks Bill in Pamplona, "Where are the foreigners?" he must be told "We're the foreigners" (154). His false sense of personal and cultural "superiority" blinds Cohn to the truth of his own meager existence; while Pedro Romero actually risks his life in the bullring, Cohn is supposedly "ready to do battle for his lady love" (178). Cohn's demeaning and vainglorious American values seem weak when compared to the values of self-dependence, pride, and passion embodied by Romero: "Because he did not look up to ask if it pleased he did it all for himself inside, and it strengthened him, and yet he did it for her, too. But he did not do it for her at any loss to himself. He gained by it . . ." (216). Cohn can retaliate only physically against Romero; he cannot spiritually match or overcome his strength: "The fight with Cohn had not touched his [Romero's] spirit . . ." (219). Aware of his spiritual shallowness, Brett says of Cohn in reference to their affair, "He can't believe it didn't mean anything" (181); and later, "I hate his damned suffering" (182). Cohn suffers for something that was never more than an image in his own mind, spurred by an American belief in just desserts and heroic honor: "Cohn is madly futile, trying to make dreams reality in a society where the nightmare is the accepted norm" (Nelson 42). By suffering for self-created false ideals, he indulges in an egotistical self-pity. Unlike Brett and Jake, Cohn cannot comprehend the pain of love without fulfillment, a pain that Brett and Jake refuse to indulge in (Spilka 82).

When Cohn seeks forgiveness and understanding from Jake, Jake observes that he is wearing the kind of shirt he'd worn at Princeton (194); the attachment of Cohn's identity to the idyllic past, to America, reasserts itself. Cohn's superficial and melodramatic sentimentality is not a basis for but a deterrent to the mutual friendship and love shared by Jake with Brett, with Montoya, and with Bill.

Jake's friendship with Bill Gorton, as opposed to Cohn, is built on a qualitative difference. Bill knows who he is and has real values. That he is reticent about his friendship with Jake stems from his acculturation in America. Finally, in another country, Bill is able to express his admiration and friendship for Jake: "You're a hell of a good guy, and I'm fonder of you than anybody on earth. I couldn't tell you that in New York. It'd mean I was a faggot" (116). Bill recognizes that his Americanness, however deplorable, is an inescapable part of his identity. When shaving, he says to Jake, "Go west with this face and grow up with the country."[2] He then looks in the mirror, a classic metaphor for internal reflection, and says, "My God! Isn't it an awful face? (102). The irony is that, even as the American philosophy tells him to escape, he is unable to escape the ugly mask of the "American."

Although Bill is sometimes viewed as the in-house humorist in the novel (Donaldson 27-28; Hinkle 85-86, 88-89), he also serves as an antithetical character to Robert Cohn as a writer and human being. Bill does not bait Romero, or Brett, or Cohn, or Mike. When he arrives in Paris in Chapter VIII, we learn that he has been traveling around Europe. Jake says Bill "was very cheerful and said the States were wonderful. New York was wonderful. . . . Bill was very happy" (*Sun* 69-70). Opposed to Robert Cohn who says he is "sick of Paris" and the Quarter and who, in fact, seems dissatisfied with everything, Bill expresses his fondness for Paris as he and Jake are crossing over to the Left Bank from the Quai de Bethune on a wooden footbridge. They stop and look "down the river at Notre Dame." "'It's pretty grand,' Bill said, 'God, I love to get back'" (77). Bill had also "made a lot of money on his last book, and was going to make a lot more" (70), suggesting that Bill, unlike Robert Cohn, is a successful writer who has written more than one book and one whom Jake admires. Viewed from this perspective, Bill is everything that Cohn is not. Although Cohn has achieved some degree of literary success in America, Jake does not hesitate to tell us that Cohn has written "a very poor novel" and that his "mother had settled an allowance on him, about three hundred dollars a month"

(5-6). When they meet in Paris, Brett takes an instant liking to Bill when they have a drink at the Closerie des Lilas, and tells Jake to bring Bill along with him when they meet later that night: "Mind you're at the Select around ten. Make him [Bill] come" (74-75).

In Bayonne, Jake and Bill meet Cohn at the station on their way to the fishing trip. In the cab to the hotel, Cohn tells Bill, "I'm awfully glad to meet you. . . . I've heard so much about you from Jake and I've read your books" (89). Cohn, in effect, acknowledges Bill's professional identity and achievement, at least suggesting that he knows who Bill is from his books. In Pamplona, Bill easily merges with the Paris crowd while Cohn antagonizes nearly everyone. Bill is a summer visitor with an expatriate's manner and attitude, which is why he fits in and Cohn does not. Bill also appreciates the ritual of the bullfights and enjoys seeing the bulls as Cohn does not.

During the days just before the fiesta begins, Jake tells us that he sometimes took a walk in the mornings and that "Sometimes Bill went along. Sometimes he wrote in his room" (150). But in the next sentence he says that Cohn "spent the mornings studying Spanish or trying to get a shave at the barbershop," thus reenforcing the notion that Bill is a serious and professional writer who works when he has an opportunity while Cohn is a dilettante and completely undisciplined in his craft. After Cohn has hit Mike and Jake and beaten Romero badly, it is only Bill who has any compassion for Cohn's bad behavior at the fiesta:

> "I feel sorry about Cohn," Bill said. "He had an awful time."
>
> "Oh, to hell with Cohn," I said.
>
> "Where do you suppose he went?"
>
> "Up to Paris."
>
> "What do you suppose he'll do?"
>
> "Oh, the hell with him" [Jake replies]. (222)

In Hemingway's dichotomous portrait, however, most Americans are shown traveling in groups, or herds. While Jake has considered the possibility of escaping himself, these people are unable or unwilling to escape each other. Unlike Jake and his friends, they have no desire for either the close intimacy Jake enjoys with Bill and Harris in Burguete or the temporary seclusion that Jake uses in San Sebastian as an opportunity to rejuvenate himself. Madame Lecomte's "quaint restaurant on the Paris quais" is crowded with Americans hoping to find a place "as yet untouched by Americans" (76). The train Jake and Bill take to their fishing trip is filled with Americans on a pilgrimage to Biarritz and Lourdes. As Bill says, "So, that's what they are. Pilgrims. Goddamn Puritans" (86). Unlike their predecessors, however, their promised land is not America. The Americans in Jake and Bill's compartment decide to pass themselves off as pilgrims in order to get a meal; Jake refuses to assume this identity even temporarily, despite the fact that he is Catholic. He is antagonistic to their assumed superiority and their exclusionary attitudes, which defy any religious ideal of brotherhood. As one of the tourists remarks,

> "It certainly shows you the power of the Catholic Church. It's a
> pity you boys ain't Catholics. You could get a meal, then, all right."

> "I am," I said. "That's what makes me so sore." (87)

At the fiesta, Hemingway similarly describes tourists as watching and observing from a distance, rather than engaging with the Spanish: "Some of the women stared at the people going by with lorgnons" (179-80), as if it were a performance put on for their benefit. Neither are they able to be emotional participants of the bullfight; like Cohn, these tourists understand neither the reality and danger of death nor the art of courage and endurance. Instead, they impose their own ignorant interpretation on the events unfolding before them: "The Biarritz crowd did not like it. They thought Romero was afraid, and that was why he gave that little sidestep each time as he transferred the bull's charge from his own body to the flannel" (217-18).

Jake is typical of a character who is defined to a large extent by loss. Yet his losses—of his "masculinity," in one sense, and of his country—have allowed him to know himself without any encumbrances and to pass through the world semidetached, without need of permanent attachments and meanings. He is an "expatriate," which means that his status in the world is defined by his oppositionary relationship to his original country. Thus, though he is external to America, he is still inescapably connected to it.[3] Jake warns Cohn: "You can't get away from yourself by moving from one place to another" (11). "Place" is differentiated and detached from "self," yet it is difficult to read this comment in the sense of radical individualism to mean that place, community, and society had no part in shaping identity. Jake's expatriate status does not so much denote a physical quest as an inward quest for self-knowledge or, more likely, simply coming to terms with the burden of oneself. In *Imagining Paris*, J. Gerald Kennedy discusses a basic "contradiction" in Jake:

If his relation to Paris thus holds the key to book one, his problem goes beyond a mechanical balancing of public and private attitudes. His troubled relation to the city derives from his simultaneous association with and antagonism for the expatriate group, as well as his perverse identification with the Montparnasse quarter, which he detests. Ulti- mately, Jake's complex attachment to Paris and the "Quarter" reveals a contradiction within the narrator himself: his perceptions of locale disclose an agonizing personal conflict. (99)

The fact that Jake has left America and lives permanently in Paris signifies his attempt to leave his American existence and social identity behind because it interferes in some manner with his quest. Why is this abandonment of America desirable? It is not because of a mere attraction to its opposite, Europe; rather, he is one of those Americans "who did not wish to go to Europe as much as they wanted to get out of the United States" (Nelson 30).[4] America in the 1920s was not the comfortable environment for artists and intellectuals that Paris was and is. Jake makes clear that the desire of tourists to "see" Europe is the legacy of the old American desire to "go West," to explore new frontiers and enact new dreams. There is perhaps nowhere left in America "commensurate with [man's] capacity for wonder," as Fitzgerald wrote in *The Great Gatsby* (189), so Europe, or an image of what Europe should be, has become the object. These American tourists do not escape themselves (as Jake warns), but bring along their American naïveté and wealth. These encumbrances act as a screen through which they view what they believe is an exotic, "virgin" land, but they are guilty of self-deception. The scene of Jake's American acquaintances meeting the prostitute Georgette, whom Jake passes off as his fiancée, illustrates the expatriate's tendency to see what their idealized vision presents rather than the facts. Georgette is a novelty for them; she becomes an "Other" to the Americans by which they conceitedly "prove" their ability to speak a "foreign" language and their cultural appreciation:

> "Oh, Mademoiselle Hobin," Frances Clyne called, speaking French very rapidly and not seeming so proud and astonished as Mrs. Braddocks at its coming out really French. "Have you been in Paris long? Do you like it here? You love Paris, do you not?"
>
> "Who's she?" Georgette turned to me. "Do I have to talk to her? . . . No, I don't like Paris. It's expensive and dirty." (*Sun* 18-19)[5]

The distinction between Jake and his "compatriots" "lies in the 'tourist-phonies' not having the right sense of values: not being in the know or not recognizing the importance of what they observe" (Peterson 30).

Regardless of Jake's cynicism and disregard for "Americans," his own "American-ness" is not extractable. It is only displaceable, in that it does not serve as a barrier to his enjoyment and understanding of the experiences that form his existence. But the freedom he has to move from place to place also holds him at a certain distance from the inhabitants who "belong" to the place, for he is, like Cohn, defined in relation to them as a "foreigner"—he can never really "belong" either in France or in Spain. An advantage of the displaced American expatriate-hero is his increased existential freedom: "One can be merely an observer or spectator if he doesn't like what is happening around him. 'In another country' the hero is not really involved unless he chooses to be" (Peterson 194).

The loss, or blurring, of Jake's sexual identity is signified at the same time by the loss of a national identity: "'You, a foreigner, and Englishman' (any foreigner was an Englishman) 'have given more than your life'" (*Sun* 31). Just as Jake must reconcile the loss of sex with his desire for Brett, so must he reconcile the loss of his country with his desire for fellowship. The journey that Jake is on has a far less superficial goal than the quest of his fellow Americans, though he shares the motivation: the need to go beyond the known and the well traveled, to push frontiers. In microcosm, Jake's quest parallels American history. As Philip Young has commented, "Once we were fully discovered, established, and unified we began to rediscover the world, and this adventure resulted in our defining ourselves in the light of people who did not seem, to us or to them, quite like us" (185).

The mentorlike figure of Count Mippipopoulos, who is accepted as "one of us" by Brett, states the philosophy of the expatriate: "You see, Mr. Barnes, it is because I have lived very much that now I can enjoy everything so well. . . . That is the secret. You must get to know the values" (*Sun* 60). The key is the plural "values"—many, not one. Unlike Cohn, Jake is not fixated on one ideal or value or philosophy. Conscious of his expatriate, or nonbelonging, status, Jake is thus able to act as a "bridge" between ever-changing places and times. He experiences many horizons and values, without ever having a permanent commitment to any: "Perhaps as you went along you did learn something. I did not care what it was all about. All I wanted to know was how to live in it. Maybe if you found out how to live in it you learned from that what it was all about" (148). This freedom is "enviable," for "he cannot be blamed much for rejecting foreign values which he dislikes; on the other hand, he is ennobled when he imposes foreign values on himself because he believes in them" (Peterson 194).

The way Jake formulates what he has experienced and how he has learned "the values," even while he is showing that the values of America have become unnecessary, shows that his American-ness provides a foundation to his "bridge." Even in Paris—"the city of light" and the center of the expatriate movement—as a way of explaining his current philosophy of living, he uses metaphors of paying and exchange that smack of American capitalism, where "value" takes on the double meaning of moral and material standards: "No idea of retribution or punishment. Just exchange of values. You gave up something and got something else. . . . You paid some way for everything that was any good. . . . Enjoying living was learning to get your money's worth and knowing when you had it. . . . The world was a good place to buy in" (*Sun* 148). To some extent, Jake is still following the American "myths" of escape and fulfillment. Cornellier argues: "Hemingway's expatriates in *The Sun Also Rises* each seek out ways to escape, to find a form of fulfillment the war and society has left void in them. . . . they find themselves victims again not only of the war but the materialistic wasteland which has emerged to replace it" (15). While he is praying in the cathedral, Jake prays not only for his friends and for the bullfighters but for money. He then becomes "ashamed, and regretted that I was such a rotten Catholic, but realized there was nothing I could do about it . . . and I only wished I felt religious" (*Sun* 97). The Catholicism he learned in America has been corrupted with materialism; it cannot provide him with that spiritual sustenance he experiences through fishing, bullfighting, and companionship.

On the bus ride with the Basques, Jake and Bill almost become one of them, learning from them, sharing their wine, and talking in their language. One of the Basques identifies them as Americans and speaks in English, thus singling them out. When the Basque speaks of his trip to America, Jake and Bill ask: "Why did you leave?" and "Why did you come back here?" (107), showing their implicit belief that America is a place to go *to*, not away from— a destiny. As Nelson has noted, "America had always been the place people went, not the place they left, especially not dissatisfied. The whole idea behind the American Dream was that there was room to do anything you wanted anywhere you wanted" (30).[6] The Americans' questions are now more appropriately directed to themselves.

The materialism of America is shown by the Basque's comments about the wine, the sharing of which betokens the friendship among the men.

When asked if they can get the wine in America, the Americans reply "There's plenty if you can pay for it" (107). Hemingway implies that American friendship, or fellowship, is not shared but bought. The American Dream has been sold, as Bill cynically observes to Jake: "You ought to dream. All our biggest businessmen have been dreamers" (124).

Better than dreams, Hemingway suggests, is Jake's possession of *aficion*, which "it was taken for granted that an American could not have." Like Cohn's devotion to Brett, "he might simulate it or confuse it with excitement, but he could not really have it" (132). Jake's dual existence as American and aficionado gives him power, for he has knowledge that threatens the values and faith of *aficion*. Montoya seeks his advice concerning the American ambassador's invitation to Pedro Romero, for Jake is an American. Jake confirms his opinion that Americans, foreigners, are a corrupting influence. Montoya replies: "People take a boy like that. They don't know what he's worth. They don't know what he means. Any foreigner can flatter him" (172). In a foreboding line, Jake warns, "There's one American woman down here now that collects bull-fighters" (172). While Cohn and Mike are crude, envious, and self-deprecatory toward Romero, Jake is able to communicate with him on several levels, in the languages of Spanish, English, and bullfighting. His opinion is respected by Romero who, to Jake, is a model of honor, strength, and courage.

Ultimately and tragically, this ideal does not succeed in filling the vacancy of a lost American dream, for Jake's "foreignness," his inescapable American identity—personified in its worst form in Cohn—has brought violence to Romero through Brett. Jake has betrayed the "very special secret" shared between Montoya and himself by exposing it to "outsiders" who do not "understand" it (131) and who were under his protective responsibility. Romero's physical pain is paralleled in Jake by a feeling of physical dislocation inflicted by memory after Cohn knocks him out.

> Walking across the square to the hotel everything looked new and changed. . . . I felt as I felt once coming home from an out-of-town football game. . . . I walked up the street from the station in the town I had lived in all my life and it was all new. . . . my feet seemed to be a long way off, and everything seemed to come from a long way off, and I could hear my feet walking a great distance away. I had been kicked in the head early in the game. It was like that crossing the square. (192-93)

In the guilt of betraying and losing his ideal, Jake is sent back, in his memory, to the origin of his innocent identity in America. The pain he seeks to cure has made him an outsider. He has again been confronted by Young's paradigm of "violence, an essential experience of the frontier, and also in our time—which is a wartime—of the American in Europe. And there is nothing triumphant about the beating which innocence takes, or about what happens to it after it is beaten" (186). As a wanderer, an expatriate, he has already understood that for him America cannot provide a sense of rootedness and belonging. But Jake always has Paris, and he will return there—and that is quite possibly more than enough for any American expatriate.[7]

By using Cohn, Jake, and Bill as representative Americans in Paris during the expatriate period, Hemingway portrayed the best and worst qualities of Americans abroad. His scathing portrait of American tourists leaves little doubt about his feelings for the huge number of summer visitors who flocked into Paris from 1920 on. As the narrator, Jake tells us "how it was," and we feel pity for him and his difficult situation. But *The Sun Also Rises* is not just a sad tale of frustrated lives and bad endings. Jake is a survivor and searches for some value to give meaning to his present existence. Cohn embodies the values and attitude of a time long past. He cannot merge gracefully into the world of the expatriates because he has all the wrong assumptions about life, about love, and about himself. His is a world long gone and he will never become "one of us," as Brett says of the count (60). Bill, on the other hand, is the American who merges into a different culture with ease because he does not hold on to the romanticized past. He enjoys life and appreciates its intensity and variety. *The Sun Also Rises* remains as a historical view of the expatriates with permanent value for those of us in the contemporary world. Hemingway's Paris and Pamplona and the expatriate life are no longer possible in quite the same way that they were for his time. But *The Sun Also Rises* lives on as a reminder of the good times in the good place. "Isn't it pretty to think so?" Jake comments to Brett at the end of the book. To that slightly ambiguous remark we might respond "yes" and reflect on our own lives and loves.

NOTES

1. Reynolds, in *"The Sun Also Rises,"* observes that "Most Americans spoke little or no French; there was no need, for they seldom engaged natives in any real conversation. Except to provide services, few native French or Spanish appear in *The Sun Also Rises*" (1).

2. Readers may recognize Bill's remark as based on a phrase mistakenly attributed to Horace Greeley in his *New York Tribune* editorial of about 1851 or 1852. The phrase was originally used by John Babsone Lane Soule in an article in the *Terre Haute* (IN) *Express* in 1851. As the saying became widespread and popular, Greeley reprinted Soule's article, to show that it was not original with him (cited in *Bartlett's Familiar Quotations*, 13th edition, under "Soule, John Babsone Lane" [585a]. Indexed under "West go, young man").

3. John W. Aldridge, however, argues that the expatriates in Europe possessed "an intellectual arrogance, a disdain for bourgeois society," that caused them to become "cosmopolitan provincials abroad; they learned to judge America by essentially elitist standards; and of course, they found America provincial. But since they were themselves provincial, their attitudes retained a dimension of ambivalence that helped to humanize their satire and finally made it seem an expression more of regret than of contempt" (116).

4. For an extensive analysis and reliable background of the expatriate milieu, see Kennedy; Reynolds, *Hemingway*; and Cowley. The collection *In Transition: A Paris Anthology* contains a special section entitled "Why do Americans live in Europe?" with responses to a survey by, among others, Robert McAlmon, Kay Boyle, Gertrude Stein, and Kathleen Cannell (217-27).

5. See Reynolds, *"The Sun Also Rises"* 75-76, on Georgette's "sickness" and the prostitute world of Paris in the 1920s.

6. For a more detailed commentary, see Cowley 36-47.

7. Although not cited herein, I am greatly indebted to the following for enlarging my understanding of the expatriate period: Roger Asselineau, Professor Emeritus of American Literature at the Sorbonne, for his work and for many conversations in the United States and France over many years; Sheri Benstock, *Women of the Left Bank: Paris, 1900-1940* (Austin: U of Texas P, 1986); Humphrey Carpenter, *Geniuses Together: American Writers in Paris in the 1920s* (Boston: Houghton Mifflin, 1988); Noel Riley Fitch, *Sylvia Beach and the Lost Generation* (New York: Norton, 1983); Jean Méral, *Paris in American Literature* (Chapel Hill: U of North Carolina P, 1989); Brian N. Morton, *Americans in Paris* (New York: Morrow, 1986); and George Wickes, *Americans in Paris* (Garden City, NY: Doubleday, 1969).

WORKS CITED

Aldridge, John W. "Afterthoughts on the Twenties and *The Sun Also Rises*." *New Essays on "The Sun Also Rises*." Ed. Linda Wagner-Martin. New York: Cambridge UP, 1987. 109-29.

Cornellier, Thomas. "The Myth of Escape and Fulfillment in *TheSun Also Rises* and *The Great Gatsby*." *Society for the Study of Midwestern Literature Newsletter* 15.1 (1985): 15-21.

Cowley, Malcolm. *Exile's Return*. 1951. New York: Penguin, 1979.

Donaldson, Scott. "Humor in *The Sun Also Rises*." *New Essays on "The Sun Also Rises*." Ed. Linda Wagner-Martin. New York: Cambridge UP, 1987. 19-41.

Fitzgerald, F. Scott. *The Great Gatsby*. 1925. The Authorized Text. Ed. Matthew J. Bruccoli. New York: Scribners, 1992.

Hemingway, Ernest. *The Sun Also Rises*. 1926. New York: Scribners, 1970.

Hinkle, James. "What's Funny in *The Sun Also Rises*." *Ernest Hemingway: Six Decades of Criticism*. Ed. Linda W. Wagner. East Lansing: Michigan State UP, 1987. 77-92.

In Transition: A Paris Anthology. Introduction by Noel Riley Fitch. New York: Doubleday (Anchor Books), 1990.

Kennedy, J. Gerald. *Imagining Paris: Exile, Writing, and American Identity*. New Haven, CT: Yale UP, 1993.

Nelson, Gerald. *Ten Versions of America*. New York: Knopf, 1972.

Peterson, Richard K. *Direct and Oblique*. Paris: Mouton, 1969.

Reynolds, Michael. *Hemingway: The Paris Years*. Cambridge, MA: Blackwell, 1989.

———. *"The Sun Also Rises": A Novel of the Twenties*. Boston: G. K. Hall, 1988.

Spilka, Mark. "The Death of Love in *The Sun Also Rises*." *Hemingway and His Critics*. Ed. Carlos Baker. New York: Hill and Wang, 1961. 80-92.

Young, Philip. "Ernest Hemingway." *Seven Modern American Novelists*. Ed. William Van O'Connor. Minneapolis: U of Minnesota P, 1964. 153-88.

CITY OF BROTHELLY LOVE

THE INFLUENCE OF PARIS
AND PROSTITUTION ON HEMINGWAY'S FICTION

C L A U D E   C A S W E L L

Paris has never had a red-light district *per se*, where the girls, seated in windows overlooking the street, could display their wares to passers-by. But there have always been *quartiers chauds*—"hot spots" in Paris. It would be boring to name them all.

—Brassaï, *The Secret Paris of the 30's*

Everything is on such a clear financial basis in France. It is the simplest country to live in. No one makes things complicated by becoming your friend for any obscure reason. If you want people to like you you only have to spend a little money.

—Jake Barnes, narrating in *The Sun Also Rises* (233)

Paris and Ernest Hemingway were a perfect match. They lived their early twenties together as twentieth-century "moderns," and their mutual fascination with prostitution was entwined deeply in their social and artistic identities. When Hemingway arrived in Paris in 1921, he encountered a

world of art in which the prostitute had been the principal visual focus for
many years. Manet, Cézanne, Degas, and Renoir—as well as a host of other
Impressionist and post-Impressionist painters—made their work synonymous with scenes of literal and implied prostitution. In Hollis Clayson's
critique of these painters and their depictions of prostitutes, *Painted Love:
Prostitution and French Art of the Impressionist Era,* she documents this "durability
and malleability of the theme of prostitution in French art" (5).

Claiming that "the attraction to prostitution was pervasive in these
years [of the late nineteenth and early twentieth centuries]—appealing
especially to avant-garde painters of modern life but to many men in the
larger culture as well" (9), Clayson writes that these artists "took up 'the
prostitute' as a standard emblem of modernity" (152) because the repressive
French system of prostitute regulation had driven so many prostitutes
underground to become "clandestine prostitutes" (152). Behind the false
front of professions for working women such as flower girl, laundress,
seamstress, hairdresser, chambermaid, shopgirl, linen maid, designer, journal saleswoman—and particularly milliner and barmaid—prostitutes
assumed a double identity of "respectability" and "availability." It was this
ambiguity of "Was she or wasn't she?" that Clayson says became a symbol
of modernity for avant-garde painters.

The young Hemingway entered this Parisian world of public sexual
ambiguity as a journalist with a keen eye for detail and nuance. Not only
did he see a body of art featuring the prostitute as a central figure, he also
found a Paris where prostitution was literally embedded in the stones of
the city's streets. Brassai (real name Gyula Halasz), the celebrated photog-
rapher who began documenting Paris nightlife in 1929, but who had been
observing it since 1924 when he arrived in Paris from his native Transyl-
vania in order to paint, wrote that in certain sections of Paris "one could
smell the fumes of venal love: the stones, the pavements, the very walls
had been impregnated with it for eight or nine centuries." (Brassai, who
took his pseudonym in honor of his native city of Brasso, employed neither
a first name nor page numbers.)

This Parisian combination of gritty reality and artistic metaphor
concerning prostitution was a magnet for Hemingway—particularly in
terms of its possibility of joining the "respectable" and the outré in
ambiguous portrayals of character. It was a synthesis of themes he had
begun in less subtle fashion even earlier in his writing life. Hemingway
began his professional interest in prostitution as an eighteen-year-old cub
reporter for the *Kansas City Star,* observing the nocturnal lifestyle of
prostitutes with a kind of eager empathy. Peter Griffin, in his biography

of the young Hemingway, writes that Hemingway learned about prostitution firsthand, not as a customer but as a fellow worker of the night: "Like most western boomtowns (the city had grown from the town of Kansas, population twenty-five hundred in 1850), Kansas City had its share of crooked politicians, prostitutes (12th Street was known as Woodrow Wilson Avenue—where one could get 'a piece at any price'). . . . he [Hemingway] covered pool halls, dance halls, and roller-skating rinks, where prostitutes did business. . . . Ernest developed a special sympathy for the prostitutes . . ." (37-41). This interest took tangible form in what Hemingway considered his best *Star* story, "Mix War, Art and Dancing" (*Cub Reporter* 56-58), which Hemingway said many years later was "very sad, about a whore" (Fenton 46). Jeffrey Meyers writes that this story, "which never explains why the woman was excluded from a fashionable dance, does not actually state she was a whore" (25).

Writing about prostitutes, but not actually stating that they were prostitutes, was a pattern that Hemingway would continue throughout his career. He also wrote about prostitutes overtly, however. In an early, unpublished story, "Crime and Punishment" (an allusion to Dostoyevsky, whose work Hemingway admired and in whose fiction prostitutes figure prominently), Hemingway wrote about a prostitute he supposedly saw in New York's Battery district just before he shipped out to Italy as an ambulance driver. She was "just as clean looking as a Madonna," he writes, and there were "thirty-seven dollars in one dollar bills in her stocking from that many sailors and she was the most beautiful girl I ever saw" (Griffin 60).

As a young writer with a reportorial mind, Hemingway seems to have conducted his own study of prostitution at an early age. Besides his acquaintance with prostitutes in Kansas City, Michael Reynolds speaks of the nineteen-year-old Hemingway's knowledge of prostitutes in Italy during World War I. Reynolds writes that in 1920, although Hemingway had "little hands-on experience" with sex, "he had detailed knowledge of sexual anatomy and techniques" which he had "learned in the army brothels in Italy and listening to soldiers talk . . ." (120).

By the time Hemingway arrived in Paris as a young married man of twenty-one, he was a sophisticated and meticulous observer of prostitution as a microcosm of social and psychological human relationships. The iconography of prostitution and the psychological idiosyncrasies of women working in the profession would also soon become a central trope in the young Hemingway's growing body of fiction. The prostitute "consciousness," as an ambivalent form of both social rebellion and "selling out"— establishment of a kind of courageous identity and yet at the same time a despairing loss of integrity—became in Hemingway's texts a key symbol of modernist reality.

That reality took shape in the character of Georgette Hobin, the first woman we meet in the company of Jake Barnes, the protagonist of *The Sun Also Rises*. Georgette is from Brussels, now working as a streetwalker in Paris. Professional, vulnerable, alone, jaded, fragile, resilient—the sick heart behind the performer's mask and at once the user and the used—Georgette Hobin enters the novel not merely as a minor, "atmosphere" character representing the Parisian underworld known to cognoscenti like Jake, but as the key to the prostitution motif pervading Hemingway's first major novel. *The Sun Also Rises* is not literally about prostitution, but it is about a world in which people buy and sell each other with a desperation and ruthless casualness associated with the demimonde. In this world of tough, hard surfaces covering the wounds underneath, the prostitute is a dominant symbolic figure against which many of the social and personal values in the novel are articulated and measured.

One of the most dramatic effects of this motif is the way Georgette foreshadows the character of Lady Brett Ashley. Georgette functions as a shadowy mirror image, a dissonant echo of Brett, playing out in miniature the role in Jake's life that Brett does on a larger scale. When Jake sees Georgette on the sidewalk in front of his café, he is trying to forget Brett and go on with his life. Revealing both his worldliness and his intense loneliness, Jake picks Georgette up, not for sex but "because of a vague sentimental idea that it would be nice to eat with someone" (*Sun* 16). His idea proves to be much nicer in theory than in practice. It has been a long time, Jake tells us, since he has "dined with a *poule*" and he "had forgotten how dull it could be" (16). Georgette, the *poule* (the French word for chicken that evolved into a slang term for prostitute), although a "good-looking girl" (14), has bad teeth and speaks in practiced clichés. When she speaks of "that dirty war" (17), Jake's protective cynicism wells up inside him: "We probably would have gone on and discussed the war and agreed that it was in reality a calamity for civilization, and perhaps would have been better avoided. I was bored enough" (15).

In the taxi on the way to the restaurant Georgette tries to do what she assumes she is being paid for. She tries to touch Jake's genitals "with one hand," but Jake pushes "her hand away." "What's the matter? You sick?" Georgette asks. "Yes," replies Jake. "Everybody's sick," Georgette says, "I'm sick, too" (15). A short time later, when Jake and Brett meet at the dance hall and decide to get away by themselves by taking a taxi ride around Paris, the taxi scene with Georgette is reenacted. When Jake kisses Brett, she says,

"Don't touch me. . . . Please don't touch me." "What's the matter?" asks Jake. "I can't stand it," Brett replies (25-26).

Although Jake has taken on Georgette's role as sexual aggressor and Brett is the "sick" one, this interaction is a thematic repetition of the first taxi scene because in both cases Jake is seeking emotional and social companionship, and in both cases he is unsuccessful because neither he nor his companion is able to "touch." The novel ends with a reprise of the same scene, with Brett and Jake in a taxi in Madrid. Brett says, "Oh, Jake, we could have had such a damned good time together." At this point Jake sees a "mounted" policeman who "raise[s] his baton"—an image that ridicules Jake's sexual impotence and calls forth Jake's sad and bitter final comment: "Yes. Isn't it pretty to think so?" (247).

The Sun Also Rises is framed literally and figuratively by these scenes in a taxi, a framing that equates Brett with Georgette. The taxi represents the transience and impersonality of venal love for Hemingway—just as it did for Flaubert in *Madame Bovary*. The taxi is for Hemingway the modern vehicle of impersonal, illicit sex, as well as a place to contract the diseases or "sickness" that Hemingway associated with prostitution. That association was made explicit in one of the *In Our Time* stories, "A Very Short Story," which was based on Hemingway's brief romance with Agnes von Kurowsky and which later became the story of Catherine and Frederic in *A Farewell to Arms:*

> The major did not marry her in the spring, or any other time. Luz never got an answer to the letter to Chicago about it. A short time after he [an unnamed "he" but consistent with the age and circumstances of the Nick Adams character] contracted gonorrhea from a sales girl in a loop department store while riding in a taxicab through Lincoln Park. (*Short Stories* 240)

What makes Brett's connection to Georgette an association with prostitution in general, however, is the number and nature of other textual references throughout the novel that surround Brett with an aura of "prostitutionality." The linguistic connection between Georgette and Brett is immediately evident even in the sound of their names. Not only do the names end in the same sound and carry an androgynous connotation, but the "-ette" ending was common among the *noms de guerre* (aliases, but literally "names of war") of French prostitutes. Alain Corbin, in his book on prostitution in France after 1850, *Women for Hire*, writes about "the large number of diminutives ending in '-ette' (Violette, Yvette, Paulette . . . Georgette . . .). In all, these account for 65 percent of the pseudonyms" (77). Corbin guesses that the purpose of these names "was probably to emphasize youth" (77), thereby contributing to the client's fantasy that he was winning the affections of an innocent young girl.

Georgette and Brett are also both expatriates—Georgette from Belgium and Brett from England—who find Paris a place of "sickness," yet who are drawn to it as a means of financial survival. Georgette calls Paris "dirty" (*Sun* 19), while Brett calls it a "pestilential city" (74). They are also similar in their circumstances, or "role," when they appear in the novel for the first and only time together. Brett arrives at the nightclub as the lone woman with a group of young gay men who seem to enjoy her as a kind of token, "straight" mascot. When these men see Georgette, an "actual harlot" (20), they rush to dance with her, at the same time that Brett detaches herself from them to talk to Jake. Jake watches Georgette's desertion of him wryly, prefiguring his view of Brett's behavior in Pamplona: "She had been taken up by them. I knew then that they [the gay men accompanying Brett] would all dance with her. They are like that" (20).

Brett jokes with Jake about bringing a prostitute into the company of his respectable friends. "Where did you get it?" she asks, referring to Georgette as a thing. She adds, "It's wrong of you, Jake. It's an insult to all of us" (22). Is Brett making a serious moral judgment? Not at all. She follows these comments immediately with "It's in restraint of trade" (22), and laughs—implying that bringing in a professional is unfair to the amateurs. At this point Robert Cohn sees Brett and looks longingly at her "as his compatriot [Moses] must have looked when he saw the promised land" (22), a reference by Jake to Cohn's view of Brett as a piece of property—a thing or "it" like Georgette—and also a reference to Jake's intuitive perception of Cohn's instantly possessive attitude toward Brett. In this way Cohn becomes the first of Jake's friends who "take up" Brett. Observing that Brett has made a new conquest in Cohn, Jake comments sarcastically: "I suppose you like to add them up" (23). Brett tells him not to talk "like a fool" (23). A few minutes earlier, Georgette had called Jake "a fool" (18) for introducing her as his "fiancée" (18). Brett, too, is a "false" fiancée, whose promiscuous behavior—and the fact that she is still married to Lord Ashley—makes a mockery of her engagement to Mike Campbell. Georgette and Brett are counterparts here. Each is "engaged" in a temporary contract, which each quickly abandons for better prospects.

Besides these circumstantial connections between Georgette and Brett, there is little doubt about the subconscious melding of the two women in Jake's mind later in the same evening when Brett comes to Jake's apartment, drunk and loud and disheveled from carousing with Count Mippipopolous. The concierge tells Jake there is a "species of woman" (32) (like an "it") to see him on some obviously "dirty business" (32). The concierge thinks Brett is a prostitute. Then Jake hears Brett's voice on the stairs below: "Half asleep I had been sure it was Georgette. I don't know why. She could not have known my address" (32).

Costumed in these textual allusions, Brett is presented to us through Jake's narrative consciousness in terms unmistakably aligning her with Georgette's social and sexual role as a *poule.* Like a prostitute, Brett is surrounded by men who want to pay her—in money or marriage—for her companionship. Count Mippipopolous, the titled Greek "sugar daddy" (he owns a "chain of sweetshops in the States" [32]), briefly becomes enamored of Brett in Paris and offers her "ten thousand dollars to go to Biarritz with him" (32). She declines because she knows "too many people in Biarritz" (33) and because she's "in love" (33) with Jake.

Jake is skeptical about Brett's sense of love, and he is particularly jaundiced not only about her motivations for sexual encounters but also about her motivations for marriage. He tells Robert Cohn that Brett married the British aristocrat Lord Ashley—from whom she got her title of "Lady"— shortly after her "own true love had . . . kicked off with the dysentery" (39). Cohn, ever the sentimentalist, refuses to believe she "would marry anybody she didn't love." "Well," Jake replies, "she's done it twice" (39). Jake's implication here is that Brett, like a prostitute, enters contracts with men for material, not emotional, reasons: money, security, and a "title" (she says a title is good for "hell's own amount of credit" [57]).

Even Pedro Romero, the young bullfighter who becomes her lover in Pamplona and who has genuine esteem for her, eventually plays the "john" role and tries to give her "a lot of money" (242). Brett will not allow Romero to give her money, of course, just as she would not accept money from Count Mippipopolous. She has her own private system of exchange. She will only allow men to pay her expenses: the Count in Paris, Robert Cohn in San Sebastian, Michael in Pamplona, and Jake everywhere. Romero, too, picks up the tab. When Jake tries to pay Brett's bill at the Hotel Montana in Madrid, he learns "the bill had been paid" (243) by Romero. Jake then joins Brett in the bar where she asks him the typical *poule* question: "*Would* you buy a lady a drink?" (244; emphasis in original). By textual transformation, the Lady with a capital "L" has become a lady with a lower case "l." Soon Jake and Brett are riding around Madrid, and what began in a taxicab ends in a taxicab, with the connotations of transience, isolation, and prostitution.

Georgette Hobin does not function solely as a reflection of Brett Ashley, however. She is also a mirror for virtually every other character in the novel, including Jake himself. In this same mirror, Jake is reflected as a prostitute figure fully as much as Brett is. When Georgette first meets Jake and he calls her a "little girl" (14), she retorts "little girl yourself" (14). Before Georgette goes to meet Jake's friends at the restaurant, she looks "in a little mirror" and "re-define[s] her lips" (18) with lipstick. Later, alone at home, Jake looks at himself naked in front of his mirror and contemplates the private "face" he does not show in public. He does not show the reader either; he only says enigmatically: "Of all the ways to be wounded. I suppose it was funny" (30). Jake is attempting here to "face" himself, but he does so with a mask of false, protective humor that he cannot sustain. In bed, "all of a sudden," he starts "to cry" (31).

Georgette and Jake are also alike in many other ways. Both are "sick"; both are casualties of the "dirty war"—the war in a larger sense being life, not only World War I. Georgette finds Paris expensive and "dirty," like the war, and is doing her best to survive in it on what little resources she has, just as Jake is. Georgette and Jake are also outsiders, both possessing the hard-shelled knowledge and wry honesty of wounded survivors who are living with an inner pain that they mask in humor and affected gaiety. When Jake introduces her as his fiancée to a party of his "respectable" Canadian and American friends at the nightclub—insulated in their superior, affluent, tourist mentality—and Georgette smiles "that wonderful smile" (18), his casual joke separates him from them and subtly aligns him with Georgette. She knows he is making fun of her, using her, but she also senses that he is making fun of his friends' inflated ideas of their social worth.

Part of Jake's mockery of the Parisian social scene during this exchange is his introduction of Georgette to his friends as "Mademoiselle Georgette LeBlanc" (18). Georgette LeBlanc was a minor celebrity living in Paris at that time. She was a singer who, as Samuel Putnam writes, was "famous for her long association with Maeterlinck" (82). Maurice Maeterlinck, a "symbolist" writer who won the Nobel Prize in 1911, was a Belgian, like Georgette Hobin. Georgette LeBlanc was also a lesbian who was Margaret Anderson's lover and who hosted meetings of the "Gurdjieff [a Turkish mystic] Circle" under the leadership of Jane Heap. Hemingway's often derogatory and crude references to lesbians (particularly in high social circles) are well known, and this case is no exception. James R. Mellow writes that Hemingway referred to LeBlanc in private "even more scurrilously as 'Georgette Mangeuse [the eater] LeBlanc'" (306). Thus by overlaying an allusion to a "respectable" living personality onto the identity of a fictional *poule*, and mocking both, Hemingway creates a composite character resonant with satirical implications in terms of the blurred boundaries of prostitution.

Georgette calls Jake "a fool" (18), but it is clear from the ensuing interaction that, for better or worse, Georgette at least has no pretensions about who she is. She suddenly seems, by contrast to this group, more perceptive and real than when she was putting on her professionally "seductive" persona for Jake earlier. Georgette sizes up Frances, Robert Cohn's fiancée, as a phony immediately. When Frances gushes sentimentally about Paris, Georgette turns to Jake and says, "Who's she? Do I have to talk to her?" (18). Without waiting for Jake to give her permission to be herself, she turns back to Frances and says frankly that she does not like Paris and finds it "dirty" (19). Frances, on the contrary, finds Paris "extraordinarily clean" (19) and suggests that Georgette must not have been in Paris "very long" (19). Georgette replies simply, "I've been here long enough" (19).

Frances and Georgette are speaking, of course, out of different class experiences, one "upper" and one "lower," but Hemingway leaves little doubt which one is more valued by Jake. Georgette may be there to bargain coarsely for whatever food, drinks, and cash she can get out of Jake, but Frances is there—in Jake's eyes—with Robert Cohn for essentially the same reason. Georgette is simply more honest, or at least unable at the moment to afford illusions; and in Jake's value system, Georgette therefore has more integrity. He also respects the rules of her *métier* enough to leave an envelope containing fifty francs at the bar for her when he leaves without her. She has gone off dancing with another group of men who seem to offer more financial promise—the joke presumably being on her, since the men are gay. Jake's instructions to the bartender are that if Georgette returns to look for him to honor her "contract" to be his social companion for the evening, then the bartender is to give her the money. If not, Jake is not obligated to pay her. He respects the code, and he pays his bills.

This concept of "payment" for one's personal involvements (romantic and otherwise) makes the prostitutional contract, whether represented by Georgette's *métier* or by Jake's "exchange of values" (148), the vernacular of all the relationships in *The Sun Also Rises*. Almost all the characters in the novel, male or female, are portrayed both as prostitutes and "johns"—sellers and buyers—victims and victimizers. Frances tries to buy marriage to Robert Cohn by using guilt as emotional blackmail. Cohn gives her two hundred pounds to go away. Jake sells his self-respect to keep Brett's "love." Brett sells her "ladyship" image to almost anyone, except to the concierge at Jake's apartment building—there she has to *buy* the concierge's compliance with a hundred francs, borrowed from the count, of course.

Even the bullfighters are depicted in terms of the prostitution contract. Belmonte's integrity has been "sold in advance" (216) because he has chosen mediocre bulls to give the crowd the illusion—the false image—of his "greatness" (216). And at first the crowd prefers Belmonte's "imitation of himself" (218) to Pedro Romero's authentic greatness, which they do not understand. Romero is the only one who has not sold out, however, because even though he has jeopardized his career by his affair with Brett and subsequent beating by Cohn, "his spirit" is not touched (219). Nevertheless, even Romero is rendered in language suggesting the sexual and contractual exchange endemic to prostitution. Not only is his bullfight narrated in sexual terms—he makes the "bull consent with his body . . . the sword went in . . . [he] became one with the bull" (218-20)—but the crowd also acts like a collective "john." They want Romero to risk his life with a bad bull because: "They've paid for him. They don't want to lose their money" (217). Then they act the same way the *riau-riau* dancers did earlier with Brett: "the crowd wanted him . . . made him go on . . . making a little circle around him . . . held him and lifted him . . ." (220-21).

In these direct and indirect ways the bartering and contracting for services in *The Sun Also Rises* is cast in terms of a prostitutional exchange integral to the novel's dialectic. Jake thinks to himself in Pamplona that relationships are: "Just exchange of values. You give up something and get something else. Or you worked for something. You paid some way for everything that was good" (148). Thus, for Jake it's not the buying and selling that makes a thing bad; it's rather the paying with your work or the integrity of your performance that makes a thing good. Mike and Brett do not work, yet they expect everyone else to pay their bills. Mike says, "I always pay everything back" (192), and Brett says, "Don't we all pay for the things we do, though?" (26)—but they don't pay. They live on credit until someone else pays. In this scenario Georgette becomes by implication an ironic touchstone of integrity for Jake, while Brett is a poor reflection of Georgette's working class values. By casting his inner dialogue about "how to live" (148) in terms of prostitution, Jake seems to embrace the most cynical common denominator of human involvement, in order to distance himself from disillusionment and to keep alive, like Romero, his conception of the most precious part of himself: his spirit, his integrity, the "non-negotiable" truth of himself.

Hemingway explored this physical and psychological territory of prostitution in other fiction that he wrote during his Paris years and throughout his career. Characters as diverse as Catherine Barkley in *A Farewell to Arms*, published in 1929 during Hemingway's last year of partial residence in Paris, and Harry in "The Snows of Kilimanjaro," written during the Key West years in the 1930s, attempt to maintain personal integrity—either by their professional detachment or by a kind of sardonic stoicism—in a "sell-out" world that has cast them, against their will, in the role of the "whore." When Frederic Henry takes Catherine to a hotel decorated in "red plush and brass" (*Farewell* 151), she recoils from the brothel decor. "I've never felt like a whore before," she says. When Frederic says she is "not a whore," Catherine replies that nevertheless "it isn't nice to feel like one" (152).

In "The Snows of Kilimanjaro," Harry is suffering for "betrayals of himself" and his writing talent "by laziness, by sloth" (*Short Stories* 158), and by love of the comfort provided by his rich lover. Harry calls himself her "possession" and says "it was strange that when he did not love her at all and was lying, that he should be able to give her more for her money than when he had really loved" (158-59). Harry's gangrenous leg is a fitting symbol for the disease of false character that is eating him to death, the way a hyena will eat itself in a feeding frenzy. Harry has become a "filthy animal" (161) (or, as he describes his days in Paris: a "cock" crowing on the "dunghill" of love [155]), like the hyena, eating carrion on the plain, instead of a snow leopard climbing toward the heights. Only in death does he regain his ascent.

Like Catherine and Harry, Hemingway's prostitutes and "prostitution-alized" characters are often sick or feel "dirty" or are somehow impaired. Brett Ashley flicks her cigarette ashes (which, like her last name, is evocative of "getting the ashes dragged," slang for sexual intercourse) everywhere and repeatedly says she "must bathe." Georgette has bad teeth and says she's sick, like everyone else (*Sun* 16). Honest Lil, the motherly prostitute in *Islands in the Stream*, has a "lovely dark face" (267) but is ashamed of the "grossness that [has] come over her body" (267) as she has grown older. In "The Light of the World," when Alice's sister prostitute, "Peroxide," calls her a "big mountain of pus," Alice counters with: "I'm clean and you know it and men like me, even though I'm big . . ." (*Short Stories* 488).

Hemingway's portrayals of prostitute characters and themes acknowledge the threat of literal disease with which prostitutes and their customers had to contend. Nick Adams learns this view of prostitutes, and by implication a view of sexuality itself, from his father—just as Hemingway probably did in conventional Oak Park. In "Fathers and Sons," Nick, as an adult with a son of his own, remembers "the sum total of direct sexual knowledge bequeathed to him by his father." Nick remembers that his father "summed up the whole matter by stating that masturbation produced blindness, insanity, and death, while a man who went with prostitutes would contract hideous venereal diseases and that the thing to do was keep your hands off of people" (*Short Stories* 589).

Far more than physical or even moral disease, however, it is the spiritual or psychological disease of the falseness of character for which Hemingway makes prostitution—but not the prostitute—a metaphor. In his texts, "selling out" or faking one's integrity, particularly in the performance of one's skill or profession, is a far worse form of corruption than sexual impropriety. Betraying and merchandising one's gifts through fakery and indolence is the real prostitution, the real moral decay, in Hemingway's fictional worlds, and this disease infects all sexes and classes equally. By means of this metaphor we can see narrator as "whore," bullfighter as "whore," writer as "whore."

Hemingway himself was concerned about becoming a "whore" as a writer. Carlos Baker highlights this concern by citing Hemingway's own experience prior to writing "Snows":

> Ernest later explained how he had arrived at the conception which governed his story. It all began, said he, with the rich woman who had invited him to tea in New York in April, 1934, and offered to stake him to another safari. Back in Key West that summer he had done some daydreaming about how things would have turned out if he had accepted her offer. The dying writer in the story was an image of himself as he might have been. Might have been, that is, if the temptation to lead the aimless life of the very rich had overcome his integrity as an artist. (289)

While Hemingway liked to see himself as a "pure" artist, as Baker suggests, he was very hard on writer friends from the Paris days who, in his opinion, sold their art or a lesser version of their art for mere money. When Don Stewart gave up bullfighting for Hollywood screenwriting, Hemingway "scorned him for selling out" (Brian 59). When Archibald MacLeish took an editorial job with *Fortune* because poetry did not pay the bills, "Ernest was scornful about 'the romance of business' . . . and took pride in his own position as a writer who had refused to compromise his artistic integrity" (Baker 206).

Part of Hemingway's sensitivity to this issue of artistic purity—and also part of the emotional background of "Snows"—was his relationship with his second wife, Pauline Pfeiffer. Pauline's family money provided Hemingway with support and luxuries he could not have afforded on his own, and he resented it even as he accepted it. More important, in his later assessment of his relationship with Pauline, expressed in *A Moveable Feast,* she was the "other woman," the temptress he met in Paris who seduced him away from the innocence of his marriage to Hadley. In his look backward, Hemingway, as Denis Brian puts it, "pictures himself as a guileless innocent, a devoted husband and father—until the other woman appears on the scene. He also sees himself as the dedicated young writer trying to live the good life, while going hungry, in a city of the decadent, the debauched, and the drug-addicted" (62-63). In this reinvention of himself, Paris itself was for Hemingway the "whore"—as Henry Miller called it literally, or as Samuel Putnam's book title expressed it only slightly less crudely: *Paris Was Our Mistress*.

The chief reasons Paris was a seductive, corrupting place for Hemingway, in his eyes, were the sophisticated, sexually assertive women who dazzled him there. Prior to Pauline, his focus was Lady Duff Twysden, the British socialite who was the model for Lady Brett Ashley. What is particularly revealing, in terms of Hemingway's Paris years, about the melding of Georgette and Lady Brett is Hemingway's relationship with Duff. In the *roman à clef* that *The Sun Also Rises* was considered to be—or as Baker puts it, the "literature of gossip" (153)—Duff's flamboyant personality, parasitic financial lifestyle, and attractiveness to men are clearly recognizable in Brett, just as Hemingway was identifiable in Jake, and Harold Loeb in Robert Cohn.

As Hadley would later say, all the characters in *Sun* were a "composite" of people Hemingway knew in Paris: "Almost none of his characters are pure Loeb or pure you or pure me. He makes a composite that fits his story" (Brian 56). What is striking about Duff's composite, however, is that it includes the image of the prostitute. Part of the reason for this synthesis may have been Hemingway's own sexual insecurities or conflicts, but the sexual milieu of Paris itself seems to have blurred for him any distinction between the "fallen woman" of the streets and the sexually liberated woman in higher social circles.

Duff Twysden may have been the epitome of the "liberated" woman of her era, yet views of her vary, depending on who is writing about her or remembering her. Hadley's biographer, Gioia Diliberto, refers to Duff and Kiki (another colorful Montparnasse figure, whom Baker calls a "sometime courtesan" [207]) as "heroines of Left Bank bohemia," while acknowledging their "sexual rapacity and alcoholism" (109). Like Brett, Duff was still married to, but estranged from, her second husband, Sir Roger Twysden, an alcoholic who abused her physically and emotionally. Duff, too, was living in seedy Parisian hotel rooms, with her cousin and fiancé, Pat Guthrie, while having affairs with other men. One of those men was Harold Loeb. Loeb theorized years later about why Hemingway made Cohn and Brett such negative characters: "I'd outraged his puritanism because I'd been off with Duff. . . . Hemingway made her into a tramp. I don't think of her that way at all. He made her promiscuous, a drunkard, all of which I can't support. She was elegant in a way" (Brian 57-58). Hadley refers to Duff as "a wonderfully attractive Englishwoman, a woman of the world with no sexual inhibitions" (Brian 55-56).

Most people who knew them during their acquaintance in Paris agree that while Hemingway did not sleep with Duff, he wanted to. Diliberto writes that "although Hadley liked Duff, she was deeply distressed by Ernest's relationship with her" (198). Years later Hadley said: "I don't know if they had an affair. I think it's perfectly possible but I don't know it for a fact" (Reynolds 157). She told Denis Brian, however, that although Ernest "adored [Duff] . . . I'm sure they didn't have an affair" (56). Hemingway's apparent lack of actual sexual experience with Duff was perhaps one of the driving forces of his portrayal of her as a promiscuous woman, a "whore." Part pique and part complex characterization, the blending of prostitute and heroine became a staple of Hemingway's prose. Baker writes that:

> Ernest's view of Duff was tinged with ambiguity. . . . Although he does not seem to have been included in the narrow circle of her amours, he felt sufficiently possessive towards her to resent Loeb's steadily developing infatuation. . . . The situation between Barnes and Brett Ashley, as Ernest imagined it, could very well be a projection of his own inhibitions about sleeping with Duff. (145, 157)

Jeffrey Meyers puts it more bluntly: "Hemingway portrays sex with women he never managed to sleep with in real life" (quoted in Brian 32).

The sad end of Duff Twysden's life makes even more striking the amalgam of her life and the life of a fictional character who was presented in ambiguous images of prostitution. Duff died of tuberculosis, a disease as common to prostitutes of that era as "black lung" was to coal miners. Corbin documents that tuberculosis was the chief killer of prostitutes in France. Duff's close relationship in Hemingway's mind with her fictional counterpart is also clear from what he told A. E. Hotchner years later: "Brett died in Taxco, Mexico. Call her Lady Duff Twysden, if you like, but I can only think of her as Brett. Tuberculosis. She was forty-three. Her pallbearers had all been her lovers. On leaving the church, where she had had a proper service, one of the grieving pallbearers slipped on the church steps and the casket dropped and split open" (48).

Whether from unrequited longing or from professional fascination— or both—Hemingway never stopped writing about the atmosphere of prostitution he inhaled from the air of Paris. The images of Paris permeated his work even when he wrote about other cities. In words strikingly similar to those of Brassai, for instance, Pilar speaks of "this odor of love's labor lost" (256) in *For Whom the Bell Tolls*. As part of her evocation of the smell of death for Robert Jordan's benefit, Pilar tells him to go "to the Jardin Botanico where at night those girls who can no longer work in the houses do their work against the iron gates of the park and the iron picketed fences and upon the sidewalks." There, Pilar says, where the prostitutes will "perform all that a man wishes," even "the great act that we are all born to," Jordan is to inhale from the "doings of the night . . . the smell that is both the death and the birth of man" (256).

This connection between sex and death was not only a function of Hemingway's sensibility as a writer, it was also part of the vernacular of Parisian prostitution. Alain Corbin writes that there was a certain marginal group of prostitutes from the middle and upper classes called *femmes gallante* who sought only "to pick up a lover who might subsidize their expenses" (136). Many of these temporary or part-time prostitutes were educated or otherwise respectable women who simply had fallen on hard financial times and did not wish to be identified as prostitutes. These were "courtesans who concealed their identity" (136) by claiming to be wives of husbands who were out of town or by posing as "unconsolable widows, who haunted the cemeteries like Les Tombales, described by Maupassant, and whom Mace calls *pierreuses de la mort* ('streetwalkers of death')" (136).

Hemingway clearly depicts Brett Ashley—and by implication Duff Twysden—as a *femme gallante*: an upper class "courtesan" who conceals her "identity," who exploits the fact that she has lost one husband to death and that her second husband is out of town, and who looks for a lover to "subsidize" her expenses. Catherine Barkley is also introduced in *A Farewell to Arms* as a faux widow who is grieving over the death of her fiancé. Catherine also, like Brett, takes on the role of prostitute. Like an actress doing research for her part, Catherine presses Frederic for details of the prostitute/"john" financial and psychological exchange: "When a man stays with a girl when does she say how much it costs? . . . Does she say she loves him? Tell me that. I want to know. . . . I'll say just what you wish and I'll do what you wish and then you will never want any other girls, will you?" (105). Catherine later tells Frederic that if she dies, she will visit him in the night like a fantasy, "prostitute" lover.

Brassai, too, refers to the language of death in connection with prostitution when he writes that the "most flourishing whorehouses in Paris were the ones known in slang as the 'slaughterhouses.'" These were the "dimestores of sex" for the lower class working men with little money, often staffed by physically scarred women who could sell themselves nowhere else. Brassai describes a scene he witnessed in one of these brothels, which he aptly calls a "descent into hell":

> In a suffocating haze of smoke so dense that the end of the room was invisible, there appeared gradually out of the crowded darkness a long line of men along one wall . . . and along the other wall a line of naked girls, some of whom wore half-open red satin kimonos to conceal a scarred breast or an appendectomy. . . . The men were not allowed to pick and choose; their partner was theirs by chance. . . . they paid the fixed price—five francs for room, trick, and tip, plus twenty-five centimes for the towel. The cash register never stopped ringing. . . . There was no time to catch one's breath, to take a minute's rest. In these "slaughterhouses," it was not unusual for a diligent girl . . . to pick up a clean towel forty or even fifty times in twenty-four hours—she was aptly called a "hustler."

"Hot and smoky" anonymous sex is an image consistently linked to brothel overtones in Hemingway's texts. Frederic Henry remembers his experiences with Italian prostitutes before falling in love with Catherine as "the smoke of cafés and nights . . . not knowing who it was with you, and the world all unreal in the dark and so exciting that you must resume again unknowing and not caring in the night" (13).

The "slaughterhouses" may have represented the sub-bargain basement of the edifice of prostitution in Paris, but there were many other floors, each more ornate, exotic, and expensive. Brassai describes these places in a chapter entitled "Houses of Illusion." They had many generic names—*maison close, maison de tolérance, maison publique, maison d'illusion,* or simply *maison* ("house")—but house of illusion seems most accurate, given their penchant for theatricality, elaborate costuming, and fantasy settings. Many were "located in the heart of Paris" and served the most powerful and prominent men of Europe. Edward VII had a special "Hindu Room" set up in the Chabanais brothel, in "homage to his mother [Queen Victoria], the Empress of India."

Owned by "respectable families and institutions, as well as by the underworld," all these exclusive bordellos had a "luxury unparalleled at the time," decorated with a "wealth of chandeliers, tapestries, Venetian mirrors, rooms with 'themes'—very much in vogue—of such elegance: Moorish rooms, Pompeian rooms, the Chinese pagoda, all with appropriate music and costumes." The women in these fantasy settings were almost never completely naked, but instead wore "sumptuous negligées . . . transparent evening dresses, with silk trains, decorated with bows, covered with lace." Each *maison d'illusion* also customarily had a "Chamber of Mirrors . . . making the entwined bodies visible from all sides, reflected a thousand times." Mirrors play a key role in Hemingway's depiction of brothel imagery. Catherine Barkley feels like a whore in the hotel room with Frederic when she sees herself "in one of the mirrors." At exactly the same instant, Frederic "saw her in three other mirrors. She did not look happy" (*Farewell* 152).

Brassai writes as well of "the inevitable torture chamber, with all its accessories: handcuffs, whips, hunting crops, flails." In one such fake "torture chamber of a medieval castle" at the Acropolis brothel, Brassai saw "fake flames" licking "fake logs" in an immense fireplace and a "wooden crucifix" upon which "a woman or man depending on whether the customer was a sadist or a masochist" could be fastened with handcuffs. The Acropolis also had a "Virgin's Room—all in white, lace, and immaculate muslins"—decorated with a "garland of orange blossoms, and next to it a bridal veil." The increasingly bizarre, theatrical nature of these brothels is best illustrated, perhaps, by "The Sphinx," which opened in Montparnasse and catered primarily to artists. Adorned only by a "glittering statue of a golden sphinx," this brothel broke with the tradition of "red velvet" sumptuousness and instead featured the decor of the modern bathroom: "enameled, waxed, white, clean, functional, hygienic." Another innovation of the Sphinx was that "men could bring their wives and children. . . . Going to the Sphinx was like a family outing." Soon the Sphinx had imitators, "bordellos that welcomed couples, who came out of curiosity and didn't go upstairs."

Whether Hemingway set foot in any of these places, we do not know for certain, partially because the women that Hemingway did *not* have sex with in "real life," ironically, appear to have been prostitutes. With all the controversy and conflicting information about Hemingway's sexuality, there is little historical evidence—and very few innuendos—that his knowledge or attitudes concerning prostitution came from actual sexual experience with women working in that profession. His many biographers do not often venture into this speculative territory. Jeffrey Meyers does assert that because Hemingway "adopted the Romantic idea that venereal disease could inspire creativity," he "cultivated a taste for the low life and prostitutes of Montmartre, but told Max Eastman that he felt disgusted by his attraction to these girls" (66). Meyers then implies, however, that Hemingway may have been making it up—engaging in the kind of myth-making braggadocio that amused him and confounded his biographers. As Denis Brian says of Hemingway's first biographer: "Baker set out to deliberately sever fact from fancy, but with Hemingway himself feeding him information, Baker was stymied and frequently admitted defeat" (6). Biographers could not rely on Hemingway to tell them the facts because he liked to make up stories. Sometimes the stories were good ones, but they were rarely completely true, as far as anyone knows. The biographers could not rely on other people, like Max Eastman, to set them straight either, because almost everyone who talked about Hemingway said something different about him—as *The True Gen* amply demonstrates.

None of the major biographies even list prostitution or prostitutes in their indices, and if they mention prostitution in the text, it is only in passing—never in detail. There appears to have been no detail to mention. Unlike Stephen Crane or Gustave Flaubert, who spent a great deal of well-documented time in brothels, Hemingway cannot ever be placed for certain in a house of prostitution. Meyers compares Hemingway to Crane by saying that "both were personally and professionally interested in the lives of prostitutes and criminals" (135)—but he provides no real detail. Baker and Reynolds do document by means of supporting evidence from Mary Welsh Hemingway that Hemingway invited Havana prostitutes to dinner. Baker writes about these encounters as social occasions; there is no mention of sex:

> While Mary was away, he did his best to keep his bad-boy reputation. A new whore whom he nicknamed Xenophobia had recently appeared in Havana and he sent his retainer, Roberto Herrara, to bring her out to the Finca for dinner. Some days later he paid a nonprofessional call on Leopoldina, who was just his age. They exchanged the local gossip and told each other what Ernest described as "sad stories of the death of kings." (475)

More typical of the biographies is to place Hemingway near a brothel and let the reader's imagination do the rest. James McLendon writes about the notorious, ornate brothels operating in Key West during the time that Hemingway lived there. McLendon calls them the "finest houses of prostitution in America" (68). After going into some detail about these establishments, however, McLendon admits that while "it is tempting to report that Hemingway . . . visited this local attraction . . . there is no evidence to substantiate the fact" (72). Also typical are the apocryphal remarks—usually traceable back to Hemingway himself—made by obscure Hemingway acquaintants. Denis Brian quotes a fisherman friend of Hemingway's, John Rybovich, Jr., as saying: "Ernest said he liked Cuba because they had both fishing and fucking there. I believe they had him try out all the houses of prostitution" (84).

The one thing that everyone who writes about Hemingway's private life does seem to agree on is that Hemingway made himself up. James R. Mellow, in writing about the gay man who successfully and illegally impersonated Hemingway for several years in the 1930s—referred to by Mellow as "Ernest's doppelganger"—says that "the irony—superb, in a way—was that Hemingway was himself creating a sometime imposter, a public persona whose reputation preceded him in his travels" (399). Carlos Baker writes about the "facets of the public image that Ernest wished to project" and says that "it was a kind of tribute to his powers of self-dramatization that almost everybody . . . took him at his word. There were probably many times when he believed it himself" (207). Lillian Ross implied that he invented an image to fulfill the desires of other people: "They didn't like Hemingway to be Hemingway. They wanted him to be somebody else—probably themselves" (190).

What is particularly relevant to the connection between Hemingway and prostitution is that as he got older, what he invented was the image of a swaggering sexual dynamo who had swashbuckled through brothels all his life. In the years between 1948 and 1961 Hemingway made a series of tape recordings featuring selections of his published work, poetry, and satirical spoofs, including the following excerpts:

> When I was a young boy, it was not necessary to pay any money to women. Later, I paid money to a few women to whom I wish all good things well. The principal woman of these was one named Alice, who weighed approximately 258 lbs. Her fee for love was two dollars, but she did not collect this fee if love was made satisfactory, and she often loaned me money to get a can of beans or something else in order that I might fight or box or attempt to fight or attempt to box in Northern Michigan. She was a very beautiful girl in spite of her weight, and I love her dearly still. . . .
>
> I never had the good fortune to know Miss Matahari . . . However, one night I fucked her very well. . . .
>
> After the war I worked in three whorehouses which were located in Billings, Montana, Red Lodge, Montana, and Cody, Wyoming. I was young at the time and trying to write, and it was difficult to preserve the balance between trying to write and working in a whorehouse where every Saturday night you broke your hand. . . .
>
> After my hands were broken and I did not think that I could continue in Billings and continue my writing, I moved to Red Lodge, where we only had to throw people out of the whorehouse on Saturday night because they were mostly thin and were usually armed with knives. . . .

> In Cody I was quite successful and met many interesting whores,
> professional whores, and since I did not believe that there were any
> good girls, and I cared nothing about the idea of them, I had already
> abandoned any hope or fear of them . . . As regards amateur whores, I
> have known a vast group of them. They are much duller than the
> professional whores because they are not truly conscious of their *métier*.
> *Métier* is a French phrase which means in Spanish *officio* and in American
> means their trade. (Transcript of "Ernest Hemingway Reads")

A. E. Hotchner writes that "one of Ernest's mischievous pleasures was the
practical-joke fantasy" (89). Perhaps the most obvious feature of this particular "fantasy" is the sexual prowess that Hemingway assigns to himself. He
is so adept that prostitutes pay *him* for sex. Another intriguing aspect of the
"tall tale" is where Hemingway places himself in the picture. He is neither
in the brothel as a "john" nor outside as a respectable "Oak Parker." He is
instead a bouncer, a fellow professional of the prostitutes and, in his role as
their protector, a sort of pimp. The third important feature is that Hemingway mentions his emotions of "hope and fear" concerning "good girls" and
then implies that all women are "whores"—only some are professionals and
some are amateurs.

The ambiguity of women's sexual conduct in his life and art was a
lifelong focus for Hemingway, but nowhere did he encounter this ambiguity
as a social reality more than he did in Paris during perhaps his most
impressionable years as a writer. Whether he experienced prostitution as an
observer or a participant—either in the streets or the brothels of Paris—we
cannot be sure. What is clear, however, is that prostitution held a central
place in the fantasy and bravado that occupied a significant portion of
Hemingway's language, in print or out. Since Hemingway, the quintessential
writer who wrote about what he *knew*, never wrote an actual brothel scene,
we might reasonably speculate that he had no experience in one. What is
more important, however, is that we do know for certain that his image of
himself as a sexually potent man of the world included fantasies of bordellos—even during his happily married Paris years. In a letter to Ezra Pound
in 1923 from the French Alps, Hemingway writes in his characteristic tone
of jocular savoir faire that "the high altitude has made me practically sexless"
and that he is considering writing a "monograph on the increasing scarcity
of prostitutes above 2000 meters" (*Selected Letters* 79). In 1924 he writes to
Pound that he "made a pilgrimage to Van Gogh's whorehouse in Arles and
other shrines" (115). In 1925, in perhaps his best-known sarcastic fantasy,
Hemingway wrote to F. Scott Fitzgerald describing his personal "heaven":

"To me heaven would be a big bull ring with me holding two barrera seats and a trout stream outside that no one else was allowed to fish in and two lovely houses in the town; one where I would have my wife and children and be monogamous and love them truly and well and the other where I would have my nine beautiful mistresses on 9 different floors . . ." (165).

In contrast to these "boy's club" inside jokes from the "bad boy" Hemingway, other views of him during his Paris years picture him as a sheltered "Rotarian" (Gertrude Stein's term, i.e., hopelessly bourgeois), far removed from illicit sex. Diliberto points out that "Hadley felt she and Ernest were the only happily married couple in town" (109). Loeb recalls that Hemingway "made himself out to be a sort of bad boy; he certainly wasn't. He was a bit of a Puritan, if anything" (Brian 48). Kiki, who knew the sexual secrets of the Left Bank as well as anyone, tweaks Hemingway in her *Memoirs* by recalling: "I saw Ernest again, looking more like a first-communion lad and friendlier than ever; I wondered if he was still a virgin" (56). These conflicting images of Hemingway's personal sexual adventurousness highlight the ambiguity about venal sex that appears in his texts. During his Paris days, at least, Hemingway seems to have been more a voyeur than a participant in the carnival of sexual experimentation going on around him. That voyeuristic distance, inherent in the impotence of the male protagonist of his first novel, makes what Hemingway *saw* in Paris stand out in even sharper relief than the direct experience of a brothel habitué.

One only had to be in Paris, after all, to see the glitter and the grotesqueness of its prostitution culture. The sale of sex and sexual fantasy was a public event, and Hemingway, like Brassai, was a keen observer. Hemingway's reportorial eye functioned with the precision and clarity of a camera, and it is perhaps not merely coincidental to his writing style that Hemingway's life chronologically paralleled the development of the movie camera, invented by the Lumiére brothers in France in 1895. Considering the avant-garde film experiments of Man Ray and Luis Buñuel in Paris in the 1920s, taking conventional ways of seeing apart the way Joyce and Stein were taking apart and rearranging language visually on the page, Paris in the 1920s could be called the Age of the Eye.

As much as any of his experimental contemporaries, Hemingway helped define this era of the eye. As a writer he was a seer, a watcher, a wandering camera—a voyeur. Vision is overwhelmingly the dominant sense in his fiction, and the eye is his primary metaphor of perception. Hemingway's "descriptions," said Janet Flanner (the "Genêt" who wrote "Letter from Paris" for the *New Yorker* for fifty years), "were like reports from the pupils of his eyes transferred by his pen onto his paper" (vii). The primacy of vision in Hemingway's experience and work is clear in his first serious Paris writing, a series of unpublished, one-sentence sketches entitled "Paris 1922," which Carlos Baker calls "the most concentrated distillation that he could make of what he had seen in Paris during five months of residence in the Latin Quarter" (90). Each sentence begins with "I" and emphasizes what the "I" saw:

> *I have seen* the favourite crash into the Bulfinch and come down in a heap kicking. . . . *I have seen* Peggy Joyce at 2 A.M. . . . in the Rue Camartin quarreling with the shellac haired young Chilean who . . . shot himself at 3:30 the same morning. . . . *I have watched* the police charge the crowd with swords. . . . I have stood on the crowded back platform of a seven o'clock Batignolles bus. . . . *I have watched* two Senagalese soldiers in the dim light of the snake house. . . . *I have seen the one legged street walker* who works the Boulevard Madelaine between the Rue Cambon and Bernheim Jeune's limping along the pavement through the crowd on a rainy night with the beefy red-faced Episcopal clergyman holding an umbrella over her. (Baker 90-91; emphasis added)

These six sentences, so close in linguistic form to the visual form of Brassaï's photographs, not only mark the beginnings of Hemingway's distinctive literary style, but they also reveal something about the nature of his approach to experience, particularly his experience of prostitution and perhaps of sexuality itself. He watches from a distance, uninvolved except in his imagination. He draws back, whether literally or in his mind, to a place where he can shape what he sees into what he desires or into themes or scenes that have dramatic power in his psyche. Each sentence is like a spotlight on a tableau or a scene in a play, the last one focusing on the tragicomedy of venal sexuality shuffling lamely toward what Pilar calls the "great act that we are all born to" (256). In the case of the streetwalker what Hemingway chooses to remember seeing is not the image of a glamorous, sexually provocative *poule* but a glimpse of a grimly working, physically impaired woman escorted ambiguously (who knows whether out of kindness or for sex?) by another person in the costume of his trade: a clergyman.

Thirty-five years later, in Hemingway's reminiscences of Paris collected in *A Moveable Feast*, he writes of his memory of another Parisian woman from what appears at first to be a far different, romanticized perspective. Even this nostalgic idealization, however, blends inevitably into a vision with overtones of prostitution. Hemingway begins the remembrance by recalling that he used to write in cafés when "all of the sadness of the city came suddenly with the first rains of winter" (4). On this particular day, as he was writing a story about "up in Michigan," a young woman came into the café and sat "by herself at a table near the window." Hemingway watched her as he wrote: "I looked at her and she disturbed me and made me very excited. I wished I could put her in the story, or anywhere, but she had placed herself so she could watch the street and the entry and I knew she was waiting for someone. So I went on writing"(5). The story "was writing itself," and Hemingway was "having a hard time keeping up with it," while drinking several "rum St. James" and sharpening his pencil frequently. He "watched the girl whenever [he] looked up" and thought to himself: "I've seen you, beauty, and you belong to me now, whoever you are waiting for and if I never see you again, I thought. You belong to me and all Paris belongs to me and I belong to this notebook and this pencil" (6).

At this point he "entered far into the story and was lost in it." He became so absorbed in the story that he did not know where he was or how much time had passed. When he was finished and "very tired," he looked up and noticed that his muse had left him, for another man, he assumed: "I read the last paragraph and then I looked up and looked for the girl and she had gone. I hope she's gone with a good man, I thought. But I felt sad." Hemingway concludes the scene with the thought that "after writing a story I was always empty and both sad and happy, as though I had made love . . ." (6).

The framing of the scene in sexual language is clear. Hemingway sees a woman who is a stranger to him, and she "excites" and "disturbs" him. He imagines she is waiting for another man. Hemingway wishes to possess her somehow, wants her to "belong" to him, but he realizes he only has voyeur status in her life. So he focuses his passion on his imagination, his writing, a process he calls "transplanting yourself" (5). He makes love to his art; he has "a hard time keeping up with it" and "enter[s] far into" it. In this way, because he has "seen" the woman, she "belongs" to him and he in turn "belongs" to his writing. Then after the frenzy of creation has spent itself, he feels bittersweet sadness and loss, as if he had "made love"— expressed in the language Hemingway characteristically uses to describe the postcoital emotions of his protagonists throughout his fiction: "always empty and both sad and happy."

The prostitutional nature of this scene is less overt than the image of the one-legged streetwalker perhaps, but it is nonetheless strongly present. A woman in public is observed by Hemingway; she is looking out a window (an archetypal brothel image) waiting, he imagines, for a man; Hemingway wistfully wishes to be with her, perhaps in a sexual way, but he becomes lost in his art; when he looks again, she is gone, an anonymous woman gone with an anonymous man. Collectively these elements have the overtones of a prostitutional encounter for Hemingway, an unrequited sexual encounter rendered in ambiguously prostitutional terms. Hemingway is not merely "projecting" here; there were many Parisian prostitutes who characteristically worked out of restaurants, so many in fact that they constituted a class of prostitutes called *femmes de restaurant.* Alain Corbin writes that "unlike the street prostitute," what the *femme de restaurant* "was really looking for, with the help of the café waiter, was a *coucher*—someone to spend the night with in a furnished room she could rent" (136).

What is even more revealing is Hemingway's identification with the woman (who "places herself" so he cannot see her face) and her ambiguously dual role, as he sees it, as desiring lover and desired object. Hemingway sees himself possessed by his work in the same sexual way that he wishes to possess her. He does not say that she is a prostitute, but Hemingway understood what the ambiguity of a woman in public meant in the cultural context of Paris. This ambiguity of the "public" woman, so integral to Hemingway's fictional portrayal of women, is also intimately connected to the brothel system embedded in the psychic configuration of Paris as Hemingway and Brassai knew it. Any study of Hemingway that attempts to place him historically in the Paris of the 1920s must recognize this powerful presence in his mind and art.

Hemingway observed prostitution closely in many places other than Paris in the 1920s. In those other cities and eras, however, prostitution was more clearly delineated from the mainstream culture. Paris was unique in the sense that the institution of prostitution was centuries old and highly complex, and the boundaries between the respectable and the outcast were blurred often beyond recognition. *Poules,* whether in the brothel or on the street, were an integral part of the "scene." Samuel Putnam writes about "the bawdyhouse that Montparnasse frequently was" (202) and the "little free-lance prostitutes of the Quarter" (253). Robert McAlmon describes the bars and how "the *poules* pranced about, dancing together and waggling their behinds with much energy to indicate that they were enjoying themselves. They laughed shrilly and were bawdy and reckless and ready for arguments or battles among themselves" (163-64). Even Hadley tasted the free, risqué air of the Quarter. Diliberto writes that when one of her priggish American cousins came to visit: "She resented his pity and enjoyed tweaking his bourgeois sensibilities by taking him to the Bal Musette next door for a turn around the smoky floor. Hadley loved to watch his pale face recoil as she danced with the rough sailors, and Ernest, she recalled, 'danced with anything he could get his hands on''' (105).

Paris in the 1920s was a city free of sexual restraint and strict rules about sexual roles. From the stylish lesbian soirées of Natalie Barney, to the bacchanalian and androgynous artists' festivals, to the ornate brothels, to the steamy *bal musette* dance halls, to the street *poules*, sexual manners and mores in Paris became a seamless costume of diverse sexual identities and practices. Ernest Hemingway had a great affinity as an artist for this blending of sexual role and sexual symbol. His work in Paris, as well as much of his later work, reveals not only the prostitute as an essential trope in his art but also the intimate influence of the demimonde on his vision of the human condition.

WORKS CITED

Baker, Carlos. *Ernest Hemingway: A Life Story.* New York: Scribners, 1969.

Brassai. *The Secret Paris of the 30's.* New York: Pantheon, 1976.

Brian, Denis. *The True Gen: An Intimate Portrait of Hemingway By Those Who Knew Him.* 1988. New York: Delta, 1989.

Clayson, Hollis. *Painted Love: Prostitution in French Art in the Impressionist Era.* New Haven, CT: Yale UP, 1991.

Corbin, Alain. *Women for Hire: Prostitution and Sexuality in France after 1850.* Cambridge, MA: Harvard UP, 1990.

Diliberto, Gioia. *Hadley.* New York: Tickner & Fields, 1992.

Fenton, Charles. *The Apprenticeship of Ernest Hemingway.* New York: Farrar, Straus & Young, 1954.

Flanner, Janet. *Paris Was Yesterday.* New York: Viking, 1972.

Griffin, Peter. *Along With Youth: Hemingway, The Early Years.* New York: Oxford UP, 1985.

Hemingway, Ernest. *Ernest Hemingway, Cub Reporter: "Kansas City Star" Stories.* Ed. Matthew J. Bruccoli. Pittsburgh: U of Pittsburgh P, 1970.

———. "Ernest Hemingway Reads." A series of tape recordings recorded 1948-61. Originally distributed by Caedmon Records. Currently copyrighted and distributed on cassette by HarperCollins Publishers.

————. *Ernest Hemingway: Selected Letters, 1917-1961*. Ed. Carlos Baker. New York: Scribners, 1981.

————. *A Farewell to Arms*. 1929. New York: Scribners, 1962.

————. *For Whom the Bell Tolls*. New York: Scribners, 1940.

————. *Islands in the Stream*. New York: Scribners, 1970.

————. *A Moveable Feast*. New York: Bantam, 1964.

————. *The Short Stories of Ernest Hemingway: The First Forty-Nine Stories and the Play "The Fifth Column."* New York: Modern Library, 1938.

————. *The Sun Also Rises*. 1926. New York: Scribners, 1962.

Hotchner, A. E. *Papa Hemingway: A Personal Memoir*. New York: Random House, 1955.

Kiki. *Kiki's Memoirs*. Tr. Samuel Putnam. Paris: Edward W. Titus at the Sign of the Black Manikin, 1930.

McAlmon, Robert. *McAlmon and the Lost Generation: A Self-Portrait*. Ed. Robert E. Knoll. Lincoln: U of Nebraska P, 1962.

McLendon, James. *PAPA: Hemingway in Key West*. Miami: E. A. Seemann, 1972.

Mellow, James R. *Hemingway: A Life Without Consequences*. Boston: Houghton Mifflin, 1992.

Meyers, Jeffrey. *Hemingway: A Biography*. New York: Harper & Row, 1985.

Putnam, Samuel. *Paris Was Our Mistress: Memoirs of a Lost & Found Generation*. Carbondale: Southern Illinois UP, 1947.

Reynolds, Michael. *The Young Hemingway*. New York: Blackwell, 1986.

Ross, Lillian. "Portrait of Hemingway." *Reporting*. New York: Simon and Schuster, 1964. 187-222.

A SHELTER FROM
THE TORRENTS OF SPRING

W E L F O R D   D U N A W A Y   T A Y L O R

1.

When Ernest Hemingway's *The Torrents of Spring* appeared in late May 1926, the Paris literary community responded with bewilderment and shock. Having established himself as a serious writer but a few months before with the story collection *In Our Time*, Hemingway had produced in the new work a slender but ruthless satire, the primary object of which was Sherwood Anderson's recent novel, *Dark Laughter* (1925). Given the evidence of Anderson themes and mannerisms in several of the *In Our Time* stories, this lampooning seemed odd, to say the least. The expatriated American literati in particular saw the parody as callous and unjustified. Several of those to whom Hemingway had shown the manuscript had advised him to withhold publication.[1] Perhaps they, as friends of both Anderson and Hemingway, had a better understanding of literary influence and loyalties. Moreover, they were aware of the older author's well-known acts of generosity to the younger and considered such a public act of renunciation unjustifiably cruel.

However, when *Torrents* appeared under the Scribners imprint, rather than that of Boni & Liveright, the publishers of Anderson and of *In Our Time*, many readers inferred a clearer motive. Whatever his unfathomable hostility toward Sherwood Anderson, Hemingway now had a new publisher, and his burlesque of the best-selling author of his former one appeared to have brought about the change.

Most investigators have accepted this as Hemingway's rationale. However, such a practical explanation fails to address—much less justify— his heartlessness toward Anderson. Nor is this fact mitigated by his weak explanation, to Anderson and others, that he had an obligation to call foul when a fine writer produced an inferior work (*Selected Letters* 206). I maintain that there was a good deal more behind the writing of *Torrents* than a desire to break with Liveright and that Hemingway's patronizing explanation, offered long *after* the decision to publish, was but one of many gestures by which he attempted not only to rationalize but to shelter himself from the repercussions of what he had come to see as only a partially successful—if not a misguided—act. The premise for this interpretation is supported in part by Anderson's unwitting connection to certain crucial events in Hemingway's artistic development at the time *Torrents* was written. It is further reinforced by the lengthy aftermath of the publication, a segment of the *Torrents* episode that has been addressed only piecemeal but that, viewed as a whole, offers a revealing exposition of Hemingway's feelings regarding Anderson and the limited success of the parody.

2.

From his newspaper days on the *Toronto Star* until the early fall of 1925, Hemingway had admired and promoted Sherwood Anderson's work. This was revealed by fellow journalists Gregory Clark, Frank Mason, and Morley Callaghan.[2] It was affirmed by Y. K. Smith, Anderson's former advertising associate, who had introduced him to the aspiring young writer in Chicago in the winter of 1920-1921. Apparently they saw each other with some frequency during this period, until Anderson and his wife, Tennessee, left for France in mid-May.

Headquartered in Paris, Anderson spent most of his three-month sojourn exploring the city and meeting members of the native and expatriate literary communities. Both in his letters and in a diary of the trip he recorded positive impressions of André Gide and the French critics Léon Bazalgette and Charles le Verrier. Of the expatriates he had mixed opinions. He fell into an easy camaraderie with Sylvia Beach, Gertrude Stein, and Alice B. Toklas, but did not take to James Joyce ("a misty gloomy Irishman") or Ezra Pound ("an empty man without fire") (Fanning 12).

Still, he returned to Chicago in the early autumn flushed with enthusiasm for Paris and buoyed by news that he had won a two-thousand-dollar award given by *The Dial* magazine for "service to letters" during 1921. Upon learning that Hemingway and his recent bride, Hadley, were planning a move to a European city, Anderson made a strong case for Paris. The Hemingways were responsive; they left for the French capital in mid-December, armed with introductory letters from Anderson to Sylvia Beach, Lewis Galantière, James Joyce, Ezra Pound, and Gertrude Stein (Somers 24).

Over the next three and a half years Hemingway made remarks to several new friends in Paris—individuals who also knew Anderson—that indicate a continuing enthusiasm for the older writer and his work and only a hint of negative undercurrent. In October 1923 he wrote in Steinese to Gertrude Stein that her recently published "Valentine for Sherwood Anderson" was "very fine and very mine" (*Selected Letters* 94). However, he had developed some private misgivings about the direction Anderson's work was taking. In mid-November 1923, when Edmund Wilson questioned him about Anderson influences he had surmised in "My Old Man," a story in *Three Stories and Ten Poems*, Hemingway replied:

> No, I don't think *My Old Man* [sic] derives from Anderson. It is about a boy and his father and race-horses. Sherwood has written about boys and horses. But very differently . . . I don't think they're anything alike. I know I wasn't inspired by him. I know him pretty well but have not seen him for several years. His work seems to have gone to hell, perhaps from people in New York telling him too much how good he was. Functions of criticism. I am very fond of him. He has written good stories. (Wilson 117)

Nevertheless, in March 1925 Hemingway published a laudatory review of Anderson's autobiography, *A Story Teller's Story* (1924). In it he referred to the experimental novel *Many Marriages* (1923) as a "poor book." However, he balanced this qualification with praise for *A Story Teller's Story*, declaring it "as good writing as Sherwood Anderson has done and that means considerably better than any other American writer has done" (Review 85). In view of statements he was to make in 1926 and later, this one should be carefully noted, as should his commendation of Anderson's authentic portrayal of "horses and women and bartenders . . ." (Review 85). This was eight months before *The Torrents of Spring* was written. Why, then, would Hemingway have so adamantly denied Anderson's influence to Wilson? I suggest that his protestations were motivated chiefly by what Wilson and virtually every subsequent critic has concluded: namely, that Anderson's influence, pervasive in Hemingway's work up to and including *In Our Time*, was a valued but increasingly sensitive factor in his artistic development. While this general finding has been voiced from the early 1920s onward, in the last thirty years it has been defined with more precision in stylistic and thematic analyses by Paul P. Somers, Clinton S. Burhans, and others. The primary exhibit is, not surprisingly, "My Old Man," with its racetrack setting, its adolescent narrator, its echoes of the Anderson stories "I'm A Fool" and "I Want to Know Why." Other identified traits include a shared use of polysyndeton, the repetition of key words, and the employment of such adjectives as "good" and "fine" to elicit sympathetic reader response. Several critics have also suggested that the structure of *Winesburg, Ohio* is reflected in that of *In Our Time*.

In the spring of 1925, after Anderson had urged Horace Liveright to publish *In Our Time* and had written an endorsement for its jacket, Hemingway wrote to thank him and added that he had "probably" been "wrong about the *Many Marriages*" (*Selected Letters* 161). Thus, when *In Our Time* appeared, Hemingway's relations with Anderson seemed amicable enough. Their letters had been warm and friendly. Hemingway's one review of an Anderson title had contained lavish praise, its single discordant note—the negative comment about *Many Marriages*—long since apologized for. There were of course expressions of resentment for having his work compared with Anderson's, but these he had made largely in private (as in the letter to Wilson cited earlier).

Therefore, the decision to write *The Torrents of Spring*, the actual composition, and the subsequent decision to submit it for publication were compressed into two brief months. Although this chain of events was driven in part by a growing urgency to be free of Anderson's influence, tempered by a certain sense of obligation, this tension was brought to a crisis point by two connected events of mid-September-early October 1925. The first, the arrival of a copy of *Dark Laughter*, sent to Hemingway at Anderson's request, occurred probably in mid-September.[3] The second, the publication of *In Our Time* on October 5, immediately elicited further and stronger comparisons with Anderson's work from reviewers. A gauge of Hemingway's resentment over this development is found in his reaction to Herbert J. Seligman's review, which, although one of the most laudatory, ended with a single qualifier—that Hemingway, "still intent upon . . . perfecting his formidable instrument . . . has not yet the big *movement*, the rich content of such a book as *Dark Laughter*"

(16; emphasis added). In one of the Fieldingesque asides in *Torrents*, the narrator promises the reader "that I am going to try and get that sweep and movement into the book that shows that the book is really a great book" (72).

Assuming that Hemingway had had good reason for thinking *Many Marriages* a "poor" performance, he had more justification for finding fault with *Dark Laughter*. Both novels represented a departure from Anderson's early mode, in which he had evoked the inner drives of his characters with an unvarnished, rather primitivistic frankness. These later novels were affected, their styles and structures obviously derivative. *Dark Laughter*, especially, exhibited a self-conscious Joycean texture with its awkward attempts at interior monologue and loosely constructed passages of stream-of-consciousness (often little more than rambling sentence fragments). Moreover, rather than focusing sharply and penetratingly upon the inner terrain of character, as Anderson had so effectively done in *Winesburg, Ohio*, his narrative focus is skewed by having "selected a focus of narration close to, but outside of, the mind of [his protagonist] Bruce Dudley" (Wylder 29). He also indulged in fanciful musings on the characters' thoughts and actions and offered ridiculous asides to the reader. All of these traits resulted in a "convoluted" (Wylder 32) structure and overall diffusion. Nevertheless, *Dark Laughter* might also be seen as a legitimate experiment in narrative technique that took Anderson out of his accustomed narrative pose and beyond his signature spheres of the provincial town and the racetrack.

Also, in all fairness, Hemingway might well have kept his reservations to himself, as he had done for the most part in the case of *Many Marriages*. But succeeding events were to make this impossible. By October *Dark Laughter* was in its fourth printing. Hemingway's resentment at this development was heightened by the slow sales of *In Our Time*, which he felt Liveright was not promoting as vigorously as he should. Another annoyance, as yet unnoted by critics, was his mother's penchant for comparing him unfavorably with Anderson. He wrote Archibald MacLeish,

> My mother sent me your review of Dark Laughter from the Atlantic Monthly. Monthly is correct. . . . My mother always sends me everything that shows up Sherwood or when he gets a divorce or anything because she has read that I am much the same thing only not so good and she naturally wants me to know how the master is getting along. (*Selected Letters* 178)

Discussions of Hemingway's motives repeat a common image: *Torrents* was a declaration of artistic independence from Sherwood Anderson's influence. In other words, the ultimate goal of the parody was to have it serve as a public renunciation while at the same time giving vent to private frustrations.

3.

Although bitter over the recent turn of events in his and Anderson's literary fortunes, Hemingway was privately grappling with more formidable and insidious pressures. On September 21 he had completed the first draft of *The Sun Also Rises*. Ostensibly a roman à clef drawn from individuals he had known in Paris, the summer fiestas he had attended in Pamplona, and the defining geography of both settings, the new novel in fact represented a decisive advance in Hemingway's artistic development in that it had grown out of extensive literary roots. The most prominent of these was Ivan Turgenev, whom Hemingway described to Archibald MacLeish as "the greatest writer there ever was. . . . Tolstoi was a prophet. Maupassant was a professional writer . . . Turgenev was an artist" (*Selected Letters* 179).

In detailing the nature of Turgenev's influence on *The Sun Also Rises*, Myler Wilkinson concentrates much of his discussion on *Fathers and Sons* (1862), the novel having the most bearing and one of two Turgenev titles that Hemingway had with him as he began revising his manuscript in Schruns in December 1925. Wilkinson identifies several manifestations of this influence: the "code" protagonist of both novels; the "common vision of man's organic place within nature, rather than his alienation from social self" (59); and the use of geography as an objective correlative, whereby "nature for both becomes an extended metaphor of man's possible self [and] terrain becomes a projection of his body . . ." (37). He also notes the imagistic trait of a "unified world" in which all elements "stand for things in themselves" (63).

Still, however pervasive the imprint of Turgenev and however great the debt to him, it was Hemingway's desire not to emulate but to supersede his model. In his own words, he was "trying to beat dead writers that I knew how good they were" (*Selected Letters* 673). Stated in terms of literary theory, he was experiencing what Harold Bloom has designated the "anxiety of influence." Citing Bloom, Wilkinson observes that it was this "anxiety which drove him to be the best" and that "the history of his relationship with writers, both dead and alive, illustrates Hemingway's attempt to project that anxiety, either aesthetically in his writing or personally in his attacks on literary forebears" (23).

In the early autumn of 1925, this anxiety was centered on not one but two sources of influence. If Hemingway's attempt at projecting his "anxiety" toward Anderson was in part justified by the artistic inferiority of *Dark Laughter*, he also recognized some familiar characteristics in the latter's story of Bruce Dudley, who flees an unhappy marriage in Chicago for his boyhood home in Indiana. There he takes a job in a wheel factory and is seduced by the wife of the passive owner, while an Id-chorus of laughing blacks notes the proceedings in mocking celebration.

In pivotal, if limited, ways these elements recalled Ivan Turgenev's novel *The Torrents of Spring* (1872),[4] whose protagonist, Dimitry Sanin, falls in love with Gemma Roselli, a young Italian woman. But while trying to sell his estate in order to finance his marriage, his wealthy and sensual client, Marya Polozova, seduces him. Thus, in the sexual theme and in such characters as the weak male, the abandoned female, and the seductress, Hemingway found the raw materials for a parody featuring the ineffectual aesthete Scripps O'Neill, an abandoned husband who takes up with two waitresses and whose sexual confusion is contrasted to the fecund primitivism of the local Indians and the black cook in Brown's Beanery.

The two texts suggested something more compelling than general parallels, however, as it is probable that Hemingway's explorations of Turgenev had begun at Sherwood Anderson's behest. Anderson, who called *A Sportsman's Sketches* "the sweetest thing in all of literature" (Howe 93) and who "raced through the pages like a drunken man" (Sutton 302) in his initial reading, had apparently discussed Turgenev and other Russian authors with Hemingway during their close association during 1921 in Chicago. In *A Moveable Feast*, Hemingway recalled that on his first visit to Sylvia Beach's bookshop, within a few days after his arrival in Paris, he had selected four titles, three of which were by Dostoyevsky, Tolstoi, and Turgenev ("the two volumes of *A Sportsman's Sketches*") (36).

Here, then, in the linking of Turgenev and Anderson, was a found opportunity, the exploitation of which might, as Hemingway saw it, free him from the shadow of both these literary benefactors, now that he had stripped them of their treasures. This does not imply, however, that *The Torrents of Spring* constituted a double-barreled attack, whereby Anderson and Turgenev received comparable assaults. For one, the influences of Turgenev on the Hemingway text now in revision were far more subtle and elusive than the obvious Anderson mannerisms in the one just published. Also, in the course of his literary apprenticeship Hemingway had developed a greater admiration for Turgenev than for Anderson. Finally, Anderson and his work constituted more of an immediate and pressing reality. Any doubts that *Dark Laughter* was the primary target are eliminated by a preface for *Torrents* that Hemingway wrote but excluded from the published text:

> Many critics commenting on a book of stories written by myself
> and published last fall remarked on how much whatever excellences
> they detected in these stories resembled the excellences of Mr. Sher-
> wood Anderson. Having just read a novel by Mr. Anderson which was
> called, I believe, Dark Laughter and which is, I believe, generally
> acknowledged to be a masterpiece and being exceedingly impressed by
> what these critics had written I resolved to write henceforth exclusively
> in the manner of Mr. Anderson. The careful reader will see that in my
> attempt to write as Mr. Anderson writes I have failed most signally. It
> is therefore to his indulgence that I commend myself most diffidently.
> ("'Author's Preface'" 112)

Turgenev's novel did not go untouched to be sure, but aside from
furnishing the title, with its metaphor of springtime amorous reawakening,
and such broad features as character types and selected themes, it escaped
major satiric attack. On the contrary, as Robert Coltrane has noted,
"Hemingway is saying satirically that Turgenev's *The Torrents of Spring* is the
work Anderson should have tried to emulate but was incapable of emulat-
ing" (150). Critical opinion is virtually unanimous in assessing Turgenev's
Torrents not only as being superior to *Dark Laughter* but also as being one of
his finest works.

It is possible that Hemingway was aware that Turgenev, like himself
a literary exile (his *Torrents* was written mainly in Germany and England),
had taken a personal incident as the basis for his plot. While passing a shop
in Frankfurt, a pretty young girl had rushed out and excitedly begged him
to save her brother, who lay unconscious in a back room. After reviving the
boy, Turgenev fell in love with the girl and decided to leave her only after
a difficult struggle with his conscience. The incident had occurred in 1840,
when he was twenty-two. Recalled thirty years later, at the height of his
powers as a novelist and with a mature, cosmopolitan discernment, Turgenev
turned it into one of his most objective and controlled narratives. Even the
original setting of Frankfurt is vividly evoked. Against its austere tidiness and
exaggerated formalities, personified in part by the priggish Herr Klüber,
Gemma's fiancé, the immigrants, both Italian and Russian, are portrayed.

The Petoskey, Michigan, setting of Hemingway's *Torrents* functions in
a decidedly different manner. Although most of the plot evolves there, the
narrative is related from a European frame of reference. Several of the
sections are introduced with quotations from Henry Fielding (a benchmark
of classic European satire, implying that Hemingway is playing Fielding to
Anderson's Richardson, his *Torrents* being the *Shamela* to the former's *Pamela*).

He also reveals in various ways that he is writing the narrative in Paris, which serves as a kind of tandem referent for satiric effects.

This apparent incongruity seems to have been suggested by several flashbacks in *Dark Laughter* (139-57) dealing with the meeting and engagement of Aline and Fred Grey in Paris following World War I. Another passage has Bruce Dudley reflecting on "a new book by the Irishman, Joyce, 'Ulysses'" (120). Such references suggest a contrasting note of sophistication to what Anderson saw as a provincial, impotent American culture. However, in Anderson's setting (some two-thirds of *Dark Laughter* takes place in Old Harbor, a nondescript Ohio River town in southern Indiana) such references seem anomalous, if not ridiculous.

It should be remembered, however, that Anderson's purpose, no less than his theme and tone, was serious. Hemingway's was satiric, and ubiquitously so, even in those elements of *Torrents* that concern his settings and even himself. Therefore, neither of his milieux, Petoskey and Paris, nor their unlikely connections was immune to spoofing. Yogi Johnson, who works with Scripps O'Neil at the pump factory, has been left impotent as the result of a sexual exploit during a visit to Paris. Diana, the elderly waitress to whom Bruce is married briefly, spins an elaborate yarn of her involvement in a hushed-up scandal during the Paris Exhibition of 1900. Even Scripps thinks of buildings in Paris but then remembers that he has never been there (26). In other words, with these unlikely characters, through which Paris is evoked as a place of scandal, intrigue, and romance, Hemingway explodes the anomaly found in *Dark Laughter*. The frozen dullness of Petoskey stands out against these collective images in mocking contrast. The snow, knee deep at the beginning, slowly yields as the chinook begins to blow and the gutters fill with dirty snow water. In this atmosphere of Midwestern *rêverie* a nude squaw enters the beanery, reawakening Yogi's suppressed libido, and Scripps takes the younger waitress, Mandy, as his "woman."

Hemingway's authorial perceptions of Paris in *Torrents* are depicted somewhat more subtly. The city he describes is characterized by its intellectuals (John Dos Passos, F. Scott Fitzgerald, Gertrude Stein); its refined cuisine and vintages; its heady talk about "Art" in such forums as the Café du Dôme. However, even these emblems are not immune to parody. Fitzgerald is pictured in a drunken prank; Dos Passos appears only long enough to proclaim "Hemingway, you have wrought a masterpiece" (71); and the author forgoes discussing Art with Dos Passos at the Café du Dôme in order to return home and get another chapter written (71). Speaking of Paris as represented by Gertrude Stein, he quips, "All that in Paris, Ah, Paris. . . . Paris in the morning. Paris in the evening. Paris in the morning again. Paris at noon, perhaps. Why not?" (75). Thus, the Paris that Hemingway presents in *Torrents* is, for all its social and cultural urbanity, a place where these attributes are assumed but are not taken seriously and where levity, libertinism, and even more serious forms of intrigue prevail.

When portraying Petoskey, however, other motives were at play. His reasons for moving northward from Anderson's Indiana setting to the lower Michigan peninsula were apparently private and had little to do with Anderson or *Dark Laughter*. Although few critics have noted the fact, Robert Coltrane has demonstrated that *Torrents* "is as personal as any of Hemingway's other works," albeit with "disguise and misdirection" (159). Hemingway had known the general area while growing up and again after his return from World War I. In *Torrents* it is embodied in both landmarks (e.g., Braun's restaurant ["Brown's Beanery"] and the Blackmer Rotary Pump Factory) and in various people he had known there. However, his close personal connections with these individuals are disguised in their satiric roles (e.g., his former lover, Pauline Snow [Diana]; the veteran Billy Gilbert [the Indian amputee]; his first sexual conquest, Prudie Boulton [the squaw clad only in moccasins]).

Also disguised is a volatile personal crisis. By October 1925 Pauline Pfeiffer's role in Hemingway's life had developed from that of casual friend into a serious romantic attachment. Hemingway now faced a trying dilemma of choosing between "the older matronly Hadley" and "the vivacious and wealthy Pauline" (Coltrane 154). More than one commentator[5] has pointed to this triangulation as the source for the theme of infidelity in *Torrents*, in which Scripps O'Neil, abandoned by his first wife, marries the elderly Diana, only to leave her for the younger and more tantalizing waitress, Mandy. It also finds an analogue in Turgenev's *Torrents* in the seduction of Sanin by the married Marya Polozova and his subsequent jilting of Gemma. Similarly, in *Dark Laughter* Bruce Dudley abandons his wife and eventually is seduced by his boss's wife, Aline.

4.

Hemingway had written numerous brief satires before.[6] But the one he composed between November 23 and 30, 1925, far exceeds the designation *jeu d'esprit* applied by Carlos Baker. Even its shortest printed state (in *The Hemingway Reader*) runs to sixty-three pages of cruelly funny parody that strikes with deadly precision. Anderson was not being self-serving when he later remarked that *Torrents* might "have been humorous had Max Beerbohm condensed it into twelve pages" (*Memoirs* 475). And even if we acknowledge, as we must, that it subsumed targets other than Anderson,[7] this effort represented a cannonade, the very scope and intensity of which reveals the hostility that had been festering in Hemingway's spleen. Kenneth S. Lynn characterizes the resulting black humor as "a substitute for pistol and ball" (305).

That sufficient pretext existed for venting this spleen there can be little doubt, and that the therapy should have taken the familiar form of satire is not in itself unjustifiable. Still, it is one thing to create satire, and quite another to make it public. And in light of the preceding explanation it seems appropriate to consider the commonly stated reason for both the composition and the decision to publish—namely, Hemingway's desire to terminate his obligation to Horace Liveright. Although one is well advised to question any statement he made on the subject at this time, there is no reason to believe that he was being insincere when he wrote Fitzgerald on January 1, 1926, that while "[*Torrents*] makes a bum out of [Liveright's] present ace and best seller Anderson[,] Now in 10th printing[,] I did not, however, have that in mind in any way when I wrote it" (*Selected Letters* 183). In other words, putting Anderson down—a sure means of inviting Liveright's rejection of his next book—was not, according to Hemingway, the primary motive. Rather, while freely voicing resentment over the success of *Dark Laughter*, he confides to Fitzgerald serious doubts about Liveright's promotion of *In Our Time*, citing the lack of advertising and the mishandling of publicity. He also expresses concern about the fiscal soundness of the firm and of Liveright himself, whose heavy losses in theatrical ventures had already forced him to sell half of his business. The concern turned out to be prophetic; by the end of the decade the firm had all but collapsed and Liveright was bankrupt.

Still, the pressured week of November 30 to December 7, 1925, was scant time for making a rational decision on a crucial matter that threatened lasting negative effects. Hemingway was incapable of seeing past the now-intimidating Anderson stigma to the sobering fact that once a therapeutic parody becomes a published work, its effects are all but impossible to remove. Therefore, I would argue that even if breaking with Liveright had not been a consideration, Hemingway would have made the same compulsive decision anyway, especially since Pauline Pfeiffer praised the work and urged publication. Thus, on December 7 he dispatched the manuscript to Liveright, who declined it on December 30. By mid-February Scribners had agreed to publish both *Torrents* and *The Sun Also Rises*.

5.

It is difficult to determine just when Hemingway began to develop misgivings over his decision; however, as publication day approached he began putting his defenses in place. These he was to express over many years in statements marked by evasiveness, contradiction, outright falsehood, and vitriolic denunciation. First, he set out upon the ethical high road, claiming in a letter to Anderson that any hand that created inferior art needed to be called, but that he meant nothing personal, and that "nothing that's any good can be hurt by satire" (*Selected Letters* 206). Anderson called the letter "gigantic . . . it was a kind of funeral oration delivered over my grave. It was so raw, so pretentious, so patronizing that in a repellant way . . . I was filled with wonder" (*Memoirs* 475). Anderson's poised response—his only negative comment on *Torrents* was "it's got the smarty tinge" (*Anderson: Selected Letters* 80)—ended with an invitation to the Hemingways to visit him at his new home in Virginia. Hemingway responded immediately, relaxing his superior stance with a cool apology, admitting that he had been a "horse's ass" for having written a "snooty" letter (*Selected Letters* 210). He wrote again in September, apologizing more pointedly for having spoken in such an "ex cathedra" manner (219).

One cause for Hemingway's moderating attitude might have been the unexpected reception of *Torrents*. Despite several positive reviews, it was being called yet another imitation of Anderson. In an unpublished chapter of his memoirs, covering a residence on the Left Bank during the winter of 1926-1927, Ralph Church noted that Lewis Galantière, "and more than a few others, eventually" charged Hemingway "with having come in that case to write too much . . . like Anderson" (29). More significantly, in the same chapter Church reveals that Hemingway himself asked Sylvia Beach to quit stocking the volume.

This must have been a consequence he had not foreseen. Another miscalculation was his underestimating of the loyalty of Anderson's friends, many of whom were not amused by *Torrents*. The most complete statement we have from one of these is Gertrude Stein's. Stein had herself been a minor target in *Torrents* ("Ah, there was a woman! Where were her experiments in words leading her? What was at the bottom of it?" [74-75]). Commenting through the fictive guise of Alice B. Toklas, Stein recalled that she and Anderson had discussed Hemingway at length when Anderson visited Paris in December 1926 (some six months after *Torrents* had been published): "Hemingway had been formed by the two of them and they were both a little proud and a little ashamed of the work of their minds . . ." (265). Both admitted to a certain fondness for Hemingway, however, "because he is such a good pupil. . . . it is so flattering to have a pupil who does it without understanding it, in other words he takes training and anyone who takes training is a favorite pupil. They both admit[ted] it to be a weakness" (265). Stein observed that Hemingway, like Derain, was successful because "he looks like a modern and he smells of the museums" (266).

They also discussed the pompous letter Hemingway had written to Anderson explaining his rationale for writing *Torrents* and agreed that Hemingway was "yellow," that he was naturally afraid when he learned that Anderson was coming to Paris; whereas "Sherwood as naturally was not [yellow]" (265). The point seemed valid. According to Anderson, Hemingway avoided him during the several weeks that Anderson stayed in Paris, but finally showed up on the last day and invited him for a drink. When they had ordered, Hemingway turned awkwardly and walked away (*Memoirs* 475). However, he immediately wrote to Maxwell Perkins, effusing over the "fine afternoons" he and Anderson had had and adding that "he is not at all sore about Torrents" (*Selected Letters* 241).

This was the first in what would become a series of untruths concerning his connection with Anderson and *Torrents*. He was to tell Ralph Church that "I'm a Fool" was Anderson's "worst" story and that its author (who had spent three years working at racetracks!) "shouldn't try to write about things he doesn't know by his own experience." Still more incredible was his claim to Louis Cohn that he had not read Anderson before he wrote "My Old Man" (Phillips 205).

In subsequent comments, falsehood often gave way to invective.[8] In 1927 he commended Wyndham Lewis for having "destroyed the . . . Black [racial] enthusiasm [in *Dark Laughter*] very finely in Paleface" and sneered at Anderson's having seen Chartres "accompanied . . . by Jewish gentlemen" (*Selected Letters* 264). Twenty years later the attitude had hardened still further, as seen in his statement to Harvey Breit of the *New York Times*, that "SA was like a jolly but tortured bowl of puss turning into a woman in front of your eyes" (862). But the harshest attack was in his description of Anderson in a letter to Bernard Berenson in 1953:

> Sherwood Anderson was a slob. Un-truthful (not just inventing untruthful; all fiction is a form of lying). . . . Also he was wet and sort of mushy. He had very beautiful bastard Italian eyes and if you had been brought up in Italy (with very beautiful Italian eyes) you always knew when he was lying. From the first time I met him I thought he was a sort of retarded character. The sort that gets to be Minister of Culture in a new chickenshit Republic where there are no standards except charm. . . . (802)

Such diatribes do not tell the complete story, however. Hemingway repeatedly offset his harsh criticisms of Anderson with compensatory compliments. As early as 1923, when responding to Edmund Wilson's suggestions of Anderson's influence, he had acknowledged that the latter had written "good stories." On March 30, 1926, while *Torrents* was in the press, he had written Edwin L. Peterson that despite the fact that *Dark Laughter* was "awfully bad," Anderson could write beautifully and had indeed written better than anyone in America.[9] One may of course contend that such statements are at best ambiguous, in that they might well have been self-serving, that is, made for purposes of evasion. On the other hand, they seem to square with comments on Anderson (and Stein) in *"Une Genération Perdue,"* a sketch in *A Moveable Feast,* which is generally regarded as Hemingway's summing-up statement on his life in Paris in the 1920s.

Not only does he extend the common thread of Anderson's stories being "beautifully written" (27-28), he also repeats the image of Anderson's "great, beautiful, warm Italian eyes" (27) that he had denigrated in his letter to Bernard Berenson. Here again he downplays this physical characteristic, along with the overall importance of Anderson the artist. He further alleges that Stein's motives were ulterior, in that she always spoke well of anyone who supported her and her work. He claims that she would not discuss Anderson's stories or novels with him, and he feels that the "stories were too good to make happy conversation" (28). He goes on to mention that when he had parodied the "terribly bad, silly and affected" *Dark Laughter,* Miss Stein was very angry. I had attacked someone that was a part of her apparatus" (28).

What is perhaps most revealing in the sketch is the implied offense that Hemingway takes to Stein's description of himself and his contemporaries as a "lost generation." The highlight of *"Une Genération Perdue"* is the account of an afternoon visit to 27, rue de Fleurus during which he and Stein argued about the irresponsibility and immaturity of Hemingway's generation. After a less than civil parting, he says that he reflected upon these same young men he had seen wounded and dying during the war: "I thought of Miss Stein and Sherwood Anderson and egotism and mental laziness versus discipline and I thought who is calling who a lost generation?" (30).

As if to counterbalance these sentiments, Hemingway addressed the *Torrents* episode again, at about the same time, in a draft preface to a student edition of his most popular stories that Scribners was planning in 1959.[10] Near the end of more than a dozen pages of condescending and occasionally cynical commentary on his own work and that of several other authors and critics are several sentences relating to Anderson the person, his work, and *Torrents:*

Writers have enough enemies without doing it to each other. . . . All really good writers know exactly what is wrong in all other good writers. . . . But writers have no business fingering another writer to outsiders while he is alive. . . . What I mean is, you really shouldn't really give it to another writer, I mean really give it to him. I know you shouldn't do it because I did it once to Sherwood Anderson. I did it because I was righteous, which is the worst thing you can be, and I thought he was going to pot the way he was writing and that I could kid him out of it by showing him how awful it was. So I wrote *The Torrents of Spring*. It was cruel to do, and it didn't do any good, and he just wrote worse and worse. What the hell business of mine was it if he wanted to write badly? None. But then I was righteous and more loyal to writing than to my friend. I would have shot anybody then, not kill them, just shoot them a little, if I thought it would straighten them up and make them write right. Now I know there is nothing you can do about any writer ever. The seeds of their destruction are in them from the start, and the thing to do about writers is get along with them if you see them. . . . All except a very few, and all of them except a couple are dead. Like I said, once they're dead anything goes as long as it's true.

I'm sorry I threw at Anderson. It was as cruel and I was a son of a bitch to do it. The only thing I can say is that I was as cruel to myself then. But that is no excuse. He was a friend of mine, but that was no excuse for doing it to him. . . . (100-1)

Though seemingly contradictory, the preceding statement and the one in *"Une Génération Perdue"* are linked by adumbrations of the anxiety of influence and by the attendant need to repudiate benefactors. They represent two final manifestations of an admiration-rejection dichotomy that Hemingway found it impossible to resolve. But if we assume that the stronger of the two needs was to repudiate, as seems to have been the intention in *"Une Génération Purdue,"* and even more so in *Torrents*, then the attempt fell far short of the mark. In addition to having been forced to recognize the artist's powerlessness to control the responses of an audience, Hemingway had come to realize the seeming inability of parody to negate a literary influence once it has been appropriated.

Or perhaps he had overestimated his own skills as a parodist. Ray Lewis White is probably correct in observing that he "was not very proud" of *Torrents* ("Explanation" 261). And Richard B. Hovey's observations, made in 1965—that *The Torrents of Spring* "has had fewer readers than any of Hemingway's other fiction" and is "the least of [his] writings to appear between hard covers" (460)—may still be said to hold. In all events, what Hemingway realized was at best a Pyrrhic victory. *Torrents* had fallen far short of providing the ultimate refutation he had sought, and the putdowns of his former mentor failed to provide him with a shelter of justification. For the benevolent specter of Sherwood Anderson would haunt his early work— and his conscience—forever.

NOTES

1. The manuscript quickly made the circuit of Hemingway's friends. Louis Bromfield and F. Scott Fitzgerald praised it. Gerald Murphy was treated to a late-night reading while Sara dozed and Ernest failed to notice. John Dos Passos, to whom Hemingway read the manuscript in the Closerie des Lilas, first laughed and then strongly urged him not to publish it. Hadley Hemingway also opposed the publication; she thought it cruel and inappropriate in light of Anderson's support and felt that it detracted from Ernest's reputation as a serious writer (Baker, *Life Story* 159-60; Dos Passos 157-58; Sokoloff 83; Tomkins 27).

2. Charles Fenton notes that during this period Hemingway "talked constantly about Anderson" (148). Frank Mason, the Paris correspondent for Hearst International in the early 1920s, was one of Fenton's primary sources. Interviewed in 1952, "Mason's most positive memory of Hemingway's interests during [the] first months of 1922 was that he spoke repeatedly of Sherwood Anderson, and, more specifically, that he expressed many times his intention to model his own literary career on Anderson's" (149). The following year, in conversations with Morley Callaghan, a Canadian newspaperman, Hemingway discussed Anderson's work "extensively" and "with sympathy and understanding" (Fenton 148).

3. Anderson's letter to Horace Liveright requesting that copies of *Dark Laughter* be sent to Hemingway and Gertrude Stein, among others, is dated August 28, 1925 (*Letters of Sherwood Anderson* 146-47).

4. Although Robert Coltrane implies (152) that Hemingway happened to read Turgenev's *Torrents of Spring* at about this time, there is strong reason to believe that he had known the work before the autumn of 1925. True, the borrowing history of Sylvia Beach's lending library is missing for 1921 through much of 1925; however, between October 8, 1925, and November 23, 1929, when this history is intact, Hem-

ingway checked out the volume three additional times (Wilkinson 95-101). Wilkinson states that "Hemingway read through Turgenev's entire *œuvre* within a short space of time [i.e., in the fall of 1925]" (63); however, this should not be seen as precluding earlier readings.

5. See Coltrane 154-55, 156-57, and Lynn 302, 305-6.

6. In addition to the satiric verse he contributed to the *Toronto Star* and *Der Querschnitt,* there is the brief story "A Divine Gesture," published in the *Double Dealer* in 1922. A pronounced satiric strain runs through his journalistic features, and Baker cites numerous examples of notebook entries that criticize their subjects in similar terms (*Life Story* 135). In 1924 Hemingway wrote a satiric account of Ezra Pound's Bohemianism. He was ready to submit this to the *Little Review* when Lewis Galantière intervened, insisting that it would almost surely be rejected, since Pound served as foreign editor of the magazine (Baker, *Life Story* 86).

7. Wylder (35) mentions such targets as H. L. Mencken, Sinclair Lewis, Harold Stearns, D. H. Lawrence, Mary Austin, and Henry Wadsworth Longfellow. Gertrude Stein is another obvious one, as is Hemingway's own love dilemma.

8. Small and Reynolds (1-11) trace an extended use of boxing metaphor in the correspondence between Anderson and Hemingway concerning the publication of *Torrents.* They further argue that Ole Andreson ("Ole Anderson" in an earlier draft), the aging and defeated fighter in Hemingway's "The Killers," is an allegorical representation of Anderson and that the latter's subsequent story "The Fight," in which a long-smoldering rivalry between two cousins erupts into fisticuffs when both are in middle age, is a retort in metaphorical kind.

9. These comments are found in a letter not included in *Anderson: Selected Letters;* however, it is paraphrased in White, "Explanation" 261-63.

10. Because of the "boastful, smug, and malicious tone" (Introduction to Hemingway, "Art" 86) of the preface Hemingway wrote, author and publisher never reached a compromise on the final text, and the project was abandoned. However, the preface was published in 1981 in the *Paris Review* as "The Art of the Short Story."

WORKS CITED

Anderson, Sherwood. *Letters of Sherwood Anderson.* Ed. Howard Mumford Jones and Walter B. Rideout. Boston: Little, Brown, 1953.

————. *Sherwood Anderson: Selected Letters*. Ed. Charles E. Modlin. Knoxville: U of Tennessee P, 1984.

————. *Sherwood Anderson's Memoirs*. Ed. Paul Rosenfeld. New York: Harcourt, Brace, 1942.

Baker, Carlos. *Ernest Hemingway: A Life Story*. New York: Scribners, 1969.

————. *Hemingway: The Writer as Artist*. Princeton, NJ: Princeton UP, 1963.

Burhans, Clinton S., Jr. "The Complex Unity of *In Our Time*." *Modern Fiction Studies* 14 (1968): 313-28.

Callaghan, Morley. *That Summer in Paris: Memoirs of Tangled Friendships with Hemingway, Fitzgerald, and Some Others*. New York: Coward-McCann, 1963.

Church, Ralph. "The Brasserie Lip[p]." In "Ralph Withington Church Reminiscences [19—]." Unpublished manuscript. Bancroft Library, U of California, Berkeley.

Coltrane, Robert. "Hemingway and Turgenev: *The Torrents of Spring*." *Hemingway's Neglected Short Fiction: New Perspectives*. Ed. Susan F. Beegel. Ann Arbor, MI: UMI Research P, 1989. 149-61.

Dos Passos, John. *The Best Times*. New York: New American Library, 1966.

Fanning, Michael. *France and Sherwood Anderson: Paris Notebook, 1921*. Baton Rouge: Louisiana State UP, 1976.

Fenton, Charles A. *The Apprenticeship of Ernest Hemingway*. New York: Farrar, Straus & Young, 1954.

Hemingway, Ernest. "The Art of the Short Story." *Paris Review* 23.79 (1981): 85-102.

————. "The 'Author's Preface' for *The Torrents of Spring*." *Fitzgerald/Hemingway Annual 1977*: 112-13.

————. *Ernest Hemingway: Selected Letters, 1917-1961*. Ed. Carlos Baker. New York: Scribners, 1981.

————. *A Moveable Feast*. New York: Scribners, 1964.

————. Review of *A Story Teller's Story*. *Sherwood Anderson: A Collection of Critical Essays*. Ed. Walter B. Rideout. Englewood Cliffs, NJ: Prentice-Hall, 1974. 84-86.

————. *The Torrents of Spring*. *The Hemingway Reader*. Ed. Charles Poore. New York: Scribners, 1953. 23-86.

Hovey, Richard B. "*The Torrents of Spring*: Prefiguration in the Early Hemingway." *College English* 26 (1965): 460-64.

Howe, Irving. *Sherwood Anderson*. New York: William Sloane, 1951.

Lynn, Kenneth S. *Hemingway*. New York: Simon and Schuster, 1987.

Phillips, William L. "Sherwood Anderson's Two Prize Pupils." *The Achievement of Sherwood Anderson.* Ed. Ray Lewis White. Chapel Hill: U of North Carolina P, 1966. 62-84.

Seligman, Herbert J. Review of *In Our Time. Critical Essays on Ernest Hemingway's "In Our Time."* Ed. Michael S. Reynolds. Boston: G. K. Hall, 1983. 15-16.

————. "The Mark of Sherwood Anderson on Hemingway: A Look at the Texts." *South Atlantic Quarterly* 73 (1974): 487-503.

Small, Judy Jo, and Michael Reynolds. "Hemingway v. Anderson: The Final Rounds." *Hemingway Review* 14.2 (1995): 1-17.

Sokoloff, Alice Hunt. *Hadley: The First Mrs. Hemingway.* New York: Dodd, Mead, 1973.

Somers, Paul, Jr. "Sherwood Anderson Introduces His Friend Ernest Hemingway." *Lost Generation Journal* 3.3 (1975): 24-26.

Stein, Gertrude. *The Autobiography of Alice B. Toklas.* New York: Literary Guild, 1933.

Sutton, William A. *The Road to Winesburg.* Metuchen, NJ: Scarecrow, 1972.

Tomkins, Calvin. *Living Well Is the Best Revenge.* NY: Viking, 1971.

White, Ray Lewis. "Anderson's Private Reaction to *The Torrents of Spring.*" *Modern Fiction Studies* 26 (1980-81): 635-37.

————. "Hemingway's Private Explanation of *The Torrents of Spring.*" *Modern Fiction Studies* 13 (1967): 261-63.

Wilkinson, Myler. *Hemingway and Turgenev: The Nature of Literary Influence.* Ann Arbor, MI: UMI Research P, 1986.

Wilson, Edmund. *The Shores of Light: A Literary Chronicle of the Twenties and Thirties.* New York: Farrar, Straus & Young, 1952.

Wylder, Delbert E. "*The Torrents of Spring.*" *South Dakota Review* 5.4 (1967-68): 23-35.

"IN THE TEMPS DE GERTRUDE"

HEMINGWAY, STEIN, AND THE SCENE OF INSTRUCTION AT 27, RUE DE FLEURUS

K I R K   C U R N U T T

Two years after Gertrude Stein's death in 1946, Hemingway complimented William ("The Kiddie") Rogers for judiciously portraying their tempestuous relationship in *When This You See, Remember Me*: "I always loved her very much," Hemingway confesses before blaming Stein for their celebrated feud of the 1930s. "She had . . . a sort of necessity to break off friendships and she only gave real loyalty to people who were inferior to her. She had to attack me because she learned to write dialogue from me just as I learned the wonderful rhythms in prose from her." He then congratulates Rogers for recognizing that his indignation at Stein's attack upon him was justified: "As you said I never counter-punched when she left herself wide open" (*Selected Letters* 649). The letter is revealing for several reasons. First and most dramatically, Hemingway goes on to confess in graphic language that he always wanted to seduce his mentor. However honest, the admission seems calculated in its crudity, as if he were trying to shock Rogers, the novice biographer whom he had never met, by informing him that the book did not tell the whole story of his Paris years with Stein. His comments further suggest that he misread Rogers's memoir, for while Alice B. Toklas eventually broke with Rogers because the latter described Stein as "aloof," the book is hardly as critical of her as Hemingway implies. Yet most subtly perhaps, his response suggests the characteristic strategies by which he dealt with the legacy of her influence after what she described as their "cooling of friendship." By claiming to have taught Stein (against her will) how to write dialogue, Hemingway effectively places her in the same ignominious position of "taking training" that he occupies in *The Autobiography of Alice B. Toklas* (216).

The claim resurfaces almost verbatim a year later in a letter to Charles Scribner granting Donald Gallup permission to quote from his letters to Stein in an article on the composition of *The Making of Americans*: "I liked Gertrude Stein very much and never counter-attacked her even when she attacked me in such force after she had learned to write dialogue from me. To learn anything from a fellow-author is evidently an unforgivable sin" (*Selected Letters* 664). If Stein's memoir labels Hemingway a good student of writing because "it is so flattering to have a pupil who does it without understanding it," she becomes in his correspondence the "rotten," resentful pupil that Alice once judged him to be (*Autobiography* 216). Significantly, this revisionary strategy of portraying Gertrude as the reluctant beneficiary of his talent was not restricted to private correspondence. As early as *Green Hills of Africa* in 1935, Hemingway publicly attempted to deny Stein's tutorial authority over him by announcing that she "never could write dialogue. . . . She learned how to do it from my stuff. . . . She never could forgive learning that and she was afraid people would notice it, where she'd learned it, so she had to attack me" (65).

Some critics have accepted these claims at face value, as when Julian Maclaren-Ross, reviewing *A Moveable Feast* for *London Magazine*, notes in passing that "Miss Stein learned to write dialogue from *The Sun Also Rises*" (Meyers, *Critical Heritage* 485). Yet there is little evidence that Hemingway taught her this art, for nothing she wrote after reading the novel—not *A Novel of Thank You, Lucy Church Amiably*, or *Mrs. Reynolds*—contains anything remotely resembling the repartee of his expatriate drama. As Edmund Wilson once observed, Stein avoids dramatizing the peculiar speech patterns of her fictional characters, fashioning instead "a sort of splintered stenographic commentary made up of [often unattributed] scraps of conversation as they reverberate in the mind and awaken unspoken responses" (194). Even in her autobiographies, the quotes attributed to friends and foes alike resonate with the trademark devices (rhythmic repetitions and gerunds most obviously) of her piquant, playful style.[1] Committed to conveying the nuance of feeling through sonic rather than psychological reference, Stein dismissed dialogue as "fabricated words" that result in "imitative emotional-ism" (*Autobiography* 119).

Yet if the evidence does not support Hemingway's claim to have instructed Stein, the insistence is nevertheless significant, for his "counter-punches" imply that he assuaged recurring anxieties over her influence by repeatedly revising the legend of his apprenticeship. In several accounts of his early Paris years, he returns to the museumesque studio where, between 1922 and 1924, Gertrude and Alice treated him and his first wife Hadley "as though we were very good, well mannered and promising children" (*Moveable Feast* 14). These remembrances constitute a leitmotif that Harold Bloom calls the "scene of instruction," in which a one-time pupil or "ephebe" reimagines his artistic development to search for the "fault that is not there" in the work of a "Great Original" who influenced him. By projecting a stylistic trait of his own like dialogue into Stein's writing, Hemingway enacts that necessary "creative correction" to her corpus that allows him to legitimate his aesthetics while distinguishing them from hers. According to Bloom, only through such a "misprision" or a strategic misreading can the student assert his artistic autonomy (30). But while the act should alleviate the guilt of throwing off her influence, breaking free proves a Sisyphean task, for no sooner does Hemingway roll the rock of independence to the peak of liberation than a sense of loyalty and obligation tumbles him back to a plateau of conflicted feeling: "It never occurred to me until many years later," he mourns in a typescript passage eventually cut from *A Moveable Feast*, "that anyone could hate anyone because they learned to write from that novel that started off with the quotation from the garage keeper" (Item 163). Assuming this tone of bewildered abandonment, Hemingway can blame Stein for their estrange-ment while implying continued fealty to her. He neither rejects her teaching nor rebels against it, he suggests. He simply has no further use for it.

Hemingway's complex defensiveness toward Stein's influence has received little substantive attention, mainly because critics draw from the mutually acrimonious *Autobiography* and *A Moveable Feast* when chronicling their friendship and feud. Recently, biographers have begun to acknowledge a lesser-known body of evidence, including the 1927 *New Yorker* essay "My Own Life," which purports to tell "The True Story of My Break with Gertrude Stein," as well as unpublished miscellanea like the two-line doggerel parody "Gertrude Stein was never crazy / Gertrude Stein was very lazy" and "The Autobiography of Alice B. Hemingway," a melancholy 1933 response to Stein's memoir. Yet these resources continue to receive only cursory mention, undoubtedly because, as James R. Mellow notes, they offer at best a "thin trail" for following "how, if never quite why," the two writers succumbed to their "spell of disaffection" (345). If we take Hemingway's comments on Stein at face value, as Michael Reynolds does, they endorse the traditional chronology of his development by confirming that "Gertrude was no longer the writer he so admired" by the mid-1920s (*American Homecoming* 84); if we read beneath their surface, as Jeffrey Meyers insists we should, they reveal that "the loss of her friendship and viciousness of her attack [in *The Autobiography*] caused a profound and permanent wound" (*Biography* 81).

The deeper importance of these fragments becomes apparent, however, when we examine the specific strategies of misreading by which Hemingway struggled to alleviate his anxieties of influence. By castigating Gertrude's work ethic, ridiculing her hunger for fame and "official recognition," even dismissing her peculiar style as a consequence of her lesbianism, he momentarily frees himself from the Gordian knot of affection and suspicion that entangles his feelings for her. Less obviously, he strives to displace the reputation of Stein's salon as the epicenter of literary Paris by contesting her territorial claim to the city. Just as writing was hers before it was his, the *ville lumière* inspired her experimentation long before he ever crossed the ocean.[2] As he describes the relationship between Paris and his prose then, his misreadings must prove that the scene of Stein's instruction was a mere detour on the route to artistic triumph. Only by remapping his expatriate apprenticeship to disassociate the rue de Fleurus from those landmarks inspiring his artistic formation can he chart the effect of the city upon the scene of his writing in statements like "all Paris belongs to me [as] . . . I belong to this notebook and this pencil" (*Moveable Feast* 6).

As J. Gerald Kennedy and I have argued, Hemingway stages his earliest, most tentative break with Stein in "Soldier's Home," the 1924 short story in which Harold Krebs struggles to reacclimate himself to the stifling domesticity of his parents' Oklahoma home after fighting in the Great War. In describing a photograph of Krebs at the Rhine in which the river "does not show" (*Complete Stories* 111), Hemingway alludes to Stein's "Accents in Alsace," a collage of closet drama and hermetic verse from *Geography and Plays* (1922) that concludes with a reference to another picture, presumably of Gertrude and Alice during a tour of the contested region in 1919, in which the river "hardly showed." If Stein limns a scene of romantic bliss "sweeter than water or cream or ice . . . sweeter than winter or summer or spring" (415), his photograph focuses upon the alienation and displacement that soldiers like Krebs suffer. Pushing her eros out of his picture allows Hemingway to assert his conviction that "war is the best subject of all" for the modern writer (*Selected Letters* 176) by equating Stein's aversion to such *inaccroachable* subjects with the shallow pieties of Harold's mother, who fails to recognize how battles at Belleau Wood and in the Argonne have scarred her son. Yet while Mrs. Krebs's inability to empathize with the horror of war anticipates Hemingway's later claim that Gertrude only "wanted to know the gay part of how the world was going; never the real, never the bad" (*Moveable Feast* 25), "Soldier's Home" also prefigures the residual dependency upon his expatriate mater that haunted him throughout his life. Although Harold attempts to shatter his mother's complacency by declaring that he does not love her, he quickly recognizes that "he couldn't tell her, he couldn't make her see," and the story concludes with his dreading the "one more scene" (*Complete Stories* 116) of conflict necessary before he can escape her suffocating influence. Although Hemingway quietly distinguishes himself from Stein, he avoids confronting the scene of her instruction by projecting his desire for autonomy away from Paris onto an American landscape (Kennedy and Curnutt 1-11).

A year and a half later, he attempted a more overt declaration of independence. In November 1925, after *In Our Time* was published and the first draft of *The Sun Also Rises* awaited revision, Hemingway rapidly wrote *The Torrents of Spring*, a parody of Sherwood Anderson's *Dark Laughter* that promised to "start plenty of rows" (*Selected Letters* 174), including one with Stein. By "show[ing] up all the fakes of Anderson, Gertrude, Lewis, Cather," he would satirize these "pretentious faking bastards" right into retirement: "I don't see how Sherwood will ever be able to write again," he boasted to Ezra Pound. Stein's "stuff," however, was so opaque that it was not "worth the bother to show up. It's easier to quote from it" (Mellow 318). The comment may explain why *Torrents* only indirectly quizzes his mentor: "Gertrude Stein. . . . Where were her experiments in words leading her?" As if to answer the question, Hemingway parodies her rigmarole style: "Paris in the morning. Paris in the evening. Paris at night. Paris in the morning again. Paris at noon, perhaps. Why not?" (74-75). Yet he chose not to locate these doubts in one of his intermittent authorial intrusions into the story, in which he describes the Paris scene of its composition, recounts convivial encounters with John Dos Passos and F. Scott Fitzgerald, and even invites the reader to mail him a writing sample in care of his private table at the Café du Dôme on the Boulevard Montparnasse. Instead, he ascribes the passage to Yogi Johnson, the former solider who prowls the outskirts of Petoskey, Michigan, while suffering the melodramatic bouts of self-inquiry that Anderson employed to excess in *Dark Laughter*. If "Soldier's Home" projects Stein's fastidiousness into Mrs. Krebs's willful ignorance, *Torrents* employs an equally allusive strategy as Hemingway conflates her experimentation with what Reynolds calls the "pointless questions" and "maundering Whitmanianism[s]" bloating Anderson's prose (*Paris Years* 335). Privately Hemingway could assuage the temptation to confront Gertrude by declaring her a "faking bastard" to Pound, yet he remained unprepared to go public with his feelings, and, as a result, she was more offended for Anderson's sake than for her own. By setting his satire in Petoskey rather than in Paris, he had again delayed the "one more scene" of conflict standing between him and his autonomy.

Only after yet another year, in late 1926, could he openly address the failures of Stein's instruction. Precipitating the break was the publication of "Composition as Explanation," her elliptical lecture, delivered at Oxford and Cambridge the previous June, in which she immodestly presented herself as the epicenter of the modernist movement by outlining how the "progress of my conceptions was the natural progress entirely in accordance with my epoch" (500). Discovering the slim volume at Sylvia Beach's Shakespeare and Company bookstore in early November, just weeks after *The Sun Also Rises* was published in America, Hemingway apparently resented the serious attention it received in England, feeling perhaps that it was stealing the spotlight from his own imminent success. Describing himself as a "man with a grudge" and a "bitter boy who is envious," he set about imitating her style in a series of therapeutic responses. As if to console himself for once believing in the merit of her method, he (subconsciously or not) invented a story in which Gertrude had betrayed him by abandoning the hard work of writing for cheap and easy fame. Contrary to critical opinion, he told himself, she "was never crazy," merely "very lazy." When he first visited the rue de Fleurus, her writing was "something and we all liked it," but now she hid behind the smokescreen of her style by describing "just how it is done and what it means" to the "new ones," her English champions. By contrast, work had remained so exhausting for him that he "rolled on the floor with pain in his eyes." Was that labor not a greater reward than the notoriety she now enjoyed? "Is it a question of how hard do we work?" he asks ("It was happy . . ." 2). In a similar fragment, he equates her aversion to work with the desultoriness of another favorite target of ridicule, those expatriate poseurs more devoted to Paris's literary lifestyle than their prose style: "If one is lazy there are other ways [of not writing] than sitting in cafes. There are other ways than talking about it. There are other ways than reading about it. There is writing about it without effort and one does not feel badly because one has written it and always finally somebody will say it is good" ("Now it is all over . . ." 2).

Throughout his career, Hemingway misread the circuitousness of Gertrude's prose as artistic sloth. By her own account, writing was a "tormenting process" (*Autobiography* 119), but it posed a different sort of work, for she was "relinquish[ing] the right to make language submit to [her] will" through a "concerted effort to *resist* mastery and control over linguistic operations" (Benstock 159-60). Hemingway was incapable of appreciating this resistance, for will, mastery, and control for him were integral measures of craftsmanship. Indeed, he cradled his professional identity in this idea of writing as a slow, painful exercise of vocational commitment. In 1928 he would lament that "I have never been able to write longer than two hours. . . . If I could only take the slight plunge to going in for not making sense I could work ten and twelve hours a day every day and always be perfectly [content] like Gertrude Stein who since she has taken up not making sense some eighteen years ago has never known a moments unhappiness with her work" (*Selected Letters* 287). Because he imagined writing as a centripetal quest to arrive at the "one true sentence," he could only misread Stein's centrifugal hermeticism as indifference to "the obligation to make her writing intelligible" (*Moveable Feast* 17). But if he boasts of having met this obligation in his later years, these 1926 fragments find him worrying that his efforts will go unrewarded. If "one can eliminate the need for [writing] to mean something and simply write" and still "new people . . . will see the greatness" ("Now it is all over . . ." 1), does his devotion have any value? If a lazy writer like Gertrude could be welcomed with open arms by stodgy old institutions like Cambridge and Oxford, would they appreciate his work?

To soothe these doubts, Hemingway imagines that, by abdicating the principles she once instructed, Stein not only abandoned him but Paris as well. Although he never mentions the city by name, he implicitly claims it as the embodiment of his literary ideals. When Stein "stopped doing it when it became hard to do," she had to avoid "other people [who] know when the things do not come out right and are failures" by replacing them with more naive readers. There "must always be new people," he writes. "And it is better for them to be English people." He refers here to Edith Sitwell, the London-based poet who, along with her brothers Osbert and Sacheverell, had championed Stein's lecture and had expedited its publication by the Hogarth Press. As pupils, these "bright English people learn very quickly but always a little late," for unlike Hemingway, they do not recognize that Gertrude is "writing without effort." Because the fame that the Sitwells offer excuses her from "feel[ing] badly" for her laziness, she need no longer "notice those" like him who "say it changed." But to continue writing without discontent, she has to transport her affection across the English Channel: "And we have the English and now it is very very easy to do and we will do it. And once it was very hard to do. And now what does it matter?" ("Now it is all over . . ." 1-2). By insinuating a geographical shift in Stein's loyalties, Hemingway could justify the distance now separating the two writers without threatening the integrity of his own vocational and emotional investment in Paris.

At the same time that he cultivated this story in private fragments, he transmuted its anger and resentment into absurdist farce for public consumption. With a title seemingly intended to announce his emergent autonomy, "My Own Life" promises to reveal the real story of his break with Stein by charting his apprenticeship from early, uncertain visits to her atelier to his professional debut.[3] He wanted a wide audience to acknowledge this declaration, for he resisted an invitation to attack Gertrude in the obscure pages of Pound's literary quarterly *Exile* in favor of "a more widely circulated medium" like the *New Republic* or the *New Yorker*. Yet the Hemingway of "My Own Life" is not as "glad to insult Gertrude Stein" (Mellow 345) as his letters to Pound claim, for instead of disparaging her work, he portrays 27, rue de Fleurus as a refuge for the artist *manqué*, a realm in which cultivating one's artistry is less important than currying the favor of Paris's imperious literary maven. Assuming the role of an eager, earnest pupil, he vents his disappointment with the scene of her instruction by satirizing it as a frivolous realm of tea parties and petty jealousies—a world, in other words, inimical to the industry that true writing demands.

He makes his point both by slapstick exaggeration and veiled but pointed inside jokes. Most obviously, he presents Stein as an eccentric recluse, temperamental and inconstant in her affections. When he first visits the salon, a maid assures him (in suspiciously bad French) that the matron of Montparnasse is not home, even though he catches her peeking out an upstairs window. Once admitted to her prandial gatherings, he proves too talented to remain a mere pupil of Stein's and is quickly disinvited. When he attempts to reingratiate himself with her expatriate circle, the maid beats him with a bicycle pump, claiming she is following her employer's orders. Ultimately Gertrude nails her doors shut and posts an attack dog to keep him away. Beneath this strained humor, Hemingway crafts a plot he would maintain until *A Moveable Feast*: Stein abandoned him out of jealousy. By going public with this true story, he is merely acknowledging the rift for which she refuses to accept responsibility. Yet the central passage of "My Own Life" suggests a deeper anxiety as Hemingway challenges Stein's right to apply "all the dirty, easy labels" of her "lost-generation talk" to his work (*Moveable Feast* 30-31). As he describes his literary aims, Gertrude abruptly intrudes to assure him that "all you young men are alike" (23), a line echoing her pithy pronouncement ("You are all a lost generation"), which Hemingway was then insisting that he had appropriated as an ironic epigraph for

The Sun Also Rises. ("Nobody knows about the generation that follows them and certainly has no right to judge," he told Maxwell Perkins, qualifying the quote [*Selected Letters* 229]). Stein's propensity for such sweeping generalizations ignores his individuality: "Frankly, I was hurt," he admits in "My Own Life," momentarily dropping its farcical tone. When Stein welcomes a coterie of *salonières* with the same greeting, Hemingway quickly distances himself from these expatriates. While he finds her remark offensive, these admirers (this time Russian instead of English) break "into eager chatters," for "it was an exciting statement. They hoped it was true. What times we would all have then" (23). By assuming the insight superior enough to see through her "splendid bombast," he distinguishes himself from the habitués of Gertrude's salon. As hopeless epigones entranced by her "prophetic roles" (*Selected Letters* 229), they have gone to Paris to be part of a movement. He, by contrast, is there to work.

By denigrating both Stein's writing and her followers, Hemingway was able during the fall of 1926 to minimize her influence in his own mind. All that remained was public recognition of their differences—a desire that would not go unfulfilled for long. In January 1927, before his satirical take on Gertrude even appeared in the *New Yorker,* he received a letter from fellow author Ella Winter, Lincoln Steffens's wife, congratulating him on the success of *The Sun Also Rises:* "Your book is a corker," she assured him. "I've read Gertrude Stein's little essay on Composition as Explanation after I read your book and I understood it. You seem to have somehow got something she's trying to put over, only having made it yours, you put it over." The compliment undoubtedly delighted him, for she recognized that he was not imitating Stein's stylistic effects but had minted them into his own literary currency. Not only had he transcended her influence, but, according to Winter, his writing was essential to making sense of hers. It was now Gertrude's turn to be grateful.

Between 1927 and 1933, Stein's influence apparently caused Hemingway little discomfort. Critical and commercial success convinced him that his *métier* was of his own making; his 1928 move to Key West with the second Mrs. Hemingway, Pauline, also seems to have granted an emotional distance from his apprentice years. Even when he returned to Paris, he could retrace the pathways of his formative period without worrying about Stein's approval. "I like to have Gertrude bawl me out because it keeps one['s] opinion of oneself down—way down," he joked to Fitzgerald after a rare dinner party at the rue de Fleurus in late 1929. Fitzgerald had worried that Hemingway was offended when Stein compared the relative "flame" of her most famous expatriate heirs to Ernest's disadvantage, but he professed to remain nonplussed by her negative opinion: "You think I shouldnt [sic] worry when some one says I've no vitality—I dont [sic] worry—Who has vitality in Paris? People dont [sic] write with vitality—they write with their heads. . . . G.S. never went with us to Schruns or Key West or Wyoming or any place where you get in shape—If she's never seen me in shape—Why worry? When they bawl you out ride with the punches" (*Selected Letters* 310-11). However atypical this diminution of the importance of Paris to his writing, the strategy is understandable, for he implies that while the city stimulates his intellect, other locales invigorate his energy and athleticism. If Gertrude fails to appreciate this vitality, he suggests, she ought to get out of the house more often. A world-traveler like himself need not bother with her criticism, for it is an obvious result of her Parisian provincialism.

But such equanimity faded upon the appearance of Stein's *Autobiography*, in which Hemingway discovered himself described as "ninety-percent Rotarian," as "smell[ing] of museums," and as "yellow" as "the flat-boat men on the Mississippi river as described by Mark Twain." Beyond such withering insults, she impugned his originality by complimenting his facility at "taking training": "Hemingway had been formed by [her and Anderson]," she boasted through Alice, "and they were both a little proud and a little ashamed of the work of their minds" (216). Her wrath caught him at an exceedingly vulnerable moment. In the midst of a harsh critical reassessment of his reputation, Hemingway found himself subjected to increasingly personal attacks: *New Republic* columnist Max Eastman recently had wondered aloud whether his infatuation with blood sports belied sexual uncertainties; syndicated columnist Heywood Broun curtly dismissed him as "phony"; most viciously, Wyndham Lewis would soon label him a "dull-witted, bovine, monosyllabic simpleton" doomed to copy the "Stein manner" that he stole from his "overmastering influence" (Meyers, *Critical Heritage* 196-97). As John Raeburn argues, these attacks hardly persuaded Hemingway "to moderate his public personality," for he answered critics with "even more strenuous"— some would say strained—"assertions" of his talent: "He would prove them wrong by giving his audience further examples of courage and stalwart behavior. His readers could decide who was telling the truth" (63).

In Stein's case, his "courage" takes the form of an ugly misogyny as he ascribes her bitterness to menopause in letters to Janet Flanner, John Dos Passos, and Maxwell Perkins throughout the spring and summer of 1933. "Suddenly," he describes the effect of Gertrude's change of life to Perkins, "she couldn't tell a good picture from a bad one, a good writer from a bad one, and it all went phtt" (*Selected Letters* 395). Retaliatory slurs crop up in odd places during the following year: In a monthly column he had recently agreed to contribute to *Esquire*, he conspicuously inserts her name into a discussion of dysentery (*By-Line* 159). In an appreciation of Joan Miró's beloved "The Farm" (which Hemingway owned) for *Cahiers d'art*, he notes that the painting required nine months to complete, "as long to make as it takes a woman to make a child . . . and a woman who isn't a woman can usually write her autobiography in a third of that time" (28). In an introductory note to Jimmie Charters's *This Must Be the Place*, he accuses Stein (though not by name) of "cashing in" on his reputation to appeal to the "clubs or guilds" that were sending the *Autobiography* into best-sellerdom (7). By 1935, as Stein told *Atlantic Monthly* interviewer John Hyde Preston that Hemingway was "no good" after *In Our Time* (191), he was dismissing her in *Green Hills of Africa* as an embittered ingrate. Not surprisingly, the acrimony provided irresistible fodder for gossip columnists, who quickly promoted their feud as the literary prizefight of the decade.

Yet Hemingway's public ire is misleading, for evidence suggests that, however willing to insult Gertrude, he was uncertain about how best to resolve the lingering question of his debt to her. Recognizing his hesitation, *Esquire* editor Arnold Gingrich spent much of 1934 obsequiously cajoling him to refute her claims: "There have been references in every piece I've read about Gertrude Stein in the papers and magazines to her 'disagreement' and 'misunderstanding' with you . . . but none of them have direct quotes" (Letter 1). Annoyed, Hemingway firmly said no: "I've written all the facts about Gertrude so they'll be on tap if anything happens to me but I don't like to slam the old bitch around" (*Selected Letters* 411).

In truth, he was uncertain whether "slamming" Stein would prove a winning strategy in their war of words, for already "on tap" were two very different rebuttals of her *Autobiography*. According to an unpublished October 1933 letter to Pauline, he planned to submit the short sketch "The Autobiography of Alice B. Hemingway" to the *New Yorker*, perhaps recalling how it had published "My Own Life." But unlike that parody, this mock memoir eschews broad farce in favor of melancholy reflection, as if, instead of launching a cathartic counterattack, he were excising the lingering sadness of his "temps de Gertrude," as he describes his early Paris years to his wife (1). Another important difference distinguishes the two works: If "My Own Life" satirizes the eccentric atmosphere of Stein's atelier, "Alice B. Hemingway" effectively bars the reader's entry into 27, rue de Fleurus, for the setting is not the famous salon but Ernest's own Paris domicile.[4] Supplanting the scene of her instruction with the idealized marital world he shares with his ever-supportive wife Alice (a conflation, apparently, of Hadley and Pauline), Hemingway effectively confronts Gertrude's influence on his home turf. Rather than dramatize her pedagogical prowess, he focuses on her flaws and failures as he casts himself as a critic keenly aware of the limitations of her lessons. No longer a "bitter boy who is envious," he projects back onto his apprentice years the certitude and confidence of a "master" biding his time until his talent reaches its zenith. This faith in his own capability, he implies, allowed him to survive Stein's pressure to emulate her prose.

Perhaps the most striking aspect of the sketch is its initial absence of malice, for rather than disparage Gertrude, he mourns her inability to measure up to his high standards. When Ernest confesses that his mentor dislikes his short stories, Alice loyally professes her affection for them, but he sides with Stein: "She's smart. . . . They are lousy" (2). Later he assures her that "Gertrude wrote some damn fine stuff." Her downfall is her unwillingness to work hard at writing: "What makes us happy? When we've worked well. All right, she invents a way of writing that she can do a lot of every day and feel good. It doesn't have to mean anything and it doesn't have to please anybody but her. . . . She makes up all sorts of reasons for writing this way but the real reason is because she is cockeyed lazy and can write that way every day and never fail." Although the complaint echoes his 1926 responses to "Composition as Explanation," here he manifests little of the resentment he voiced when accusing her of abandoning her precepts. Instead, he pities her unwillingness to confront the failure that a "real writer" inevitably confronts in his work: "All good writers fail. . . . All bad writers succeed. A real writer . . . is never satisfied with anything he has written." Suggesting that Stein writes as she does because she fears dissatisfaction, he turns her accusations of cowardice back upon her. The subtle strategy allows him to assume the moral high road, for when Alice asks why he hesitates to talk publicly of her failure, he says, "Because I like her" (4).

Despite this professed fondness, Hemingway does indulge in two highly personal insults. At one point, he reports that Stein is angry because he is forever fatigued during her lectures. Alice knows why: "Why shouldn't you be when you've finished a days [sic] work?" Knowing that Gertrude could never empathize with his exhaustion, he asks, "And how am I going to tell her what else we do? They don't know what it's about baby" (3). Equating the hard work of writing with his own heterosexuality, he suggests that Stein's lesbianism prevents her from properly valuing literary labor. Elsewhere, he dismisses her infatuation with language with an ethnic slur: "Did you ever notice that when people become very romantic about the english [sic] language it is usually because that language has not been in their family very long?" Attributing the "difficulty" of her style to her family's immigrant history (Stein was a first-generation American), he equates her abstract style with faulty translation, for "unless that language has been their language for a long time, they can never tell very many stories in it clearly." Because imagination is a "racial experience," he rejects the very premise of Stein's intent to liberate language from its referential obligations: "No one can make up something that has not happened or its parrallell [sic] and you have to do it in words, you know" (4).

If "Alice" portrays Hemingway as a master rather than a pupil, another unpublished piece (most likely written in the fall of 1934)[5] admits his debt to Stein but vociferously rejects the assumption that he was "formed" by her. Instead of lamenting her cowardice, he tries here to ameliorate his student status into a position of power. Although Gertrude exaggerates her influence by "implying that given half a chance [he] would pop eagerly back into her womb if he could find it," Hemingway, as a self-described "noble chap," will readily admit "that he learned a lot from her." Unfortunately, Stein's ego prevents her from reciprocating the gesture: "The literary racket being what it is and Stein one of the smartest practitioners she knew some bright lad would pounce on this resemblance [of her writing to his] so she proceeded to attack him as a personal, literary, and physical phony to cover herself. This is called in the prize contest business beating him to the punch and in the literary world is known as gratitude" ("Mr. Heywood Broun . . ." 1). Further stripping the stigma from the pupil role to which she relegates him, he claims that a real writer is always learning—a fact that Stein refuses to admit. While he "still likes to learn and has a lot to learn," Gertrude believes that "the one unforgivable sin is to teach your elders anything." Her talent failed to mature because she assumed that she long ago learned all she needed to know about writing (2).

Why Hemingway suppressed these sketches is unknown, but their varying mood suggests recurrent doubts about how best to correct the derisive image Stein had painted of him. The conciliatory tone of "Alice B. Heming-way" may have left him feeling vulnerable to further attack, while he perhaps assumed that the second piece would merely prolong the squabble by "giv[ing] the critics something to burp about" (*Selected Letters* 423). Whatever the specific motive for not publishing a full-length response amid the controversy, Hem-ingway seems to have recognized that by boasting of her influence Stein had irrevocably tarred his reputation. When Perkins objected to his calling her a "bitch" in the galley proofs of *Green Hills*, Hemingway warily agreed to mute his anger by substituting a less pungent put-down. Denouncing her as a "female," he sarcastically assured his editor, "will make her angrier than bitch, will please you by not calling a lady a bitch, will make it seem that I care less about her lying about me, and will please everyone but me who cares only about honesty" (*Selected Letters* 423-24). The comment reveals the frustration he felt at being forced to respond to her canards. Stein lied about the extent of her influence, he insisted, but even worse, few readers were interested in the truth—at least the truth as he imagined it.

Ultimately, he seems to have decided that the best strategy was to contest Gertrude's claims indirectly, for echoes of the "Alice" satire reverberate in his October 1935 *Esquire* contribution, "Monologue to the Maestro" (*By-Line* 213-20), in which he asserts his tutorial authority by instructing *his* obedient pupil in the fundamentals of writing.[6] Although only internal evidence links the two essays, "Monologue" can be read as refuting Stein's artistic imperatives as Hemingway implicitly contrasts the efficacy of his "practical advice" to what she calls in the *Autobiography* her "general principles." If there she boasts of "never correct[ing] any detail of anybody's writing . . . stick[ing] strictly to . . . the way of seeing that the writer chooses to see, and the relation between that vision and the way it gets down" (214), he promises his apprentice "some of the information" that "would have been worth fifty cents" when he was "twenty-one" (*By-Line* 215). (He was actually twenty-two when he first met Gertrude.) Not the abstract parlor trick of Parisian salons, writing is a "five finger exercise" analogous to virile pursuits like hunting and deep-sea fishing; as if to emphasize the connection between art and these strenuous, worldly activities, Hemingway stages his scene of instruction as he and his student set sail from Key West to Cuba.

The lessons that he offers reiterate ideals articulated in "Alice." Most important, he measures a writer's "true seriousness" by his willingness to work hard at revision: "After you learn to write your whole object is to convey everything, every sensation, sight, feeling, place and emotion to the reader. To do this you have to work over what you write." Nor does a real writer envy the success of a contemporary, for literary "fame is created by critics who always need a genius of the season, someone they understand completely and feel safe in praising, but when these fabricated geniuses are dead they will not exist." In the clearest echo of his satire, he again defines imagination as "racial experience," though the phrase here is less of a racial slur than a synonym for the mimetic fidelity to which "serious" writing aspires: "If [the writer] gets so he can imagine truly enough people will think that the things he relates all really happened and that he is just reporting" (*By-Line* 215-18). Hemingway states his aesthetics here without censure or challenge; in fact, his pupil wholeheartedly agrees with his judgment. Yet establishing this mastery forced Hemingway to forfeit his emotional ties to the city of his apprenticeship, for he could not reconcile his current status as a teacher with the site of his earlier instruction. He had admitted as much in a previous *Esquire* essay, "A Paris Letter": Paris "was a fine place to be quite young in and it is a necessary part of a man's education," he wrote in early 1934. "But . . . she has other lovers now." His art having matured, he finds other locales more inspiring: "I like it better on the ranch [in Wyoming], or in Piggott, Arkansas, in the fall, or in Key West, and very much better, say, at the Dry Tortugas" (*By-Line* 155, 158).

More than twenty years later, however, as he sketched his last and most notorious remembrance of Stein, he returned to the *ville lumière* to reassert its pivotal role in the shaping of his aesthetics. As Kennedy notes, Hemingway "obviously foresaw the end of his career" as he began *A Moveable Feast* in the late 1950s, and the desire to "recover . . . his earlier relationship to writing" (*Imagining Paris* 140) undoubtedly compelled him to denigrate fellow expatriates whose presence in Paris might threaten the connection he imagined between the city and his art. While many of his vignettes linger lovingly upon the cafés, quads, and walkways from which he drew his inspiration, the three chapters that portray Stein's salon insist that he merely tolerated her preceptorial rectitude. Although he enjoyed browsing in her art collection, appreciated the tasty liqueurs she served him, and recognized the potential of the rhythm and repetition with which she experimented, he claims her lectures were "merely interesting to listen" to. Confident of his burgeoning literary beliefs, he would not bother to debate Gertrude: "I did not argue . . . nor try to explain what I was trying to do. . . . That was my own business" (15). Much like his "Alice" parody, Hemingway presents himself as a tyro savvy enough to recognize that Gertrude "talk[s] a lot of rot sometimes" (31). Unlike other literary neophytes who "took on trust writing of hers that they could not understand because of their enthusiasm for her as a person," he withstood the sheer force of her personality because he understood her debilitating disinterest in revision produced a mass of unpublished manuscripts that a "less lazy writer would have put in the waste basket" (17-18).

Yet *A Moveable Feast* departs from earlier reminiscences of Stein's salon in one important way: For the first time, Hemingway takes credit for ending their friendship. Unlike earlier pieces that portray Gertrude as abandoning him out of jealousy, he insists here that any serious respect he held for her vanished when he caught her and Alice in flagrante delicto. Claiming to have inadvertently overheard Gertrude "pleading and begging" with Alice, who spoke as "I had never heard one person speak to another; never, anywhere, never," he implies he was repulsed by their sapphic intimacy: "It was bad to hear and the answers were worse" (118-19). At the same time that he exposes Stein's lesbianism, he condemns her via her emotional dependency upon her lover; in her most unguarded moment, he suggests, Gertrude proved less of a "master" than a passive object of Alice's amorous intent. If, as many critics have suggested, the veracity of the scene is suspect, Hemingway's strategy is fascinating, for he tears away the veil of her imperiousness by reducing her to a suppliant who will "do anything" if only Alice promises not to act upon some unspecified threat. The maliciousness of his denunciation suggests how he was compelled, even a decade after Gertrude's death, to deny her influence. For thirty years he had struggled to qualify her role in the growth of his artistry. In the end, only by bitter insult could he convince himself (if not subsequent readers) that, among the many sites and scenes of his Paris apprenticeship, the rue de Fleurus had proved a cul-de-sac on the road to literary triumph.

NOTES

This essay could not have been completed without a generous research grant in 1993 from the John F. Kennedy Library Foundation. Special thanks to Stephen Plotkin, curator of the Hemingway Collection, for his help in locating unpublished materials.

1. When Stein accuses Hemingway of "kill[ing] a great number of his rivals and put[ting] them under the sod," he defends himself by claiming not to have "seriously killed anybody but one man and he was a bad man and, he deserved it, but if I killed anybody I did it unknowingly, and so I am not responsible" (*Autobiography* 220). One assumes here that Hemingway was not so obsequious as to address the matron of Montparnasse in the style for which she was famous; instead, she wreaks revenge upon those who question her methods by forcing them to speak in a Steinian tongue.

2. Kennedy's *Imagining Paris* is essential to understanding how differently Paris affected each writer's sense of place and identity. By "committing herself to [the] absolute interiority" of her abstract style, Stein characteristically assumes an "imaginative detachment" from its sights and sounds by transforming the "actual, physical milieu" into an "imagined space of writing, a city of words." This "repudiation of place . . . becomes an index of integrity, a sign of commitment" to the literary aesthetics by which she challenges her contemporaries (44). Hemingway, by contrast, typically focuses on realistic details to craft a "collage of images" that "projects a frenzied, cosmopolitan city of violent contrasts" (90). As Kennedy demonstrates, Hemingway internalized these contrasts to distance himself from the provincialism of his Oak

Park, Illinois, upbringing and experiment with Paris's "dangerous" qualities (the sexual ambiguity of androgyny in particular).

3. As its subtitle notes, "My Own Life" is a homage to Frank Harris's sexually explicit memoir *My Life and Loves,* whose first volume Hemingway had encouraged Sylvia Beach to publish in 1923. There can be little doubt that the piece offered a cautiously indirect way of breaking ties with Paris acquaintances he felt he had outgrown—including not only Stein but Hadley too, from whom he had recently separated. The third section of the parody, "How I Broke with My Children," was in fact originally titled "How I Broke with My Wife." (See Item 593a in the Hemingway Collection.)

4. Which of the two apartments Hemingway occupied during his apprenticeship is dramatized here is unclear. Most likely, the setting is his first Paris home at 74, rue du Cardinal Lemoine, where he and Hadley lived in 1922-1923. He wrote most of the *In Our Time* stories, which he certainly would not dismiss as "lousy," when he resided at 113, rue Notre-Dame-des-Champs (1924-1926).

5. This piece was undoubtedly intended for *Esquire;* Hemingway was apparently struggling to respond to Stein, Broun, and Eastman in one fell swoop, as Gingrich was encouraging him to do. In fact, Gingrich forwarded several copies of the syndicated column in which Broun denounced Hemingway as a "phony" to Key West. (Broun's piece created a minor controversy in the columns of New York dailies; Gingrich's correspondence even includes a reply by then-journalist Ed Sullivan.) "How many more do I have to send you before you get sore enough to do a piece on them?" Gingrich demanded when the desired response failed to materialize (see his unpublished letter of September 4, 1935).

6. Hemingway based "Monologue" on an actual voyage he took in the summer of 1934 with Arnold Samuelson, whose dubious dexterity on the violin earned him the ironic nickname Maestro.

WORKS CITED

Benstock, Shari. *Women of the Left Bank: Paris, 1900-1940.* Austin: U of Texas P, 1986.

Bloom, Harold. *The Anxiety of Influence: A Theory of Poetry.* New York: Oxford UP, 1973.

Gingrich, Arnold. Letters to Ernest Hemingway, August-November 1934. Unpublished. Hemingway Collection, John F. Kennedy Library, Boston.

Hemingway, Ernest. "The Autobiography of Alice B. Hemingway." Unpublished. Item 256. Hemingway Collection, John F. Kennedy Library, Boston.

——. *By-Line: Ernest Hemingway. Selected Articles and Dispatches of Four Decades.* Ed. William White. New York: Scribners, 1967.

——. *The Complete Short Stories of Ernest Hemingway: The Finca Vigía Edition.* New York: Scribners, 1987.

——. *Ernest Hemingway: Selected Letters, 1917-1961.* Ed. Carlos Baker. New York: Scribners, 1981.

——. "The Farm." *Cahiers d'art* 9.1-4 (1934): 28-29.

——. *Green Hills of Africa.* New York: Scribners, 1935.

——. Introduction to *This Must Be the Place: Memoirs of Montparnasse by Jimmie the Barman* by Jimmie Charters. Ed. Morrill Cody. London: Herbert Joseph, 1934. 11-13.

——. "It was happy & it was something. . . ." Unpublished. Item 524. Hemingway Collection, John F. Kennedy Library, Boston.

——. Letter to Pauline Hemingway, ca. October 1933. Unpublished. Hemingway Collection, John F. Kennedy Library, Boston.

——. *A Moveable Feast.* New York: Scribners, 1964.

——. "Mr. Heywood Broun calls your correspondent a phoney. . . ." Unpublished. Item 588. Hemingway Collection, John F. Kennedy Library, Boston.

——. "My Own Life." *New Yorker,* February 12, 1927: 23-24.

——. "My Own Life" [manuscript]. Unpublished. Item 593a. Hemingway Collection, John F. Kennedy Library, Boston.

——. "Now it is all over. . . ." Unpublished. Item 622a. Hemingway Collection, John F. Kennedy Library, Boston.

——. *The Torrents of Spring.* New York: Scribners, 1926.

——. Unpublished. Item 163. Hemingway Collection, John F. Kennedy Library, Boston.

Kennedy, J. Gerald. *Imagining Paris: Exile, Writing, and American Identity.* New Haven, CT: Yale UP, 1993.

——, and Kirk Curnutt. "Out of the Picture: Mrs. Krebs, Mother Stein, and 'Soldier's Home.'" *Hemingway Review* 12.1 (1992): 1-11.

Mellow, James R. *Hemingway: A Life Without Consequences.* Boston: Houghton Mifflin, 1992.

Meyers, Jeffrey. *Hemingway: A Biography.* New York: Harper & Row, 1985.

Meyers, Jeffrey, ed. *Hemingway: The Critical Heritage*. London: Routledge & Kegan Paul, 1982.

Preston, John Hyde. "A Conversation." *Atlantic Monthly* 156 (1935): 187-94.

Raeburn, John. *Fame Became of Him: Hemingway as Public Writer*. Bloomington: Indiana UP, 1984.

Reynolds, Michael. *Hemingway: The American Homecoming*. Cambridge, MA: Blackwell, 1992.

———. *Hemingway: The Paris Years*. Cambridge, MA: Blackwell, 1989.

Stein, Gertrude. *The Autobiography of Alice B. Toklas*. New York: Random House, 1933.

———. "Composition as Explanation." *Gertrude Stein: A Stein Reader*. Ed. Ulla E. Dydo. Evanston, IL: Northwestern UP, 1993. 493-504.

———. *Geography and Plays*. Boston: Four Seas, 1922.

Wilson, Edmund. *Axel's Castle: A Study in the Imaginative Literature of 1870-1930*. 1931. New York: Flamingo, 1984.

Winter, Ella. Letter to Ernest Hemingway, January 11, 1927. Unpublished. Hemingway Collection, John F. Kennedy Library, Boston.

THE OTHER PARIS YEARS OF ERNEST HEMINGWAY: 1937 AND 1938

W I L L I A M   B R A A S C H   W A T S O N

Perhaps no two years were as critical to the ultimate success of Ernest Hemingway's career as a writer as were 1937 and 1938. These were the years in which he immersed himself in the events of the Spanish Civil War and out of which, paradoxically, came a renewed dedication to the craft of fiction and a stunning achievement of that dedication, *For Whom the Bell Tolls*.

Prior to that war, Hemingway's status as the premier American writer of the century, so recently celebrated, was in doubt. Indeed, throughout most of the 1930s, Hemingway's reputation as a writer of fiction was patently in decline, and the appearance of *To Have and Have Not* in 1937, his first novel in eight years, did nothing to revive it. Three years later, however, his reputation suddenly soared once again with the publication of *For Whom the Bell Tolls*, the enormously successful novel he fashioned out of his Spanish Civil War experiences. Its critical success permanently established Hemingway as a major American author of the twentieth century.

What happened, therefore, to transform a distracted and failing writer, so evident in the mid-1930s, into a writer obviously hitting his stride once again is of more than passing interest. The rediscovery of his commitment to the craft of fiction—or as Edmund Wilson put it, "Hemingway the artist is with us again" (591)—was in fact a triumph over a variety of obstacles, not the least of which was his involvement in the politics of the Spanish Civil War. This struggle to rediscover his true vocation—one could even say the center of his true being—is unconsciously revealed through the changing character of the short stories he wrote during that war. Most of these stories were not written in Spain or in Key West, where he spent most of his time in 1937 and 1938, but rather in Paris, the site of so much of his good writing in the 1920s.

Hemingway was in and out of Paris about eight times between March 1937 and November 1938, either on his way to or coming back from the civil war in Spain. During these mostly brief visits to Paris, he managed to write, surprisingly enough, just about as much fiction as he did there in the winter and spring of 1924, the acknowledged period of his greatest productivity as a short story writer. Six of the eight short stories he wrote during the Spanish Civil War were written in Paris, as were two chapters of a novel, all in a total of about four months scattered over a year and a half.

Quantity, of course, is not quality. The novel chapters never did become a novel; a story manuscript titled "Landscape with Figures" was abandoned, only to be published many years after his death; and "Nobody Ever Dies," which was published by *Cosmopolitan* in March 1939, should, in my judgment, have been abandoned as well. But the three Chicote's Bar stories (so-called because they were all set in this famous Madrid cocktail bar), if not among his best, are arresting sketches of war-torn Madrid, and "The Chauffeurs of Madrid," which was first published as a news dispatch, is a masterful character portrait, as good in its way as the character portrait in "Old Man at the Bridge," his first story to be published as such during the war. Whatever their varying quality, these stories nonetheless provide revealing portraits of a writer struggling to discover his *métier* and his proper place as a writer in the turbulent world about him.

Since so many of these stories were written in whole or in part in Paris, it is necessary to see, first of all, just how much Paris and the world and Hemingway himself, for that matter, had changed since the late 1920s when he left this beautiful and stimulating city for America. These, therefore, are the *other* Paris years of Ernest Hemingway's writing career, years that are not well known and are not at all like those of the 1920s.[1]

THE CONTEXTS

The Paris Hemingway returned to in 1937 must have looked much the same as the Paris he left nine years earlier—the same cafés and bars, many of the same restaurants and hotels, perhaps even most of the same waiters and bartenders. But behind the façade of continuity and familiarity lurked another Paris seething with resentment and anger, a city on the verge of exploding into violent class warfare. Paris, and much of France as well, had profoundly changed in less than a decade.

The mid-1920s had seen the beginning of a *belle époque* for France. It combined relative economic stability with an increased sense of security, generated by such international agreements as the Locarno Pact of 1926. The 1920s in Paris were in many respects also the "mad years" in music, in art, and in fashion. These were the years of the Surrealist and Dadaist revolutions and of the great modernist experiments of Joyce and Pound, among others. Josephine Baker arrived in Paris in 1925 as the lead dancer in *La Revue Nègre* and, as her son and most recent biographer puts it, all hell broke loose (Baker and Chase 3-7).

By contrast, the depression-wracked and politically violent 1930s were nothing like the prosperous and playful late 1920s. By the time Hemingway returned to Paris in 1937, the spirit of playfulness and the passion for experimentation had all but evaporated. Only three years before, an enraged right-wing mob had almost succeeded in storming the Chamber of Deputies. The electoral victory of the Socialist-Radical Popular Front in June 1936 set off a wave of strikes that convinced the moneyed interests and the conservative classes that France was on the verge of open civil war. As an artistic movement, surrealism was now virtually dead, and "art for art's sake" had become an irresponsible, even dangerous, slogan in the eyes of many artists turned activists. Artists and writers, like most everyone else, had other things to worry about, among them the dread of another war among nations. It hung over Europe like a dirty, ugly cloud. Indeed, for many Europeans and Americans, Hemingway among them, that war had already begun in Spain in the summer of 1936.[2]

Not only had Paris and France and much of the European world changed, but so had Ernest Hemingway. He was richer, fatter, and more arrogant than he was in 1928 when he left for America, and he was no longer in love with the woman for whom he had ended his first marriage in 1926. Above all, he was no longer the barely recognized and still uncertain writer he had been throughout much of his earlier stay in Paris. The Hemingway of the 1920s was a committed experimentalist trying to establish for himself an authentic and distinctive way of observing and writing about the world. The Ernest Hemingway of the 1930s was not just an established writer; he was also a famous personality. His fame, oddly, derived less from his success as a writer than from the things he had done, the places he had visited, and the life of sport and adventure he had led throughout much of the 1930s. This transformation of the writer into an international celebrity made a profound difference in the way he approached the world and, above all, in the way the world approached him.

As a consequence, the people who now surrounded Hemingway in Paris, who sought out his company and his talent, had also changed. With a few exceptions, they were not the familiar American expatriates of the 1920s—the Great Depression had summoned most of them home—nor were they writers and artists, for the most part, but rather political and business-people, almost all of them involved in one way or another with the Spanish Civil War. And they all wanted something from him: an article, a speech, his name, his money, anything that could help the cause of the Spanish Republic.

The demands began even before Hemingway left the United States. When the news that he was going to the Spanish Civil War got about, the list of people who wanted something from him lengthened enormously. Among those who succeeded in recruiting his services or enrolling his name in their causes was Jack Wheeler, who wanted him as a correspondent for NANA, the North American Newspaper Alliance. The Friends of Spanish Democracy wanted him to sponsor a medical unit with his name and his money. The Medical Bureau of the North American Committee to Defend Spanish Democracy wanted him to buy ambulances for the Loyalists and to lend his name to their fund-raising campaigns. His old friends John Dos Passos and Archibald MacLeish wanted to enlist him in the film projects of their new venture, Contemporary Historians. Arnold Gingrich and David Smart of *Esquire* wanted biweekly articles from him for their new political magazine, *Ken,* and even persuaded him (briefly, as it turned out) to serve on its editorial board. And so it went—demands for talks here, appearances there, and pieces for this or that publication—an incessant drumbeat from almost the first day it was known he was headed for Spain.

The people who wanted him most and in some respects got the most out of him were the Communists. By Communists I mean the Communist International, or the Comintern, as it was then called. Ever since the triumph of the Nazis in Germany in 1933, the Comintern had been operating out of Paris an energetic and effective propaganda bureau under the direction of that wizard of agitation and propaganda, Willi Münzenberg. I am quite certain that when it was learned in late February 1937 that Hemingway was going through Paris on his way to the Spanish Civil War, the Comintern propaganda bureau set out to make sure that the famous American writer received an appropriate introduction to the war. Münzenberg was a master at enrolling famous people in his left-wing causes, especially famous writers and intellectuals, and he would have been derelict had he not made an effort to recruit Hemingway. In the manipulation of fellow travelers, Münzenberg left nothing to chance. He arranged his celebrities into guided and controlled networks, and he assigned agents (or what today the intelligence community calls "case officers") to their management.[3]

Almost certainly it was Joris Ivens who volunteered or was assigned to be Hemingway's case officer in the Spanish Civil War. The Dutch filmmaker was then in Paris working on a documentary of the war for Contemporary Historians—the production company set up in New York by MacLeish, Dos Passos, and others—and was intimately associated with the Communists. When Hemingway's imminent arrival in Paris was made known, Ivens immediately changed his plans to resume his filming in Spain and instead met up with Hemingway in Paris. He then followed Hemingway to Spain; for several days escorted him around various government ministries in Valencia and then accompanied him to Madrid, virtually never leaving his side for the next five weeks. Because Ivens had privileged access to the Communist commanders on the Madrid front and to the Russians installed in Gaylord's Hotel, he proved extremely useful to Hemingway.[4]

As a result of the efforts of Ivens and others, Hemingway became deeply immersed in the war's international politics. In his dispatches, and even more so in the articles he wrote for *Ken* magazine, there emerged a consistent portrait of the war as an *international* struggle—not an internal *Spanish* struggle—a struggle between democracy and fascism, a struggle in which the Spanish Republic was being attacked by foreign invaders from Germany and Italy. In this sense Hemingway became, at least in his nonfiction writing and in his public appearances, a cooperative, indeed eager, contributor to this international antifascist cause whose most energetic leaders were the Communists. He had become, in fact, a participant in a propaganda war that was being waged throughout the world, and his participation was as important to the outcome of that war, at least in the eyes of the Comintern, as was that of any front-line soldier in Spain.

This, then, is the powerful political and psychological context in which Hemingway wrote his short stories of the Spanish Civil War and from which he struggled, successfully, to free himself as a writer.

THE SHORT STORIES

The Spanish Civil War stories evolved through several phases. The first two, written in the midst of Hemingway's reporting on the war, are what I would call "witness stories"—personal testaments to the human drama in which Hemingway was himself caught up.

He wrote the first of these stories at the beginning of May 1937, probably just after he returned to Paris from his first visit to the Madrid front. Although it was originally published as a newspaper dispatch, "The Chauffeurs of Madrid" was not sent out to the North American Newspaper Alliance by cable, as had been all the other dispatches from this visit, but rather was submitted as a long, professionally typed manuscript. There is good circumstantial evidence, moreover, that it was composed in Paris over a period of about four days, although it may have been revised slightly on the boat going back to America (Watson, "Hemingway's Spanish Civil War Dispatches" 43). In short, Hemingway had time, as he usually did not with his regular news dispatches, to give this quite personal and charming account of the chauffeurs he encountered in Madrid the shape and feel of a good short story.

After experiencing several unreliable and nearly worthless chauffeurs, a couple of whom provide comic relief in the midst of the murderous shelling of Madrid, the narrator of the story receives the services of a chauffeur with the improbable name of Hipolito. "Hipolito is the point of this story," Hemingway advises the reader, and goes on to describe a very short man who "looked carved out of a granite block." Unlike the previous chauffeurs, "He knew motors, he could drive, and if you told him to show up at six a.m. he was there at ten minutes before the hour." Throughout a prolonged, nineteen-day shelling of the city, Hipolito proved that "he was as solid as the rock he looked to be cut from, as sound as a good bell and as regular and accurate as a railway man's watch" (46).

The enduring qualities of this exemplary chauffeur rapidly emerge through a series of brief comic exchanges between the narrator and Hipolito. On a day when some 300 shells had hit the city, one of them landing, unexploded, on the sidewalk right beside the hotel in which the narrator is staying and only fifteen feet from where Hipolito was sitting in a parked car, the rather skittish and understandably concerned narrator rushes down from his room to get the chauffeur to move the car farther down the street, but the imperturbable and utterly fearless Hipolito shrugs off the whole thing: "'Don't be foolish,' he said. 'Another one wouldn't drop here in a thousand years. Besides it didn't explode'" (46).

When it comes time for lunch, the still cautious narrator has worked out a tortuous but safe route to the restaurant through the back streets of Madrid, but the confident Hipolito will have none of it. He orders the narrator to get in the car, and they drive down the rubble-strewn main street of Madrid solely on the chauffeur's assertion that the shelling has stopped because the enemy is eating lunch too (46-47).

After lunch, the narrator has another scare. The shelling has resumed while they were still eating, but Hipolito, having finished early, decides to leave the basement restaurant and wait for the others in the car. When the others emerge from the restaurant, the first thing they see is the car covered with dust and rubble from a nearby shell and Hipolito lying with his head back in the driver's seat. "My God," the narrator says. "They've got Hipolito." Hipolito, it turns out, is simply taking his after-lunch siesta. "I am always accustomed to sleep after lunch if I have time," he explains matter-of-factly to the relieved narrator, who admits he "had gotten very fond of Hipolito" (47).

The story ends with a little lesson in integrity. As the narrator is leaving Madrid, he tries to give Hipolito some money, but the chauffeur refuses. "I don't want anything from you," he says, and when the narrator tries to insist on at least giving him something for his family, Hipolito still says no. "Listen, we had a good time didn't we?" he asks rhetorically (47). Between equals there could be no exchange of money; it would have corrupted their relationship, as Hipolito instinctively knows and as the narrator immediately recognizes.

In many respects, "The Chauffeurs of Madrid" resembles "Old Man at the Bridge," a short story Hemingway wrote almost a year later, not in Paris but in Barcelona. Both stories are based on a real person and on an actual encounter: Hipolito was actually a chauffeur named Hipolito Maeso y Maeso assigned to Hemingway in the spring of 1937 (Watson, "Hemingway's Spanish Civil War Dispatches" 47), and the old man with steel-rimmed spectacles, although unnamed, appears so described in Hemingway's field notes for a trip he made to the Ebro River at Amposta on Easter Sunday of 1938 (Watson, "Old Man at the Bridge" 123-24). In technique, too, the two stories resemble each other by the way in which Hemingway uses brief, entirely focused exchanges between the narrator and these individuals to sketch their characters and to intensify the human drama in which they and the narrator are involved.

In effect, these two stories form mirror images of each other. Both use the character and situation of an individual to represent the larger realities of the war and the fate of many others like them. But whereas "The Chauffeurs of Madrid" pays tribute to the defenders of Madrid through the character of Hipolito, "Old Man at the Bridge" eulogizes the victims of war by concentrating on the plight of an old man of seventy-six driven from his home by the approaching enemy forces. These are the two sides of the same coin of war: the one comic in its affirmation of the spirit of resistance and the other tragic in its acknowledgment of the consequences of defeat.

The endings of both stories drive home their different temperaments and outlooks. At the end of "The Chauffeurs of Madrid," the narrator, having witnessed the imperturbable conduct of his chauffeur, affirms his confidence in the defenders of the city: "You can bet on Franco, or Mussolini, or Hitler if you want. But my money goes on Hipolito" (47). "Old Man at the Bridge," on the other hand, ends in somber judgment, as though pronouncing some awful and unalterable fate: "There was nothing to do about him. It was Easter Sunday and the Fascists were advancing toward the Ebro. It was a gray overcast day with a low ceiling so their planes were not up. That and the fact that cats know how to look after themselves was all the good luck that old man would ever have" (58).

Not only did Hemingway write these stories in the midst of the war, he wrote them from the center of his being. To me they represent the best that committed writers can offer their readers: honest and emotionally engaged portraits of some of the most important realities of war, its heroes and its victims. In the spring of 1937, when there was still hope of victory, there could still be indomitable heroes like the chauffeur Hipolito; in the spring of 1938, a year later, when that hope was disappearing for the Spanish Republic, there could only be, for Hemingway at least, tragic victims like the old man at the bridge.

He wrote the next several stories—the Chicote's Bar stories—over the summer and fall of 1938, mostly in Paris. These stories are somewhat disengaged from their subjects, as though Hemingway were trying to back away a step or two from the lives of the people about whom he was writing. The narrator is still involved in the stories, but reluctantly and more often as a spectator rather than as the directly engaged and compromised participant he had been in the first two witness stories. The Chicote stories describe, moreover, some of the uglier and more perplexing realities of the war, realities that wartime propaganda had to suppress and that partisans of the Spanish Republic chose to ignore. In fact, their subjects seem downright perverse in view of the ongoing struggle of the republic to save itself from annihilation. They deal with such topics as the denunciation of a former friend who has become a spy, the murder of a prankster in a burst of short-tempered violence, and the cowardice and superstitious fatalism that afflict soldiers the night before they go into battle. These subjects are not the stuff of propaganda, nor are they inspirational in any political or moral sense, as were the witness stories. They are best described as counterpropaganda pieces, explorations of the dark underside of war and, as such, affirmations of a realism too often suppressed in the clamor of partisan politics.

The Chicote's Bar stories are also agitated by matters that seem to have a more personal and troubled relevance to Hemingway himself than was the case with the first two witness stories. In "The Denunciation," the first of the Chicote stories, the narrator, a foreigner named Enrique Emmunds, is asked to take part in denouncing a former friend from the old days in Madrid who is now clearly engaged in spying on the Republic. At first he refuses to have anything to do with denouncing his old friend, claiming that the problem is a matter for the Spaniards and not for him, but this posture of noninvolvement does not last very long. Under continued pressure from one of the bar's old waiters and from his own troubled conscience, Enrique gives the waiter a telephone number and a name he knows will soon lead to the arrival of the security police to arrest his former friend. Enrique leaves Chicote's before the police arrive, but a short while later, before going up to his room in the hotel, he stops in the lobby to call his friend Pepe at security headquarters to insist that it was he and not the old waiter who denounced Delgado. His friend at security is justifiably puzzled, for what difference will it make to the prisoner? He will soon be shot. The narrator says only that it makes a difference to him, and the matter is dropped. As he climbs the stairs to his room, Enrique feels much better. Luis Delgado had been a good client of Chicote's, "and I did not wish him to be disillusioned or bitter about the waiters there before he died" (428). Chicote's, after all, had once been the best bar in Spain and, the narrator thinks, one of the best bars in the world.

This rather bizarre, sentimental ending does not really make much sense in terms of the war then being fought in Spain. Although espionage and denunciation were common phenomena during the spring of 1937 when Hemingway first arrived in Madrid, sentimentality about former friends who had turned traitors clearly was not. Politics had long ago broken friendships, and the savagery with which the war was being waged made the kind of gesture Enrique was willing to make for Luis Delgado almost impossible to conceive of under the circumstances. Hemingway knew this perfectly well.

Obviously, then, "The Denunciation," unlike the witness stories, is not an impassioned statement about the realities of war, although some of the war's starker realities are present. Rather it seems to be exploring other, more personal, matters. The story appears to be related to a bitter conflict that took place in Spain between Hemingway and his former friend, John Dos Passos, over the wartime disappearance of Dos Passos's translator and friend, José Robles. That Robles was executed by the Republic's internal security police is now almost certain, but how and why he was arrested is today, as it was then, unknown. Hemingway refused to get involved in any inquiry into the man's disappearance and even warned Dos Passos to lay off raising the matter with Republican authorities for fear of jeopardizing the film project they were working on together with Joris Ivens. Dos Passos left Spain shortly thereafter, thoroughly disillusioned with his old friend and with what he perceived to be the Communist stranglehold on Republican affairs. Hemingway kept his own counsel, but the dispute and the issues it raised clearly bothered him, for he kept coming back to the questions of loyalty and disloyalty, of denunciations and security police conduct, in a variety of writings over the next year and a half, most transparently in *The Fifth Column*, the play he wrote in his Madrid hotel in the fall of 1937.

"The Denunciation," finished a year later in Paris, is a subtle and veiled exploration of these same issues, and it can be read, in part at least, as an analog to the Robles affair. In the story, Luis Delgado is clearly guilty of spying and deserves to be denounced; in Spain, José Robles was justifiably denounced because he, too, Hemingway had to believe, must have been guilty of some crime against the Republic. Despite Delgado's obvious guilt, Enrique is reluctant to get involved, believing that it is a matter for the Spaniards to settle among themselves; Hemingway may very well have felt the same about the Robles affair. At the end of the story, Enrique recognizes that he has to turn against Delgado because his loyalty to the Republican cause supersedes his former friendship. Hemingway, too, may have realized that his commitment to the Republican cause was so public and so entrenched that it required him not to denounce his old friend Dos Passos but to deny him support when he most needed it. In the sentimental ending to the story, Hemingway invents a kind of resolution to his conflict with Dos Passos that was not, in reality, available to him. Enrique's final gesture to Delgado contains, I believe, an encoded plea to Dos Passos not to become disillusioned with Spain (Chicote's Bar) or with its people (the old waiters). If you have to be disillusioned, the message reads, be disillusioned with me, for I'm the one who turned against you. It was a sentimental gesture, the most he could muster for his old friend and literary rival of more than a decade.

"The Butterfly and the Tank," the second of the Chicote's Bar stories, also explores matters of direct relevance to Hemingway. The first part of the story tells how a prankster goes around squirting the waiters at Chicote's with eau de cologne from a flit gun until everyone's patience runs out and one of the patrons shoots him dead—a poignant vignette of the tension that penetrated every recess of shell-shocked Madrid in the spring of 1937. The second part has to do with what a writer could and could not properly write about in wartime and is obviously relevant to Hemingway's own changing relationship to the war: How free as a writer was he?

The unnamed narrator, who is a writer, tells his drinking companion shortly after the shooting that he thinks "the whole thing was a pretty good story" and that he "would write it sometime." His companion, a rather severe woman who works for the government's radio services (and is quite likely a Communist, although the story does not say so), is shocked and tells him that he "could not write it because it would be prejudicial to the cause of the Spanish Republic." This sets off a not-too-friendly debate, with the narrator asserting that "if I saw a comic shooting in Chicote's during the war I could write about it just as though it had been in New York, Chicago, Key West or Marseilles. It did not have anything to do with politics." Although he recognizes that other people will also say he should not write the story, something important is clearly at stake here: the independence and integrity of the writer (433).

As was often the case with Hemingway, however, an important and sensitive subject is raised only to be touched upon briefly and then deflected onto some related but innocuous topic. Here Hemingway diverts the important question of a writer's independence versus his political responsibilities onto the equally charged but politically neutral question of style—symbolism versus realism—and treats it with a bemused sense of irony.

The narrator returns to Chicote's the next day around noon "to try a little gin and tonic before lunch" (433) and falls into an amiable conversation with the bar's manager that eventually veers around to the subject of writing. The manager has no objection to the narrator writing a story about the shooting; on the contrary, he already has an elegant title for it: "The Butterfly and the Tank." As the manager readily explains, the gaiety of the man with the flit gun "comes in contact with the seriousness of the war. . . . You see it? Like a butterfly and a tank" (435). The narrator sees it all too clearly and wants nothing to do with this clumsy symbolism that virtually eradicates the reality of what happened. But he is in a cheerful mood and the manager is an old friend who is pleased to be making literature together with this writer, so the writer goes along. The story concludes, however, as the writer, the realist, cannot help thinking "of the wife kneeling there and saying, 'Pedro. Pedro, who has done this to thee, Pedro?' And I thought that the police would never be able to tell her even if they had the name of the man who pulled the trigger" (436).

This grim, final realism, so in contrast to the lighthearted discussion between the manager and the writer that preceded it, reminds the reader that despite its airiness their discussion still deals with the same serious subject raised earlier in the story—a writer's integrity. A writer of integrity could not gloss the shooting as a comedy, as Hemingway in the end does not. In the manuscript version of this story the discussion between the manager and the writer becomes an extended debate between symbolism and realism, and it is much more serious than the bantering exchange that was published (Pencil draft). Even so, the published version reveals that although the realist is willing to surrender the title to the symbolist, he will corrupt nothing else. The title then becomes ironic, almost mocking. The flit-gun man was no butterfly, and although titles may be elegant and literature beautiful, life is not. The ending brings us back to the first and main subject of the story: the unexpectedly violent nature of tension in a war-torn city.

Although "The Butterfly and the Tank" is not one of Hemingway's strongest stories, it nonetheless marks an important milestone in the gradual transformation that takes place in his outlook on the war and on himself as a writer. By the fall of 1938, when Hemingway was in Paris writing this story, it was apparent to most independent observers that the Republican cause was virtually lost. If there was any doubt on the matter, the surrender of Czechoslovakia to Hitler at Munich at the end of September made it absolutely certain that the Western democracies were not going to come to the rescue of the Spanish Republic—its only real hope then. For Hemingway, as for many others, the war in Spain as a cause worth fighting for or worse, risking one's life for, was over. His first priority now was to commit himself to his own writing, to free himself from all political commitments and propaganda writing, to recover, in short, the independence and integrity that were the fundamental, uncompromising conditions of his craft. Although the ostensible subject of "The Butterfly and the Tank" is still the war in Spain, its most important subject is its affirmation of a writer's autonomy and integrity.

The last and by far the longest of the three Chicote's Bar stories is "Night Before Battle." Very little happens in this story, and what little action there is is seen from a distance or from the present looking into the day's events already now part of the past. The story seems rather like a memoir of Hemingway's own experiences in Madrid in the spring of 1937, an effort on his part to recapture as faithfully as he can the sights and sounds—especially the moods and conversations—of those eventful days before they faded into oblivion.

"Night Before Battle" also introduces a subject that Hemingway had not touched upon before in his stories: the fear of dying. Al Wagner, a tank man who has just come out of the thwarted offensive in the Casa de Campo, runs into the story's narrator, a filmmaker named Edwin Henry, in Chicote's and proceeds in a variety of ways to make it clear that he thinks he is going to get killed in the next day's attack. He is a brave man and does not mind dying. "Dying is just a lot of crap," he says. "Only it's wasteful. The attack is wrong and it's wasteful" (443). The mercenary pilots who have congregated in Edwin Henry's room at the Hotel Florida do not admit that they are afraid of dying, but one of them who had parachuted to safety after his plane was shot down earlier in the day is now completely drunk and the others, who had signed up for six months, "soldiered good for five," Al observes, "but now all they want to do is live through the last month and go home" (444).

By the fall of 1938, when Hemingway wrote this story, it would have been difficult for him not to think of himself dying in Spain as wasteful and unnecessary. As the narrator says at the end of the story, "You get angry about a lot of things and you, yourself, dying uselessly is one of them" (459). Hemingway did return to Spain for one more visit in November of that year, but not to report on the war and certainly not to risk his life uselessly. He was in Spain for only five days just to say good-bye to some wartime comrades.

Seen together in this way, the three Chicote's Bar stories reflect the various forms and stages by which Hemingway gradually extricated himself from the political commitments and psychological compromises that had enveloped him since the winter of 1937. He is no longer the engaged participant of the witness stories, and he is certainly not the propagandist of his narration for "The Spanish Earth" (Joris Ivens's brilliant documentary film) or of his fund-raising speeches or of the articles he wrote for *Ken* magazine. He has become the detached observer and commentator, a writer searching for some distance and once more asserting his independence. His only obligations from now on will be to himself and to his writing.

The last group of three stories, two of which were written in Paris, are inquiries into the nature of death and dying: how it happens, what it looks like, and the justifiable necessity of avoiding it, if one can. The two written in Paris are the weakest of all the Spanish Civil War stories. They seem rushed and somewhat superficially developed, perhaps because they were written either in the midst of or shortly after the greatest war scare Europeans had experienced in the twentieth century—the so-called Munich Crisis at the end of September 1938. The terror provoked by this crisis has been largely forgotten today, but to contemporaries it seemed that Europe, if not the entire world, was about to be engulfed in another devastating war. Less than a year later, of course, what everyone feared had come to pass.

This context does not rehabilitate a weak story, but it helps to explain the title and the implicit subject of "Landscape with Figures," the one Spanish

Civil War story Hemingway decided not to publish, perhaps because Martha Gellhorn, Hemingway's companion at the time, objected to the way Hemingway seemed to characterize their relationship as the all-knowing male correspondent instructing the innocent girl correspondent in the realities of war. The literal landscape in the story is the open parkland of the Casa de Campo in the northwest section of Madrid in which a fierce battle is being fought. The figures in this battle-torn landscape are the dead and dying. In the story, the narrator (once more the thinly disguised Hemingway) is trying to instruct an American girl named Elizabeth (an equally thinly disguised Gellhorn) about the realities of combat. Even at a distance it is horrible to see men being killed and wounded, and eventually the girl, who wants to know what war is really like, has to put down the field glasses, her eyes filled with tears (593).

The narrator and the girl are correspondents who are paid to go there to see and write about the realities of war. So, too, was the author of this story, and he sees and writes here about combat as convincingly as he ever did in his news dispatches. Yet, however much the story is focused on the events of a particular day in Madrid, behind this landscape of warfare lies a consciousness that the next one would soon include all of Europe and that the figures of death would someday be strewn across every European landscape. I think Hemingway fully expected he would be there to report that war.

The other story written in Paris at this time is a strange bit of experimentation, a strenuous effort on Hemingway's part, it strikes me, to escape the oppressive realities of the impending defeat of the Loyalists in Spain and the threatened devastation of Europe. It has about it a surrealistic air of disaster and defeat that can be explained only by the contemporary events that surrounded him. "Nobody Ever Dies" was not a successful experiment and probably should not have been published, but it is nonetheless interesting as Hemingway's first *direct* effort (the Chicote's Bar stories were indirect efforts) to reestablish the freedom of his imagination. Related indirectly to events of the Spanish Civil War, the story is set in far-off Cuba, as though he needed a refuge for his imagination.

The underlying subject matter, however, is still death, but this time the subject is treated ironically and perhaps even satirically. Although the title says that nobody ever dies, it is quite evident that a great number of Cubans, both beloved and politically important, have died in Spain. The protagonist, a Communist Party militant who has just returned to Cuba from the war in Spain, justifies these deaths as both worthwhile (because the individuals died in the cause of liberty) and unimportant (because what is important is what must be done now in Cuba, not what was done then in

Spain). The protagonist is such a caricature of the party automaton that it is hard to believe Hemingway meant him to be anything more than an object of ridicule.

As for the protagonist's female counterpart, Maria, her insistence that the dead, no matter how they died, are a true loss to their families and to the Communist Party of Cuba (for they were the best the party had to offer) would be convincing were it not for her epiphany near the end of the story, when she miraculously seems able to communicate directly with these dead comrades and believes wholeheartedly that they can come to her assistance as she herself is about to be captured and perhaps killed by the Cuban police. Hemingway's comparison of this communication with the spirits of dead Cuban revolutionaries with the inspiration that Joan of Arc received in her time of need (479-80) is so far-fetched and so uncharacteristic of his own sardonic views of the world that one wonders if he meant this as a bit of satire.

Whatever its limitations, "Nobody Ever Dies" is best read as an exercise in rejection, ridiculing not only some of the most characteristic ideas and slogans of the Communist Party but also the tough-minded realism of Hemingway himself. He seems to be trying, in some perverse way, to reject everything he was involved with in Spain, including his own artistic standards.

These last two Paris stories reflect the conflicted ending of Hemingway's involvement in the Spanish Civil War. Although he believed that the immediate future of Europe, perhaps the world, was at stake in that war, he recognized that he personally had paid a price for the services he had rendered. He may not have believed that he had sold out to the agents of propaganda and to the Communists in particular, but he now had to wonder what were the limits of his obligations to the Spanish cause. After the Munich debacle at the end of September—that "carnival of treachery and rottenness," he called it—there was no point to the Spanish cause anymore. And there certainly was no point in risking his life when he had other obligations as an artist, not the least of which was the obligation to write as true a novel as he could about this war, a novel that, if successful, would rescue his declining reputation as a novelist.

Hemingway's last short story of the civil war, "Under the Ridge," was written in Cuba in February 1939. Among several admirable characters in the story is a French volunteer of the International Brigades who, with total justification and complete dignity, deserts his unit just before an attack that he knows is pointless and can only lead to the death of himself and of many others. In contrast to the honorable French volunteer are the battle police who patrol the front lines looking for deserters. They hunt the Frenchman down (with no help from the narrator, again our easily recognizable author), and when they catch up with him, they shoot him in cold blood. The battle police are not Spaniards but foreigners with thick accents. Anyone with knowledge of the realities of the Spanish Civil War would know that these policemen are Soviet operatives (463-65).

Although Hemingway wrote this story more than three months after he left Spain for the last time, his own walking out of the war months before it ended appears to be still very much on his mind. Like the desertion of the French volunteer, Hemingway's own withdrawal from the war, the story implies, could be regarded as a reasonable and honorable act. Like the French volunteer, he could do nothing more to alter the course of events. To walk away, then, in order to write the truth about the Spanish Civil War could certainly be justified. And as if to provide a sample of what that truth might include, Hemingway exposed the brutality of the Soviet battle police and the Spaniards' fierce, accumulated hatred of them.

CONCLUSION

In reviewing these eight Spanish Civil War stories, one can see that Hemingway, after the first two witness stories, was writing himself out of the war in order to return to it on his own imaginative terms. He had taken a certain risk in engaging as actively as he had in the political struggles surrounding the war in Spain, the danger being that he would become, whether he wanted to or not, an agent of the cause he chose to serve and thus no longer a wholly independent actor. If, moreover, one is the kind of writer who fears, as apparently Hemingway always did, that a writer can be easily corrupted— by money, by fame, by Hollywood, and, in the turbulent 1930s, by politics—then the risks of corruption loomed all that much larger for him than they did for most others. Had Hemingway not succeeded in overcoming the dangers of corruption posed by his political involvement in the Spanish Civil War, he could not have written the compelling novel he did and his standing today as a novelist would be much diminished. Through the short stories he wrote between 1937 and 1939, most of which were written in Paris, he managed to recover the integrity and discipline of his craft and thus restored his literary reputation to its former preeminence, a preeminence confirmed for all time by *For Whom the Bell Tolls*. These latter Paris years were not as brilliant in terms of literary achievement as were the Paris years of the 1920s, but in their own way they were as critical to the development of Hemingway's career and to his lasting reputation as a great writer of fiction as were those earlier years.

Much had changed, as we have seen, in the decade separating the Paris years of the 1930s from those of the 1920s. Yet for Hemingway one thing seems *not* to have changed: Paris in the late 1930s was still a good place for a writer to do his work. Despite all the demands being made upon him by the war in Spain and by the threat of another world war (and despite some profound changes in his personal life as well in these years), Hemingway found in Paris, as apparently he could not in Madrid or in Key West, the right setting in which to forge once more the craft of fiction that defined him as a writer. It was work he knew he had to do, and what better place to begin doing it again than in Paris?

NOTES

1. Wagner and Josephs are the only other critics to have commented previously on these stories as a group.
2. For a reliable summary of the transformation of French society in the 1930s, see Wright, chapters 30 and 31.
3. For the best recent account of Münzenberg's activities in Paris in the 1930s, see Koch, chapter 1. Koch, however, had only limited access to the Comintern archives. Other parts of his book should be used with great caution because of the large number of unsubstantiated assertions and allegations.
4. A more detailed account of the effort made by Ivens to introduce Hemingway to the political intricacies of the Spanish Civil War can be found in my article "Joris Ivens and the Communists."

WORKS CITED

Baker, Jean-Claude, and Chris Chase. *Josephine: The Hungry Heart*. New York: Random House, 1993.

Hemingway, Ernest. "The Butterfly and the Tank." *The Complete Short Stories of Ernest Hemingway: The Finca Vigía Edition*. New York: Scribners, 1987. 429-36.

———. "The Chauffeurs of Madrid." *Hemingway Review* 7.2 (1988): 43-47.

———. "The Denunciation." *The Complete Short Stories of Ernest Hemingway: The Finca Vigía Edition*. New York: Scribners, 1987. 420-28.

———. "Landscape with Figures." *The Complete Short Stories of Ernest Hemingway: The Finca Vigia Edition.* New York: Scribners, 1987. 590-96.

———. "Night Before Battle." *The Complete Short Stories of Ernest Hemingway: The Finca Vigia Edition.* New York: Scribners, 1987. 437-59.

———. "Nobody Ever Dies." *The Complete Short Stories of Ernest Hemingway: The Finca Vigia Edition.* New York: Scribners, 1987. 470-81.

———. "Old Man at the Bridge." *The Complete Short Stories of Ernest Hemingway: The Finca Vigia Edition.* New York: Scribners, 1987. 57-58.

———. Pencil draft of "The Butterfly and the Tank." Unpublished. Hemingway Collection, John F. Kennedy Library, Boston.

———. "Under the Ridge." *The Complete Short Stories of Ernest Hemingway: The Finca Vigia Edition.* New York: Scribners, 1987. 460-69.

Josephs, Allen. "Hemingway's Spanish Civil War Stories, or the Spanish Civil War as Reality." *Hemingway's Neglected Short Fiction: New Perspectives.* Ed. Susan Beegel. Ann Arbor, MI: UMI Research P, 1989. 313-27.

Koch, Stephen. *Double Lives.* New York: Free P, 1994.

Wagner, Linda W. "The Marinating of *For Whom the Bell Tolls.*" *Journal of Modern Literature* 2 (1972): 533-46.

Watson, William Braasch. "Hemingway's Spanish Civil War Dispatches." *Hemingway Review* 7.2 (1988): 4-92.

———. "Joris Ivens and the Communists: Bringing Hemingway into the Spanish Civil War." *Hemingway Review* 10.1 (1990): 2-18.

———. "'Old Man at the Bridge': The Making of a Short Story." *Hemingway Review* 7.2 (1988): 152-65.

Wilson, Edmund. "Return of Ernest Hemingway." *New Republic* 103 (October 28, 1940): 591-92.

Wright, Gordon. *France in Modern Times: 1760 to the Present.* 1960. Chicago: Rand McNally, 1995.

PART III

FITZGERALD AND FRANCE

FITZGERALD, PARIS, AND THE ROMANTIC IMAGINATION

R U T H   P R I G O Z Y

Most readers of F. Scott Fitzgerald's fiction are struck by the author's skill at evoking a particular locale, particularly by his ability to infuse a place with an aura of otherworldliness. Fitzgerald's Paris and other locales that convey his sense of romantic wonder (New York, the Riviera, Lake Forest) derive from three sources: from tourist brochures and other aspects of popular culture celebrating the glamour of travel abroad and in the United States, from literary sources as embodied in lyric poetry (Keatsian, as many have noted), and from an Emersonian extension of the self into, as Richard Poirier has identified it, "a world elsewhere" (3-4). Further, Fitzgerald's depiction of place is closely tied to his familiarity with particular environs: New York, Hollywood, as well as certain areas in the Midwest that he renders less as a tourist than as places to which he goes as a visitor filled with romantic wonder. Paradoxically, the less he knows about a place, the more romantic it is envisioned. Matthew J. Bruccoli, commenting on the short story "Not in the Guidebook" (1925), believes that the lack of a rich description of Paris reflects the author's unfamiliarity with the city, having, at the time of its publication, spent only a few days there (Fitzgerald, *Price* 162). André Le Vot makes the same point about Paris in "Babylon Revisited" (1931): "The city might just as well have been London or Rome, a mere backdrop for

Fitzgerald's imagination, a stimulus for his sensibility, playing the role New York had played from 1922 to 1924 before he came to France" (66).

Similarly, describing Fitzgerald's treatment of Paris, J. Gerald Kennedy observes, "Judged by locodescriptive criteria, Fitzgerald's representation of Paris in *Tender Is the Night* seems comparatively superficial. The author did not possess that attentiveness to the inner life of the city which excited [Henry] Miller; he never shared Hemingway's fetish for geographical precision . . ." (218). Kennedy finds Fitzgerald curiously indifferent to aspects of daily life that intrigued Stein, Hemingway, and Miller (he attributes this indifference to Fitzgerald's drinking) and describes Fitzgerald's attitude toward the city as "bourgeois conventionality" (194). Yet Kennedy also sees the Paris of Dick Diver and his expatriate friends as a "theater of dreams, a scene of fantasy and excess which becomes a terrifying site of violent change" (219). For Kennedy, Fitzgerald is ultimately a "rich tourist" in "a random quest for absolute freedom and pleasure . . . a life based on a hedonistic impulse facilitated by wealth, without regard for local customs or cultural differences" (195), a position I do not dispute, but one that describes only partially the author's relationship with that city or other cities which serve as backdrops for Fitzgerald's fiction.

Henry Dan Piper, like Le Vot, remarks on the distinctive quality of Fitzgerald's settings, the surprise at finding "that an author whose fiction is so notable for its brilliant settings —Paris, Hollywood, the Riviera—took so little interest in places apart from their human aspects. Places held little interest for him until they acquired associations through personal relationships" (297). Place for Fitzgerald was the locus of feeling; if he had to portray an event occurring in a particular locale, and that event had to be described simply to move the narrative forward, he could be as literal and realistic as the occasion required. ("News of Paris—Fifteen Years Ago" [posthumously published in 1947] describes the city in both concrete detail and in brief evocative suggestions [*Afternoon* 221-27].) The relationship that inspired the most imaginative settings, the most lyrical prose, the most elaborate flights of fancy, is a love affair. Fitzgerald's view of Paris, or of any of his favorite settings, is that of a tourist; but he projects imaginatively depending on the degree to which a romantic mood requires that projection.

Before discussing the influence of tourism and popular culture on Fitzgerald's description of place, we should first consider the most familiar characteristic of his prose as it relates to place and milieu: Its poetic lyricism, as Richard Lehan notes, is "inflated to create a moonlit, magical heightened world of youthful splendor" (42). If Romanticism, as Hoxie N. Fairchild has defined it, is "the endeavor . . . to achieve . . . [the] illusioned view . . . of human life which is produced by an imaginative fusion of the familiar and the strange, the known and the unknown, the real and the ideal" (251), then, Lehan concludes, "F. Scott Fitzgerald is a Romantic" (3). In *Tender Is the Night* (1934), Fitzgerald's prose is clearly within this tradition in scenes associated with romantic love. Even Kennedy sees the external scene in the novel as a mere extension of Rosemary's desire as, for example, in the description of "a huge horsechestnut tree in full bloom bound for the Champs-Elysees" (*Tender* 79) with which she identifies. When Rosemary sits with the Divers, secretly in love with Dick, Fitzgerald's lyricism is expressed in images of a river shimmering with lights, cradling "many cold moons" (59). This extraordinary lyric passage, copied with a few changes by Fitzgerald from "Babylon Revisited," illustrates the connection between romantic love and poetic lyricism. Similarly, he describes the lovers inside the taxi, pressed for time, while outside, the leisurely grandeur of Paris mocks the haste of their passion: The lovers "fell ravenously on the quick seconds" inside while the world outside is slowly fading from twilight into night revealing the grandeur of the hues of sunset against the enchantment of Paris—"the green and cream twilight faded, and the fire-red, gas-blue, ghost-green signs began to shine smokily through the tranquil rain. It was nearly six, the streets were in movement, the bistros gleamed, the Place de la Concorde moved by in pink majesty as the cab turned north" (73). In "Babylon Revisited," this same passage reflects Charlie Wales's remembrance of his lost love (*Short Stories* 617).

In "One Trip Abroad" (1930), Fitzgerald compares a boat ride on the Seine to a child's dream out of the Arabian Nights, with, extending the imagery of childlike wonder, champagne moving past "in platoons like a drill of bottles" and soft music drifting from the upper deck "like frosting drifting over a cake" (*Afternoon* 159). Here Nicole Kelly is tired, having recently given birth, and emotionally exhausted from the dissipation of the past years and the concomitant strains on her marriage. For a moment, the setting stimulates her romantic imagination, enabling her momentarily to rediscover her lost youth. Fitzgerald's imagery makes palpable the contrast between the Kellys' jaded lives and the innocence with which they had once embarked on their trip abroad. Indeed, later in the same story, the couple find new hope looking at the lake and the moon after the storm has lifted over the Dent du Midi, a hope that is directly linked to the childlike imagination: "the music and the far-away lights were like hope, like the enchanted distance from which children see things" (164). Again, in "Love in the Night" (1925), Fitzgerald links the romantic lights of Cannes with "the irresistible ineffable love in this air . . ." (*Bits of Paradise* 71). Through evocations of place, Fitzgerald creates the heightened world of youthful splendor so characteristic of his romantic imagination.[1]

A second impulse in Fitzgerald's imaginative treatment of place has been outlined by Richard Poirier, the idea that "through language it is possible to create environments radically different from those supported by economic, political, and social systems is one of the sustaining myths of any literature" (16). In his prose, Fitzgerald creates a world elsewhere, a fairy-tale world replete with its own conventions and milieus, free of the tensions in his familiar environment; he projects his imagination through the rhetoric of longing and nostalgia so deeply and so frequently into the past, into a never-never land of beauty, stupefying luxury and fulfillment, idyllic and exotic, so that it might, through re-creation, erase forever the unimaginable present.[2] Fitzgerald's other world is a refuge from fear and anxiety, satiety and void; it is his response to deterioration and death. Through a profusion of words, images—especially the sights, sounds, and smells of luxury—perhaps existence itself might assume new meaning and possibility. In any event, the words themselves might provide a refuge from his personal storm. Fitzgerald's imaginative possession of another world may be looked upon as an "expansion of the self. . . . In works where this expansion of self occurs there is less a tendency to criticize existing environments . . . than an effort to displace them" (Poirier 6).

Poirier notes that in both Emerson and Fitzgerald, the relation to landscape is established by gazing at it, by an "'aesthetic contemplation' rather than by more palpable and profitable claims to ownership" (61). Thus, in *The Great Gatsby*, when Nick looks at the inessential houses they begin to melt away, just as his own identity has earlier melted into the Wisconsin landscape and finally into a spiritual union with the timeless and mythologized Dutch sailors. As Poirier explains, "Disintegration of fabricated forms like houses and boundaries is the precondition both in Fitzgerald and in Emerson for a new integration that occurs in the contemplative aesthetic-poetic eye" (61). Indeed, locale for Fitzgerald is typically moonlight, starlight, lazy rivers, warm sultry afternoons, colors, scents, and sounds of the real world that, transformed by his imagination, take on new and magical properties. The loss of the self in the natural or enhanced natural world is characteristic of Fitzgerald's treatment of locale, and it is always associated with the heightened sensibility of the truly romantic imagination: in "A Freeze-Out" (1931), after describing the "starry and crystalline" nights of a "magical" February, feeling the "cold glory" of the town, "an ecstatic pantheism for his land and its weather welled up in him." It is through love that he is able to find his identity with this place: "She had brought him finally back to it; he would live here always" (*Price* 395).

Fitzgerald brought that Emersonian vision to Paris, where "before you *melt* out into the green-and-cream Paris twilight you will have the feel of standing for a moment at one of the predestined centers of the world" ("A Penny Spent" [1925] [*Bits of Paradise* 111]; emphasis added). Even in *Tender Is the Night*, Fitzgerald views both the Riviera and Paris through the lens of romantic wonder, allowing his characters to melt into their worlds. The magic of a Mediterranean night "*melted* into the two Divers and became part of them" (34; emphasis added). And in Paris, Dick realizes that his and Rosemary's love will be consummated when she realizes that external splendor becomes part of the self, "something in the heart"; at that moment, when she has "*melted* into the passion of the universe" (63; emphasis added), their love will attain a transcendent dimension, free of guilt or remorse. It is indeed that "ecstatic pantheism" that enables Nick to project the vision that ultimately defines the meaning of Gatsby's life and dream.

Not unlike Huck Finn's raft or Hemingway's big two-hearted river, Fitzgerald's world elsewhere is charged with ecstasy. But paradoxically, despite the "inessential houses" in *Gatsby*, he carries into his imagined world as many of the trappings of luxurious, sophisticated society as it can possibly contain. The societies in Mark Twain's and Hemingway's works were free in large part because civilization and its symbols were left behind. And both writers found solace and refuge in a close communion with an unspoiled nature. For Fitzgerald and his heroes, the imagined world is resplendent with the things money can buy: diamonds, yachts, glittering mansions, marble balconies, satin and silk draperies, diaphanous gowns, silky furs, swift automobiles, gold and crystal chandeliers—a profuse, lavish, and unrestrained display of wealth. Rather than seeing Fitzgerald's Paris and other romantic locations, as Kennedy does, as part of the hedonistic impulse, I would argue that wealth and the things that money can buy enable Fitzgerald's protagonists to enter a world of beauty and romantic possibility, as they do for Jay Gatsby.

Fitzgerald's Keatsian and Emersonian visions are ultimately filtered through those of the newest leisure industry, another world elsewhere, and one that offered popular visions of romantic possibility to an eager audience—tourism. Kennedy is correct in describing Fitzgerald's view of Europe as that of a rich tourist. When the Fitzgeralds left the United States for Europe (the first of three trips for both of them—he would return to the United States alone for his father's funeral in 1931 while Zelda Fitzgerald was hospitalized in Switzerland), they were the quintessential tourists, expecting from their travels the excitement and romance shared by others of their generation who went abroad not simply to work (as Fitzgerald did in the beginning when writing *Gatsby*) but to partake of a glamour lacking in America, a glamour celebrated by movies, magazines, and advertisements for the growing tourist industry.

Prohibition not only made the decade following the war a confusing era but also, as travel historian Horace Sutton notes, "a well-traveled one" (130). In addition to the stimulation to travel effected by Prohibition, the Nineteenth Amendment stirred new interests in American women. Among the freedoms that now beckoned was the freedom to travel, first accompanying husbands and fathers and later without escorts. The Cunard Line reported that in the early 1920s, 60 to 65 percent of their passengers were women, many of them young, traveling either alone or in groups (Sutton 133). The freedom to be found abroad, the sense of adventure and romantic possibility, was advertised to Americans by steamship companies' travel guides. Cunard's copywriters described the Aquitania as "the aristocrat of the sea" and promised voyagers proximity to people distinguished by "blood and achievement" (Feifer 209). Even more exciting, as travel writer Basil Woon wrote in his guidebook *The Frantic Atlantic* (1927), these apparent bluebloods might really be former masseurs and now gigolos, fan dancers masquerading as heiresses, and tycoons whose money came from unexalted, perhaps shady dealings. Among these pseudocelebrities, he promised, one would undoubtedly brush up against the real thing—genuine peers and movie stars. But Woon advised patience while waiting for celebrities to appear and, in the meantime, to follow the advice of the Cunard's advertisement, to admire the wood paneling, the furnishing of the cabins, "the dignity united with exquisite taste and severe simplicity" (quoted in Feifer 209). The ideal trip, as described by travel writer Maxine Feifer, was "to cross the Atlantic from New York to London in summer on the Aquitania . . . then to connect with the Golden Arrow train from London to Paris; and then the Train Bleu to the Riviera. . . . it was really more like a series of still lifes" (209).

In 1928 the Department of Commerce reported that more than 437,000 American had sailed abroad, and the favorite destination was France (Sutton 134). Sutton notes that the greatest pleasure American tourists seemed to derive from their travels was to sit around hotel lobbies with other travelers whom they had just met, comparing sightseeing, shipboard experiences, and cities, "and commenting to each other on the superiority of all things American" (137). Because Americans seemed unwilling really to enter the world they visited, they soon became the source of resentment among the residents, particularly in France, where in the summer of 1926, angry Parisians attacked American tourists at their sightseeing buses at the Place de l'Opéra. Fitzgerald captures that view of the American tourists invading

Parisian streets in *Tender Is the Night*, where groups grew from twelve, to sixteen, then joined by others "as if by magic," some dropping out to be succeeded by other people "so that it appeared as if the freshness of each one had been husbanded for them all day" (76). Throughout the novel, Americans are waiting for the boat train; and in "Not in the Guidebook" (1925), Fitzgerald notes, "it was thrilling to be in Paris when it seemed that all the world was there, when each arriving boat dumped a new thousand into the pleasure ground, when the streets were so clogged with sight-seers that . . . busses were reserved for days ahead" (*Price* 171).

The couple on "One Trip Abroad" decide over a flask at dinner to settle in Paris, because it promised "metropolitan diversion, friends of their own age, a general intensity that Italy lacked" (*Afternoon* 145). But the offensive American tourist is epitomized in the portrait of Mrs. Miles who complains about the sameness of every place, declaring that the only thing that matters is "who's there. New scenery is fine for half an hour but after that you want your own kind to see." She concludes that the place itself is unimportant; travel for her is about whom one meets at each site (145). Fitzgerald is thus consistently ambivalent about travel and tourism. He ridicules tourists yet shares their perspective—even the most frivolous expectations of the newest waves of travelers. He expresses his double perspective in "Not in the Guidebook" and "One Trip Abroad," in the former, mocking the "rich old ladies" playing Samaritans at the American Aid Society because they are "tired of the Louvre and the Tuileries, and anxious for something to do" (*Price* 169), and, in the latter, evoking the pleasure that Paris initially promised: "But doesn't somebody first decide that the place is nice," says Nelson. "The first ones go there because they like the place" (*Afternoon* 145). Rosemary and her mother, in *Tender Is the Night*, fail to respond wholly to Paris because they bring the perspective of the tourist to the city (Kennedy 202). They do respond to Paris as Fitzgerald does, but differently from noted expatriate writers. Their response is comprised of such images as Fitzgerald created in his magazine fiction, images deriving from the glamorous world of movies, popular songs, and illustrations like those that graced the pages of his own stories in the *Saturday Evening Post*. Our appreciation of Fitzgerald's romantic evocation of place and locale must take into consideration some of these sources in popular culture that fueled his imagination.

The era of travel abroad, particularly to France—with Paris as the ultimate mecca—was preceded by the war years when popular images of the city were celebrated in song, most of them gently ridiculing the doughboy's flirtations with French women. The titles of those songs indicate the fun and amatory excitement likely to be found in Paris—and these songs, all published around 1917, were extremely popular in America: "Oh, Frenchy!" (Sam Ehrlich and Con Conrad), "How Ya Gonna Keep 'Em Down on the Farm, After They've Seen Paree?" (Walter Donaldson, with Sam M. Lewis and Joe Young), "And He'd Say Ooh-La-La Wee Wee" (George Jessel), "When Yankee Doodle Learns to Parlez-Vous Français" (William Hart and Ed Nelson), and "Oui, Oui, Marie" (Alfred Bryan, John McCarthy, and Fred Fisher). The *Ziegfeld Follies* and other Broadway musicals incorporated numbers that celebrated the heroism of our troops and the excitement promised by France (Ewen 235). Indeed, the *Follies*, annual Broadway musicals, were fashioned on the *Folies Bergères*, popular for years with tourists in Paris. France as a destination, Paris as a hub of pleasure and romance amid the grim actualities of the war, were part of American popular culture, epitomized by the finale of Irving Berlin's 1918 hit *Yip, Yip, Yaphank* as the whole company, in full regalia for overseas service, sang "We're On Our Way to France" (Ewen 236). And George Gershwin's "An American in Paris" (1928) is the composer's attempt to give expression to the feelings of an American tourist as he strolls along the boulevards of Paris (Ewen 263).

As early as 1909 in the silent film *Les Miserables,* an image of Paris began to appear on American screens. The city became synonymous with glamour and adventure, with an abandoned nightlife that often led to a sad aftermath—even tragedy. The great German director Ernst Lubitsch (1892-1947) created for the screen in *Passion* (1920), the story of Madame DuBarry, a Paris that would feed the imagination of crowds of filmgoers with scenes of famous Parisian cafés and a sultry seductress played by Pola Negri, who seemed to symbolize the temptations of the city itself. (Pratt 308-11). He followed this film with *The Flame of Love* (1922), also known as *Montmartre,* again with Negri, and in America in 1926 gave audiences a sophisticated romantic comedy, *So This is Paris,* that offered a contemporary vision of Paris, fixing its romantic possibilities in American minds. *The Hunchback of Notre Dame* (1923) was a great success for Lon Chaney and for the spectacular sets that evoked Paris. As the *New York Times* critic noted, "no pains or money have been spared to depict the seamy side of old Paris. . . . If there were nothing else to see in this film it would be worth while to gaze upon the faithful copy of Notre Dame" (Pratt 294). Even Charlie Chaplin succumbed to the lure of Paris, creating several splendid scenes in an expensive restaurant in his film *A Woman of Paris* (1923). Although the film, a tragedy, was not successful (audience expectations of a Chaplin film were quite different), it nevertheless was treated respectfully by critics, and it certainly maintained the trend to picture Paris as enchanting, fulfilling, and yet tragic at the same time.

Although impelled by the same impulse to travel that tourist brochures and popular culture had stimulated six years earlier, Fitzgerald by 1931 had soured on tourism and on Americans who had clambered aboard those luxury liners in search of free-living fun in the 1920s. He recalls, in "Echoes of the Jazz Age" (1931), "Americans were wandering ever more widely. . . . by 1928 Paris had grown suffocating. With each new shipment of Americans spewed up by the boom the quality fell off, until toward the end there was something sinister about the crazy boatloads" (Wilson 20). Thus in *Tender Is the Night*, the party, descriptively resembling the first big party in *Gatsby*, is a tourist's party, roaming over the city. When Rosemary Hoyt is sitting in the Café des Alliés on the Croisette at the French Riviera, the background seems to have come from a romantic movie: "the trees made a green twilight over the tables and an orchestra wooed an imaginary public of cosmopolites with the Nice Carnival Song and last year's American tune" (13).

Similarly, the Paris in the nine stories and one novel of Fitzgerald's set there is filled with images from the sources in popular culture I have described. In "A New Leaf" (1931), the line "It was the first day warm enough to eat outdoors in the Bois de Boulogne, while chestnut blossoms slanted down across the tables and dropped impudently into the butter and the wine" (*Bits of Paradise* 298) might be the advertising copy for a Parisian holiday, and in "The Intimate Strangers" (1935), Fitzgerald invokes the movies to describe the city: "In the movies it is so simple to tell of time passing—the film fades out on a dressing station behind the Western Front, fades in on an opera ball in Paris with the punctured uniforms changed into tail coats and the nurses' caps into tiaras. And why not? We only want to hear about the trenchant or glamorous moments in a life" (*Price* 615). The sounds of Paris are those of popular mythology (Gershwin certainly used them in his tone poem of Paris): "the teacups being gathered up in cafes on the Champs-Elysées . . . the chatter of people pouring from the stores at five-thirty . . . the clink of tables being laid for dinner at the Ritz and Ciro's—then the clack of plates being piled and taken away . . . black bells strike the hour, then taxis without horns . . ." (*Price* 617). The association of Paris with music would persist into the films made decades later (*An American in Paris* [1951], *Love in the Afternoon* [1957]). Fitzgerald's sounds of music are drawn from the popular music that he used to accompany a cinematic moment, as in "Not in the Guidebook": "From a high window the plaintive wail of a violin drifted down into the street, mingling with practice chords from an invisible piano and a shrill incomprehensible quarrel of French children over the way. The twilight was fast dissolving into a starry blue Parisian evening . . ." (*Price* 172).[3]

Whether the "evening gem play of New York" in "Diagnosis" (1932) (*Price* 407) or the sultry South of "The Last of the Belles" (1929), or the "soft air, aching with enchantment," of the Riviera of "Love in the Night" (1925) (*Bits of Paradise* 71), Fitzgerald's romantic imagination is far more complex than most critics have perceived. To ignore the vision derived from popular culture and tourism in Fitzgerald's treatment of place is to devalue the authenticity of the experience he describes as it reflects the dreams, aspirations, and beliefs of a particular culture—not that of Hemingway to be sure—but a culture shared by thousands of Americans of Fitzgerald's era who could best express their dreams in the language that by the 1930s had become their vocabulary of desire. I will conclude with a passage from "Love in the Night" that in its evolution from lyrical romanticism, through an Emersonian projection of self, to images purveyed by tourism and popular culture conveys the intensity of a passion for romantic ecstasy and thrilling adventure that Americans embarking for France—not the least of whom was F. Scott Fitzgerald—brought with them:

> From the open-air cafés, vivid with dresses just down from Paris, came a sweet pungent odor of flowers and chartreuse and fresh black coffee and cigarettes—and mingled with them all he caught another scent, the mysterious thrilling scent of love. Hands touched jewel-sparkling hands upon the white tables. . . . The luxury of music and bright colors and low voices—they were all part of his dream. They were the essential trappings of Love in the night. (*Bits of Paradise* 68-69)

NOTES

1. The connection between romantic love and poetic lyricism, or that between any strong feeling and its symbolic projection onto a place or locale, is not restricted to Paris or the Riviera. Young Basil Duke Lee, thrilled at his visit to New York City, sees it as "the very stuff of romance" filled with the "vast, breathless bustle" of "metropolitan days and nights that were tense as singing wires" (*Afternoon* 34).
2. For an analysis of Fitzgerald's use of the past, see Morris 157-70.
3. For a discussion of Fitzgerald's use of popular music in his fiction, see my essay "Poor Butterfly."

WORKS CITED

Ewen, David. *All the Years of American Popular Music.* Englewood Cliffs, NJ: Prentice-Hall, 1977.

Fairchild, Hoxie N. *The Romantic Quest.* New York: Columbia UP, 1931.

Feifer, Maxine. *Tourism in History: From Imperial Rome to the Present.* New York: Stein and Day, 1985.

Fitzgerald, F. Scott. *Afternoon of an Author.* Princeton, NJ: Princeton U Library, 1957.

———. *The Great Gatsby.* 1925. The Authorized Text. New York: Scribners, 1992.

———. *The Price Was High: The Last Uncollected Stories of F. Scott Fitzgerald.* Ed. Matthew J. Bruccoli. New York: Harcourt Brace Jovanovich, 1979.

———. *The Short Stories of F. Scott Fitzgerald: A New Collection.* Ed. Matthew J. Bruccoli. New York: Scribners, 1989.

———. *Tender Is the Night.* 1934. New York: Collier Macmillan, 1986.

Fitzgerald, F. Scott, and Zelda Fitzgerald. *Bits of Paradise: 21 New Stories.* London: Bodley Head, 1973.

Kennedy, J. Gerald. *Imagining Paris: Exile, Writing, and American Identity.* New Haven, CT: Yale UP, 1993.

Lehan, Richard. *F. Scott Fitzgerald and the Craft of Fiction.* Carbondale: Southern Illinois UP, 1966.

Le Vot, André. "Fitzgerald in Paris." *Fitzgerald/Hemingway Annual 1973:* 49-68.

Morris, Wright. *The Territory Ahead.* New York: Harcourt, Brace, 1958.

Piper, Henry Dan. *F. Scott Fitzgerald: A Critical Portrait.* New York: Holt, Rinehart and Winston, 1965.

Poirier, Richard. *A World Elsewhere: The Place of Style in American Literature.* New York: Oxford UP, 1966.

Pratt, George C. *Spellbound in Darkness: A History of the Silent Film.* Greenwich, CT: New York Graphic Society, 1966.

Prigozy, Ruth. "Poor Butterfly: F. Scott Fitzgerald and Popular Music." *Prospects* 2 (1976): 41-68.

Sutton, Horace. *Travellers: The American Tourist from Stagecoach to Space Shuttle.* New York: William Morrow, 1980.

Wilson, Edmund, ed. *The Crack-up.* New York: New Directions, 1945.

T E N

"FRANCE WAS A LAND"

F. SCOTT FITZGERALD'S
EXPATRIATE THEME IN *TENDER IS THE NIGHT*

J O H N F . C A L L A H A N

1.

In the Ritz bar in July 1994, during the Hemingway/Fitzgerald International Conference, looking over his shoulder as if his subject were off in a dark corner listening, Budd Schulberg recounted memories of F. Scott Fitzgerald. He called *Tender Is the Night* a "kind of scripture," and revealed that for all the years since Fitzgerald's death in 1940, he has continued to keep that haunting novel on his desk. "It doesn't matter what page the book falls open to," he said that soft Paris evening, the beauty and feeling of the writing beckon the reader toward the French doors leading into Fitzgerald's soul. As Schulberg spoke, the violet hour of Parisian twilight darkened to evening, and you half heard Fitzgerald's voice from the late 1930s call *Tender Is the Night* "a confession of faith" (*Letters* 363).

Fitzgerald never elaborated on his intriguing characterization. For years I've regarded his words as gospel even while puzzling over their meaning. Did he mean he had kept faith with his craft and written something lasting and lovely from the pain of his and Zelda's dissolving lives and his remorse over having been only a sporadic, mediocre caretaker of his talent? Or did he mean that in *Tender* he had kept faith with his responsibilities as a man by virtue of going on as a writer? "[O]ur united front is less a romance than a categorical imperative" (*Letters* 500), he wrote Richard Knight in 1932, of his life with Zelda, after he was going full tilt on *Tender Is the Night*, just as in the novel Dick Diver tells an infatuated Rosemary Hoyt: "Nicole and I have to go on together. In a way that's more important than wanting to go on" (136). And did Fitzgerald's "confession of faith" also mean he thought that by touching the bone of his own life and times he had extended his reach as a novelist nearer "the model for the age that Joyce and Stein are searching for, that Conrad didn't find" (*Letters* 182)?

Whatever he meant after the fact, persevering with *Tender* was a categorical imperative for Fitzgerald during insomniac nights at Rodgers Forge, where the spires of Baltimore were visible through the fog. With the brilliant intuition of his last-minute change of title from "Doctor Diver's Holiday" to *Tender Is the Night*, he paid homage to Keats's "Ode to a Nightingale," a poem Fitzgerald could never read, he told his daughter, without tears in his eyes. What saves Keats's narrator from disabling melancholy is not wine but the act of literary creation. For Fitzgerald, who often lost battles with Bacchus, the tenderness attained was only a brief respite from care. In Keats and Fitzgerald, the night blooms with tenderness because of the sensibility each writer brought to the pigments of language and the natural world. Just as Fitzgerald's Keatsian title draws attention to *Tender*'s disequilibrium of history and personality *within* the equilibrium of nature's cycles of existence, the "lush midsummer moment outside of time" (175) lived through by the characters in the novel before they know it is over recalls the finely tuned self-consciousness of Keats's narrator.

In both works a sense of landscape heightens consciousness, but the settings in *Tender Is the Night* do not recapitulate the lush "verdurous glooms" of Keats's ode. The latter evokes many places and no particular place, whereas Fitzgerald's moment owes much of its magic intensity to the sensuous palpability of France. From the Riviera of Cannes and Nice, to the ancient hill villages above the Mediterranean, to the public splendors and private nooks and crannies of Paris, to provincial towns like Amiens beyond the raw, unhealed battlefields and tranquil graveyards of World War I, the spirit of France moves through *Tender*. France is there grounding the lyrical melancholy Fitzgerald imbibed from Keats and from his sense that in his middle thirties he had lost his way in a strange wood. Written, or at least rewritten and revised in America, where in 1932 and 1933 Fitzgerald sometimes felt as much of an exile as he had in France, *Tender Is the Night* possesses a vividness of place that intensifies its American characters' sense of alienation from self and country.

2.

"France was a land," Fitzgerald wrote in 1929, "England was a people, but America, having about it still that quality of the idea, was harder to utter" (Wilson 197). But Fitzgerald did utter it. And the name he gave to that national ideal pursued by Americans from Abraham Lincoln to the country boys who died in the Argonne "for a phrase that was empty before their bodies withered," and by fictional heroes like Jay Gatsby and Dick Diver, was "a willingness of the heart" (Wilson 197). Fitzgerald's characterization of America throws his observation about France into sharp relief. Throughout the French landscapes of *Tender Is the Night*—the "warm, strident" nights of Paris (156), the "echoing purple town[s], still sad with the war" (120), "the tragic hill of Thiepval" (117), or the Riviera with its "diffused magic of the hot sweet South" (91)—Fitzgerald expressed his sense that France was a land palpably different from Switzerland and the other countries traversed in the novel, including America, that familiar, distant, simultaneously ever more beckoning and remote homeland.

In Book I of the revised version of *Tender Is the Night* that Fitzgerald shaped in the late 1930s, and in Book Two of the 1934 first edition, he put readers onto the scent of France through the perspective of the young, about-to-be-expatriate psychiatrist, Doctor Richard Diver. Back in Zurich in 1919 after a stint with a neurological unit in Bar-sur-Aube, Diver, "missing something," at length "perceived that it was the sense he had had in finite French lanes that there was nothing more" (7). The young man who had gone to Zurich two years before with "illusions of eternal strength and health, and of the essential goodness of people— . . . the illusions of a nation" (5) now misses the here-and-now quality of finitude engendered by the French landscape. In Zurich, however, "there was a lot besides Zurich"; there the eyes traveled up and up until life "was a perpendicular starting off to a postcard heaven. The Alpine lands, home of the toy and the funicular, the merry-go-round and the thin chime," Fitzgerald observes from underneath Diver's skin, "were not a being *here*, as in France, with French vines growing over one's feet on the ground" (7). The contrast between French and Swiss landscapes throws into relief Diver's imminent observation to Nicole that he hasn't "heard a thing." "Nor known, nor smelt, nor tasted" (27), Fitzgerald adds, revealing that life's experience and sensuous pleasures, especially love, had eluded Dick back in America to the point of impoverishment. "A being *here*": the phrase implies a mingling of sensuous with psychological experience and an attendant grounding of personality sought, seemingly found, then lost by Dick Diver and, to a greater or lesser extent, the other American characters in *Tender Is the Night*.

After Zelda's second mental breakdown in February 1932 and his growing feeling that his novelist's talent and vocation were slipping away, F. Scott Fitzgerald, too, longed for a center, a matrix from which to live and work. (How bitter this feeling must have been for the writer who regarded *The Great Gatsby* not as a culmination but as his "true beginning" as a mature novelist.) "La Paix (My God!)," he scrawled across the top of a letter to Edmund Wilson in 1933 (*Letters* 345) as he bled out *Tender Is the Night* from his study in the large, sprawling, rented house of that name on the Turnbull estate outside Baltimore. Who can calculate how much that French word for peace resonated with Fitzgerald as a reminder of possibilities and hope dissipated bit by bit into depression and despair and, equally awful, creative inertia as his long-awaited, self-ballyhooed novel lay stalled, far from complete? Perhaps, as Fitzgerald took stock in early 1932 and sat down to write his new plan for *Tender* (then called "The Drunkard's Holiday"), France became the center of gravity for many of the individual scenes in what Milton R. Stern has called "the great American novel of history in the twentieth century" (30).

As he did in much of his work, in *Tender Is the Night* Fitzgerald turned familiar landscapes and personal situations into representative expressions of his generation's experience. Most of Fitzgerald's fellow expatriates were provincials. Indeed, like him, many were Midwesterners who, fed up with so-called American normalcy, fled eastward to France, permanently some of them thought, in the 1920s. Perhaps the persistence of France as a land— not a covenant but a place—liberated, then chastened, and finally enabled Fitzgerald to put in relief that "quality of the idea" in American life that he found so hard (and so vital) to utter.

Ironically, very little of this novel of American history takes place in America. Even Fitzgerald's cinematic projection of Dick Diver's exile to the Finger Lakes section of upstate New York is largely referential, allusive, merely suggestive. It is the novel's aesthetic paradox that the remoteness of Fitzgerald's settings permitted him imaginative and emotional intimacy with his characters' inner lives. As Fitzgerald's finite country of the imagination, France kept him honest about Dick Diver and the America to which that fallen, submerged man returns in decline. The vivid sensuousness of the

France discovered, shared, enjoyed, and finally left for good by Dick lends an almost unbearable intensity to the taut account, seen through Nicole's eyes on the Riviera, of his ironic homecoming at the end of the novel. The lovely, lost small towns of upstate New York that he is transient in give little prospect of becoming the living homeland that the "low-forested clayland of Westmoreland County" had been to his ancestors—those seventeenth-, eighteenth-, and early nineteenth-century Virginians who, he imagines, mingled with the ground under their descendants' feet in a community and a continuity reminiscent of the Jeffersonian American dream.

On that occasion in two vivid paragraphs Fitzgerald brings to life Diver's brief intense identification with his ancestral American landscape. The feeling of being at home in the world, reminiscent of the "transitory, enchanted moment" of "aesthetic contemplation" that Nick Carraway imagined for the seventeenth-century Dutch sailors at the end of *Gatsby* (137), vanishes once Diver travels beyond "the magnificent facade of the homeland" (*Tender* 222) glimpsed from New York harbor aboard ship. But "once ashore the feeling vanished" (222), and only in Westmoreland County, homeland of his paternal ancestors (and George Washington), does he "feel once more identified with his surroundings" (222).

On another occasion Dick notices a group of World War I Gold Star mothers in an elegant Paris restaurant, and their presence prompts him, involuntarily, to recover childhood memories and caress the past: "Momentarily, he sat again on his father's knee, riding with Mosby while the old loyalties and devotions fought on around him" (162). In a number of places, Fitzgerald hints that Diver's allegiance is divided between the view that a certain grace and ease—sentiment perhaps—had gone out of America after the demise of the old South in the Civil War and a historical consciousness respectful of Lincoln's struggle on behalf of the Union exemplified by his First Inaugural's appeal to national sensibility in the form of a call to "the better angels of our nature." In any case, as Fitzgerald observes more than once, except for more and more remote memories, in America Dick Diver lacks the sense of "a being here" that he associates with France, especially the French countryside. After Diver buries his father, Fitzgerald writes that "Dick had no more ties here now and did not believe he would come back" (222). "Of all natural forces, vitality is the incommunicable one," he later wrote in "The Crack-up" (Wilson 74), and for Dick Diver the loss of vitality is his worst, most irreversible loss. Fitzgerald's ability to come into imaginative possession of the vital ground of France may tell much about why America ceases to be a true homeland for Diver and for so many other characters in *Tender Is the Night*.

3.

From the time of his marriage to Nicole, Dick Diver links his destiny to the possibilities of love and work in Europe—first in Switzerland, then in France. In a reversal of the east-to-west movement and metaphor of the frontier, he regards America as the old world, Europe as the new. If he, and through his example, Nicole, will live with vigilance and discipline, Diver believes in an expatriate life compatible with his desire to be independent of the ducal Warrens and their robber baron family fortune. In Zurich, however, before long Nicole pushes her money and her point of view: "Why should we penalize ourselves just because there's more Warren money than Diver money?" (*Tender* 54). As life flows on, Nicole's relapse into darkness after the birth of their second child leads her farther away from the simple, spare arrangement they had agreed on: "We must spend my money and have a house—I'm tired of apartments and waiting for you. You're bored with Zurich and you can't find time for writing here and you say that it's a confession of weakness for a scientist not to write" (56).

Later she presses for a move to France, and her intentions, like Dick's, seem consistent with his work and her health, as if she knows that their marriage depends upon a common discipline. "This is going to be Dick's work house. Oh, the idea came to us both at the same moment," she says, voicing the expectation that the France they inhabit will be the rooted France of disciplined, experimental work rather than the leisure-class world of dalliance and dissipation. "No one comes to the Riviera in the summer, so we expect to have a few guests and to work" (56), she explains. Yet, as Fitzgerald recapitulates the matter in "Echoes of the Jazz Age" (1931), most of the Americans flowing to France in 1926 and after did not go there to work: "Pretty much of anything went at Antibes—by 1929, at the most gorgeous paradise for swimmers on the Mediterranean no one swam any more, save for a short hang-over dip at noon." Perhaps in remembrance of his own bizarre, self-destructive antics and anticipation of what he intended to make of Dick Diver, Fitzgerald wrote that "one could get away with more on the summer Riviera, and whatever happened seemed to have something to do with art" (Wilson 19).

In the novel, after Nicole's collapse in Paris where, to protect Rosemary's reputation from scandal, Dick makes his wife a co-conspirator in his cover-up of the circumstances behind a black man's murder, the Divers' move to the Riviera is rehearsed again, this time from Dick's point of view: "The inception of the idea of the cliff villa, which they had elaborated as a fantasy one day, was a typical example of the forces divorcing them from the first simple living arrangements in Zurich" (*Tender* 183). Diver's bitterness is palpable, though more than a little occasioned by his desire for Rosemary and the youth he's missed as well as by his flagging appetite for scientific work: "'Wouldn't it be fun if—' it had been; and then, 'Won't it be fun when—.'" But, as he notes, recapitulating the declining trajectory of his life in the midst of the finite beauty and vitality of France, "it was not so much fun" (183).

What happens to Dick Diver's American "willingness of the heart"? Back in Switzerland, he dreamed of doing the work of genius. "I've only got one, Franz," he replies to his friend and colleague's question about his postwar plans, "and that's to be a good psychologist—maybe to be the greatest one that ever lived" (22). For a while his ambition soars higher than the mountains towering above the Zurichsee. Later, recalling their early years in Switzerland, Nicole reflects that Dick had "taught me that work is everything" (56)—and for a time love and work did curve the Divers' lives into an arc of nourishment. In Nicole's case, only through work and discipline—the craft of self—could she recover and not merely turn back into the lovely, carefree rich girl from Lake Forest whom she had been before her violation and illness, but become a whole, responsive person capable of contributing to the world.

In France, however, Dick's work gradually yields to the sinister, gilded texture of the "leisure-class" background that Nicole's money and their mutual ingenuity turn into a milieu. "Like so many men," Dick comes to realize that "he had only one or two ideas—that his little collection of pamphlets now in its fiftieth German edition contained the germ of all he would ever think or know" (177). In the meantime his work has become confused with Nicole's psychological problems; in addition, "her income had increased so fast of late that it seemed to belittle his work" (183). Nevertheless, Nicole, whose resurgent Warren nature pushed the move to the French Riviera, sees, possibly more clearly than Dick, his emergent displacement and attenuation of work and love. There was, she reflects in Paris about the time Dick begins to yield to his infatuation with Rosemary, "a pleasingness about him that simply had to be used—those who possessed that pleasingness had to keep their hands in, and go along attaching people that they had no use to make of" (149).

Living in France in a world also apart from France, the energy behind Diver's scientific writing and psychiatric attention shifts to a performance of a different kind, one where charm does duty for love, respect, and discipline, and where the need to be loved substitutes for the tougher work of loving. In time, Dick's dissatisfaction with his compromises leads to antisocial, indeed eventually pathological, behavior and the self-destructive capacity "to make nothing out of something" (*Stories* 389)—the careful definition Fitzgerald gave to dissipation in "Babylon Revisited," a short story set in Paris, written in 1931 before he had settled on the true shape and theme of *Tender Is the Night*.

Although he has a workhouse at the Villa Diana, bought and paid for with his own money, Dick's focus on personality changes from the healing scrutiny of the psychiatrist to the ambivalent, somewhat self-serving ministrations of a master of ceremonies showing off the pleasures of France for uninitiated Americans like Rosemary Hoyt. Perhaps unable to inhabit the leisure-class world truly, either in work or in idleness, the man who will tell Rosemary, "Don't you know you can't do anything about people?" (*Tender* 140), tries to do something for various aspiring people and, by doing so, shore up his own diminished ego. "Rosemary," Nicole observes, "was one of a dozen people [Dick] had 'worked over' in the past years: these had included a French circus clown, Abe and Mary North, a pair of dancers, a writer, a painter, a comedienne from the Grand Guignol, a half-crazy pederast from the Russian Ballet, a promising tenor they staked to a year in Milan" (149).

What does it mean to "work over" someone? And who, one wonders, is using whom? Especially when this list is put next to the list of processes and persons who "gave a tithe to Nicole . . . as the whole system swayed and thundered onward" (113-14). The "system" behind Nicole is a vast network of international corporations controlled wholly or in part by the Warren family fortune. And increasingly, Dick lets down his guard in his role of expatriate patron with Warren money until his apparent tithe to Nicole's health and happiness has ominous consequences for her, for them, and, most irreparably, for him. The person Dick should "work over" is himself; instead, gradually he neglects intimacy with his work and with Nicole in favor of a Parisian "postcard heaven" that mocks the France of his true memory and experience.

4.

Despite his early sense of the differences between France and Switzerland, Dick Diver's transition from one country to the other is blurred. In the novel's first version, initial glimpses of Doctor Diver give little or no sense that he is a prominent, active, contributing psychiatrist; we are introduced to him in his role as a kind of minister of hospitality without portfolio who inspires in his guests a healthy enjoyment of each other and the world. To be sure,

Dick's expenditure of charm is bound up with his desire to be loved; "[h]e sometimes looked back with awe at the carnivals of affection he had given, as a general might gaze upon a massacre he had ordered to satisfy an impersonal blood lust" (*Tender* 84).

France is where the action is in *Tender Is the Night*, and Dick practices his craft of personality in places that comprise Fitzgerald's tableau of France. Both the Riviera and Paris can be hospitable and enervating to creative experience. Whether unsettled, worldly, and adrift like Abe and Mary North or naive and young with the innocence of sudden celebrity like Rosemary Hoyt, the Americans coming through are missing something. An observation Fitzgerald makes about trains also describes something of the incompleteness felt by those taken up by Dick Diver: "Unlike American trains that were absorbed in an intense destiny of their own and scornful of people on another world less swift and breathless, this [French] train was part of the country through which it passed" (70). But Diver's guests are not part of the country they pass through, and only his gift of sensibility—"some heightened sensitivity to the promises of life" (*Gatsby* [4])—makes it possible for them to know the difference between spending time and passing time and on that basis to mingle with the world around them.

No scene in the novel illustrates the possibilities of France for Americans more exhilaratingly and poignantly than the dinner party at the Divers' Villa Diana above the Mediterranean. On this occasion before heading to Paris, Diver deliberately throws together a disparate array of guests, some intimates, others held in ridicule and disfavor, and some hostile to those in the charmed circle. They are mostly Americans, and in her wonderment, soon-to-be-eighteen Rosemary Hoyt experiences "a conviction of homecoming, of a return from the derisive and salacious improvisations of the frontier" (91). Directly and indirectly, the French settings of *Tender* suggest something gone wrong or unfinished and incomplete about the rhythm and quality of American life, at least as it is lived by those seeking the "uniqueness of their destinies" in France (84). But for a while in the Divers' garden, Fitzgerald shows what is possible in a civilized and elegant social gathering. "They had been at table half an hour and a perceptible change had set in," he writes with that keen sense of social observation that comes from his preoccupation with the harmonies of friendship—"person by person had given up something, a preoccupation, an anxiety, a suspicion, and now they were only their best selves and the Divers' guests" (89). The change of feeling from conviviality to sentiment occurs because Dick and Nicole, almost without knowing it, flow into the landscape and the night around them. These acts of living well among people—not just between two lovers—take place in *Tender Is the Night* only during what Fitzgerald calls "the lush midsummer moment outside time" (175).

Here and elsewhere, French places are hospitable to the nourishing companionship that complements the solitude necessary for creative work. So catalytic to modern art and artists, the intimate, measured beauty of the French earth and sky is reassuring in its limits, its finitude. (Would cubism have attained its surety without the amazing mosaic of tiny white squares that appear from time to time like a magic quilt in the Parisian evening sky?) Fitzgerald's seldom-achieved sense of living well rises poignantly from the bistros of Paris—like the early-morning smells of coffee and bread. "To Gerald and Sara: Many Fêtes," Fitzgerald dedicated *Tender* in a simple, moving tribute, and in response Murphy wrote back that "I now know that what you said in *Tender Is the Night* is true. Only the invented part of our life—the unrealistic part—had any scheme, any beauty" (Miller 151). Like the Murphys, Dick Diver, in his hunger for "a being *here*" (7), regards food, drink and conversation as prerequisites to the repose, ease, and serenity that he partially, briefly attains and falsely, fatally regards as his permanent possession.

Keeping faith with one's place and being is a continuing response to life's sensuous and imaginative possibilities. Such a response, the Divers show for a while, involves a work and discipline of its own, and it also involves giving up something. Perhaps here Fitzgerald is close to the bone of what the France of his imagination—as realized not during his years of dissipation in France but in the novel he created later back in America—had to teach the rootless, uncertain Americans of *Tender Is the Night*: To be complete, a person accepts vulnerability and surrenders some of the self's armor: "a preoccupation, an anxiety, a suspicion" (89). In short, a person accepts and takes a certain pleasure from the very finitude that the romantic impulse tries to overcome in the first place.

Ironically, Diver, who, after his first encounter with France, missed the "finite" quality of the French countryside, makes less and less effort to blend his work and self with his surroundings while he lives in France. During Dick's subsequent disastrous interval in Rome, Fitzgerald remarks that "he was scarcely conscious of places except for their weather, until they had been invested with color by tangible events" (239). Moving his caravansary to Paris, for the most part Dick begins to experience the American surfaces of the city while Fitzgerald counterpoints the trivial, transient doings of his characters against French settings, merging nature with a sense of history and architecture. In Paris, the Divers seem more and more like sophisticated tourists sampling the best of the city, giving little or nothing back. Diver knows better. He knows that despite—and because of—Nicole's great wealth, their lives depend upon an alliance with "the simplicity of behavior" and "emphasis on the simpler virtues" (77) offered by France. But "swayed and driven as an animal" by his passion for Rosemary (152), Dick surrenders to an ersatz "being here" that dissipates his earlier sense of France as the best of the sensuous, palpable natural world, expressed by "French vines growing over one's feet on the ground" (7). Much more than in 1919, when, after having administered a temporary coup de grace to Nicole's love for him, he felt as if he were "hovering between being centripetal and centrifugal" (36), six years later with Rosemary in Paris Dick struggles to keep his balance.

Paradoxically, the more dissociated Diver becomes from places, whether the America to which he returns to bury his father or the Riviera village and beach he leaves at the end of his marriage to Nicole, the more intensely, vividly, unbearably Fitzgerald renders the natural world. He keeps his novelistic balance, and in his prose nature comes alive always as simultaneously related to and independent of the human scene. But the color and texture of the natural world—sky and sea and land—are a consolation to the reader more than to Dick Diver. Back at the Villa Diana after Nicole's collapse in Paris, Dick finds little or no succor in the world around him—as if his diminishing sense of self diminishes the power and responsiveness of his senses. Matters only worsen when the Divers return to the Riviera after the several years' reprieve that Warren money buys at a Swiss clinic. As if in human reversal of nature's serenity and form, Dick's self-indulgence veers him toward jarring, destructive syncopations of his previous elegant, nourishing rhythm. As Dick altogether stops doing his psychiatric writing and ceases using his personality to make life secure and interesting for Nicole, the Riviera he had once enhanced becomes a lovely, bitter mockery of his increasing emptiness of body and mind, heart and imagination. Bereft of his margin of self, on a yacht of the same name he responds to the brilliant, starlit night by dashing Nicole's kind words and grabbing her arm as if to propel them both overboard. Then, as if even this human contact is beneath him, he turns away from death to embrace a cold emotional indifference in life.

5.

For his part, Fitzgerald strives in *Tender Is the Night* for a consciousness beyond the forgetting of Keats's narrator in "Ode to a Nightingale." His authorial observations occasion a return to time and history. The sense of place inspirits his prose and gives his theme of dissolution a certain tenderness. Fitzgerald was in France from May 1924 to December 1926,

April to September of 1928, and, finally before and after Zelda's first breakdown, in France and Switzerland from May 1929 to January 1931. Like his subsequently realized character Dick Diver, he veered between competing centripetal and centrifugal forces of self. He was unable to integrate life's pleasures with the discipline and routine necessary to his novelist's calling. Unlike the Murphys, who also experienced more than their share of personal tragedy, Fitzgerald did not master the art of living well. His letters home to America from France during the mid- and late 1920s are full of reassurances and sometimes boasts about his new novel. In May 1925, in the afterglow of *Gatsby* (and perhaps the lingering bitter aftertaste of Zelda's possible affair with Edouard Jozan), he writes his editor, Maxwell Perkins, that "the happiest thought I have is of my new novel—it is something really NEW in form, idea, structure" (*Letters* 182). Don't worry, he closes letter after letter to Perkins, my novel is fine. His novel is good, he insists, puffing it up in descriptions that recall the obligatory happy refrains of popular songs. But the letters rarely provide details either of the novel or the country he was living in. Far from being a place where Fitzgerald felt the ground under his feet, France and Paris appear most often as vague backdrops for scenes of dissipation, lethargy, little work, and despite the desperate parties and drinking bouts, very little pleasure on his part.

Only in America with his back against the wall did Fitzgerald begin to tap into the deep well of his experience. From January 1932 until the publication of *Tender* in April 1934, he never looked back, though the writing was slowed by drink, depression, and the fragility of Zelda and his household. Having played hooky from his novel and, for that matter, from a whole-souled response to France while living there, Fitzgerald, not without melancholy regret, put a true expatriate feel for France into scene after scene of *Tender Is the Night*. To his surprise perhaps, evocations of French places render American contemporary experience and the history it echoes more harrowing and intense than had been the case in his previous books.

In *Gatsby*, for example, Fitzgerald indicates American reversals of racial hierarchy through a succession of comic touches. A white chauffeur drives a carful of blacks in refutation of Tom Buchanan's "impassioned gibberish" (99). But in *Tender Is the Night* Fitzgerald recapitulates Emancipation and the Reconstruction by having Abe North, a caricature of Lincoln and Grant, refuse to pay his bill in an "alcoholic fog" at a jazz bistro (perhaps inspired by Bricktop's), prompting the French police to arrest "the prominent Negro restaurateur, Freeman" (168). In the end, black friends of Freeman's track down and murder Jules Peterson, "a small manufacturer of bootblack polish," who has foolishly thrown in his lot with Abe. This farcical yet violent parody of American race relations resonates more richly because Fitzgerald situates it in Paris, the City of Light where Americans are supposedly unshackled from the chains of their history. Just as the flagrant bloody shirt belied the complexities of Reconstruction politics, the bloody sheet from Rosemary's bed at once underlines and obscures the trauma of Nicole's history. And Diver's harsh assurance that the murder is "only some nigger scrap" (172) triggers Nicole's terrified memory of her incestuous seduction—another, seemingly unrelated, suppressed act of violation and violence.

So it goes. Throughout *Tender*, Fitzgerald's intense imagination of France peels back layer after layer of painful reality long denied or repressed by his characters, especially Dick Diver. France is indeed a land in *Tender Is the Night*. Thinking himself emancipated from Victorian inhibitions, Diver acts more and more as if he were on vacation from the American moral stance Ralph Ellison, remembering Henry James, has identified with "conscience and consciousness" (423). Intellectually knowing the truth of his behavior, emotionally Diver rationalizes his self-indulgence—"I've wasted nine years teaching the rich the A B C's of human decency, but I'm not done" (219).

Fitzgerald, on the other hand, while he writes the novel, digs a sense of France out of his lyrical imagination and purgatorial memory. The elusive vividness of France detaches Fitzgerald from Diver and intensifies the dying fall of the novel's ending. Identified with his hero, he feels, as he said of Wordsworth's intimations of *mortality*, "no compulsion to pass away with [him]" (Wilson 81). At the last, Fitzgerald follows Diver home only as an artist. Because of the ambiguities of place in *Tender Is the Night*, it is fitting that Fitzgerald leave readers the task of discovering America and breathing life into Nicole's indefinite, merely suggestive details concerning the upstate New York site of Diver's exile. In a brilliant touch for this novel of places lost and found, Nicole's only knowledge of the Finger Lakes section comes through an atlas. Diver's arrested sense of history and place, alongside Fitzgerald's complex, continuing evocation of Europe and America, urges us, at however high a cost to our illusions—"the illusions of a nation" (*Tender* 5)—to fashion a true sense of history. And perhaps the quality of the finite early absorbed by Dick Diver from French lanes and felt elsewhere in Fitzgerald's evocations of France may serve as cautionary ground under one's feet in the unfinished American quest to apprehend the immensities of the new world.

WORKS CITED

Ellison, Ralph. *The Collected Essays of Ralph Ellison*. Ed. John F. Callahan. New York: Random House, 1995.

Fitzgerald, F. Scott. *The Great Gatsby*. 1925. *Three Novels of F. Scott Fitzgerald*. New York: Scribners, 1953.

————. *The Letters of F. Scott Fitzgerald*. Ed. Andrew Turnbull. New York: Scribners, 1963.

————. *The Stories of F. Scott Fitzgerald*. New York: Scribners, 1951.

————. *Tender Is the Night*. 1934. Ed. Malcolm Cowley. *Three Novels of F. Scott Fitzgerald*. New York: Scribners, 1953.

Miller, Linda Patterson, ed. *Letters From the Lost Generation: Gerald and Sara Murphy and Friends*. New Brunswick, NJ: Rutgers UP, 1991.

Stern, Milton R. ed. *Critical Essays on F. Scott Fitzgerald's "Tender Is the Night."* Boston: G. K. Hall, 1986.

Wilson, Edmund, ed. *The Crack-up*. New York: New Directions, 1945.

THE FIGURE ON THE BED

DIFFERENCE AND AMERICAN DESTINY
IN *TENDER IS THE NIGHT*

F E L I P E   S M I T H

In F. Scott Fitzgerald's *Tender Is the Night,* the murder of a black European in a Parisian hotel sets in motion the climactic revelations of Book One, particularly the fact that Doctor Dick Diver is not simply the husband of Nicole Diver but also her psychiatrist. The murder of Peterson serves simultaneously as a distraction from and as a catalyst to the dramas playing out in the lives of the central figures: Dick's fling with teenage movie starlet Rosemary Hoyt; Nicole's jealous suspicions and consequent mental break-down; and Abe North's self-destructive moral free-fall. Fitzgerald sheds light on one of Peterson's plot functions late in Book Three when Dick, showing off for Rosemary, explains to her an acting insight gained from years of self-conscious role-playing as husband and doctor to Nicole:

> "The danger to an actress is in responding. Again, let's suppose that somebody told you, 'Your lover is dead.' In life you'd probably go to pieces. But on the stage you're trying to entertain—the audience can do the 'responding' for themselves. First the actress has lines to follow, then she has to get the audience's attention back on herself, away from the murdered Chinese or whatever the thing is. So she must do something unexpected. If the audience thinks the character is hard

she goes soft on them—if they think she's soft she goes hard. You go
all *out* of character—you understand?" (288)

Dick's hypothetical scene, recalling the murder of Jules Peterson, opens up
several interpretive possibilities. It had been Dick's idea to move Peterson's
body from Rosemary's bed into the hotel corridor, but his subterfuge triggers
Nicole's recollection of her sexual exploitation by her father. Thus Nicole,
who had tried to scare off Rosemary very early in the novel by telling her
"I'm a mean, hard woman" (21), does indeed bring attention to herself by
going "soft," in Dick's terminology. She goes all *out* of character—out of her
mind, in fact.

Yet in the very act of calling attention to the convention of the
expendable exotic outsider, Fitzgerald ironically tips off a more involved
connection between Peterson and the Diver group. Dick's casual substitution
of the phrase "the murdered Chinese or whatever the thing is" for the
expression "Your lover is dead" reintroduces the scandalous insinuation of
interracial sex that his own "rescue" of Rosemary had originally sought to
prevent, almost as if in his attempt to demonstrate how she might fashion a
realistic response to the timeworn artifices of her profession, Dick has
exposed his own deepest fears about Rosemary's real "character" behind the
"Daddy's Girl" persona. That this conversation occurs just before Dick finally
admits he cannot save anyone as flawed as Rosemary suggests that the two
scenes are part of a calculated pattern of exposition.

Despite such hints, critical discussions of the novel have uniformly
ignored Peterson's brief, curious arrival and exit from the novel. Mary E.
Burton's psychoanalytic treatment of the novel's love relationships, "The
Counter-Transference of Dr. Diver," summarizes the scholarly puzzlement
and, finally, disinterest in Peterson:

> The inclusion of the Negro murder remains mysterious; one can
> only conjecture back from Fitzgerald's early notebooks on the pro-
> jected novel, all of which involved a murder. In the final shaping, it
> seems, he could not fit it into the heart and soul of the novel, but felt
> impelled to include a murder somehow—perhaps quickly to bring the
> reader up against the unreality and "enchanted" quality of the Divers'
> lives by a shocking intrusion of reality from the passions and problems
> of another class and race. (469)

In her discussion of the intricacy of Fitzgerald's psychoanalytic themes,
Burton confines this observation to a footnote near the end of her article,

an indication that she has accepted at face value Dick Diver's claim about Peterson's unimportance to their lives. Yet despite her extensive examination of the novel's phallic symbolism, including the word play implicit in Dick Diver's name, Burton somehow overlooks the pun that links a character named *Jules* (Jewels?) *Peterson* to a character named Dick. Burton thereby misses the evidence of "reaction formation" signaling Dick's unconscious identification with the man on Rosemary's bed when he tries to placate Nicole by telling her "Look here, you mustn't get upset over this—it's only some nigger scrap" (*Tender* 110).

Clearly, the figure of the dead black man sprawled on the white starlet's bed is much too charged an image in the national historical consciousness (and in Dick Diver's as well, as I will show) to be expelled from critical discussion as "just some nigger scrap." In accordance with Burton's surmise that the murder scene is a survival from heavily revised earlier drafts, the following close examination of the manuscript history of Fitzgerald's American expatriate novel, supported by material drawn from his essays, correspondence, and other writing from that period, will reconstruct the conceptual evolution of the published novel's intersecting concerns with nationality, race, ethnicity, gender, and sexuality, for which the Peterson murder serves as a nodal episode. Throughout this manuscript history, Paris serves a crucial function as the place where American idealism, as exemplified by Dick Diver, begins a protracted and painful decline. I will argue that Fitzgerald stages the Peterson murder as a quintessentially American sex/race dilemma in Paris first to demonstrate the way that Paris exacerbated disturbing American Jazz Age social trends and second to illustrate that the "freest" of Americans, having escaped the imaginative limitations of their native institutions by fleeing to this expatriate paradise, thereby only accelerated their decline.

AMERICANS IN PARIS

In order to assess the importance of the Paris setting of Book One's climactic scenes, it will first be helpful to review Fitzgerald's impressions of France covering the years of the novel's action, many of which alternately reflected his discomfort with the French population and his strong admiration for some of the Americans with whom he became acquainted there, including Gerald and Sara Murphy on the Riviera and Ernest Hemingway in Paris. In the volatile friendship between Fitzgerald and Hemingway, 1925 and 1926 were the critical years establishing the shift in their respective reputations as "the man to watch" among American writers. Late in 1925 T. S. Eliot had written Fitzgerald to praise *The Great Gatsby* as the "first step that American fiction has taken since Henry James" (Wilson, *Crack-up* 310). As Hemingway worked in 1925 on *The Sun Also Rises*, soon to become the essential American expatriate novel of the 1920s, Fitzgerald set out to fulfill the promise he had made after the publication of *Gatsby* that his next novel, a tale based on his experiences in France, would be "something really NEW in form, idea, structure—the model for the age that Joyce and Stein are searching for, that Conrad didn't find" (Kuehl and Bryer 104). That both Americans staked their hopes for preeminence in American literature upon novels written in France and set largely in Paris speaks to the city's importance in this phase of modernism. But while Hemingway wrote the first draft of *The Sun Also Rises* in two months and published it within a year, Fitzgerald struggled for nine years to complete his artistic response to the novel that Hemingway half kiddingly referred to as "A greater Gatsby" (Bruccoli, *Fitzgerald and Hemingway* 76).

In their own ways, Hemingway's novel and Fitzgerald's unfinished expatriate project exemplify Donald Pizer's contention that, among American expatriate writers, "Paris encouraged not so much the expression of new and radical faiths as the restatement of traditional [American] beliefs in the new and radical forms of an open sexuality and an evocative Paris locale" (178). Hemingway claimed that he had set out in *The Sun Also Rises* to delineate a new code of disciplined self-sufficiency in defiance of Gertrude Stein's pompous declaration that theirs was a "lost generation" (Hemingway 29-30). But Fitzgerald's unfinished drafts, highlighting the expatriate night life in Paris to the same degree as *The Sun Also Rises*, were clearly intended to demonstrate the "lostness" of the pleasure-seeking Americans abroad. Their differences in tone about what was significant in the expatriate lifestyle derived from Hemingway's adoption of a savvy insider's posture toward the city in contrast to Fitzgerald's marked ambivalence.

Fitzgerald's first trip to France on his inaugural European tour in 1921 had been less than a success. He wrote a splenetic letter from London after his first visit to his old Princeton friend Edmund Wilson, perhaps because Wilson had recommended travel in Europe to him and because he had expected at some point to rendezvous with Wilson in Paris. Fitzgerald's letter adopted the tone of someone with unfulfilled expectations, someone determined to set the record straight: "God damn the continent of Europe. It is of merely antiquarian interest. . . . The negroid streak creeps northward to defile the Nordic race. Already the Italians have the souls of blackamoors." Fitzgerald warned Wilson that America should "raise the bars of immigration and permit only Scandinavians, Teutons, Anglo-Saxons and

Celts to enter," going so far as to suggest that it might have been better after all if the Germans had been allowed to conquer Europe. Fitzgerald also leveled his strongest condemnation of the French in terms of "racial" unfitness, as he had with the Italians, leaving little doubt that his newfound preference for German domination took comparative ethnology as its starting point: "I believe at last in the white man's burden. We are as far above the modern Frenchman as he is above the Negro" (*Letters* 326). Fitzgerald's letter reveals not only his strong sensitivity to racial and ethnic difference; it also shows his tendencies to use Africanness as a term of ultimate disapprobation and to see hierarchical classifications of race and ethnicity as absolute measurements of human worth. Wilson decided that Fitzgerald and his wife, Zelda, had had the language and culture problems typical of many first-time visitors, which accounted for the mood of Fitzgerald's letter (Wilson, *Letters* 63, 73). Although his later visits to France would provide him with numerous English-speaking companions who helped to ease his sense of alienation, Fitzgerald's extended stays in Paris and the Riviera would never permit him anything approaching Hemingway's professed level of acclimation.

By the time Fitzgerald wrote *Tender Is the Night* he had been to Europe on four separate occasions—five voyages in all, including his brief return to the States for his father's funeral while Zelda was hospitalized in Switzerland—and he remained in Europe for long stretches in the years between 1924 and 1931. His twenty or so months aggregate in Paris were comparable to the nearly eighteen months he spent in various Riviera locations intermittently over the years. This is quite a long time to spend voluntarily in a place that one despises, and indeed, his new friendships with the Murphys in the summer of 1924 and with Hemingway in the spring of 1925 must have gone a long way toward changing his first impression. "I've gotten to like France," Fitzgerald assured Edmund Wilson in May 1925 (*Letters* 342), but by December of that same year, he was insisting to Maxwell Perkins that the thought of returning to America "revolts me as much as the thought of remaining in France" (Kuehl and Bryer 126). His interview with the *New York World* in 1927 stressed what must have emerged during these early years of friendship with Hemingway as a fairly important consideration in France's favor, besides the inevitable quest for *valuta*. Fitzgerald had found in France a land commensurate with his need for intellectual freedom: "The best of America drifts to Paris. The American in Paris is the best American. It is more fun for an intelligent person to live in an intelligent country" (Bruccoli and Bryer 276). This shift in attitude from his 1921 letter to Wilson, in which he had proclaimed that "France made me sick" with its "silly pose as the thing the world has to save," however, contains a significant qualification: One goes to Paris for the "best of America," not the best of France.

"France was a land, England was a people, but America, having about it still that quality of the idea, was harder to utter. . . ."—this was Fitzgerald's formula for distinguishing national character in his conclusion to the short story "The Swimmers," written in France in 1929. Amending his 1927 interview, Fitzgerald declared in "The Swimmers," "The best of America was the best of the world" (Bruccoli, *Epic Grandeur* 281). Behind this contradictory assortment of impressions lurks a discernible fantasy of a France without the French. In his generally vicious portrayal of Fitzgerald in A *Moveable Feast*, Ernest Hemingway re-created him as a stubborn outsider who blamed his inadequacies as a writer and as a man on "Paris, the town best organized for a writer to write in that there is" (182). Hemingway noted that Fitzgerald's problems with Paris in part derived from his hatred of and condescension toward the French, of whose culture and language he neither had nor wanted more than an inkling (168). For all its mean-spiritedness, Hemingway's charge agrees with Wilson's surmise of Fitzgerald's intense culture shock. Because it was not French life itself that primarily interested Fitzgerald, the importance of the French settings in *Tender Is the Night* must largely be established with regard to the way that they enabled the flourishing of certain possibilities latent in American culture, some of which Fitzgerald welcomed and others that he obviously feared.

In every draft version of *Tender*, the characters based on Gerald and Sara Murphy epitomized "the best of America" living in France. In the early drafts, written prior to Zelda Fitzgerald's first mental breakdown in Paris in 1930, Fitzgerald called the couple Seth and Dinah Roreback (or Piper) and later Lew and Nicole Kelly. Only after Zelda's prolonged institution-alization provided him with a new metaphor for the American moral collapse in the boom era did he reconceptualize the story around the lives of Dick and Nicole Diver. Although Gerald Murphy is the model for Dick Diver in his role as the cultured doyen of the expatriate community in the published novel, Fitzgerald's depiction of Dick's personality disintegration borrowed heavily from the early drafts of the novel that featured a young American southerner named Francis Melarky, who shared Fitzgerald's given name, his alcoholic bingeing, and his xenophobia. He was to have suffered a breakdown while dissipating in Paris and there murdered his manipulative mother in a climactic scene that Fitzgerald never got around to writing. When Fitzgerald revised the novel into the Dick Diver version, the matricide plot disappeared in favor of Dick's protracted, self-destructive breakdown along the lines of Melarky's. Apparently, this unwritten murder scene is what Burton considers to be the origin of the Peterson episode.

The Paris setting for the Peterson murder evolved less from this unwritten scene, though, than from Fitzgerald's association of Paris in the mid-1920s with self-destructive behavior and moral disintegration. When Fitzgerald began the Melarky drafts in 1925, he announced in a letter to Maxwell Perkins that the new novel was "about Zelda + me + the hysteria of last May + June in Paris. (Confidential)" (Kuehl and Bryer 120). The novel would have documented a period that was, according to Matthew J. Bruccoli, a "time of heavy drinking and almost no work for Fitzgerald," when he "began to remain drunk for a week at a time, and his behavior . . . became increasingly erratic" (*Composition* 18). Fitzgerald's correspondence and other comments about this, his second trip to France in 1924, describe him as being drawn into a never-ending spree. "1000 parties and no work," he wrote in his ledger for June and July of 1925 (Bruccoli, *Epic Grandeur* 229). "Paris has been a madhouse this spring," he wrote to John Peale Bishop in August, "and, as you can imagine, we were in the thick of it" (*Life in Letters* 126). By December of 1925, Hemingway, having known him for only slightly more than six months, had seen enough to assure Fitzgerald that he and his wife, Zelda, would "be a damned sight better off on the Riviera than in Paris. . . . Paris is poisonous for you" (Bruccoli, *Fitzgerald and Hemingway* 42). Hemingway's description in *A Moveable Feast* of Fitzgerald transformed into a "death's head" after consuming a negligible quantity of alcohol in the Dingo Bar is a striking portrait of the man he thought of as having been "poisoned" by Paris (152).

"[T]he mind of the confirmed alcoholic," Fitzgerald wrote to Zelda's psychiatrist in 1931, "accepts a certain poisoned condition of the nerves" (*Life in Letters* 206), but along with this acquiescence came lifestyle compromises required for the indulgence of that condition. A "poisonous" atmosphere to Fitzgerald, therefore, was one like the New York of 1927, which he described in "My Lost City" as a place where "the catering to dissipation set an example to Paris" (Wilson, *Crack-up* 30). "Whole sections of [New York] had grown rather poisonous," Fitzgerald noted, transferring his disgust over his uncontrolled drinking to the social environment that enabled it. Associating the increased opportunity for self-destructive behavior with some essential quality about the place itself, Fitzgerald judged France unfavorably as well, in part because Paris's reputation for "open" lifestyles collapsed social boundaries in a fashion that exposed the "best of America" to the rest of America. As the Melarky drafts reveal, the "poisoned condition" of Francis Melarky's nerves in Paris derived partly from the physical and emotional aftereffects of alcohol but mostly from his fears about the way the decade-long postwar spree was eroding his conviction that he controlled his own destiny.

"ECHOES OF THE JAZZ AGE"

To get a clearer reading of this aspect of the Melarky material, I will turn for the moment to Fitzgerald's most revealing statement on the moral climate of the 1920s. In his 1931 "Echoes of the Jazz Age," written while he was fashioning the final version of *Tender Is the Night*, Fitzgerald began by gazing nostalgically back at the era that "bore him up, flattered him and gave him more money than he had dreamed of, simply for telling people that he felt as they did, that something had to be done with all the nervous energy stored up and unexpended in the War" (Wilson, *Crack-up* 13). But the end of the era that began with America acknowledged as the most powerful nation witnessed the exhaustion of national energy into economic depression through the depredations of "a whole race going hedonistic, deciding on pleasure" (15). For Fitzgerald, the squandering of newfound might and prestige was not simply the result of a mindless dedication to the pleasure principle. Indeed, he asserted that "petting parties" had been a common diversion of wealthy adolescents before the 1920s, that movies did not titillate the masses as much as moralizers pretended, and that women's discovery of sex as something to be enjoyed rather than endured was a positive development of the era's new frankness.

Fitzgerald felt, however, that an unhealthy tendency toward excess began to dominate American sexual expression in an era whose trendsetters, the "girls [who] dramatized themselves as flappers," succeeded in "corrupting [their] elders and eventually overreach[ing themselves] less through lack of morals than through lack of taste" (Wilson, *Crack-up* 15). Housewives calculating the timing of their first adulterous affair, "the whole upper tenth of a nation living with the insouciance of grand ducs and the casualness of chorus girls" (21)—these phenomena were not so much causative as symptomatic of the age's abdication of moral leadership from its social and cultural elite. In fact, whatever direction the Jazz Age received was from forces below and outside of the American mainstream: "By 1926 the universal preoccupation with sex had become a nuisance. . . . For a while bootleg Negro records with their phallic euphemisms made everything suggestive, and simultaneously came a wave of erotic plays—young girls from finishing-schools packed the galleries to hear about the romance of being a Lesbian" (18). The sequencing here is equally as interesting as the data: Jazz, which Fitzgerald had previ-

ously described as "progress[ing] toward respectability" from being a metaphor for sex to finally becoming a style of music (16), had opened the door
for an ethnic music, the blues, which had not similarly shed its class and race
origins before being bootlegged, like alcohol, into white society. Simultaneously, the normal, heterosexual groping of teens in automobiles gave way
to the glamorizing and legitimizing of lesbianism. Bootleg alcohol had
created a cultural opening for corrupting, "bootleg" sex.

Fitzgerald completes his explication of the American preoccupation
with sex by citing the sensational case of Ruth Snyder, whose lover, Judd
Gray, had killed her husband. Both Gray and Snyder, in unsuccessful
attempts to escape the electric chair, had accused the other of psychosexual
manipulation, explanations that the jury accepted without deciding which
was primarily at fault (Douglas 126-27). One of the case's allegorical
underpinnings was the murder of the archetypal Successful Man by his
vampirish wife and her lover, both of working class origins, spicing the thick
oedipal overtones of the press coverage with a dash of economic determin-
ism (Douglas 250-51). The implied connective among these instances of
what went wrong with the Jazz Age is its indulgence of new and corrupting
forms of sexuality by previously suppressed social forces—blacks, lesbians,
heterosexual women—all in revolt against social propriety. Fitzgerald gives
an early instance of what amounts to a conspiracy against white male
authority when he cites as an inaugural event of the Jazz Age the "poisoning"
of President Harding by his wife, "upon the advice of the female Rasputin
who then made the ultimate decision in our national affairs" (Wilson, Crack-
up 14). Subsequently, the flappers, more reckless than sinister, would go on
to corrupt their elders and the American stage to the insistent rhythm of
black sexual innuendo. Fitzgerald's anecdote of the man who wrote persua-
sively about the revitalizing power of native American soil from a sanitarium
where he was recovering from nervous exhaustion (Wilson, Crack-up 19-20)
suggests that if the postwar era had dawned with Americans in possession
of a surfeit of "nervous energy," by 1926 white males could no longer claim
a monopoly on the supply.[1]

For Fitzgerald, "such phenomena as sex and murder" had become
"more mature, if much more conventional," by the mid-1920s, indicating a
lessening of their shock value through familiarity (21), during which time
"contemporaries of [his] had begun to disappear into the dark maw of
violence" (20). Paralleling the way that he viewed American libido as having
taken on female, gay, and black attributes, Fitzgerald's examples of his
generation's violent demise portray American loss of vitality as a white male
phenomenon, including his story of the friend beaten in a speakeasy who

dies trying to reach the symbolic safety of the Princeton Club. Fitzgerald later fashioned the speakeasy murder of Abe North in *Tender* from this incident, a fitting end for the person whose dissipation exposed the exclusive world of the Divers to the intrusion of violent blacks.

In "Echoes of the Jazz Age," Lindbergh's flight seems a poetic last gasp of the old American masculine pioneering spirit, defying the impending, inevitable "Crash." The curious thing about this precipitous plunge in American vitality is that it occurred simultaneously at home and abroad. Precisely at the time that sex and violence had become nuisances in American life, those whom Fitzgerald called "the gay elements of society" began abandoning American cities for exclusive enclaves in Palm Beach and farther afield in France. Those who had gone toward the "summer Riviera," where "pretty much of anything went at Antibes" (19), were the first to show signs of softening up under the regimen of all-out hedonism. Thus France presented a critical perspective from which to view the depletion of America's energy resources because it was there that the final phase of the process begun in America took place. The Melarky material, begun in the years that he saw as the last shining moment of the "best of America" who had fled to France, is Fitzgerald's fictional exploration of this squandering of American vitality.

THE MELARKY PAPERS

Francis Melarky is a young southerner caught up in the wild expatriate spree in France yet temperamentally at odds with the modern world, given his pronounced sensitivity to what Fitzgerald had earlier called "the white man's burden." Francis goes to the "summer Riviera" after being savagely beaten in Italy. In the flashback material on Rome, Fitzgerald establishes early Francis's hatred of Italians. The indigenous Italian population detracts from the "antiquarian interest" of Rome, it seems, as Francis's tour of the famous cathedrals gets spoiled by all of the "wops" around. Francis meets and then loses a tempting, ephemeral blond English girl, subsequently getting into an argument with a cab driver and the police during which he resorts to "violence, the honorable, the traditional recourse of his land" (Fitzgerald, *Tender: Facsimile* I: 21). The beating that Francis receives from the police results in a humiliation that he is unable to endure as a "Western man." In a later draft, Fitzgerald strikes "man" and replaces it with "Aryan" (293), although in the published *Tender Is the Night*, in which much of this Melarky material survives intact as Dick Diver's ill-fated trip to Rome, the wording is "mature Aryan" (233). Thus, over the nine-year history of the writing of *Tender*, Fitzgerald increasingly associated Francis's humiliation in Rome (and the drunken 1925 episode in his own life upon which he based it) with a historical turning point in the future well-being of the "Aryan" male.[2]

On the French Riviera coast, Francis finds an American colony in place, first encountering the parvenu group headed by Albert McKisco, including the two men who were, in a telling combination of traits, both "effeminate" and "ambiguous as to nationality" (*Tender: Facsimile* I: 57). In the published text of *Tender*, Abe North uses a one-liner straight out of a blackface minstrel sketch to convey, by analogy, that the presence of these homosexuals was the moral equivalent of racial integration. When Dick notices "the two young men" reading "the Book of Etiquette together," Abe wisecracks in stage black dialect: "Planning to mix wit de quality" (20). It's a throwaway line, on the one hand, but it effectively signals Abe's disapproval in racial terms that prefigure his own deterioration. The social-climbing McKisco party represents the "worst" of America on the Riviera, but even the ultrasophisticated Pipers participate in the anything-goes expatriate mentality. Francis quickly falls in with both groups of Americans, who carouse, duel, plot adultery, and generally live lives of restless intrigue.

Despite the rather farcical duel on the Riviera, which survives largely intact in *Tender*, the "hysteria" of expatriate life doesn't truly emerge until Francis travels to Paris with his friends. There are hints that Seth has an interest in Abe Grant's wife, and both Abe and Francis try to seduce Dinah Piper, who halfheartedly encourages Francis. Dinah takes Francis on a shopping trip, during which they visit the arty salon of a "Miss Retchmore," who surrounds herself with lesbians, parasites, and other generally aggressive women, an event "not very different from many teas just at that season" (*Tender: Facsimile* II: 124). There Francis responds angrily to the gossiping about the Pipers, calling the women in one crossed-out section "a bunch of cows," a "bunch of horrors" (125). These women "would like to have been [Dinah], but not to have paid the price in self-control" (242), corresponding to the Americans that Fitzgerald complained of on his return to Paris in 1925: "I'm filled with disgust for Americans in general after two weeks' sight of the ones in Paris—these preposterous, pushing women and girls who assume that you have any personal interest in them. . . . If I had anything to do with creating the manners of the contemporary American girl I certainly made a botch of the job" (*Letters* 342). Two years later on his return to America, Fitzgerald would present an entirely different impression with his public statement that "The American in Paris is the best American," but the Melarky materials that treat the Paris expatriate scene emphasized instead the threat posed to American moral character by these "preposterous, pushing women and girls."

Subtly, the scene jabs at Gertrude Stein, whose well-known artistic salon not only must be counted among "many teas just at that season," in Fitzgerald's delicate phrasing, but actually set the tone for American expatriate social gatherings. That Stein, with her unabashed lesbian lifestyle, pontificated over the aesthetics of the community of American writers in France in her salon was yet more proof that women had pushed their way to the top of the social order, forcing public acceptance of previously censored forms of sexual expression in the process. According to J. Gerald Kennedy, "In this feminized space, so clearly the expression of her modernist tastes and lesbian tendencies, Stein receive[d] male aspirants eager to signify their association with the new and the modern, . . . [in] a cultural landmark, a site of instruction and convocation for young men . . . bent on achieving brilliant things in Paris" (69). Fitzgerald's singling out of the lesbian salon scene as one of the disagreeable aspects of Paris expatriate life strongly hinted that if the postwar generation was indeed "lost," Stein herself was partly responsible.

Fitzgerald planned for Francis to kill his mother as the culmination of his struggle against the general assertiveness of modern "pushing" women. Explaining in a 1923 interview with B. F. Wilson (published as "All Women Over Thirty-Five Should Be Murdered") that reading Freud had unleashed the "repressed" libidos of American women, Fitzgerald observed that due to postwar fatigue and disillusionment, white males had "subconsciously helped the independence of the girls along," and that unchecked, American women would "use their leisure and exuberant vitality only in some form of excess" ending in "some sort of catastrophe" (Bruccoli and Bryer 265). It was Francis's mother, Charlotte Melarky, whom Fitzgerald had originally described as "the American woman, . . . the righteous cleansweeping irrational temper which has broken the moral back of a race + made ninnies out of a generation + a nursury [sic] out of a continent," a significance later attached to Nicole's sister Baby Warren in the Dick Diver version (*Tender: Facsimile* I: 43, 46). Whether adulterous like Ruth Snyder, or lesbian like the habitués of the Retchmore salon, sexual betrayal was the ultimate expression of white female assertiveness. Paris, in Fitzgerald's outline of the moral crisis of the modern experience, was an appropriate setting for the triumph of American womanhood, therefore, because of its advertisement of free sexual expression and experimentation. Fitzgerald was indignant about lesbianism because, like Francis Melarky, he found himself in a sexual rivalry with lesbian acquaintances of Zelda's in Paris. The salon of lesbian Natalie Barney was an expatriate gathering place visited by the Fitzgeralds on several occasions and probably was the site of Dolly Wilde's attempted seduction of Zelda in May 1929 (Donaldson 75-76). Zelda's lesbian inclinations may or may not be related to her mental breakdown, but her preoccupation with homosexuality had certainly driven her husband to distraction, especially after she accused him of being a "fairy" (Bruccoli, *Epic Grandeur* 293, 299).

The first three Melarky drafts populated the expatriate wasteland with Italians, lesbians, aggressive women, and gays, all of whom contributed to Francis's demoralization and eventual breakdown. Beginning with the fourth draft (written in the summer of 1929, three and one-half years after he had begun), Fitzgerald introduced new episodes involving ethnic Americans as symptoms of and contributors to the postwar malaise in Paris. The evening after the Retchmore salon visit, the Piper party embarks upon "a quick Odyssey over Paris," as magical events unfold. One of the people captured in Francis's "waiter trap," a maze of curtain cords, is a "large oil-Indian with many faults" named John T. Spotted-Bear (George T. Horseprotection from the fourth draft on), who joins the group. "I was a little ashamed of him," the narrator confides,[3] but the Englishman in the group insists on having him, so he stays and becomes their guide to a "last call" Montmartre cabaret called the Georgia Cabin (*Tender: Facsimile* II: 133, 251). Horseprotection takes them to an area in Pigalle that Gwendolyn Bennett, in a 1926 story, called "the Harlem of Paris" (Fabre and Williams 95). Bennett intended the term as a compliment, since she was a contributor in 1925 to the artistic manifesto of the Harlem Renaissance, *The New Negro*, an anthology edited by Alain Locke. But Locke's own analogy of Harlem to an emerging "race capital" in upper Manhattan (7) had either an heroic or a terrifying aspect, depending upon one's opinion of the black migration. In 1926, the same year as Bennett's story, Fitzgerald wrote from Juan-les-Pins to congratulate Carl Van Vechten on the success of his new novel *Nigger Heaven*, telling Van Vechten of sitting up all night to read the book. To Fitzgerald, attempts to impose "our civilization" on "the nigger in New York" had produced "a new and more vivid and more poignant horror as if it had been dug out of its context and set down against an accidental and unrelated background" (*Letters* 490). Fitzgerald may have intended that the "accidental and unrelated" presence of black Americans in Paris would therefore convey a similar "horror," as the presence of a largely American black contingent in these drafts of the Melarky version calls attention to Paris's allure for yet another socially marginalized group.

But blacks, as Fitzgerald hinted in "Echoes," were not at all "unrelated" to the deterioration of Jazz Age Americans. In the earliest Melarky draft,

Fitzgerald had already signaled the relation between black music, alcohol, and white male deterioration on the occasion of Francis's beating in Rome. In a drunken state, Francis inexplicably invites a black man—the orchestra leader—to share his table before he realizes what he has done: "He was a Bahama nigger, stuck-up and disagreeable," and Francis gives him money to go away (*Tender: Facsimile* I: 13). Inviting the black musician to his table is the result of a momentary loss of control induced by the Jazz Age ambiance. The retributive loss of Aryan manhood is swift in coming when the Italian police beat Francis shortly thereafter. The episode, which Fitzgerald salvaged for the published novel from the Melarky drafts, shows that the erosion of Aryan personality follows shortly upon violation of the southern tradition prohibiting "social equality" between the races, but since the very essence of Jazz Age American culture was the inevitability of racial interaction on terms of increasing equality, the compulsively self-destructive nature of the joyless expatriate dissipation that Fitzgerald documents returns again and again to this pattern.

In his 1929 fourth draft of the Melarky story, for example, Fitzgerald expanded the "odyssey" of Francis's motley crowd as they made their way through the Harlem of Paris using a similar triggering event, the invitation to the "oil-Indian" Horseprotection to their table where he soon becomes "one of us." As they sit inside the club, the narrator offhandedly notes the rather interesting procession of luminaries outside, seeing "through the yellow smoke of dawn" Josephine Baker and "Pepy" (Pepito Abatino, Baker's European "husband" and promoter [Rose 110-17]), and later Albert McKisco and the King of Sweden, all apparently attracted to black Montmartre's concentration of all-night jazz bistros. At that instant, the narrator notices "a big black buck, with his arms around a French girl, roaring a song to her in a deep beautiful voice and suddenly all Melarky's Tennessee instincts were aroused" (*Tender: Facsimile* II: 251-52).[4] Fitzgerald had initially written "French tart," but decided perhaps to make the sexually charged interracial encounter more dramatic by removing any imputation of financial transaction. By making the encounter a "seduction," Fitzgerald may have hoped to provide another instance of white womanhood reduced to moral dereliction through the suggestive crooning, no doubt, of an assortment of "phallic euphemisms." As Francis and his party get up to leave before his "Tennessee instincts" can get the better of him, a black musician entering the club accidentally brushes his horn case against the southerner's leg, and Francis pushes him down the stairs.

Horseprotection gets Francis into a cab before the other blacks in the club can retaliate, promising Francis "Now Ah'll take you to a real joint"

(*Tender: Facsimile* II: 254). To calm Francis's sincere remorse over attacking the innocent black man, Abe offers a cautionary account of his own misadventures: "'I'm all through with niggers—no more niggers,' said Abe. 'Once I had two [*sic*] many, more than you ever saw so I had to hide in my apartment and the maids were all furnished with a color chart so nobody could get in below a certain shade of tan.'" Abe goes on to explain that he had had a row with a "nigger that I thought had stolen a thousand francs," and complains that "the most trouble was a Copenhagen nigger named Hedstrum," (the prototype for Jules Peterson in *Tender Is the Night*). Abe concludes with the recollection, "I got so I wouldn't see any of them, innocent or guilty" (256). The point of this anecdote is to reassure Francis that attempts to establish a distinction between the "buck" and the innocent musician are both futile and dangerous.[5] Granting any liberties, as, for example, inviting blacks to share the social space of a table or a hotel room, leads inexorably to social chaos. The line has to be drawn firmly or not at all. Expanding and dramatizing Abe's tale of being pursued by blacks, Fitzgerald made Abe's compulsive slumming the cause of the breakdown of the color line in *Tender Is the Night* that leads to Peterson's murder.

The autobiographical event upon which Fitzgerald based this incident shows how he created emotional leverage in his fiction through strategic use of his own experiences. In his ledger, Fitzgerald made the following notations for May 1929: ". . . Lunch Bishop, Ernest + Callaghans. Nigger affair—Buck, Michell [*sic*] in prison. Dane . . ." (183).[6] "Buck" is likely not a name, but Fitzgerald's habitual term for a black man, especially a vaguely threatening one. In the fictional account of the incident, three men go to jail: two different men whom Abe suspects, and when the man "Mitchell" goes to get his friend out of jail, the gendarmes hold him as well.[7] What was different about black Montmartre from even Harlem was that the rigid separation of races in Harlem's whites-only clubs like Connie's and the Cotton Club defined all racial interaction through performer/audience roles that Paris did not require (Lewis 209-11). Fitzgerald's reference to Josephine Baker and her European lover reinforces the racially and sexually transgressive tenor of the Pigalle nightlife. Baker's name brings connotations that the name of Bricktop (a performer also associated with black Montmartre with whom Fitzgerald had friendly and rather formalized relations) would not have registered with American readers (Rose 75-76).[8] Conceptually, the relatively shocking breach in racial etiquette by Baker and Abatino merely sets the stage for the revelation of the greater "horror" of black male/white female sexual alliances, a progression designed to convey modernity's slippery slope of social experimentation. Paris's legendary status as a site for the

social and sexual emancipation of white women and black Americans alike
makes intelligible the potential for scandal to Rosemary in *Tender* if Peterson's
body had been discovered on her bed. But Dick's swift action to "erase"
Peterson's presence further suggests that he could not dismiss the possibility
of such an alliance out of hand.

The first-person narrator's relative indifference to these sights bal-
ances Francis's hysteria in a fashion that imaginatively evokes the distinction
between Hemingway's and Fitzgerald's disparate reactions to Paris, perhaps
resulting in an unconscious adoption by Fitzgerald of a Hemingwayesque
narrative tone.[9] Certainly the narrator's stated aversion to the "oil-Indian"
derives from one of Hemingway's own peeves about Paris, the openness of
its gay life. These indications that Hemingway may have been the model
for the narrator of the first-person versions of the Melarky drafts is important, for it will be from the distance achieved by this narrative innovation
that Fitzgerald will attempt to clarify the meaning of Francis's experiences
in Paris. At the conclusion of Abe's "no more niggers" story, the full enormity
of their mistake in "ma[king Horseprotection] one of us" becomes apparent
when the party arrives at the "real joint" he has promised: "[S]uddenly [they]
were in a world of fairies" (*Tender: Facsimile* II: 257). Fitzgerald's narrator strives
mightily for humor in his social satire of gays, cataloged according to body
types and nationalities. The phrase "world of fairies" itself burlesques one of
Fitzgerald's working titles for the novel—"The World's Fair"—indicating an
ironic return to the "world-as-carnival" motif that he had employed in
"Absolution" and *Gatsby*.[10] The episode concludes with Horseprotection
dancing wildly with a transvestite. Though Fitzgerald had already begun to
single out gays for ridicule in the earliest Melarky drafts, Zelda's accusation
that he was homosexual and malicious gossip about his relationship with
Hemingway spread by expatriate writer Robert McAlmon (satirized by
Fitzgerald in *Tender* as the bisexual Albert McKisco) raised the emotional
stakes for him (Bruccoli, *Fitzgerald and Hemingway* 43, 144-50). He may have
felt that he could not afford to appear indifferent to the active gay community in Paris. "Paris swarms with fairies," he wrote in 1930, "and I've grown
to loathe it" (*Life in Letters* 199).

Disgusted by Horseprotection, Abe, Francis, and the narrator leave
Montmartre and go to the Ritz bar for coffee. Surveying the toll of such
evenings on Abe and Francis, the narrator wonders why Abe has not gotten
beyond such experiences at his age, and why Francis wasn't off somewhere
with a girl. His observations bring Fitzgerald as close as he would come to
having a character explicitly announce the nature of the unnameable compulsion in the American character toward self-destructive hedonism:

There was an element at work in each of them, making them do things they didn't want to do and in the sensitized mood of the moment I saw them as drifting like America itself toward some ignoble destiny of their own that they could not evade—anyhow there they were, with an apparently irresistible impulse to waste themselves, dissipate their time and forces—certainly not on pleasure, for neither was having a good time. (*Tender: Facsimile* II: 260-61)

Because their dissipation was compulsive and gave no pleasure, it was a squandering of forces analogous to the national exhaustion of energy during the boom era, an inevitable and seemingly inescapable road toward "some ignoble destiny."

Here Fitzgerald's social vision, comparatively bleaker than Hemingway's, comes through. The narrator's focus on Abe and Francis as "very vital, very masculine" men (*Tender: Facsimile* II: 136) who were "wast[ing] themselves" relies on Hemingway's formula that all they need to do is gain some self-control and better direct their energy. But in Fitzgerald's vision, forces beyond Abe and Francis's control have taken possession of them, so that even when Francis does go "off with some girl" the next evening, putting his time and energy to the use the narrator suggested, it simply leads to the same inevitable American destiny. Fitzgerald describes the evening following the Montmartre fiasco in great detail, as Francis has a calamitous date with Wanda Breasted, whom he met at the Retchmore salon. The evening immediately turns into a sparring session between Francis and Wanda's gay and lesbian friends who crash the date, collectively discomfiting Francis by flouting the "legendary aberration" of humanity's "other face" (178). Fitzgerald here too takes pains to define the episode's meaning as a reflection of an American cultural transformation. Given clues like Wanda's "Bryn Mawr 1924" coverlet, Francis knew that "they were girls of some distinction," not simply "blue stockings or Lesbians. They were three tall rich American girls," which meant "developing an attitude toward 'this man's world' that might be confused with anything" (175). Francis, sensing a general conspiracy against himself as a would-be shareholder in "this man's world," turns predictably violent after one girl gathers Wanda into an unambiguously amorous embrace, and he throws the girl from their cab into a gutter. His desperation reflects the fact that whether in the company of Indians or Bryn Mawr debutantes, all roads seemed to take him to the sexual sewers of Paris.

Chagrined by the confrontation between Francis and the women and by her own susceptibility to lesbian overtures, Wanda toys with the idea of suicide. But her protracted argument with Francis over her handling of a loaded gun employs phallic symbolism to make the point that she will not surrender her newfound power without a fight. Francis blunders by revealing to Wanda that he is "tired," perhaps from his long night out in Montmartre the previous evening. This gives Wanda, who is anything but "tired," a psychological advantage in the ceaseless scrimmage between the genders: "[H]er nerves were crowded with feverish traffic. She tried to think of some mischief" (*Tender: Facsimile* II: 184). When she begins a pointless argument, Francis reflects that he hates Wanda, "a rotten hysterical Lesbian" who has entangled him in such "sordidness" that he can only think of hitting her, his second such response of the evening (185). His final comment upon his escape from her apartment at dawn, their mutual lusts unconsummated, is "God damn these women" (186).

Wanda Breasted's name suggests, in addition to the obvious sexual connotations, an elaborate pun on an important moment in Fitzgerald's earlier novel, *The Great Gatsby*, when Nick Carraway compares Gatsby's romantic idealism to the Dutch sailor spying something commensurate to his capacity for "wonder": the fresh green "breast" of the New World. Here in the Old World, Wanda Breasted becomes both a participant in and the object of an undignified struggle between the genders. The scene has much in common with others by American expatriates in which, according to Pizer, "the sexuality of Paris becomes the symbolic analogue not of creative energy and freedom but of a bitterly ironic failure to achieve what is so urgently desired" (181). Paris conveys the shock of modernity to Francis, straining his Victorian sensibilities through serial encounters with displays of adulterous, interracial, homosexual, and lesbian sex. The "open sexuality" of Paris "mocks" Francis's loss of vitality and ineffectualness with Wanda, due entirely to the epidemic confusion of gender and racial roles. Fitzgerald clearly planned through the lesbian scenes and the matricide plot to sound an alarm about women venturing into direct competition with men for the world's pleasures and privileges. He would make no advance in the plot beyond this scene until after Zelda's hospitalization, though he would continue to work on fleshing out and adding prior scenes.[11]

In one scene which takes place earlier on the day of Francis's date with Wanda, Fitzgerald hints at the reason that Abe had not been able to put nightly carousing "behind" him either. Shortly after the long night of the Montmartre episode, Abe and Dinah Piper go to the Gare St. Lazare to wait for Abe's boat train. During the scene at the station when he is preparing to depart for America, Abe attempts one last seduction of Dinah Piper, who fends him off with banalities like "People have got to have self-controll [sic]." Abe's challenge to her is that since "we're all getting old, . . . Everything ought to happen"

(*Tender: Facsimile* II: 152). Urging Dinah to "Do whatever you want," Abe echoes
the subterranean message of Jazz Age culture: "Follow your own impulses"
(153). The parallels between this scene and Francis's impending date with
Wanda are important, for both men admit to a "tiredness" confirmed by the
failure of their sexual advances. It perhaps explains why Fitzgerald struck the
reference to Abe and Francis as "very vital, very masculine men" in the next
draft because it clashed with his intent to show their utter exhaustion in the
face of the newly vitalized segments of American society.

Had Abe's conversation with Dinah stood on its own, it would have
explained much about Fitzgerald's thinking on the meaning of the Jazz Age.
But Fitzgerald gives it additional import by bracketing this discussion of
America's Jazz Age moral "drifting" with ominous hints about what America
would be like after the collapse of "Aryan man." As Dinah and Abe converse,
the station fills with other passengers: "There were a lot of ~~Jews~~ very new
looking baggage going past now. Hurrying along beside it were passengers
with little dark bodies and beady ~~levantine~~ eyes" (*Tender: Facsimile* II: 151).
Later, after Abe's talk with Dinah, the narrator notes that "The people were
coming fast now—~~lots of Jews~~ substantially dressed people already feeling
American" (157). Fitzgerald eventually edited out explicit references to Jews
without entirely changing the scene's "sinister" connotations. The published
text of *Tender* continues the wording of Fitzgerald's fifth draft, which used
phonetic spelling to imply a Jewish speaker whose boisterous yelling in the
station to someone named "Jules" ingeniously retains the word "Jew" in the
phrasing: "prospective passengers with dark little bodies, were calling: 'Jew-
uls-*Hoo-oo!*' in dark piercing voices" (80). Even if he intended no ironic
foreshadowing of the later appearance of Jules Peterson, Fitzgerald at the
very least reinforced the threat behind the "dark little bodies" making their
way to America. This attention to the ethnicity of the travelers bound for
America makes the point explicitly rendered in "Echoes of the Jazz Age" that
while "Americans" were declining through dissipation and exhaustion, a new,
hard, acquisitive, and racially alien social order was embarking to replace
them. "Americans were getting soft," Fitzgerald opined in that essay, so soft
that "real" Americans had to be replaced on the Olympics team by "fresh
overseas blood" with "few vowels in their names" (Wilson, *Crack-up* 19).
Because he salvaged the Rome beating, the lesbian salon, and the scene in
the train station from these early drafts into the published text of *Tender Is
the Night*, Fitzgerald clearly thought of such moments as crucial, defining
events in sorting out the meaning of the Jazz Age.

Fitzgerald's "Echoes of the Jazz Age" reflects also the influence upon
his thinking of Oswald Spengler's *Decline of the West* (1918).[12] Spenglerian

pessimism about the "organic" exhaustion of Western civilization enters into Fitzgerald's description of the changing character of Americans arriving in Paris, including many "new Americans" returning to Europe to show off their newfound economic power:

> [B]y 1928 Paris had grown suffocating. With each new shipment of Americans spewed up by the boom the quality fell off, until toward the end there was something sinister about the crazy boatloads— . . . . fantastic neanderthals . . . [like] an Italian on a steamer who promenaded the deck in an American Reserve Officer's uniform picking quarrels in broken English with Americans who criticised their own institutions in the bar. I remember a fat Jewess, inlaid with diamonds, who sat behind us at the Russian ballet and said as the curtain rose, "Thad's luffly, dey ought to baint a bicture of it." This was low comedy, but it was evident that money and power were falling into the hands of people in comparison with whom the leader of a village Soviet would be a gold-mine of judgment and culture. There were citizens travelling in luxury in 1928 and 1929 who, in the distortion of their new condition, had the human value of Pekinese, bivalves, cretins, goats. (Wilson, *Crack-up* 20-21)

Francis's and Abe's exhaustion in the Melarky drafts is a telltale sign of the Spenglerian decline that they share with other "Aryan" males. Fitzgerald's idea of calling the expatriate novel "Our Type" may in this way be linked to his belief that "This civilization has nothing more to produce. 'We threw up *our fine types* in the eighteenth century, when we had Beethoven and Goethe. The race had a mind then.' All there is left to do is go in a period of universal hibernation and begin all over" (Bruccoli and Bryer 275; emphasis added).

In *Tender Is the Night*, the episode in the Gare St. Lazare on the occasion of Abe's departure shows Fitzgerald attempting to engage the problem of American national character in an era of diminishing ethnic identification with Northern Europe. As in "Echoes of the Jazz Age," he uses the backdrop of populations in transit to intensify the sensation of social flux, calling forth the idea that "the first impression of their immaculacy and their money" cannot obscure "the vague racial dusk" of the "dark little bodies" going back and forth to America, so that although they were "travelling in luxury," their inauthenticity as real Americans stands out as the central fact, "blind[ing] both them and their observers" to all other considerations (*Tender* 83). Fitzgerald specifically exempted the mom-and-pop variety of Americans from his criticism, insisting instead that the misrepresentation of America abroad was by those elements of society which could not even properly speak the language, let alone articulate the true American ethos. The arrival of the "sinister" boatloads re-created the very social atmosphere that had driven the "gay elements of society" away from America, though with its more relaxed social attitudes, Paris proportionately intensified the "suffocating" trends. It had ceased to be a place to consort with the "best of America" in cultured surroundings and had become a place that permitted the extension of shared traditions of egalitarianism to a disastrous conclusion.

A reconstruction of the Melarky versions illustrates the deterioration of American moral fiber in the Jazz Age. Beaten in Rome by "wops," Francis, "sick with the Latin world" and suffering a "distinct lesion of vitality" (*Tender:* Facsimile I: 13), left for a France still pretending to be "the thing the world has to save." But the summer Riviera and the expatriate American scene in Paris could not be saved from the "pushing" women and the intrusive outsiders. Cheap alcohol had made loss of restraint fashionable, and the endless bouts of uncontrolled debauching had emboldened society's perennial misfits. Wealth and power were in the hands of aimless, hysterical girls from Bryn Mawr, artistic types whose excess of energy got them into promiscuity, lesbianism, and other "mischief." Parvenu Jews were lining up at the docks, first to gain admittance into America and almost immediately to return to Europe masquerading as "real American" success stories who would launch even more "sinister, . . . crazy boatloads." Released from the Jim Crow rules of etiquette that governed black/white interaction even in the segregated exotic clubs of Harlem, black Americans in Paris were free to give open sexual pursuit to white women, while "oil-Indians" squandered wealth siphoned from American energy reserves in gay bars. Exhausted from carrying "the white man's burden" of imposing order upon the world, white American males found themselves too tired to compete with women, what with having to compete *for* women with swarthy ethnic types and women themselves.

The Rome beating, the Riviera duel, the "odyssey" to black Montmartre, and the date with Wanda Breasted show that every step toward Francis's breakdown in Paris was to have been punctuated by some form of physical violence. But more important was the psychic violence to Francis as "Western man" on the brink of a new world order. In *Tender Is the Night,* Fitzgerald expanded the action beyond France, using "Teutonic" Switzerland as a zone of moral recuperation from the debaucheries of Paris and the humiliations of Rome. Significantly, Fitzgerald would transform Francis Melarky into Rosemary Hoyt in the published novel (Bruccoli, *Composition* 95-96), a gesture entirely in the spirit of his theme of the loss of American male vitality. Fitzgerald would diminish the attention to lesbian and gay expatriate life in *Tender*, but he would expand the episode involving blacks in Montmartre. The murder of Jules Peterson by "rioting" black American expatriates plays on their "accidental and unrelated" presence in Paris for a certain shock value, but the fact that Dick is incapable of preventing their invasion of his exclusive world certifies their role in the inescapable American destiny awaiting Dick and his group. The Melarky material, read against Fitzgerald's correspondence and commentaries on the Jazz Age, strongly suggests that all along, the encroachment of all forms of "difference" into the preserve of white male privilege was an essential component of Fitzgerald's vision of how the "best of America" lost its way in a labyrinth of Paris bistros.

From this perspective, the Peterson episode is central to a social vision that remained largely unchanged from the earliest to the final drafts of *Tender Is the Night*. Peterson, a harbinger of the "negroid streak" that had apparently already worked its way up to Stockholm, attaches himself to Abe North in hopes that North "can set him up in business in Versailles" (106). Compared to a border state Negro Republican ward heeler, Peterson perishes in what amounts to Fitzgerald's restaging of America's post–Civil War Reconstruction as a riot by newly emancipated blacks. Although he shifted the scene of Abe's encounter with the black expatriate community from Montmartre to Montparnasse in *Tender*, Fitzgerald's handling of Peterson's alliance with Abe and his later death show more explicitly than the Melarky episodes the moral consequences of Abe's drunken meandering across social boundaries. Peterson's murder foretells the inevitability of Abe's beating death outside of a speakeasy, his disappearance into the "dark maw of violence."

But if Peterson has a special significance for Abe, he has a more explicit relationship to Dick Diver's fate. The bed on which Peterson dies is the very one on which Rosemary had almost succeeded in seducing Dick before Peterson's intrusion. Peterson's rags-to-riches dream of entrepreneurship in Versailles—in addition to the French aristocracy, it had housed the postwar conference that made inevitable the global victory of the "rising tide of color," according to Fitzgerald's fellow Scribners author Lothrop Stoddard[13]—echoes the success mythology of American popular culture that had previously motivated Dick to rise from obscurity by marrying into money. In this regard Peterson resembles too the "fantastic neanderthals" traveling in luxury to Europe after 1928 who had reduced American idealism to "something vague, that you remembered from a very cheap novel" (Wilson, *Crack-up* 20). Peterson's and Dick's separate arrivals on Rosemary's bed demarcate the stages in the starlet's transfiguration from "Daddy's Girl" into a mature femme fatale. For Dick's unsatisfied desire turns Rosemary into an embodiment of the seductive yet "poisonous" life of moral dereliction: "all the world's dark magic; the blinding belladonna, the caffeine converting physical into nervous energy, the mandragora that imposes harmony" (164). Associating Rosemary with the "female Rasputin" who poisoned Harding and with the young women of the 1920s who squandered America's surfeit of energy pursuing mischief, Fitzgerald transforms Dick into a death-in-life replica of Peterson after Dick finally sleeps with her in Rome. "I guess I'm the Black Death," Dick says meaningfully, downcast at discovering that Rosemary has also shared her bed with her "spic" costar on the set of her movie about the decline of the Roman Empire.

Immediately following Dick's discovery of his loss of potency, Fitzgerald writes him into the old Francis Melarky episode describing an uncharacteristic attempt to befriend the unpleasant black Bahamian musician, followed by the beating at the hands of Italian police. Dick's mimicry of Abe's race-mixing in Paris, followed by his failure to rise to the challenges of "Aryan manhood" in his battle with the "wops," signals his resignation to his fate as an "homme epuisé," an "exhausted man."[14] Poisoned by his surrender of control to Rosemary, Dick has failed to interpret the meaning of the dark figure on the movie star's bed until far too late to prevent his own "dying fall" (Bruccoli, *Epic Grandeur* 372). It is no surprise, then, that in his exhaustion, he loses his children, his livelihood, and his reputation. As a result, all of the women that he had loved form sexual alliances with "dark" men. Rosemary behaves as if she sees no distinction between Dick and her "spic" lover, while Nicole gives herself "spiritually" to the swarthy Tommy Barban, whose skin just missed "attaining the blue beauty of Negroes" (269). Mary North, the last of the women of Dick Diver's exclusive party, loses little time after Abe's death, marrying an Asiatic tycoon "not quite light enough to travel in a pullman south of Mason-Dixon" (258), and putting Abe's own "anything goes" philosophy into action, punctuating her moral emancipation in a lesbian debauch with a titled Englishwoman.

Rather than failing to fit the episode "into the heart and soul of the novel," this reconsideration of the Peterson murder scene in *Tender Is the Night* shows that Fitzgerald succeeded in reclaiming and expanding the core of the social vision he first sketched in the Melarky drafts. The Paris setting for the Peterson episode is crucial in the sense that Paris, with its reputation for sexual license and interracial socialization, serves as a snapshot of the future America Fitzgerald feared, a hedonistic paradise without social boundaries. The Americans who had drifted to Paris in the 1920s clustered there in mutually accessible microcolonies no longer stratified by law, custom, or violence into a manageable social hierarchy. Seeking an expatriate utopia, they discovered themselves instead "drifting like America itself," compulsively, violently finding their way to each other to enact what Fitzgerald imagined would be the final chapter of Western civilization.

NOTES

1. See Dijkstra's *Evil Sisters*, which traces the early twentieth-century obsession with women's theft and squandering of male vitality in both academic writing and popular culture. Dijkstra discusses Fitzgerald's earlier novel *The Beautiful and Damned* (1922) in detail, illustrating women's roles in the physical and social deterioration of wealthy heir Anthony Patch, along with works on this theme by Hemingway, Faulkner, and others (349-91).

2. Fitzgerald's own beating at the hands of police in Rome while he was preparing *The Great Gatsby* for publication exacerbated his hatred for Italians, whom he had earlier reviled as having "the souls of blackamoors [*sic*]" (Bruccoli, *Epic Grandeur* 211). "I hate Italy and the Italiens [*sic*] so violently that I can't bring myself to write about them for the *Post*—unless they'd like an article called 'Pope Siphilis the Sixth and his Morons,'" Fitzgerald wrote to Harold Ober (*Life in Letters* 94).

3. The first-person narrator version of the Melarky material encompasses the third (holograph) and fourth (typescript) drafts, composed between 1926 and 1929 (Bruccoli, *Composition* 38-58).

4. See also Fitzgerald, *Notebooks* 229, where the passage is repeated with "buck" changed to "a huge American negro."

5. In *American Body Politics: Race, Gender, and Black Literary Renaissance*, I have described this principle as "undifferentiated difference," the idea that, in sum, all blacks are alike. Whites routinely justified all forms of segregation on the grounds that blacks were as indistinguishable from each other physically, mentally, and morally as they were different in these regards from whites.

6. Canadian writer Morley Callaghan, who saw Fitzgerald the day after the incident, gave this secondhand account of the "nigger affair": "Last night [Fitzgerald] had been in a nightclub, he said. His wallet had been stolen. He had accused a Negro, the wrong Negro, and the police had come, there had been a humiliating scene, then long hours of police interrogation as he tried to undo his false accusation yet prove his wallet had actually been stolen. The accused man and his friends had

turned ugly. Dawn had come. The questioning, the effort to make an adjustment, had gone on, and he had despaired of ever getting out of the humiliating dilemma" (191-92).

7.   Bruccoli reports that Fitzgerald changed the name "Mitchell" to "Freeman" in *Tender* "because there actually was a Negro named Mitchell who operated a Paris club" (*Composition* 54). He assumes that Fitzgerald changed names to avoid confusion, but Fitzgerald was not only aware of this fact in his original fictional account, he makes Abe very explicit in his identification of Mitchell: "You know Mitchell the most important nigger in Montmartre." Thus it seems likely that the real-life Mitchell *was* the person involved and that Fitzgerald changed the name to "the prominent Negro restaurateur Freeman" for practical and artistic reasons. According to Fabre and Williams, Louis Mitchell had been the first to bring American jazz to Paris in 1917 with Louis Mitchell's Jazz Kings, playing at various Montmartre nightspots until the mid-1920s, when he opened an all-night place called Mitchell's American Restaurant (95, 98). The restaurant was at 35, or 37, rue Pigalle.

8.   Bricktop was less useful in this regard because of the way she catered to her largely white clientele with a down-home folksiness that contrasted with Baker's sexually aggressive primitivism. See Stovall (88-89) for Bricktop's appeal to white audiences. However, as Stovall reports, even Bricktop participated in interracial sexual fraternization in Paris, although not as publicly and spectacularly as Baker (74).

9.   See Bruccoli, *Composition* 119, for Fitzgerald's warning note to himself in one draft of *Tender* to "beware" a tendency to adopt Hemingway's style.

10. See "Absolution" in *The Stories of F. Scott Fitzgerald* 171.

11. Hemingway's theory in *A Moveable Feast* was that Fitzgerald's struggle with Zelda was his greatest obstacle to finishing the novel (180-81). If Fitzgerald himself came to believe that Zelda's competitiveness in establishing her own artistic career was an inhibiting factor in his rise to literary preeminence, this pronounced theme of female assault on masculine authority as a sign of an ongoing social catastrophe may have been one of the forms that his resentment took.

12. See Bruccoli, *Epic Grandeur* 206-7. See also Sklar 222-26 for a discussion of Fitzgerald's interest in Spengler.

13. In *The Rising Tide of Color against White World-Supremacy*, Stoddard insisted that "the wretched Versailles business will have to be revised" to avoid a series of "cataclysms which will seal the white world's doom" (307).

14.   Fitzgerald uses this term to describe Dick in a March 1934 letter to Edmund Wilson (Wilson, *Crack-up* 278).

WORKS CITED

Bruccoli, Matthew J. *The Composition of "Tender Is the Night": A Study of the Manuscripts.* Pittsburgh: U of Pittsburgh P, 1963.

———. *Fitzgerald and Hemingway: A Dangerous Friendship.* New York: Carroll and Graf, 1994.

———. *Some Sort of Epic Grandeur: The Life of F. Scott Fitzgerald.* New York: Harcourt Brace Jovanovich, 1981.

Bruccoli, Matthew J., and Jackson R. Bryer, eds. *F. Scott Fitzgerald in His Own Time: A Miscellany.* Kent, OH: Kent State UP, 1971.

Burton, Mary. "The Counter-Transference of Dr. Diver." *Journal of English Literary History* 38 (1971): 459-71.

Callaghan, Morley. *That Summer in Paris: Memoirs of Tangled Friendships with Hemingway, Fitzgerald, and Some Others.* 1963. Harmondsworth: Penguin, 1969.

Dijkstra, Bram. *Evil Sisters: The Threat of Female Sexuality and the Cult of Manhood.* New York: Knopf, 1996.

Donaldson, Scott. *Fool for Love: A Biography of F. Scott Fitzgerald.* New York: Congdon & Weed, 1983.

Douglas, Ann. *Terrible Honesty: Mongrel Manhattan in the 1920s.* New York: Farrar, Straus and Giroux 1995.

Fabre, Michel, and John A. Williams. *Way B(l)ack Then and Now: A Street Guide to African Americans in Paris.* New York: Center for American Culture Studies, Columbia U, 1992.

Fitzgerald, F. Scott. *The Basil and Josephine Stories.* Ed. Jackson R. Bryer and John Kuehl. New York: Scribners, 1987.

———. *F. Scott Fitzgerald's Ledger: A Facsimile.* Washington, DC: NCR/Microcard Editions, 1972.

———. *The Great Gatsby.* 1925. New York: Scribners, 1969.

———. *The Letters of F. Scott Fitzgerald.* Ed. Andrew Turnbull. New York: Scribners, 1963.

———. *A Life in Letters.* Ed. Matthew J. Bruccoli, with the assistance of Judith S. Baughman. New York: Scribners, 1994.

———. *The Notebooks of F. Scott Fitzgerald.* Ed. Matthew J. Bruccoli. New York: Harcourt Brace Jovanovich, 1979.

————. *The Stories of F. Scott Fitzgerald*. New York: Scribners, 1951.

————. *Tender Is the Night*. 1934. New York: Scribners, 1962.

————. *Tender Is the Night* (Facsimile). Vol. 4a, nos. 1 and 2. New York: Garland, 1990.

Hemingway, Ernest. *A Moveable Feast*. New York: Scribners, 1964.

Kennedy, J. Gerald. *Imagining Paris: Exile, Writing, and American Identity*. New Haven, CT: Yale UP, 1993.

Kuehl, John, and Jackson R. Bryer, eds. *Dear Scott/Dear Max: The Fitzgerald-Perkins Correspondence*. New York: Scribners, 1971.

Lewis, David Levering. *When Harlem Was in Vogue*. New York: Knopf, 1981.

Locke, Alain, ed. *The New Negro*. 1925. New York: Atheneum, 1983.

Pizer, Donald. "The Sexual Geography of Expatriate Paris." *Twentieth Century Literature* 36 (1990): 173-85.

Rose, Phyllis. *Jazz Cleopatra: Josephine Baker in Her Time*. New York: Random House, 1989.

Sklar, Robert. *F. Scott Fitzgerald: The Last Laocoön*. New York: Oxford UP, 1967.

Smith, Felipe. *American Body Politics: Race, Gender, and Black Literary Renaissance*. Athens: U of Georgia P, 1998.

Spengler, Oswald. *Decline of the West*. 2 vols. New York: Knopf, 1926.

Stavola, Thomas J. *Scott Fitzgerald: Crisis in an American Identity*. New York: Barnes and Noble, 1979.

Stoddard, Lothrop. *The Rising Tide of Color against White World-Supremacy*. New York: Scribners, 1920.

Stovall, Tyler. *Paris Noir: African Americans in the City of Light*. Boston: Houghton Mifflin, 1996.

Wilson, Edmund. *Letters on Literature and Politics, 1912-1972*. Ed. Elena Wilson. New York: Farrar, Straus and Giroux, 1973.

Wilson, Edmund, ed. *The Crack-up*. New York: New Directions, 1945.

THE INFLUENCE OF FRANCE ON NICOLE DIVER'S RECOVERY IN *TENDER IS THE NIGHT*

J A C Q U E L I N E   T A V E R N I E R - C O U R B I N

The influence of place on personality and attitude can be profound, particularly when it calls forth a person's inner nature, which may have been repressed by education and an uncongenial physical or social background. Numerous writers have dramatized the impact of the physical background and the intense effects it may have on the individual for both good and ill. One need only mention Albert Camus's *l'Etranger* and *le Malentendu* in which the presence or absence of the sun results in murder; André Gide's *L'immoraliste*, where Michel is deliberately responsible for the premature death of his wife, Marceline, because of his relentless search for the sun, the heat, and young boys; Kate Chopin's *The Awakening* where the sea, the heat, and the more relaxed aspects of nineteenth-century Creole society on summer vacation, when flirtation was an accepted form of diversion, bring out Edna's latent sensuality; and Jack London's Martin Eden who loses both joie de vivre and the will to live as a result of his being transplanted into the middle class and "intellectual elite."

Zola's belief that human beings are fashioned by their heredity and environment, both physical and psychological, and that circumstances often work as catalysts in the development of personality is clearly exemplified in these works, just as it is in *Tender Is the Night*, where we witness Nicole Diver's coming to term with psychological trauma partly as a result of life in a new, more sensual, and less morally repressive setting: France and, especially, the Côte d'Azur. France offers Nicole a society which accepts sexual desire as a normal fact of life, and deals with it in practical terms, not as something to be ignored or covered up with layers of false pretenses, and provides her with an intelligent and self-disciplined man who does not question his own physical desires and faces problems without evasions. This is not to say that French society in the 1920s was more immoral or tolerant than any other society, be it American or Swiss (to name the others which had an impact on Nicole). Rather, it was less evasive when confronting realities linked to sex, whether in its acceptance or its condemnation, and did not believe in "the essential goodness of people" nor "crooned falsely," like "generations of frontier mothers . . . that there were no wolves outside the cabin door" (*Tender* 117). Moreover, Provence and the Côte d'Azur offer a hedonistic background and erotic incidents which nudge Nicole to recovery by bringing her closer to a simple acceptance of human nature. The hot sensuality of the Mediterranean, so sharply described by Fitzgerald, and even more so by André Gide and Albert Camus, allows Nicole to come to terms with her own sensuality and with the conflict between amoral sexual desire and a late puritan background that denies its existence.

Critics often tend to blame Nicole for Dick Diver's decline into obscurity and mediocrity, finding its causes both in his yielding to the corrupting influence of her money and in his doctor/husband relationship with her.[1] Fitzgerald, of course, repeatedly provides ammunition for such a reading, even having, at one point, Nicole wonder whether she might be responsible for having ruined Dick (267); but there is little need to blame Nicole for Dick's degeneration. His own deep-seated psychological problems, added to his self-indulgence, his excessive self-confidence, and his "genteel" upbringing are enough to account for it. Both Nicole and Dick come into their own, asserting their true selves, and Nicole is no more the cause of Dick's degeneration than Tommy Barban is the reason for her own recovery. Her involvement with Tommy Barban is a symptom of her recovery, just as Dick's pursuit of Rosemary is an indication of his loss of self-control. Indeed, Nicole is a far stronger and more complex character than she is usually given credit for. She is inherently strong and a natural survivor who sank into neuroticism as a result of one ugly incident and the conspiracy of silence surrounding it on the part of both her family and her doctors. In fact, one might argue that Nicole recovers in spite of the psychiatrists rather than because of them, with the French background acting as a stimulus and contributing factor to her recovery.

Nicole is both simple and deep, a primal force belonging to the sun and sea of warm climates which was tamed, blindfolded, and locked up for years in "Victorian side chambers" (143).[2] Her natural closeness to nature is epitomized by her "lovely grassless garden" and the house "from which it flowed and into which it ran, on two sides by the old village, and on the last by the cliff falling by ledges to the sea" (25). Both garden and house are an outgrowth of natural needs instead of a construction of the mind. They melt into nature and the old village—"the exterior walls . . . untouched so that from the road far below it was indistinguishable from the violet gray mass of the town" (26)—and into a past solidly grounded in the earth. There is nothing modern, flashy, or artificial about either. The wonderful Mediterranean garden is untamed, hard with rocks and dryness, but rich with the bright colors of flowers, and inhabited by small animals—pigeons, rabbits, and a parrot. Nicole belongs here, far more than in the world of mental illness embodied by the sanatorium, in the glitzy and superficial world of her sister, or in the more complicated intellectual world of Dick.

Nicole is a commonsensical, perceptive, sensual, and passionate woman who is, by nature, happy and satisfied and has no interest in glibness and social pretense;[3] her down-to-earth awareness is illustrated time and again in the novel. When Dick is trying to pretend that he is not attracted to her, she brings him right back to reality in "succinct Chicagoese": "Bull! . . . You don't think I've got any common sense—before I was sick, I didn't have any, but I have now. And if I don't know you're the most attractive man I ever met you must think I'm still crazy. It's my hard luck, all right—but don't pretend I don't know—I know everything about you and me" (*Tender* 154).

She knows from the outset that Tommy Barban is in love with her—"She knew, as she had always known, that Tommy loved her; she knew he had come to dislike Dick, and that Dick had realized it before he did. . . ." (276)—and, in her certainty, she has no need to verify it through action. When she first sees Rosemary, her instinct tells her that trouble is afoot: "Yes, she's lovely, but there can be too many people" (162). She also knows immediately that Rosemary wants Dick—"Oh, she chose him, and Nicole, lifting her head saw her choose him, heard the little sigh at the fact that he was already possessed" (19-20)—and that Dick has fallen in love with Rosemary and keeps lying about it, just as she later knows that he is flirting with some of his female patients, such as the "flirtatious little brunette" whom he kissed in "an idle, almost indulgent way" (187) while giving her a ride into Zurich.

She confronts Dick's lies concerning his aimless philandering, his dismissal of his accuser as a "mental patient," and his claim that his flirting with the brunette is a delusion of Nicole's, by accurately pointing out that the lying is "an insult to [her] intelligence" and that "[i]t's always a delusion when [she] see[s] what [he doesn't] want [her] to see" (189-90). Her crashing the car is a loss of control and an exaggerated reaction of anger at being blatantly taken for a blind idiot more than it is a sign of neurosis.

In every way, Nicole is the opposite of Dick. Despite his learning and protectiveness, he is elusive, charming, impalpable, like an "easily forgotten dream"—an organizer "of private gaiety, curator of richly incrusted happiness" (76)—and, as soon as his charm loses its edge, he is quickly rejected by all the people for whom he gave "carnivals of affection" (27), all those for whom he put on practically "the best show in Paris" (72). Ironically, his performance is both brought to light and shattered by his emotional involvement with another entertainer. Unlike him, Nicole does not naturally live in a world of illusions, and she tends to confront her problems head on, very much like Tommy Barban, when she is not hindered by ignorance, family, and doctors. Her relationship with Tommy reveals the *real* Nicole and suggests that, had she not been kept in the dark as to the amoral nature of sexual desire at the time of the rape/incest, she would probably have been able to handle the trauma and come to terms with it.

Tommy, "less civilized [superficially], more skeptical and scoffing" (19)—more French than American—embodies a more Latin attitude toward life, harboring fewer illusions about the essential innocence and goodness of people, and believing in the curing of emotional ills through "physical therapy." Indeed, Tommy suffers for years from his unrequited love for Nicole, but does not drown his pain in a bottle like Abe North and Dick Diver. Instead, he deals with it in a direct and effective way: by externalizing it and fighting it out of his system in a real war, rather than by destroying himself in an internalized war. The sex/warfare correlation here is simple and harmonious: "When I'm in a rut I come to see the Divers, because then I know that in a few weeks I'll want to go to war" (30). Far from being stupid or uneducated, Tommy accepts the world as it is and does not need to re-create it. He is sure of his identity, knows his strengths, wants Nicole for herself, not for her money or her social position, and loves her for what she is—a beautiful crook with white eyes—not for what she needs. He recognizes Nicole as a basic force and promises to deal with her in a basic way:

> "It's very hard taking care of white eyes—especially the ones made in Chicago."

"I know all the old Languedoc peasant remedies." (295)

This reference to "peasant remedies" brings up once more an underlying theme in the novel—that of the essential nature of people coming to the fore. When Dohmler first hears of the rape/incest, he sharply applies the epithet of "Peasant" to Mr. Warren in condemnation (129). When Nicole feels Dick escaping her in the early stage of their relationship, she is tempted to tell him "how rich she [is], what big houses she live[s] in, that really she [is] a valuable property"—making "herself into her grandfather, Sid Warren, the horse-trader. But she survive[s] the temptation to confuse all values . . ." (143). Her world is falling to pieces, and even though there seems to be "no home left to her, save emptiness and pain" (143), she does have the strength of her grandfather and the discernment to know that buying love, or attempting to do so, is not an acceptable solution. When she finally takes control of her own destiny, she accepts her heritage and voices her choice in terms of heredity: "[B]eing well perhaps I've gone back to my true self— I suppose my grandfather was a crook and I'm a crook by heritage . . . better a sane crook than a mad puritan" (292-93). The very words she uses link madness to puritanism (a relationship of cause and effect which works both ways) and sanity to an acceptance of reality and, in particular, evil. This "peasant" nature clearly entails a certain vitality and strength, and it is partly Dick's and the other psychiatrists' lack of recognition of it in Nicole which brings about improper therapy. Equating "peasant blood" with "big thighs and thick ankles" (185), Dick does not recognize it in Nicole's startling beauty and apparent vulnerability; nor does he see that, like her father, she could virtually walk off her deathbed and take "punishment . . . on every inch of flesh and spirit" (185), as long as the punishment was clear to her.

This is why Tommy's primitivism suits her, for, unlike Dick's "kindness," it does not do violence to her nature. He does not want to change her or control her, tame her or bully her. If there is combat between them, it will be fought in the open, not in the unconscious by controlling her self-image. With Tommy, Nicole is "ever nearer to what she ha[s] been in the beginning, prototype of that obscure yielding up of swords that [is] going on in the world about her" (298). Fittingly their first sexual encounter takes place in a setting of almost ascetic simplicity. However, it is not the severity of moral convention but the starkness of nature which needs no frills to perform the most basic and natural of all acts—a small shore hotel at the foot of the Corniche on a blunt peninsula overlooking the shiny Mediterranean: "Their room was a Mediterranean room, almost ascetic, almost clean, darkened to the glare of the sea. Simplest of pleasures—

simplest of places" (294)— "a wonderful room [according to Nicole] . . . like the bare tables in so many Cézannes and Picassos" (295). Nicole, indeed, proves to be an apt priestess in Tommy's pagan world. Her desire for him is purely erotic— "[she] did not want any vague spiritual romance—she wanted an 'affair'" (291)—and she prepares herself knowingly and carefully for love, bathing and anointing herself in a sensual way that takes the reader back to a time and place when society accepted the basic instincts of life and turned them into beauty and art. Throughout, it is Nicole who takes the initiative, even hurrying the outcome—"Have we *got* to go all the way to your hotel at Monte Carlo" (294)—and it is with relief that she welcomes his nonintellectualization of their passion: "Tangled with love in the moonlight, she welcomed the anarchy of her lover. . . . Still attuned to Dick, she waited for interpretation or qualification; but none was forthcoming. Reassured sleepily and happily that none would be, she sank low in the seat and drowsed . . ." (298). This straightforwardness and honesty about physical needs corresponds far more to the French than to the American society of the 1920s, and Jean Bessière is right when he writes that the "Riviera of Tom is different from that of the expatriates; unlike theirs, it is a place of sensual pleasure where Nicole's rebirth is possible without any brutality or any romantic illusions. Tommy succeeds where Dick failed, in loving a woman without controlling her or becoming dependent on her."[4]

While Nicole's upbringing and background helped her develop strength and self-discipline, it also crippled her emotionally and prevented her from developing the simple acceptance of sexuality which her happy, relaxed, and sensual nature needed. As the granddaughter of a robber baron who made his fortune ruthlessly, survived, and prevailed in a world of predators, she was prepared for a harsh world where the strong survive and control the weak. Fitzgerald clearly foreshadows her future recovery in his description of her background:

> For her sake trains began their run at Chicago and traversed the round belly of the continent to California; chicle factories fumed and link belts grew link by link in factories; men mixed toothpaste in vats and drew mouthwash out of copper hogsheads; girls canned tomatoes quickly in August or worked rudely at the Five-and-Tens on Christmas Eve; half-breed Indians toiled on Brazilian coffee plantations and dreamers were muscled out of patent rights in new tractors—these were some of the people who gave a tithe to Nicole. . . . (55)

This naturalistic passage establishes a background of ruthlessness and strength where the deterministic law of the survival of the fittest prevails. Moreover, the education received by Nicole and Baby was one of strict discipline, which hardly encouraged softness or self-indulgence; witness Baby who, suffering from appendicitis, was forced to dance all night at a court ball in Berlin, with an ice pack strapped on her stomach under her gown, because she had three royal princes on her dance card. Their mother was indeed another type of frontier mother who, instead of protecting her children from reality, hardened them to ensure that they would be able to handle any challenge. Nicole was thirteen at the time of Baby's stoic endurance of pain at the ball and, at that age, could not but have also felt the effect of her mother's iron hand. Mrs. Warren was very much like Mrs. Speers, who, by not sparing Rosemary, had made her hard and taught her self-control.

However, this education had one blind spot: sex. Mr. Warren's blindness to the facts of life and his self-delusions are astounding. This man finds himself with a daughter of thirteen[5] when his wife dies and, somehow, considers her a baby: "After her mother died *when she was little* she used to come into my bed every morning, sometimes she'd sleep in my bed. I was sorry for *the little thing*" (129; emphasis added). He clearly refuses to acknowledge that she is turning into a young woman and that being repeatedly in bed with a beautiful teenage daughter is, at best, unhealthy and a way of tempting fate. This sublimation of physical attraction into fatherly love and mother substitution seems complete and sanctioned by a puritan society fundamentally evasive where sex is involved:

> "[W]henever we went places in an automobile or a train we used to hold hands. . . . We used to say, 'Now let's not pay any attention to anybody else this afternoon—let's just have each other—for this morning you're mine.' . . . People used to say what a wonderful father and daughter we were—they used to wipe their eyes. We were just like lovers—and then all at once we were lovers—and ten minutes after it happened I could have shot myself." (129)

The incest/rape was the natural consequence of a self-delusional blindness to the presence of physical urges. Clearly what was wrong was not the existence of a basically amoral instinct shared by the whole of humanity—the mutual attraction of a strikingly handsome man of forty and a seductive young woman—but the ignoring of that physical reality as well as the indulging of it under the cloak of an ideal father/daughter relationship. Warren should have known better than to pretend for several years that the normal impulses of nature did not exist, while putting both himself and Nicole in high-risk situations which could only lead to a catastrophe sooner or later. Feeling sexual desire is uncontrollable; putting oneself in situations where one will almost assuredly yield to it is controllable. The burden of responsibility is squarely on Warren's shoulders and on a society which pretends that amoral sexual desire is not a fact of life.

This is the reality which brought about Nicole's psychological breakdown, and this is the reality she must learn to accept if she is to get well, further denial not being the way to psychological health. Unfortunately, avoidance of the real issue is what Nicole gets from everyone. Instead of talking to her and assuming the responsibility for the act, her father pretends nothing happened, and believes that she is still "the same loving *little girl*" to him (126; emphasis added), who tells him "Never mind, never mind, Daddy. It doesn't matter" (129). But it mattered, and pretending it did not was the straightest road to neurosis. Her sister is kept in the dark, and, having no way of understanding what is going on, she keeps blundering and treating Nicole as if she were insane. The doctors who treat her in America are not told the truth; neither are Doctor Dohmler and Franz. Essentially, Warren tries to pass on his problem to them without giving them the means to solve it, and it is only because Dohmler and Franz realize that they have not been told the truth that he finally acknowledges it. Their early diagnosis is correct: "La peur des hommes est un symptôme de la maladie, et n'est point constitutionnelle" (128). Unfortunately they too reinforce denial, and Dick does the same thing throughout his marriage to her.

Nicole needed a dose of common sense; instead she got rhetoric and denial.[6] The psychiatrists insist she not see her father for at least five years and tell her that her duty is now to herself, a wonderfully empty phrase given the situation. Despite her illness, Nicole well knows she is not being told something important, as evidenced in her letters to Dick:

> Last year or whenever it was in Chicago when I got so I couldn't speak to servants or walk in the street I kept waiting for some one to tell me. It was the duty of some one who understood. The blind must be led. Only no one would tell me everything—they would just tell me half and I was already too muddled to put two and two together. . . . I grew sicker and there was no one to explain to me. (122)

> Here I am in what appears to be a semi-insane-asylum, all
> because nobody saw fit to tell me the truth about anything. (123)

Having to deal with the doctors' "harping constantly" on the problem that
brought her to the clinic but not giving her the tools to understand it and
solve it, she keeps yearning for her father. Subconsciously and confusedly,
she realizes that he is the reality she must come to terms with and that she
will never get well without him: "I will be here always on this green hill.
Unless they will let me write my father, whom I love dearly" (122).

The words that escape her in the bathroom—after the violent murder
of Peterson in Rosemary's room and the sight of the bedspread with blood
on it have triggered a temporary relapse—suggest that Nicole would have
been able to deal with what had happened between her and her father, if
only it had been confronted openly:

> "—it's you come to intrude on the only privacy I have in the
> world—with your spread with red blood on it. I'll wear it for you—I'm
> not ashamed, though it was such a pity. On All Fools Day we had a
> party on the Zurichsee, and all the fools were there, and I wanted to
> come dressed in a spread but they wouldn't let me—. . . ."

> ". . . —so I sat in the bathroom and they brought me a domino
> and said wear that. I did. What else could I do?" (112)

At the outset, it seems that she is willing to deal with reality, is not
ashamed and wants to accept her own responsibility: She wanted to wear
the spread. But her father's[7] and society's denials prevent her from assuming her identity: They gave her a domino and told her to wear it—that is,
they made her assume a fake identity, a farcical one, which allowed them
to continue in their own denials at the cost of her sanity. In essence, she
is kept in an infantile state by her father and society and never allowed to
grow up. At this stage, Nicole is no Hester Prynne; nor is her society
willing to let her wear her scarlet letter in public.[8] However, when Nicole
is finally ready to live on her own terms and is cured of believing in her
own insanity, she immediately lays claim to her sin and casually accepts
her incestuous past. When Dick typically tries to avoid playing a song in
which there is the word "father," she exclaims in exasperation: "'Oh, play
it! . . . Am I going through the rest of my life flinching at the word 'father'?"

(290). Of course, this does not mean that she is happy about the incest, merely that it is a reality and has been accepted as such.

Her assessment of what Dick and the psychiatrists have done for her— "take[n] power from [her], pervert[ed] and discipline[d] [her] natural tastes, civilize[d] and sterilize[d her]" (290)—is fairly accurate and corresponds to Tommy's own judgment:

> "Why didn't they leave you in your natural state? . . . You are the most dramatic person I have ever known. . ."

> ". . . All this taming of women!" he scoffed. . . . "Especially this 'kind' bullying—what good does it do anybody?" (293)

Actually, both Baby and Dick, consciously or unconsciously, come to question the value of the therapy applied to Nicole, which is one of overprotectiveness and dissimulation. When Dick assesses the case of a young American girl of fifteen who had just hacked off her hair with nail scissors, he indirectly describes the very way he and the psychiatrists have treated Nicole: They tried to protect her from "life's troubles and succeeded . . . merely in preventing [her] from developing powers of adjustment to life's inevitable surprises" (186)—and, in Nicole's particular case, from understanding life's past surprises. It is indeed a fine line between protecting wealthy patients from hurt and keeping them just sick enough so that they might remain "wealthy customers." As Franz fairly cynically tells Dick: "[W]e're a rich person's clinic—we don't use the word nonsense" (119)— that is, we don't tell it as it really is.

Nicole's relationship with Dick is also one of reliance, projection, and escapism—a relationship encouraged by Dick's own needs. Had he helped her to be self-reliant and accept the reality of amoral sexual desire, she would have had no need for him. This overprotectiveness toward Nicole is in fact deeply destructive and inhibiting, and, paradoxically, Dick's falling in love with Rosemary and losing his grip on the situation is probably the best thing that could happen to Nicole, in that it forces her to turn to her own resources and realize that "[she] had somehow given over the thinking to him. . . . Yet think she must; she knew at last the number on the dreadful door of fantasy, the threshold to the escape that was no escape. She knew that for her the greatest sin now and in the future was to delude herself. . . . Either you think—or else others have to think for you . . ." (289-90). Like most human beings, Nicole does what comes easiest and relies on Dick as long as he provides protection and a life-model to look up to and emulate. But it is clear that she will not follow him on the road to self-destruction: "If you want to turn things topsy-turvy, all right, but must your Nicole follow you walking on her hands, darling?" (162). As Robert Sklar notes, Dick's role "was to serve as a smokescreen to cover up the truth Nicole so tragically discovered, to divert energies and desires into harmless pursuits through the power of his romantic imagination" (283-84). Dick, indeed, keeps hiding reality from her and avoiding the real issues. During a luncheon in Zurich, "when a stranger stared at her from a nearby table, eyes burning disturbingly like an unchartered light," Dick explained cheerfully to Nicole: "He was just a peeper. . . . He was just looking at your clothes" (137). He ignores this opportunity to be honest and talk to her about lust, and opts instead for the easy way out for himself and, eventually, the hard way out for her. Their whole marriage functions on that basis: keeping her in the dark, psychologically dependent, in close touch for years with mentally sick people, and attributing often fairly normal, if perhaps exaggerated, reactions to mental illness. Her postnatal depression, for instance, is seen as a recurrence of her neurosis, and references to her father or to fathers in general are avoided.

It is hardly surprising that, surrounded by walls of deception and obfuscation, Nicole should periodically throw a fit in a subconscious attempt to break through to the truth and the light behind the walls. Kaethe Gregorovius is quite right when she says spitefully that "Nicole is less sick than any one thinks" but wrong in believing that she "cherishes her illness as an instrument of power" (239). Dick has set himself up as Nicole's life buoy. She has become used to relying on its support and has been told repeatedly that she needs it. It is only when it fails her that she realizes that she can swim and perhaps could all along. Indeed, "the source of her disintegration lies in the same dissimulation which [Dick's] social role was made to bolster" (Sklar 285). It is only by breaking through what Dick represents that she can get well.

For Nicole to discard the cloak of socially accepted puritan manners and values which have tamed and sterilized her, accept her physical self as well as her heritage without apologies, and break through to reality, a background which exalts instead of inhibits sensuality is required. Clearly the blinding sunlight of the Riviera is more appropriate for such an awakening than Chicago or a Swiss mental institution. Indeed, France and the Côte d'Azur offer Nicole a civilization which is in closer harmony with the body, where people live more openly, and where a romantic past permeates the consciousness. Amusingly, her emancipation is heralded by her throwing a jar of camphor rub to Tommy in a direct challenge to Dick's wishes. This gesture, reminiscent of Stanley Kowalsky's throwing a package of meat to Stella in *A Streetcar Named Desire*, suggests that "physical therapy" will now take precedence over psychotherapy.

Characteristically, everyday life in Latin civilizations includes much outdoor activity, owing to the climate and a more hedonistic tradition. People eat and drink outdoors, in sidewalk cafés and restaurants, or simply outside their homes, simultaneously enjoying the food, the weather, and the setting—various forms of sensual pleasures being thus enjoyed openly and at the same time. Rosemary is sensitive to this at the beginning of the novel: "It was pleasant to pass people eating outside their doors, and to hear the fierce mechanical pianos behind the vines of country estaminets. When they turned off the Corniche d'Or and down to Gausse's hotel through the darkening banks of trees, set one behind another in many greens, the moon already hovering over the ruins of the aqueducts . . ." (15). This teeming, more sensuous life is clearly connected with a past, "the ruins of the aqueducts," which lives on in terms of beauty. It is a life lived in closer harmony with the body and with nature, where the emphasis is on *being* rather than on *doing*, which disconcerts Americans. After lunch, Rosemary and her mother are both "overwhelmed by the sudden flatness that comes over American travellers in quiet foreign places. No stimuli worked upon them, no voices called them from without, no fragments of their own thoughts came suddenly from the minds of others, and missing the clamor of Empire they felt that life was not continuing here" (13). J. Gerald Kennedy appropriately sees this as evidence of an American indifference to place "endemic to the moneyed expatriate" and as "a crass preference for excitement" (202). But it goes deeper, to the core of two contrasting modes of life: the constant American need for activity (purposeless if need be) where doing inhibits contemplation, as opposed to the Latin need for periods of quiet and silence (even during the day) which allow for the simple sensual pleasures of being, feeling, and thinking. The first is exemplified by Dick's strategy of always keeping Nicole busy to prevent her from brooding and thinking (*Tender* 95). The second, however, is clearly congenial to Nicole, who is usually active but also gives an "impression of repose . . . at once static and evocative" (26) and who yearns for peace and warmth— "We'll live near a warm beach where we can be brown and young together. . . . I am here on this tranquil beach with my husband and two children. Everything is all right. . . . My toes feel warm in the sand" (161-62).

France also offers Nicole a setting where sensuality and physical attraction are traditionally expressed more openly. People *look* at one another; men express admiration for a woman's beauty, even if they have not been introduced. Women usually accept that admiration as a natural tribute (and worry when it is not forthcoming)—that is, people verify their images in the eyes and words of others constantly as in a mirror. In this respect, Nicole, Mary North, and Rosemary are contrasted with other North American women, in that instead of feeling threatened by it, they derive strength from this reflected image of themselves (53). Not being neurotic, Rosemary is more clearly conscious of this than Nicole, and relishes it: "[She] saw him look her over from head to foot, a gesture she recognized and that made her feel at home, but gave her always a faint feeling of superiority to whoever made it. If her person was property she could exercise whatever advantage was inherent in its ownership" (23). While she is still fragile, Nicole accepts it readily, as long as it is not directly sexual: At Voisins in Paris, she sees from the eyes of her friends "how beautiful she [is], [and] she thank[s] them with a smile of radiant appreciation" (52-53). But when the desire is clearly sexual and pointedly directed at her by an unknown man, instead of Dick or Tommy in whose love she feels secure, she shrinks back. This is the case when a French sergent-de-ville, an "ill-smelling, handsome man," wakes her up, looking for Abe North: "He showed his palms, puffing out his closed mouth. He had begun to find her attractive and his eyes flickered at her. . . . Nicole pulled her dressing gown closer around her and dismissed him briskly" (96-97). This apparently minor incident foreshadows Nicole's breakdown in the bathroom a few hours later and serves to remind her that she is a sexual object—the very thing she still has to come to terms with. Kennedy is indeed right in indicating that the more relaxed morality of the Paris section "allows the unconscious to manifest itself repeatedly" (217) and that the city of Paris is increasingly linked "with the eruption of forbidden impulses" (204).

The Riviera has the same effect, but Nicole reacts more positively, perhaps because of the different context—its greater openness and closeness to nature. The hot Mediterranean summer offers a naturally erotic setting: Emphasis is on the body and bodily awareness, sensations are overpowering; and the harsh sensuality of the Mediterranean, where the sun plays an almost phallic role, is virtually palpable through Fitzgerald's prose:

> . . . the Mediterranean yielded up its pigments, moment by moment, to the brutal sunshine.

> ... The water reached up for her,[9] pulled her down tenderly out
> of the heat, seeped in her hair and ran into the corners of her body. She
> turned round and round in it, embracing it, wallowing in it. (4-5)

Sensuality pervades Book One of *Tender Is the Night*—a sensuality which is essentially that of Provence, of Fitzgerald's sensitivity to it, and of his ability to make the reader and his characters receptive to it. Everything is described in terms of physical sensations, beauty, light, and life: the "old villas rott[ing] like water lilies among the massed pines," the "pink and cream of old fortifications," the "purple Alps that . . . lay quavering in the ripples and rings sent up by sea-plants in the shallows" (3); "the diffused magic of the hot sweet South . . . the soft-pawed night and the ghostly wash of the Mediterranean far below" (35), lying "awake, suspended in the moonshine. Cloaked by the erotic darkness . . ." (39). This setting, where life is vibrant and sensual, finally brings to the fore Nicole's repressed conflict and allows her to deal with it on her own terms and in harmony with nature.

Again, an apparently minor incident of a sexual nature acts as a catalyst for Nicole's final emancipation, epitomizing the simple eroticism of the Mediterranean. She overhears a conversation between two gardeners:

> "I laid her down here."
>
> "I took her behind the vines there."
>
> "She doesn't care—neither does he. It was that sacred dog. Well,
> I laid her down here—"
>
> "You got the rake?"
>
> "You got it yourself, you clown."
>
> "Well, I don't care where you laid her down. Until that night I
> never even felt a woman's breast against my chest since I married—
> twelve years ago." (277)

This is the first time Nicole hears the principle of basically amoral sex voiced openly—sex not associated with love or romance but with simple physical pleasure—and in a non-threatening manner since it is not aimed at her, in dramatic contrast with the French sergent-de-ville episode.[10] She is merely a bystander who is offered an insight into a simple man's world where sex is natural and uncomplicated; and she is the one who establishes the link with herself and her own needs: "It seemed all right what they were saying." This episode functions as a green light to Nicole's already well-advanced eman-cipation and verifies the "rightness" for her of an affair with Tommy Barban: "She reasoned as gaily as a flower, while the wind blew her hair until her head moved with it. Other women have had lovers. . . . Why shouldn't I?" (276-77). Indeed, an intense, completely erotic and nonromantic sexual experience is in harmony with the white sun, the burning beach, and the beautiful and stark nature of Provence, away from the complicated and intellectual world of Dick Diver, which dissolves like fog in the blinding sunlight. An elemental physical response following simple psychological roadways is the path to mental health for Nicole, and Tommy Barban is the proper guide into this new pagan, primitive, and, at the same time highly civilized, world.

It is a world where sexual matters are seen for what they are and are neither shunned nor ignored. Nicole has no problem accepting Tommy's past affairs and sees the situation clearly: She is "glad he [has] known so many women, so that the word itself mean[s] nothing to him; she [will] be able to hold him so long as the person in her transcend[s] the universals of her body" (296). Both she and Tommy also accept perfectly casually the intrusion of a group of "poules" wanting to wave good-bye to their sailors from the bedroom where they have just made love for the first time. While two American women sitting on the balcony below are trying to talk the matter "out of existence," whether because they do not want to spoil their economical holiday, as Tommy surmises, or because they are too puritan to accept what is going on at face value and be amused by it, Tommy matter-of-factly compares the quality of the "poules" with that with which he is himself familiar: "One would think with their pay they [the sailors] could find better women! Why the women who followed Korniloff! Why we never looked at anything less than a ballerina!" (296). This attitude is worlds removed from that of Dick Diver, who pretended that the man in Zurich was merely looking at Nicole's clothes.

The French setting (including in particular Paris and the Côte d'Azur) and a "Frenchman"[11] have much to do with Nicole's recovery in that they allow and encourage her true nature to reveal itself. It probably also had a strong influence on F. Scott Fitzgerald, as evidenced by the complexity of *Tender Is the Night* and its greater sensuality in comparison with his earlier fiction. The complexity of its psychological revelation places it in a class with French works such as François Mauriac's *Thérèse Desqueyroux* and with Camus's, Gide's, and Proust's novels, some of its more challenging aspects probably finding their origins in Fitzgerald's unconscious rather than in his conscious mind—in his reluctant awareness that Zelda, like Nicole, might well have been better off with a man like Edouard Jozan, the French pilot with whom she had fallen in love, than with himself. Fitzgerald's receptivity to the atmosphere of life in France, and in particular that of the more relaxed and sensual Côte d'Azur, is evidenced by the sensual beauty of the descriptions, and one cannot but wonder at the extent of its influence on Fitzgerald's own art and vision of life.

NOTES

1. The view that Nicole has used Dick until he is drained of energy, and that he has cured Nicole by an almost mystical transference of his own powers, was widespread among critics up to about fifteen years ago. See, for instance, and among many, Bruccoli (96, 132) and Savage (150). More recently, however, the characters are no longer seen in black and white, Nicole as selfish and destructive and Dick as self-denying. See, for instance, Coleman, Dudley, and Tavernier-Courbin.
2. Interestingly, this expression is used by Fitzgerald at a time when Nicole is tempted to use her money to seduce Dick while he is visiting her at the Swiss clinic: ". . . for a moment she made herself into her grandfather, Sid Warren, the horse-trader. But she survived the temptation to confuse all values and shut these matters into their Victorian side-chambers. . . ." This horse-trader self—the hard, down-to-earth self which deals with realities instead of pretenses—is Nicole's core and that which will allow her to recover and prevail. It is the self she will claim as her heritage when she recovers her mental health. "Tamed" refers to Tommy's derisive comment at the beginning of his affair with Nicole: "All this taming of women!" (293).
3. See, for instance: "She was smart as a whip and happy as the day is long. . . . [She] was the only one of our children who never cried at night" (126); "[Baby] had not liked Nicole's free and easy manner as a child" (157); and "[Nicole] knew few words and believed in none, and in the world she was rather silent, contributing just her share of urbane humor with a precision that approached meagreness" (26).
4. Bessière 158: "La Côte d'Azur de Tom diffère de celle des expatriés; elle est le lieu du plaisir où la renaissance de Nicole est possible, où l'amour peut exister hors de toute brutalité et de tout romanesque; Tom

réussit où Dick a échoué: aimer une femme sans la contraindre à rien ni devenir dépendent d'elle."

5. Fitzgerald indicates that Nicole is sixteen when her father takes her to Switzerland and that she was eleven when her mother died (126). However, according to Nicole, she was thirteen when she was in Berlin shortly before her mother died (55). The "rape" then may well have taken place when she was nearly nineteen.

6. It is noteworthy that some therapists are now willing to admit that "psychoanalysis is ultimately a system of defenses, bolstered by appropriate theories, whose real purpose is the avoidance, not the revelation of painful truths. . . . psychoanalytical practice serves to cement, not resolve, damage caused in childhood" (Miller 4).

7. Clearly, Mr. Warren pretended he had nothing to do with the problem: "[We] know Nicole had some shock and my opinion is it was about a boy, but we don't really know. Father says he would have shot him if he could have found out" (152).

8. While the sins of adultery and incest are of course different, it is not so much the nature of the sin that is important as the attitude of society toward sin. The contrast between the two characters and social stances is revealing of the evolution of American society from an early Puritan society that was intolerant of sin, condemned it violently, but was determined to expose it and reared its children in full awareness of it, to a more contemporary version of puritanism which is evasive and prudish, and attempts to keep its youth from even suspecting the existence of evil. While Hester challenges society from the beginning, wearing her scarlet letter as a badge of courage and independence rather than one of sin, Nicole can only do so after a long psychological struggle with a family and a native background which demand concealment.

9. This passage deals with Rosemary's sensations, but it might as well deal with Nicole's. Moreover, since Book One is largely narrated through Rosemary's eyes, the sensuality of the setting is logically presented through her perceptions rather than Nicole's.

10. The sergent-de-ville episode and the conversation overheard by Rosemary in the basement of Voisins, near the vestiaire, during which Dick and Nicole express their desire for each other, both have something faintly illicit about them.

11. Interestingly, European critics tend to see Tommy in a far more positive light than do American critics. For a sample of European

readings of Tommy see Bessière 143 and Poli, Le Vot, Fabre, and Fabre
310.

WORKS CITED

Bessière, Jean. *Fitzgerald: la vocation de l'échec.* Paris: Larousse, 1972.

Bruccoli, Matthew J. *The Composition of "Tender Is the Night": A Study of the
Manuscripts.* Pittsburgh: U of Pittsburgh P, 1963.

Coleman, Tom C. III. "Nicole Warren Diver and F. Scott Fitzgerald: The
Girl and the Egotist." *Studies in the Novel* 3 (1971): 34-43.

Dudley, Juanita. "Dr. Diver, Vivisectionist." *College Literature* 2 (1975): 128-34.

Fitzgerald, F. Scott. *Tender Is the Night.* 1934. New York: Scribners, 1962.

Kennedy, J. Gerald. *Imagining Paris: Exile, Writing, and American Identity.* New
Haven, CT: Yale UP, 1993.

Miller, Alice. *The Drama of the Gifted Child: The Search for the True Self.* New York:
Basic Books, 1994.

Poli, Bernard, André Le Vot, Geneviève Fabre, and Michel Fabre, eds. *Francis
Scott Fitzgerald.* Paris: Armand Colin, 1969.

Savage, D. S. "The Significance of F. Scott Fitzgerald." *F. Scott Fitzgerald: A
Collection of Critical Essays.* Ed. Arthur Mizener. Englewood Cliffs, NJ:
Prentice-Hall, 1963. 145-56.

Sklar, Robert. *F. Scott Fitzgerald: The Last Laocoön.* New York: Oxford UP, 1967.

Tavernier-Courbin, Jacqueline. "Sensuality as Key to Characterization in
Tender Is the Night." *English Studies in Canada* 9 (1983): 452-67.

PART IV

INTERTEXTUAL FRENCH CONNECTIONS

STRANGE FRUITS IN
THE GARDEN OF EDEN

"THE MYSTICISM OF MONEY,"
THE GREAT GATSBY—
AND *A MOVEABLE FEAST*

JACQUELINE VAUGHT BROGAN

Since its posthumous publication, *The Garden of Eden* (itself a highly problematic text) has proven equally problematic and enigmatic to Hemingway scholars.[1] Depending on the critic, the center of *Garden* has been described as the heroic development of David (one of the main characters), of David's liberation from binary sexual and cultural constraints, as a focus on sin, as an exploration of blackness (in the most culturally encoded of terms, "Africanism"), or as simply a text obsessed with the missionary position and its inversion.[2]

Given this critical complexity, I wish to begin with a couple of obvious facts in order to provide the background for what I believe is both a new and correct insight into the connection between Hemingway's *Garden of Eden*, including the internal "African Story," Fitzgerald's *Great Gatsby* (1925), and a relatively unknown essay, Harold Loeb's "The Mysticism of Money" (1922).[3] This already complicated intertextual matrix has important bearings on the equally complicated relationship of *The Garden of Eden* to Hemingway's concurrently written *A Moveable Feast*. Taken together, these connections point to extremely interesting issues which, as the conclusion shows, merit much more future attention, both in terms of these texts in particular and in terms of Hemingway's attitude toward these issues in general.

1.

First, I think it fair to say that Hemingway was continually revising or rewriting Fitzgerald. The multiple connections between the two authors may not have been quite so evident in their own times, but they certainly have become so in the latest of Hemingway criticism. Following the insights of Peter L. Hays, Michael S. Reynolds (*Hemingway's Reading* 26), and Abby H. P. Werlock, I want to suggest that Hemingway was in fact "rewriting" *The Great Gatsby* when composing his enigmatic, unfinished yet enticing novel, *The Garden of Eden*.

Perhaps the most obvious connection between these two novels is found in their mutual indebtedness to Joseph Conrad's *Heart of Darkness*. Fitzgerald's relation to Conrad in this regard is well known, including, as it does, the ambiguous moral relationship that the narrators Nick and Marlow have, respectively, to the main characters Gatsby and Kurtz.[4] In numerous ways *The Garden of Eden* appears equally indebted to *Heart of Darkness*. At the level of the main plot, at least, we witness Catherine descending into her heart of darkness and its "horror," much as we witness the same process in Kurtz. In the internal story, sometimes called "An African Story," we find ourselves specifically in the continent of Africa, moving deeper into the interior—a journey motivated in part by the quest for money and conquest (a subject to which I will return)[5] and recounted by a narrator, the young David Bourne, who notably develops once again a highly ambiguous moral relation to a leading male character—this time his father. In fact, as David thinks negatively about his father and Juma—*and* as he variously changes his stances or his modes of behavior toward them—the narrator emerges as a character who is uncannily like the narrator Nick, in relation to Gatsby, who in turn of course is much like the narrator Marlow in relation to Kurtz.[6]

To give but a brief example, midway through the story, midway through the hunt, David thinks about Juma and his father: "Now he knew they would kill the elephant and there was nothing he could do about it. He had betrayed the elephant when he had gone back to tell them at the shamba. They would kill me and they would kill Kibo too if we had ivory, he had thought and known it was untrue" (*Garden* 197-98). Here, as in *Gatsby* and

Heart of Darkness, we are confronted with the moral liability of the narrator—as well as that of the presumed subject of the story. This somewhat murky question of moral responsibility is a major crux of the main plot as well: Just what is David's responsibility to, and in, the degenerating relationship with his wife, Catherine, and her strange replacement in the figure of Marita? Although David at times tries to avoid apportioning blame to either Catherine or Marita, he most consistently avoids assigning blame to himself for his own actions, particularly in terms of his relationship to Marita. For example, we are told explicitly that "he thought of them [Catherine and Marita], not critically, not as any problem of love or fondness, nor of obligation nor of what had happened or would happen, *nor of any problem of conduct now or to come*, but simply of how he missed them" (132; emphasis added). Only a few lines later we are told that "He did not have to examine his conscience to know that he loved Catherine nor that it was wrong to love two women and that no good could ever come of it" (132). Much later in the novel, when Catherine's disintegration is so complete that she begins to appear both "dead" and "damned," David's sense of his own moral responsibility is truncated to the somewhat insipid thought that "he began to realize what a completely stupid thing he had permitted" (178).

Such attention to the moral culpability of the main character offers, of necessity, a very different interpretation of David's relation to Catherine and *that* relation's to his writing (or actually rewriting) the African Story at the end of the novel than either the positive reading given to us by James Nagel or the negative one by Steven Roe.[7] Although Nagel argues that the suffering David endures in the breakdown of his marriage to Catherine releases the repressed suffering he had experienced on the elephant hunt as a child, thereby enabling him to become a better writer, David appears primarily interested in pursuing his own desires (regardless of the consequences to other individual human beings), as is true of both Jay Gatsby and Kurtz in *Gatsby* and *Heart of Darkness* respectively. It would appear that David uses people for his own private ends, even for the production of his own writing. As he says at the moment he exhibits anger toward both Marita and Catherine, "I wish I'd never seen any of you. . . . You know it isn't true. *I'm only getting ready for work*" (*Garden* 194; emphasis added).

However, I wish to distinguish this more negative interpretation of David's moral culpability from that of Steven Roe, who regards David as exhibiting rather categorically a "despotic brutality" (53). David may be in part responsible for what happens in his marriage, but he is equally vulnerable as well—a fact which ultimately aligns David more with Fitzgerald's Gatsby than with Conrad's Kurtz. At the very least, if David uses Catherine and later Marita, he is equally used by them as well. He is at least partially correct when he says to Catherine, "You want everything so much and when you get it it's over and you don't give a damn" (196)—a remark that might apply equally well to Daisy Buchanan in relation to Jay Gatsby.

Nonetheless, the particular connections among *Heart of Darkness*, *Gatsby*, and *The Garden of Eden*, although important and intriguing, are ultimately not the most revealing facts about the thematics of Hemingway's novel. At the heart of the novel is the fact that if Catherine is jealous of David's writing (and particularly of the good reviews his writing receives) and utterly indifferent to his writing's making money, David is completely jealous of Catherine's having the money in their relationship and particularly desirous that his writing become commercially successful. When Catherine actually says "If the reviews had said it was worthless and it never made a cent I would have been just as proud and just as happy," David's internal response is "I wouldn't. . . . But he did not say it" (25)—a highly cryptic remark that he notably represses.

In fact, I wish to argue that *The Garden of Eden* is at least in part the culmination of Hemingway's long-held desire to outdo F. Scott Fitzgerald in writing "the great literature of money"—something which Fitzgerald had managed to do in the 1920s with *The Great Gatsby* and something which Hemingway would continually try to match, in varying degrees, from the early *The Sun Also Rises* (1926), through various short stories such as "The Snows of Kilimanjaro" (1936), to the doubly entwined late texts, *A Moveable Feast* (overt in its contempt for the damage money does to an artist) and *The Garden of Eden* (quite subtle in its indictment of the artist as a necessary participant in a money-making system). Although the subject of money was itself a popular topic during the 1920s (from the general Marxist movement through such particulars as Ezra Pound's "Hugh Selwyn Mauberly" [1920]), the specific provocation for this ongoing literary boxing match between Fitzgerald and Hemingway may well have been a now little-known, but then highly influential, essay by Harold Loeb entitled "The Mysticism of Money." It is an essay which rather surprisingly laments the lack of the great "literature of money" (while praising the output from various other media in this regard) as well as actually listing the basic characteristics that would typify this new literature (characteristics, I should add, that apply to *Gatsby*, to many of Hemingway's works, and certainly to *Garden*).[8]

Although I cannot prove conclusively that Hemingway read "The Mysticism of Money," the likelihood of his having done so seems almost certain for a number of reasons. We could begin with the sheer proximity of Fitzgerald and Hemingway in Paris in the mid-1920s, precisely when

Harold Loeb was editing the then-famous journal *Broom*. I cite the humorous and anecdotal evidence of this connection as articulated in Gertrude Stein's *The Autobiography of Alice B. Toklas*[9]: "In the meantime McAlmon had printed the three poems and ten stories of Hemingway and William Bird had printed In Our Time and Hemingway was getting to be known. He was coming to know Dos Passos and Fitzgerald and Bromfield and George Antheil and everybody else and Harold Loeb was once more in Paris" (205). Only a few paragraphs later Stein has "Alice" write that Stein and Hemingway "talked endlessly about the character of Harold Loeb" (206). However, for our purposes here, the importance of this connection between Loeb and Hemingway and between Loeb and Fitzgerald is not in Loeb's being the editor of *Broom* but rather in his being the author of what I think is one of the most important pieces published in it—"The Mysticism of Money."

In fact, among the numerous essays he published in *Broom*, "The Mysticism of Money" was one of Harold Loeb's personal favorites—so much so that one evening during his affair with Duff Twysden at St. Jean-de-Luz (an affair subsequently satirized by Hemingway in *The Sun Also Rises*), Loeb by his own account ran upstairs to get this particular essay to share with her. Specifically in the context of their discussing Hemingway and how hard he works, Loeb writes that "Wanting to show her [Duff] something I had done, I hurried upstairs two steps at a time and dug down in my trunk until I came upon the issue of *Broom* that contained 'The Mysticism of Money.'" Her subsequent response that the essay "'has a beautiful make-up'" was "not," Loeb reports, "the praise I wanted" (*Way It Was* 272-73).

As humorous as this anecdote may seem years later (as in "Come upstairs and I'll show you my essays"), "The Mysticism of Money" is actually a profoundly provocative essay published, notably, in 1922, the year Charles Scribner III says "Fitzgerald was just beginning to conceive" *Gatsby* (vii). Beginning with a citation from Nietzsche,[10] Loeb notes that

> "The prerequisite of all living things and of their lives is: that there should be a large amount of faith, that it should be possible to pass definite judgments on things, and that there should be no doubt at all concerning values. Thus it is necessary that something should be assumed to be true, not that it is true." This need has been satisfied in the past by what is termed religion. It is filled to-day in America by the *Mysticism of Money*. ("Mysticism" 117)

As the title of the essay implies, Loeb argues that in America, money has become "mystical," replacing the relation religion had to society at all levels in former times. While certainly more complex than I can convey here, Loeb's essay presents the following salient points: Whereas the art of Europe is in a "decadent" decline, America (in 1922) is "in the midst of a formative-creative art epoch" (115). Loeb then convincingly argues that money is "mystic" in America because "the validity of the money standard and the intrinsic merit of money making are accepted on faith, extra-intellectually," because "Business and state are now as closely knit as church and state in the middle ages," because in "national emergencies such as the late war, public opinion does not turn to teachers or statesmen, but to business men," and because—as may be obvious—the very founding of America was based on "one of the first modern business wars, 'no taxation without representation'" (118-19).

The intriguing extension Loeb draws from the preceding argument is that what we might now think of as capitalist production had in fact become the impetus for the great outpouring in America of art in the round, including the "great innovation" of "applied sculpture" in the "combining of movement and form"—by which he literally means the steam shovel, the gold dredge, and the threshing machine (120). As he notes, "Some of to-day's forms have, I believe, plastic import even judged statically as we judge an antique statue" (120). He equally embraces advertising (as did others, by the way) as serious art derived from the mysticism of money, praising both its visual and literary merits.[11] Other art forms he finds in America include "office buildings, lofts and apartment houses," also "factories, and bridges, aqueducts and tanks" (122-23). In a rather complicated move, Loeb finds jazz, as opposed to "genuine folk music" (124), equally indebted to the mysticism of money. What is curious about this stance is that Loeb sees the thriving American art epoch as one integrally (and positively) related to money as the inspiration, as well as the support, of art.

However, for our purposes, it is when Loeb turns to the art of writing that the essay becomes most interesting. First he notes that the mysticism of money has already affected American writing by changing the language to something "Vigorous, crude, expressive . . . resembling Elizabethan rather than Victorian English" (125). Second, he argues, a "new narrative technique has crystallized," the essential ingredient of which is "speed, accomplished by elimination of data which usually accounts for logical continuity"; and third, it has resulted in the creation of "types"—"Ignoring the European tendency of the last centuries, America has conventionalized several striking characters which can easily be recognized even though disguised by the borrowed, narrative or theatrical realism of Europe" (125-26). One can think of virtually every character in *Gatsby*, published only three years later, in this regard—from Jordan Baker to Myrtle Wilson, from George Wilson or Meyer Wolfshiem to the main characters themselves. Loeb's description of the "villain" proves especially intriguing in relation to the character of Jay Gatsby and his complicated relation to Tom and Daisy Buchanan: "More interesting than these [the heroes] are the villains. The fortune-hunter, [*sic*] slightly resembles Ulysses and Robin Hood. His enemies are the powers that be, and so he attacks the money system, exhibiting wonderful cunning to keep within the letter of the law. He is quite irresistible to the purer sex and usually pals with the villainess" (126).

However—and this is *crucial* to both *The Great Gatsby* and *The Garden of Eden*—Loeb insists that despite its obvious effects on writing in America, "*The Mysticism of Money has not as yet produced a literature*. No Shakespeare has emerged to bind together into a whole, the vigorous language, the speedy narrative form, and the conventionalized characters" (127; emphasis added). In fact, in this regard, Loeb's article seems to call for a great American prose writer, much as Emerson (from a very different mystical perspective) called for the great American poet in the preceding century. And it is to this call that I believe Fitzgerald responded, writing immediately thereafter the work we really can call "the great novel of money." Though I shall not belabor the point here, money *is* the plot, the heart, the compulsion, the mystique, the mysticism, the moral quandary of *The Great Gatsby*. It is even the sound of Daisy's voice. (As Gatsby tellingly notes, "Her voice is full of money" [106].) With Loeb's 1922 article in mind, and specifically with the narrative and stylistic strategies of the new American writing he outlines in mind, we can clearly see *The Great Gatsby* as Fitzgerald's answer to Loeb's call for the missing artistic link. Furthermore, Fitzgerald's response to "The Mysticism of Money" may well explain where he derived certain ideas or techniques that account for the radical differences between *This Side of Paradise* (1920) and *Gatsby*, the latter of which he himself described as a "consciously artistic achievement" (Scribner vii).

However, I should clarify, both for Fitzgerald's handling of the theme of money in *Gatsby* and for Hemingway's subsequent handling of this theme, that Loeb concludes this otherwise laudatory essay on the "mysticism of money" by noting that "the Mysticism of Money is shaken, due to moral grounds . . ." (130). Although Loeb is specifically referring to laborers who are "dispensed with" when their services are no longer required in the "law of supply and demand" (129)—a moral dilemma somewhat obliquely configured in *Gatsby*—it is ultimately Hemingway far more than Fitzgerald who relentlessly examines how the morality of the writer himself is shaken by participating in this very "mysticism."

2.

From the moment he first read *The Great Gatsby* (and for a number of different reasons, both professional and personal—including Fitzgerald's early monetary advantage over the young Hemingway's supposed poverty), Hemingway continually tried to outdo his literary opponent's achievement in answering Harold Loeb's call for the great literature of money. Hemingway's first reaction in this regard appears to have been the obvious denigration of Harold Loeb in *The Sun Also Rises* in the form of Robert Cohn. Subsequently the *subject* of money, particularly the supposed moral and creative impoverishment an artist faces when (like Fitzgerald, at least according to Hemingway) the artist writes *for money*, remains a recurrent and sensitive topic throughout Hemingway's corpus—from various essays and short stories (though most notably in "The Snows of Kilimanjaro") and subsequent novels including *Green Hills of Africa* (1935), *A Moveable Feast,* and certainly *The Garden of Eden.*[12] In fact, it is possible that Hemingway's reading of Fitzgerald's *Tender Is the Night* (1934)—another novel, notably, in which a woman's wealth is the downfall of a man—encouraged the quite vituperative accusations Harry Walden makes against his wife and her money in "The Snows of Kilimanjaro" (begun only a short time later). Although Hemingway had certainly indicted the pursuit of money itself in *Green Hills of Africa,* saying that "We destroy them [American writers] in many ways. First, economically. They make money. . . . they have to write to keep up their establishments, their wives, and so on, and they write slop" (23), it is not until "The Snows of Kilimanjaro" and then *The Garden of Eden* that he fully explores through a character's demise the moral quandaries or moral compromises that money entails for a writer. In this sense, of all Hemingway's works, *The Garden of Eden* provides the most compelling parallels to the demise of the main character in *The Great Gatsby.*

While the subject and pursuit of money is quite obviously germane to *Gatsby,* it may be less obviously so to *The Garden of Eden.* And yet from the beginning of the novel, when Catherine says "If you'd been a European with a lawyer my money would have been yours anyway" (27), to the end, when she justifies her burning of David's stories by saying she paid for them (220) and will also now reimburse him (226), money is a motivating factor for the characters' actions and decisions in a highly erotic, even "Africanized" world.[13] Notably, Marita (the outsider in the novel's ménage à trois who is called "Heiress" by

Catherine) "inherits" the role or function of being a wife as if it were money. As Catherine says to David at the first mention of marrying Marita:

> "I'm still your wife. . . . We'll start with that. I want Marita to be your wife too to help me out and then she inherits from me."
>
> "Why does she have to inherit?"
>
> "People make their wills," she said. "And this is more important than a will." (144-45)

Hemingway even suggests that the disintegration of Catherine's personality is somehow connected to her dispensing of money to David—although this suggestion remains quite tentative and very complicated.[14] When David remarks that she takes "wonderful care of everybody," Catherine responds, "I'm going to but I was so tired and there wasn't any time and I knew it would be so humiliating if the money ran out and you had to borrow and I hadn't fixed up anything nor signed anything and just been sloppy the way I've been" (163). Certainly the pursuit of money is at the heart of Hemingway's "inner story," perhaps with a rather obvious connection here to Fitzgerald's plot in *Gatsby* (and, behind that, to Kurtz's pursuit in *Heart of Darkness*), the elephant's tusks weighing an unusual "two hundred pounds apiece" (173), thereby making them not only valuable but also almost excessively phallic.

Similarly, like Fitzgerald's novel, Hemingway's (including the inner story) is constructed with characters who are clearly "types" in precisely the way Loeb called for—despite the fact that in some ways this novel could legitimately be called a psychological novel (rather than a novel of action). As enticing and enigmatic as David and Catherine may be, they certainly do not yield to us what we might call depth of character. Nor do Marita, the Colonel, the father, or even Juma (about whom the young David merely thinks, "If they kill him [the elephant] Juma will drink his share of the ivory or just buy himself another god damn wife" [*Garden* 181]). And although Catherine may certainly represent one manifestation of the "rich bitch" in both "The Snows" and *Gatsby*, it is quite notably David, as the older person, who also regards the sleeping Catherine as a "beautiful rumpled head that looked like an ancient coin lying against the white sheet . . ." (57).

Furthermore, in the novel itself Hemingway self-consciously has David describe the narrative device of "elimination" in a way quite reminiscent of Loeb's essay. While there is a larger context for both of these last points, including the influence of Gertrude Stein herself, Hemingway pointedly has David warn himself early in the novel to "Be careful. . . . it is all very well for you to write simply and the simpler the better. But do not start to think so damned simply. Know how complicated it is and then state it simply" (37). Perhaps even more to the point is that in the writing of the inner story, David "knew what his father had thought and knowing it, he did not put it in the story" (146-47).[15] Not only do these statements correspond to Loeb's description of the art of elimination, but they also describe Hemingway's own relation to both Loeb and Fitzgerald in the theme, techniques, and plot of *The Garden of Eden.*

The suggestion that *Eden* is intimately related to *Gatsby* as a contender for the great American novel of money becomes especially tenable if we consider *The Garden of Eden* and the concurrently written *A Moveable Feast* as complementary texts, in which one text frequently questions and undermines the terms of the other. In fact, Hemingway produced a really remarkable entwining of texts in which, in a Kierkegaardian fashion, *both* narratives may be seen as countertexts *to each other* and as simultaneous attempts to outdo Fitzgerald's success with *The Great Gatsby*—*The Garden of Eden* in a highly encoded and even private way and *A Moveable Feast* in a very overt and public way.[16]

3.

The concurrent writing of *A Moveable Feast* answers the nagging question of why, with *The Garden of Eden*, Hemingway was still trying to outdo Fitzgerald in writing the great literature of money so late in his life. Obviously, *Garden* is based in part on Hemingway's memories of his early years in Paris, as Carlos Baker (454-55) and others have pointed out. However, it is equally notable that in *Feast*, which Hemingway began to write concurrently with *Eden* over a number of years, the author's memories of those Paris years became particularly focused. Initially, *Feast* seems simply to set out to fill in the missing stories—the Paris stories—that Hemingway did not write during the "Paris Years," a period dominated by Ford Madox Ford, James Joyce, Gertrude Stein, Harold Loeb, and F. Scott Fitzgerald (to name only a few of the writers Hemingway denigrates in *Feast*). Most specifically, *A Moveable Feast* covers the years of Hemingway's apprenticeship as a writer that would culminate in his novel *The Sun Also Rises*, before his involvement with Pauline and breakup with Hadley. But it was also during those specific years that Loeb's ideas and Fitzgerald's novel were very much in the air, and it is thus quite significant that during that time Hemingway had tried to "outdo" Loeb (as well as Fitzgerald) by denigrating Loeb in the fictionalized Robert Cohn. Dwelling so intensely on those Paris years, while quite consciously writing a narrative in which he publicly creates himself as *the* great writer of the century, and a writer notably indifferent to or abhorrent of money, Hemingway simultaneously engaged in a more private battle involving the same issues in the unfinished *The Garden of Eden*.[17] As such, *Garden* is a novel that questions, undermines, or even exposes the narrator/author's quasi-ethical stance toward money, writing, and relationships in the companion and more public text.

Once observed, the interconnections between Hemingway's last two extended works, and between them and Fitzgerald's novel, are so numerous as to appear nearly inexhaustible. First, like *The Great Gatsby* and *The Garden of Eden*, *A Moveable Feast* is marked by narrative speed, by the creations of "types" (consider Hemingway's treatment of other major writers in the book, such as Gertrude Stein or Ford Madox Ford, of such minor characters as Blaise Cendrars—the "only poet" he knew and one with a "broken boxer's face" [81]—or Harold Stearns, "who would want to talk horses" [101], or of the "pilot fish" [207] at the end), and most certainly by elimination. Not only does he talk overtly about his theory of omission in relation to "Out of Season" (75), Hemingway's conclusion that "I worked well and we made great trips, and I thought we were invulnerable again" (211) is also itself a masterpiece of elimination, in which the real and traumatic breakdown of a marriage is silently evoked—much as the breakdown of David's future ability as a writer is evoked at the end of *Garden*. At least as edited, the final sentence, in which we find that David "wrote on a while longer now and there was no sign that any of it would ever cease returning to him intact" (247), certainly implies that his ability to be a successful writer is in fact doomed—as was Hemingway's marriage at the end of *A Moveable Feast*.

In addition to corresponding to the characteristics that Loeb had outlined for the new literature of money years earlier, at the level of plot, both of Hemingway's last works repeat, in varying ways, specifics from love triangles and interest in "bobbed hair" to lost manuscripts and the status of authorship in a capitalist system. In fact, the actual subject of money (in addition to writing and love) is a major theme running throughout *A Moveable Feast*. If Daisy's voice sounds like money in *The Great Gatsby*, an anonymous girl's face is as "fresh as a newly minted coin" (5) in the opening pages of *Feast*. Ultimately, the pollution of acquiring money proves to be the crux of *A Moveable Feast*—as it is in all the texts mentioned in this essay. In fact, the spectral subtext of *Garden* allows us to see the young Hemingway's "sin" in

Feast not as being his participation in the love triangle to which he obliquely refers at the end of the book, not as his betrayal of Hadley nor of his marriage vows, but precisely as being a participant (as in *The Garden of Eden*) in an exploitative capitalist economy by writing to make money. Although the older Hemingway claims that the younger Hemingway of the text "would be damned" if he would write a novel "because it was what [he] should do if we were to eat regularly" (76), he also has Evan Shipman late in the narrative voice the reality of the necessity of money: "The completely unambitious writer and the really good unpublished poem are the things we lack most at this time. There is, of course, the problem of sustenance" (146). This quasi–"double-take" on the subject of the writer's moral culpability or innocence is, of course, much akin to that recently explored by Robert Fleming in *The Face in the Mirror*.[18]

Conversely, the specter of an almost excessively macho and hetero-sexual "Hemingway" in *A Moveable Feast* allows us to see more precisely one of the other important facets of *The Garden of Eden*: namely, Hemingway's great anxiety about simply inverting sexual roles if, as in *Feast*, those roles seem almost doomed to ultimate failure. That is to say, if the excessively "masculine" Hemingway fails ethically in the narrative of *Feast*, it is equally true that his counterego in the far more sexually liberal and experimental figure of David Bourne fares no better. In fact, as James Phelan has convincingly argued, in most of Hemingway's texts there exist simultaneously an "authorial" presence and an audience undermining the "narrative" presence and audience in his works—an insight which has specific ramifications in terms of both *Feast* and *Garden*. Following Peter Rabinowitz in *Before Reading*, Phelan notes that "The narrative audience is the one implicitly addressed by the narrator; it takes on the beliefs and values that the narrator ascribes to it. . . . The authorial audience takes on the beliefs and knowledge that the author assumes it has, including the knowledge that it is reading a con-structed text" (5).

Phelan's observation exposes both the similarities and the compli-cated "countermoves" of the narrative structures of Hemingway's last two works. If in *A Moveable Feast*, we find an older (and presumably more moral) voice criticizing (while sympathizing with) a younger Hemingway's eth-ical choices and mistakes, there is from the beginning an "authorial" Hemingway outside the text who implicitly invites us to share in the knowledge that this supposedly ethical tale is very much a constructed text, not necessarily a genuine autobiography. In fact, in the preface, Hemingway stresses that fact and fiction are combined: "If the reader prefers, this book may be regarded as fiction. But there is always the chance that such a book of fiction may throw some light on what has been written as fact" ([ix]).[19] While possibly a defensive strategy, the preface nonetheless keeps the fictional construct of the work very much in focus, allowing us to suspect the older and wiser moral claims made by the "narrator" Hemingway. As a consequence, we remain doubtful about the accuracy of the older Hemingway's assessment that the younger Hemingway was merely "stupid" (72), merely a fool, and merely a victim of others' capitalist/sexual games.[20] When, at the end of the chapter entitled "A False Spring," the narrator/older Hemingway writes, "But Paris was a very old city and we were young and nothing was simple there, *not even poverty, nor sudden money*, nor the moonlight, *nor right and wrong nor the breathing of someone who lay beside you in the moonlight*" (58; emphasis added), the real ethical responsibility of the young Hemingway in the decisions that constitute Hemingway's actual life remain very murky, very undecidable from the narrative point of view. At the same time, these very issues appear intensely damaging and genuinely painful from the authorial point of view, in which Hemingway as the actual author seems acutely aware of the real "someone" he would really hurt in the very actions omitted from *A Moveable Feast*.

Similarly, in *The Garden of Eden*, the author outside the text appears to criticize the self-defensive and justifying posture of David, who is, in turn, telling—or "writing"—the story of his own earlier years. Only, in the case of *Garden*, the author and narrator (and, therefore, the "authorial audience" and "narrative audience") are the same—entirely divorced from the David who, as internal author, remains quite conscious of the fictional status of his writing and of the fictional and sexual reversals of gender in which he and his wife engage. Significantly, the ménage à trois and burned manuscripts of *Garden* repeat, but in radically different forms, real events in Hemingway's life that may themselves have been somewhat fictionally shaped in *A Moveable Feast*, thus making the question of moral liability and/or culpability all the more complicated, undecidable, *and* at the same time *critical*. From such specifics to the larger themes, the narrative structures of *Feast* and *Garden* are simultaneously similar, entwined, and radically different.

To add to, or alter, Rabinowitz's theory, it seems that *The Garden of Eden* does employ a two-tiered audience of the kind he notes. While we cannot quite call it a "narrative audience," there is an imaginary audience, supposedly supportive of David, and an "authorial audience," quite mindful of David's ethical failures. However, in *A Moveable Feast*, we have a three-tiered audience: an "internal audience" sympathetic to the young Hemingway's naïveté, a "narrative audience" sympathetic to the older Hemingway's rejection of money and infidelity, and an "authorial audience" highly suspicious of the

narrator's moral stance since, *as author*, Hemingway is continuing to participate in the very structures (including monetary structures) his older Hem-
ingway-as-narrator denounces.

Thus, as opposed to other critics' interpretations with which I began,
it seems to me that the "center" of *The Garden of Eden* is, especially in relation
to *A Moveable Feast*, not a center at all, but rather a dialogue about the ethical
status of authorial production—including the writing of gender and race—
and its complicity in a monetary or capitalist and even racist structure, with
precisely the moral quandaries Loeb noted in his 1922 essay "The Mysticism
of Money."[21] Specifically in relation to the economic positions of different
races in America, Harold Loeb had earlier concluded his provocative essay
with the indictment that "the Mysticism of Money is shaken, due to moral
grounds" (130)—a fact that *The Great Gatsby*, *The Garden of Eden*, and *A Moveable
Feast* make abundantly clear.

In this sense it is important to stress that as texts "countering" each
other, the last two major works of Hemingway's career are not simply
oppositional—never simply *Either/Or*.[22] Both *Garden* and *Feast* strongly
suggest that money corrupts. Both question the position of a corrupting
capitalism within a larger heterosexual economy. While at first glance,
Garden dramatically appears to critique, even totally dismantle, the "macho"
stance of *Feast* (since, in the economic and sexual exchange between
Catherine and David we find a writer completely at odds with the
"Hemingway" of the countertext), both David and the "young" Hemingway of *A Moveable Feast* suffer ironic emasculations of sexual and authorial
prowess and prominence. Taken together, these two late works may well
show Hemingway's enormous anxiety about instituting any "other" sexual/
textual/political structures in *The Garden of Eden*, even as he was posturing
those very structures in the figure of the young (and somewhat destructive)
Hemingway of *A Moveable Feast*.

Hence, although Steven Roe may well be right in asserting that
Catherine of *The Garden of Eden* is closest to Hemingway and his moral
concerns (54), she also represents an irresolvable dilemma—both in terms
of the novel and in terms perhaps of Hemingway himself. Victim of the
macho world of authorship figured in *A Moveable Feast*, Catherine can be
neither the writer nor the dispenser of money. The larger culture undermines
her position as a woman, as both writer and owner. But we should note that
her attempts at a differently gendered—and perhaps even racial—performance from that macho world also fail.[23] If her ethical position counters
that of *A Moveable Feast* (an admittedly very phallic text overwriting all sorts
of unethical dealings, from the opening scene in which upon simply seeing

a "girl . . . in the cafe," the young Hemingway thinks, "I've seen you, beauty, *and you belong to me now*" [5-6; emphasis added], to the implied infidelity at the end of the novel), Catherine's countermoves in a different sexual politics and economy are not successful.[24] She remains, as does Caddy in Faulkner's *The Sound and the Fury*, what recent feminists might call an "empty cipher." These texts cannot, then, be seen in terms of "Either/Or." Both Catherine and the "young Hemingway" of *A Moveable Feast* fail. And David fails, as does the "older Hemingway," and as does the "authorial" Hemingway, the one writing both the public and private narratives tracing problematics defined in the "Mysticism of Money."

In sum, these two late works of Hemingway's career suggest that his deepest anxiety was not guilt over sexual choices made in his life, or fear of either homosexuality or experiments in gender roles, but rather the fear that the act of writing (whether of fact, fiction, or gender performance) is itself "the sin." For at its heart, even the fictional act *of writing oneself into a writer of fiction*—for that is very much the "story" Hemingway set out to construct for himself—is deeply involved with and even constitutive of a deeply sexist and perhaps equally racist capitalist structure. The "sin," both for David and in different ways for the "young" Hemingway, is to have written at all. Both *A Moveable Feast* and *The Garden of Eden* are marked by the radical failure of writers intricately involved in an unethical system they both need to create themselves as writers and help to create by producing works for consumption.

I do not mean to imply, however, that the texts fail. They are, in fact, infinitely fascinating, and worthy of much more attention than I have given here. I simply mean, as in the Kierkegaardian tradition I have invoked, that we find no final answers in the "strange fruits" motivating and moving Hemingway's last works. To see the interplay between these two texts in terms of issues raised in other texts earlier in the century is to see behind them an Ernest Hemingway who admittedly fits, initially, a highly distorted stereotype of "Papa": Hemingway certainly was engaged in a literary boxing match in *A Moveable Feast* in which he was trying to knock out every twentieth-century contender, and most particularly F. Scott Fitzgerald. But the interplay between the texts also allows us to see more clearly a Hemingway we have only recently begun to see—a Hemingway deeply involved with ethical issues, incessantly questioning (not asserting) the codes of values inherent in his culture, in his own writing, and perhaps in his own personal life. In the end, I am forced to conclude—however ironically—that Hemingway really was his best ethical self when writing, especially in the complicated "commentaries" *The Garden of Eden* and *A Moveable Feast* make about the act of writing itself, in a culture so relentlessly committed, as Harold Loeb rightly noted, to valorizing "the mysticism of money."[25]

NOTES

1. I will be citing the published text of *The Garden of Eden*. I am at a certain disadvantage insofar as I am not working with the longer, unedited manuscript of *Garden*, but rather am using the Scribners version. However, from what I have read of the original manuscript, the points I make are actually enhanced, not diminished, within the context of the larger, unfinished work.

2. See, respectively, Nagel, Willingham, Morrison, and Rudat (especially 10-12).

3. Note that the "African Story," which constitutes the "inner story" of *The Garden of Eden*, is reprinted as "An African Story" in *The Complete Short Stories* but is called "Eden" by Morrison and "The Hunting Story" by Nagel.

4. See Miller, who details Conrad's influence on Fitzgerald, and more recently, Skinner.

5. Note that Steven Roe usefully aligns "egoism and imperialism." Although my interpretation of the character David (both as writer and as character within the internalized story) differs from Roe's, I agree with him that behind *The Garden of Eden* is a "thematic design that ultimately implicates political ideologies of appropriation and domination" (58).

6. The connection made earlier between *The Garden of Eden*, *The Great Gatsby*, and *Heart of Darkness* dovetails with Ross's suggestion that *Heart of Darkness* influenced Hemingway's *The Sun Also Rises* (the text of which was written during the period recounted in *A Moveable Feast*, which in turn was being written concurrently with *Garden*). Ross specifically connects Jake with Marlow as "first-person narrators whose motives we suspect" (28)—a point I am making about David Bourne. Reynolds provocatively notes that *The Sun Also Rises* is really a story about Jake Barnes (the narrator), "just as Fitzgerald's *The Great Gatsby* was about its narrator, Nick Carraway" (*The Paris Years*, 319). Reynolds also discusses the continuing importance of Conrad for Hemingway (224-26).

7. As Nagel argues, "What is most significant about the conclusion [of the novel], however, is not that the marriage has come to its predict-

able end but rather that David has been able to transform the difficulties of his present life into significant art [i.e., the 'hunting story'] by using present emotions to capture the feelings of the past" (337). My point, however, is that there may well be far more ethical culpability in David's *use of Catherine* to become a writer than Nagel's argument suggests—even if David is clearly used by Catherine as well. It is not, as Nagel posits, that David realizes his marriage is over at the end of the novel when Catherine burns his manuscripts. Rather, at the end of Chapter One, as Catherine has just persuaded David to transgress sexual boundaries and identifications for the first time, we find David verbally reassuring Catherine while his "heart said goodbye my lovely girl goodbye and good luck and goodbye" (18). However, I am not persuaded that David's complicity in what happens between him and Catherine thereafter justifies Roe's conclusion that "There is, to be sure, a despotic brutality in David's character, a desire to master and control otherness, to preside over the world rather than participate in it" (53). My perspective is most closely aligned to the recent work by Robert Fleming, who finds that David may be corrupted by Catherine's money and sexual experiments but also "by his own narcissistic devotion to his art rather than to emotional relationships" (139).

8. It is of course quite possible that the characteristics of this new literature that Loeb describes are intended to justify the plot, characters, and theme of his own novel *Doodab* (1925). Notably, *Doodab* includes a meditation on money—on "gold" and "greenbacks," on how the past "race" is already "awfully far away," and on how the "automobile" had "ruined it" (162). In addition, Hemingway seems to have parodied the conclusion of Loeb's novel in the last lines of *The Sun Also Rises:* Loeb's novel concludes with the ironic statement, "Good, I knew you'd come. It will be *so* nice" (287)—a statement that is similar, both in tone and words, to Jake Barnes's ultimate dismissal of his relationship with Brett.

9. It would be well worth noting in this regard that Harold Loeb, the source for Robert Cohn in *The Sun Also Rises,* may also be through the fictional creation of Cohn a mask for Gertrude Stein. (See Wagner-Martin 39-41.) Reynolds suggests that Hemingway, who was already friends with Harold Loeb, became acquainted with Fitzgerald in the spring of 1925 (*The Paris Years,* 282). Finally, in "Life with Father," William Carlos Williams's son remembers his mother's recalling a tennis match "in Paris in the early twenties. . . . William Carlos Williams and Harold Loeb vs. Ford [Madox Ford] and Ernest Hem-

ingway. Feeling ran high, *because Loeb was Hemingway's financial crutch in those days,* and furthermore had swiped Hemingway's girl . . ." (Terrell 77; emphasis added).

10. Loeb cites the internal quotation as coming from Nietzsche's *Will to Power.* It will be obvious in the following discussion that Loeb was heavily influenced in his thinking by Karl Marx as well.

11. See Coady, Cowley, Josephson, as well as Joseph Stella's early work on factories and bridges (the "Brooklyn Bridge" notably appearing in the first issue of *Broom* [1921]).

12. The subject of money remains a recurrent theme in numerous articles reprinted in *By-Line: Ernest Hemingway*—from Hemingway's covering the Genoa Conference in the early 1920s to his writing nostalgically of the "Great Blue River" or the Gulf Stream in the late 1940s. However, we should also note that while Hemingway would specifically condemn writing for money in his autobiographical novel *Green Hills of Africa,* he "was dreaming of [making] $10,000 or even fifteen or twenty [thousand dollars]" from the novel, and angrily "settled for $5,000" for its publication by Scribners (Baker 270).

13. Willingham has noted correctly that "The motifs of money, spending, and gift giving which pervade *Garden* have great significance in terms of a feminist and post-structuralist hermeneutic" (55). However, I disagree with her conclusion that Catherine "enriches David's life" by allowing him "to see beyond restrictive binaries" (60). As implied in my disagreement with Nagel and with Roe, I find David, Catherine, and their relationship to be intensely complex and ambiguous—both for Hemingway and in the text itself—precluding simple praise or denigration of any of the characters. In addition to the problem of gender in this text, we should also note that Morrison has correctly identified the movement within the novel of the characters toward "blackness" in a largely stereotyped way. Although I disagree with her interpretation of the inner story as being one of "male bonding" (when in fact it records the rupturing of the relationship between father and son), Morrison's attention to the presence of Africa and Catherine and David's increasing darkness as they physically move closer to the continent is compelling indeed (80-91).

14. As I will discuss more fully later, it is interesting to note Hemingway's clearly negative attitude toward the "pollution" of money in *A Moveable Feast,* suggesting that money—regardless of the sex who has it—is corrupting, although the sexual politics of monetary domination is the most critical point in *The Garden of Eden.*

15. Hemingway obviously describes both his process of "elimination" and the challenge of writing "simply" in his concurrently written text, *A Moveable Feast*. In fact, for someone who was supposedly "made . . . sick" if people talked to his "face" about his writing (127), *Feast* shows the same kind of narcissistic obsession with the craft and consequences of his writing that is typical of David in *Garden of Eden* (however different, sexually, the macho Hemingway of *Feast* appears to be from the sexually experimental David of *Eden*).

16. I am referring here to Kierkegaard's well-known practice of publishing works under his own name that were simultaneously challenged or undercut by other publications criticizing his work, but which he wrote himself, under such pseudonyms as Johannes Climacus or C. Constantine.

17. The corruption that money brings both to writing and to relationships is obviously a major theme throughout *A Moveable Feast*, though perhaps most forcefully toward the end when Hemingway says "Then you have the rich and nothing is ever as it was again" (207)—a consequence, he suggests, of having finally written a novel (208).

18. Although Fleming's subject is not exactly that of the relation of the writer to the corruption of money, his insights into the literal moral cost of being a writer—when the writer uses people and relationships to fuel his writing—have interesting points of similarity with my argument here. Fleming specifically notes that "In creating his portrait of the ideal artist in *A Moveable Feast*, Hemingway deliberately denied and reversed the serious theme of the writer's failed relationships, a notion that had haunted his last two unfinished novels [*Islands in the Stream* and *The Garden of Eden*]" (165).

19. As with *The Garden of Eden*, the editing of *A Moveable Feast* poses some problems in interpretation. According to Jacqueline Tavernier-Courbin, Hemingway actually wrote that the latter book "is fiction," but that the statement was altered by Mary Hemingway in the published book (44).

20. I have cited only one instance of the older Hemingway's description of the younger Hemingway as being merely "stupid." However, Hemingway uses this particular word several times in the novel—including the very end, where he apparently justifies what will happen to him and to Hadley, in terms of Pauline, by noting "Under the charm of these rich I was as trusting and as stupid as a bird dog who wants to go out with any man with a gun . . ." (209).

21. While this last observation may be taking us into new territory, as
     suggested in note 13, issues of race in *The Garden of Eden* are in fact quite
     important, particularly in terms of capitalist production—as they are,
     I would add, in *The Heart of Darkness, The Great Gatsby,* and *A Moveable
     Feast,* though in varying ways and degrees.

22. First published in 1842, an excellent reprint of Kierkegaard's *Either/Or*
     is the 1987 Princeton University Press edition.

23. As indicated in note 13, Morrison has convincingly elaborated a racial,
     even racist, dynamics at work in this novel in which, as Catherine and
     David become increasingly destructive, they also become increasingly
     "dark." Space prohibits my exploring this aspect of the novel in this
     essay, though I would like to stress it is an important one that needs
     much further elaboration—particularly in terms of the moral under-
     mining of the "mysticism of money."
         In addition to considering the Africanist performance in which
     Catherine and David engage (according to Morrison), it is useful to
     look at Strychaez, who makes it clear that conquest and trophy-
     hunting are aligned to anxiety about male performance—specifically
     that "manhood is not an essence" but rather a public performance
     signified by "trophy-hunting and display" (37). These insights clearly
     have bearing on the internalized "African Story" of *The Garden of Eden,*
     but with ramifications extending to the larger story in which both
     maleness and femaleness are very clearly categories of public—and
     private—display (and consequently open to the rupturing of those
     categories, as David's and Catherine's relationships with each other
     and with Marita well demonstrate).

24. The extremity of the almost hyperphallic posturing the narrator
     Hemingway asserts in *A Moveable Feast* is made clear in the supposed
     antagonism that the young Hemingway takes toward homosexuality
     in the chapter "Miss Stein Instructs." Not only does he reject homo-
     sexuality, but he also describes the need (not spoken directly to
     Gertrude Stein) to be able "to kill a man" who, working with other
     men on a lake boat, might say "Oh gash may be fine but one eye for
     mine" (18-19). Obviously, the pseudo-homosexual relation between
     Catherine, when she "changes," and David, when he does not, offers
     a compelling counterplay with Hemingway's public (and published)
     stance, but one which is clearly not successful either for Catherine or
     for David.

25. See Spilka, especially his "Appendix B—A Retrospective Epilogue: On
     the Importance of Being Androgynous" (an epilogue which discusses

The Garden of Eden and Catherine's reconfiguration of several important women in Hemingway's life). Spilka clearly makes the point that Hemingway was, finally, his best ethical self when writing, even if not in person.

WORKS CITED

Baker, Carlos. *Ernest Hemingway: A Life Story.* New York: Scribners, 1969.

Coady, R. J. "American Art." *Soil* (December 1916). Rptd. in Jacqueline Vaught Brogan. *Part of the Climate: American Cubist Poetry.* Berkeley: U of California P, 1991. 286-88.

Cowley, Malcolm. "Portrait by Leyendecker." *Broom* 4 (1923): 240-47.

Fitzgerald, F. Scott. *The Great Gatsby.* 1925. The Authorized Text. New York: Scribners, 1992.

Fleming, Robert. *The Face in the Mirror: Hemingway's Writers.* Tuscaloosa: U of Alabama P, 1994.

Hays, Peter L. "Hemingway and Fitzgerald." *Hemingway in Our Time.* Ed. Richard Astro and Jackson J. Benson. Corvallis: Oregon State UP, 1974. 89-97.

Hemingway, Ernest. *By-Line: Ernest Hemingway. Selected Articles and Dispatches of Four Decades.* Ed. William White. New York: Scribners, 1967.

——. *The Complete Short Stories of Ernest Hemingway: The Finca Vigía Edition.* New York: Scribners, 1987.

——. *The Garden of Eden.* New York: Scribners, 1986.

——. *Green Hills of Africa.* New York: Scribners, 1935.

——. *A Moveable Feast.* New York: Scribners, 1964.

Josephson, Matthew. "The Great American Billposter." *Broom* 3 (1922): 304-12.

Kierkegaard, Sören. *Either/Or.* 1842. Princeton, NJ: Princeton UP, 1987.

Loeb, Harold. *Doodab.* New York: Liveright, 1925.

——. "The Mysticism of Money." *Broom* 3 (1922): 115-30.

——. *The Way It Was.* New York: Criterion, 1959.

Miller, James E., Jr. *F. Scott Fitzgerald: His Art and His Technique.* New York: New York UP, 1964.

Morrison, Toni. *Playing in the Dark: Whiteness and the Literary Imagination.* Cambridge, MA: Harvard UP, 1992.

Nagel, James. "The Hunting Story in *The Garden of Eden.*" *Hemingway's Neglected Fiction.* Ed. Susan F. Beegel. Ann Arbor, MI: UMI Research P, 1989. 329-38.

Peters, K. J. "The Thematic Integrity of *The Garden of Eden.*" *Hemingway Review* 10.2 (1991): 17-29.

Phelan, James. "What Hemingway and a Rhetorical Theory of Narrative Can Do for Each Other: The Example of 'My Old Man.'" *Hemingway Review* 12.2 (1993): 1-14.

Rabinowitz, Peter. *Before Reading: Narrative Conventions and the Politics of Interpretation.* Ithaca, NY: Cornell UP, 1987.

Reynolds, Michael. *Hemingway: The Paris Years.* Cambridge, MA: Blackwell, 1989.

———. *Hemingway's Reading, 1910-1940: An Inventory.* Princeton, NJ: Princeton UP, 1981.

Roe, Steven. "Opening Bluebeard's Closet: Writing and Aggression in *The Garden of Eden.*" *Hemingway Review* 12.1 (1992): 52-66.

Ross, Charles. "'The Saddest Story,' Part Two: *The Good Soldier* and *The Sun Also Rises.*" *Hemingway Review* 12.1 (1992): 26-35.

Rudat, Wolfgang E. H. "The Other War in *For Whom the Bell Tolls*: Maria and Miltonic Gender-Role Battles." *Hemingway Review* 11.1 (1991): 8-24.

Scribner, Charles III. "Introduction." *The Great Gatsby.* 1925. The Authorized Text. New York: Scribners, 1992. vii-xx.

Skinner, John. "The Oral and the Written: Kurtz and Gatsby Revisited." *Journal of Narrative Technique* 17.1 (1987): 131-40.

Spilka, Mark. *Hemingway's Quarrel with Androngyny.* Lincoln: U of Nebraska P, 1990.

Stein, Gertrude. *The Autobiography of Alice B. Toklas.* 1933. *The Selected Writings of Gertrude Stein.* Ed. Carl Van Vechten. New York: Vintage, 1990. 1-237.

Strychaez, Thomas. "Trophy-Hunting as a Trope of Manhood in *Green Hills of Africa.*" *Hemingway Review* 13.1 (1993): 36-47.

Tavernier-Courbin, Jacqueline. "Fact and Fiction in *A Moveable Feast.*" *Hemingway Review* 4.1 (1984): 44-51.

Terrell, Carroll F., ed. *William Carlos Williams: Man and Poet.* Orono: U of Maine P, 1983.

Wagner-Martin, Linda. "Racial and Sexual Coding in Hemingway's *The Sun Also Rises.*" *Hemingway Review* 10.2 (1991): 39-41.

Werlock, Abby H. P. "Gender Anxiety in Fitzgerald's *Tender Is the Night* and Hemingway's *To Have and Have Not.*" Unpublished paper presented at the "Lost Generation" session, NEMLA. Philadelphia, 1993.

Willingham, Kathy. "Hemingway's *The Garden of Eden*: Writing with the Body." *Hemingway Review* 12.2 (1993): 46-61.

FOURTEEN

THE SUN ALSO RISES
AS "A GREATER GATSBY"

"ISN'T IT PRETTY TO THINK SO?"

JAMES PLATH

Paris provided the site for the historic first meeting between Ernest Hemingway and F. Scott Fitzgerald, and if Hemingway's correspondence with his mother can be trusted, it also provided an informal "arena" where he taught boxing to various people, including Fitzgerald (Bruccoli, *Fitzgerald and Hemingway* 21). But it appears to have provided the site for a literary bout between them as well—and perhaps another lesson in "manhood."

When Hemingway wrote Fitzgerald that he was going to pay him tribute by adding a subtitle in the eighth printing of his novel to read "THE SUN ALSO RISES (LIKE YOUR COCK IF YOU HAVE ONE) A greater Gatsby (Written with the friendship of F. Scott Fitzgerald (Prophet of THE JAZZ AGE)" (*Selected Letters* 231), he seems to have been pulling Fitzgerald's leg—if not another part of his anatomy. But what if, in his letter "thanking" the more established author for ten pages of suggested *Sun* revisions, Hemingway wasn't really joking? What if, rather than the hypothetical plural, the "you" were singular, aimed at a writer whom Hemingway later portrayed in *A Moveable Feast* as "a drunk, a weakling, a hypochondriac, an irresponsible writer, a nuisance, an embarrassment, both sexually insecure and wife-dominated" during those early Paris years? (Bruccoli, *Fitzgerald and Hemingway* 1).

Although Fitzgerald never got around to telling his side of the story, Hemingway's version of their first meeting in late April 1925 at the Dingo Bar on the rue Delambre has Fitzgerald annoying him with a sexual/moral question: Did he sleep with his wife before they were married? (*Moveable Feast* 130). In his "memoir" of those early Paris years, Hemingway also alleged that Scott was troubled by Zelda's remark that the way he was built he could never make any woman happy. By Hemingway's ribald account, Fitzgerald was so troubled, in fact, that the pair had to adjourn to *le water* so that Hemingway could check out Fitzgerald's plumbing and subsequently reassure him that he was normal (171).

Hemingway's irritation with Fitzgerald apparently continued days later at the Closerie des Lilas, where he recalls Fitzgerald pulled out an advance copy of Gilbert Seldes's gushing review of *The Great Gatsby* (134), published in the magazine which had recently rejected Hemingway. Even describing it years later, Hemingway's resentment still showed when he wrote, "It could only have been better if Gilbert Seldes had been better" (*Moveable Feast* 134). If Hemingway felt a gauntlet had been thrown down then, he most assuredly picked it up.

Never mind that Fitzgerald may not have known that Hemingway was on Seldes's s-list, or that *The Dial* had just rejected several of Hemingway's poems and stories—"The Undefeated" was turned down less than a month before, in fact—"with politeness but with, nonetheless, definiteness, and without an invitation to submit future work" (Joost 248). Never mind that Fitzgerald may only have known of Edmund Wilson's favorable review of *Three Stories & Ten Poems* and *in our time*, which appeared in the October 1924 *Dial*—the same month Fitzgerald began hounding Scribners editor Maxwell Perkins about the talented Hemingway. Nevertheless, when Fitzgerald produced a copy of Seldes's *Dial* review, it must have gotten a "rise" out of Hemingway to read how "Fitzgerald has more than matured; he has mastered his talents and gone soaring in a beautiful flight, leaving behind him everything dubious and tricky in his earlier work, and leaving even farther behind all the men of his own generation and most of his elders." Seldes added that Fitzgerald's "technical virtuosity is extraordinary" and singled out two elements as causes behind the effect: "The novel is composed of an artistic structure, and it exposes, again for the first time, an interesting temperament . . . Fitzgerald regarding a tiny section of life and reporting it with irony and pity and a consuming passion. *The Great Gatsby* is passionate . . ." (162).

In a brief note, Matthew J. Bruccoli was the first to recognize sarcastic allusions to the Seldes review in *The Sun Also Rises*, in which Jake Barnes and his friend Bill Gorton are in Burguete preparing for a day's fishing. Amid morning banter about breakfast and tackle and bait, Bill suddenly says, "Work for the good of all. . . . Show irony and pity" (113). He presses Jake— Hemingway talking to himself, more likely, with Seldes and Fitzgerald as the intended audience—"Aren't you going to show a little irony and pity?" The answer, interestingly enough, employs the same language Fitzgerald used to describe early satirical sections of *Sun* that he advised Hemingway to cut because they were "nose thumbings"—I would argue, at Fitzgerald (Svoboda 138). Jake tells the reader that "I thumbed my nose," but Bill says, "That's not irony" (*Sun* 113). As Jake reports, Bill belabors the point in a curious way:

> As I went downstairs I heard Bill singing, "Irony and Pity. When you're feeling . . . Oh, Give them Irony and Give them Pity. Oh, give them Irony. When they're feeling . . . Just a little irony. Just a little pity . . ." He kept on singing until he came down-stairs. The tune was: "The Bells are Ringing for Me and my Gal." I was reading a week-old Spanish paper.
>
> "What's all this irony and pity?"
>
> "What? Don't you know about Irony and Pity?"
>
> "No. Who got it up?"
>
> "Everybody. They're mad about it in New York." (114)

In addition to the irony-and-pity ditty with its emphatic capitalization, the sexual innuendo in "who got it up" is certainly obvious and evocative of Hemingway's teasing letter. But there are more subtle references in this passage to Fitzgerald and *Gatsby*. Although Hemingway's allusion to a lyric is a technique he hadn't used before, it was one which Fitzgerald had recently employed in *Gatsby*. Hemingway's "coupling" of the Seldes blurb and a wedding-bell song seems indeed a parodic jab at *Gatsby* and the grand romance contained therein—which is made more evident if one tries actually to sing Bill's "lyric" to a melody that simply won't accommodate it rhythmically. Likewise, the phrase "mad about it in New York" digs gently at both Seldes's literary crowd and the West and East Egg crowds in *Gatsby*. Even more telling, in that same scene, Bill continues to prod Jake:

> "Say something ironical. Make some crack about Prio de Rivera."
>
> "I could ask her what kind of a jam they think they've gotten into in the Riff."

"Poor," said Bill. "Very poor. You can't do it. That's all. You don't understand irony. You have no pity. Say something pitiful."

"Robert Cohn."

"Not so bad. That's better. Now why is Cohn pitiful? Be ironic." (114)

More than a few critics have noticed parallels between *Gatsby* and *Sun*, between the romantic characters of Jay Gatsby and Robert Cohn. Bruce Stark argues that the similarities reflect Hemingway's "indebtedness" to Fitzgerald for providing a structural model to follow, enabling him to move beyond short *in our time*–style vignettes. Paul Lauter sees Hemingway's appropriation as "partly a commentary" on Fitzgerald's novel but mostly the borrowing of a time-honored thematic construct: "the search of an innocent outsider to achieve his ideal in an alien social world" (338). Michael Reynolds, meanwhile, sees pointed allusions to Fitzgerald as Hemingway's "jesting" notice that he had arrived, that he had served his apprenticeship and was ready for "a challenge of eminence" (120).

While, as Lauter observes, "there is probably now no way to prove that Hemingway wrote his book partly as a commentary on Fitzgerald's, can the parallels in hero, . . . narrative technique, and subject be altogether accidental?" (339). I would like to pursue the matter further. Hemingway's own sense of himself as a writer was such that wholesale literary borrowings would have been unacceptable to him, even, one might say, emasculating. But what if the initial impetus behind *The Sun Also Rises* was a parodic jab at Fitzgerald and at the novel that *The Dial* had reviewed so favorably that Hemingway, obviously stung, felt compelled to include an extended allusion in what is widely regarded as his first "real" novel? (*Sun* 113-15). What if Robert Cohn's character, though apparently patterned in part after the real character of Harold Loeb, also incorporated some not-so-subtle or gentle swipes at Fitzgerald and his *Gatsby*? In the irony-and-pity section, Cohn is pointedly identified as a character who is naturally pitiful and subject, as a result, to ironic interpretation. I'm suggesting, then, that Hemingway's tongue-in-cheek attack against Seldes and Fitzgerald occurs throughout the novel, and not just in the irony-and-pity section. Considered as a "Greater Gatsby," Hemingway's portrayal of Men With Women becomes a comic exaggeration, emphasizing the "pitiful" way that Gatsby and Cohn are rendered socially and emotionally impotent by unrequited love. Both men have, respectively, a tragic and seriocomic idealism which causes them to place a greater value on their "love" than actually exists or to exalt the object of their affection beyond all reason. Neither man can accept that his great love had a sexual or romantic past, and neither can accept that they presently have a rival for their beloved's intentions—or rivals, in Hemingway's parodically exaggerated version.

Gatsby's unreasonable love of Daisy has made him, in mere anticipation of their first meeting alone, "pale as death, with his hands plunged like weights in his coat pockets . . . standing in a puddle of water glaring tragically into [Nick's] eyes" (*Gatsby* 80). Unlike Jake, who has to be reminded by Brett what happened the last time they tried to move beyond friendship, Gatsby is so obsessed by Daisy that he measures time by her absence. When Daisy, at that reunion, casually announces to Nick that she and Jay haven't met for years, Gatsby offers a precise tally: "Five years next November" (81), something that catches both Nick and Daisy by surprise.

Cohn, who thought "true love would conquer all" (199), becomes even more incapacitated: "When he fell in love with Brett his tennis game went all to pieces. People beat him who had never had a chance with him" (*Sun* 45). Hemingway's version underscores, in comic fashion, how debilitating and emasculating the condition can be. Unlike Jake, who cries occasionally during the night—perhaps justifiably so, given his extreme physical defect which allows him to become aroused but prevents him from experiencing satisfaction or release—Cohn is emotionally impotent. Though physically more "manly," with his Tom Buchanan-like strength and brutality and his ability to have sexual intercourse, he cries easily and often, by day and in front of the women he has loved.

That Cohn's exterior physical strength is less important than an emotional and inner strength is emphasized throughout the novel. When a nonadmirer like Harvey Stone is openly insulting to Cohn and the latter makes veiled threats about hitting him, Stone quips that "it wouldn't make any difference to me. I'm not a fighter. . . . It doesn't make any difference to me. You don't mean anything to me" (44). That language is echoed later when a drunken Mike Campbell gleefully tells Cohn that his Lady Love is with the bullfighter and, after Cohn reacts violently, says, "Oh, don't stand up and act as though you were going to hit me. That won't make any difference to me" (142). When Cohn does behave badly in the company of Brett's former or current lovers, he breaks into tears and instantly seeks forgiveness. After the fight with Romero,

> Cohn was crying, and Brett had told him off, and he wanted to shake hands. . . . Brett wasn't having any shaking hands and Cohn was crying and telling her how much he loved her and she was telling him not to be a ruddy ass. Then Cohn leaned down to shake hands with the

bull-fighter fellow. No hard feelings, you know. All for forgiveness.
And the bull-fighter chap hit him in the face again. (202)

While this section is reminiscent of Cohn's need to make amends with Jake
after causing him personal injury (195), it also seems a parodic echo of
Gatsby's insistent politeness with Tom and the need to see more of him after
he had begun seeing Daisy (*Gatsby* 92-93), or of Gatsby's intitial nervous
reaction after being re-introduced to Daisy, when Nick "thought for a
moment he was going to shake hands" (83). Taken as parody, it could also
be Hemingway's comment on Gatsby's insecurities and on the falseness that
accompanies such mannered handshakes. Though outwardly reflective of a
"better man," they instead betray an almost infantile need for reassurance—
the kind of need Hemingway later wrote in *A Moveable Feast* that he saw in
Fitzgerald, who, in Paris and Lyon, had to be reassured about his manhood,
his health, his writing, and his bad behavior under the influence of alcohol.

It was clear to Hemingway that "Zelda was jealous of Scott's work"
(*Moveable Feast* 180) and "Scott was very much in love with Zelda and he was
very jealous of her" (*Moveable Feast* 181). Given that unhealthy co-depen-
dency, Hemingway writes, "Becoming unconscious when they drank had
always been their great defense," and they "would go to sleep like children"
(181). True or not, it was clear to Hemingway that the love between them
had ended. According to Hemingway's memory of those Paris years, Fitzgerald "told me many times on our walks of how she had fallen in love with the
French navy pilot. But she had never made him really jealous with another
man since. This spring she was making him jealous with other women and
on the Montmartre parties he was afraid to pass out and he was afraid to
have her pass out" (181). Hemingway was incredulous, wondering "how, if
this story [of Zelda's affair] was true and it had all happened, could Scott
have slept each night in the same bed with Zelda" after her affair? (173).

Like Fitzgerald—at least the Fitzgerald seen through Hemingway's
eyes—neither Gatsby nor Cohn can perceive or accept when "love" has
ended or even sense when their presence is unwanted. Gatsby, after one
suspects Tom has already perceived something between them, is so intent
on confronting the husband of his intended that he accepts the polite but
insincere invitation of a socialite to join them on horseback, leaving Tom to
exclaim, "My God, I believe the man's coming. . . . Doesn't he know she
doesn't want him?" (*Gatsby* 93). Such incredulity is echoed by Campbell:
"Tell me, Robert. Why do you follow Brett around like a poor bloody steer?
Don't you know you're not wanted? I know when I'm not wanted. Why don't
you know when you're not wanted?" (*Sun* 142).

Both men stand in sharp contrast to Hemingway's "Greater Gatsby" character, the bullfighter Romero. He also passionately loved Brett, because, as Jake notices, when he fought in the ring, despite being beaten so badly by Cohn the night before that he can hardly see to fight, "everything of which he could control the locality he did in front of her that afternoon. Never once did he look up. He made it stronger that way, and did it for himself too, as well as for her." In short, "Pedro Romero had the greatness" (*Sun* 216). His inner strength is later summarized: "The fight with Cohn had not touched his spirit but his face had been smashed and his body hurt" (219). In Romero, there is none of the empty gesture—no shaking of hands and no reaching out toward a symbolic light on the end of a dock, arms "trembling" (*Gatsby* 31).

That Hemingway resented Fitzgerald's idealism is clear from a letter sent to Fitzgerald in Paris the day before Hemingway's party left for Pamplona that summer of 1925, in which Hemingway, having recently read *The Great Gatsby*, sarcastically attacked Fitzgerald's Roman Catholic values: "I wonder what your idea of heaven would be—A beautiful vacuum filled with wealthy monogamists, all powerful and members of the best families all drinking themselves to death. And hell would probably [be] an ugly vacuum full of poor polygamists unable to obtain booze or with chronic stomach disorders that they called secret sorrows" (*Selected Letters* 165).

That language was echoed in *Sun*, both when Brett calls love "hell on earth" (27) and in an excised segment where Jake writes not "from a desire for confession, because being a Roman Catholic I am spared that Protestant urge to literary production . . . nor any other of the usual highly moral urges, but because I believe it is a good story" (Svoboda 134). It is also reflected in a letter to Fitzgerald which followed on the heels of one in which Hemingway had joked that he would dedicate *Sun*, a collection of "instructive anecdotes," to his son, Bumby (*Selected Letters* 199). In the follow-up letter written from Paris in May 1926, Hemingway explained, "I'll be glad to hear from Max Perkins what they think of Sun etc. It is so obviously *not* a collection of instructive anecdotes and is such a hell of a sad story—and not one at all for a child to read—and the only instruction is how people go to hell—(Doesn't it sound terrible, I can hear you say) that I thought it was rather pleasant to dedicate it to Bumby" (204-5). After hinting that Fitzgerald's moral constitution was as weak as a child's, Hemingway added that he would bring a carbon of his novel with him to the Riviera that Fitzgerald could read "at Juan les Sapins if there aren't proofs before then" (205). He signed it "Ernest M. Shit," and at that point, he certainly was.

Though earlier, in November 1925, Fitzgerald had written from Paris that he was "crazy to read the comic novel" (*Letters* 295), Hemingway was reluctant to let him see it. As he wrote *Little Review* editor Jane Heap, he didn't want "to show it to anyone until it is done" because, he said, "I don't want all my great literary friends giving me good advice. Want it to have all its defects" (Reynolds 314). Then, in a December 15, 1925, letter to Fitzgerald, having completed both *Sun* and *Torrents of Spring*, he mentioned the former but not the latter—perhaps because of the guilt he felt in portraying Fitzgerald as a drunk in an author's note to the reader in *Torrents*. It was an overt attack that would be repeated in *A Moveable Feast* and "The Snows of Kilimanjaro," the latter of which would eventually prompt Fitzgerald finally to beg Hemingway to "please lay off me in print" (*Letters* 311). But in this December 1925 letter, Hemingway also built himself up the way an athlete will sometimes make an easy maneuver seem more heroic by exaggerating the degree of difficulty. In talking to Fitzgerald about good and bad subjects, Hemingway concluded, "A dull subject I should say would be impotence" (*Selected Letters* 177)—meaning, of course, that to write effectively about a dull subject would also constitute "A Greater Gatsby."

Hemingway was quite open about his borrowing the structure and characters Fitzgerald used in *The Great Gatsby* to fashion a novel which he apparently felt was "greater," among other things, by virtue of its less idealistic (and therefore more accurate) viewpoint, one where, often, he doesn't mince words. Grit replaces romance. Instead of the discomfort Nick felt at having been asked to play matchmaker for Gatsby and Daisy (*Gatsby* 74), Jake's similar introduction of Romero and Brett leads to a blunt assessment from an indignant Robert Cohn who says, "You damned pimp" (190).

In the May 1926 letter joking about dedicating *Sun* to his son, Hemingway launched a series of serious jabs—not only at *Gatsby*, but at Fitzgerald's work-in-progress:

> If you are worried it [*The Sun Also Rises*] is *not* a series of anecdotes—nor is it written very much like either [Dos Passos's] Manhattan Transfer nor [Anderson's] Dark Laughter. I have tried to follow the outline and spirit of the Great Gatsby but feel I have failed somewhat because of never having been on Long Island. The hero, like Gatsby, is a Lake Superior Salmon Fisherman. (There are no salmon in Lake Superior). The action all takes place in Newport, R.I. and the heroine is a girl named Sophie Irene Loeb who kills her mother. The scene in which Sophie gives birth to twins in the death house at Sing Sing where she is waiting to be electrocuted for the murder of the father and sister

of her, as then, unborn children I got from Dreiser but practically everything else in the book is either my own or yours. I know you'll be glad to see it. The Sun Also Rises comes from Sophie's statement as she is strapped into the chair as the current mounts. (*Selected Letters* 200-1)

Under the guise of another joke, Hemingway openly addressed the matter of literary borrowings and also cruelly alluded to Fitzgerald's then-stalled "The World's Fair," one of the working titles of a novel which eventually evolved into *Tender Is the Night*—inspired at first by a sensational newspaper account—which Fitzgerald originally planned to end in "matricide," according to Turnbull (208).

Never mind that through "fall 1924-spring 1925 Fitzgerald reminded Perkins about Hemingway while revising *The Great Gatsby*" (Bruccoli, *Fitzgerald and Hemingway* 10), or that after reading the carbons of *The Sun Also Rises* he advised Hemingway to cut the beginning (*Letters* 208). Hemingway made the cuts, apparently with some reluctance, but could not resist another letter-jab at the author who was trying to help him:

I cut The Sun to start with Cohn - cut all that first part. Made a number of minor cuts and did quite a lot of re-writing and tightening up. . . . I hope to hell you'll like it and I think maybe you will.

Have a swell hunch for a new novel. I'm calling it the World's Fair. You'll like the title. (*Selected Letters* 217)

Fitzgerald would eventually write that he did not realize Hemingway "had stolen" *Gatsby* from him but added, in the same joking manner as Hemingway, that he was "prepared to believe that it's true and shall tell everyone" (Turnbull 298-99). Yet a 1928 letter from Fitzgerald to Perkins indicates that the author knew exactly what lay beneath the joking surface of their relationship. "Remember," he wrote Perkins about his latest work-in-progress, the "novel is confidential, even to Ernest" (*Letters* 213). In a letter he wrote from Delaware to Hemingway, still in Paris, he used Hemingway's joking manner to address the issue upon publication of Hemingway's *Men Without Women*: "I like your title—*All the Sad Young Men Without Women* [a reference, of course, to Fitzgerald's much earlier *All the Sad Young Men*] and I feel my influence is beginning to tell. Manuel Garcia [the bullfighter hero of 'The Undefeated'] is obviously Gatsby" (*Letters* 301; brackets added).

And so, I repeat: What if *The Sun Also Rises* was begun as Hemingway's parodic version of a realistic hell-on-earth, as opposed to what he apparently felt was Fitzgerald's romanticized and all-too-heavenly vision of the world? Young writers are as prone to take up the parodic pen as a way of grappling with inevitable influences and imitations as post-Freudian sons are to finish off their fathers. In Hemingway's case, his first published fiction, "Judgment of Manitou," was as clearly derivative of Jack London's Klondike tales as his "My Old Man" was of Sherwood Anderson's racetrack stories. Likewise, Hemingway's "Ring Lardner Jr." columns for *The Trapeze* positively rang of Lardner, as did his later "You know me, Al" correspondences for *Ciao!* As biographer Jeffrey Meyers notes, "*Torrents* was a natural development of this tendency" toward parody (167). And since Hemingway wrote this parody of Anderson's *Dark Laughter* between the first and final drafts of *The Sun Also Rises,* parody was certainly much on his mind.

Hemingway's sarcastic references to Seldes's review in *Sun* were so important to him that he would eventually insist to Perkins that "If the Irony and pity ditty bothers there are a couple of things you could do—reduce the size of the dashes and omit periods after them. Or just run it all in together. . . . I don't care what happens to that as long as the words are not changed and nothing inserted" (*Selected Letters* 215). Since the Seldes review was still gnawing at him a full year after he first read it, one could easily argue that Hemingway was obsessed by Seldes's praise of Fitzgerald and his own desire to produce "a greater Gatsby." In a letter Hemingway wrote to Fitzgerald after he had finished *Sun,* but before Fitzgerald read the typescript at Juan-les-Pins, he "joked" about a local boy "who was admired by Gilbert Seldes, if that means anything to you" (*Selected Letters* 204).

While the motive to out-*Gatsby* Gatsby and the opportunity for parody were certainly tempting, to Hemingway's credit he followed Fitzgerald's suggestion to cut the opening of *The Sun Also Rises,* explaining to Perkins in a November 1926 letter that the

> point of the book to me was that the earth abideth forever—having a great deal of fondness and admiration for the earth and not a hell of a lot for my generation and caring little about Vanities. I only hesitated at the start to cut the writing of a better writer—but it seems necessary. I didn't mean the book to be a hollow or bitter satire but a damn tragedy with the earth abiding for ever as the hero. (*Selected Letters* 229)

Though it's not clear who Hemingway meant by "better writer," surely it wasn't the writer of his own first drafts—for all of his manuscripts show Hemingway to be a tireless and painstaking revisionist. And, of course, though Hemingway often referred to himself by playful nicknames, he was not in the habit of referring to himself in the third person. Perhaps, then, the remarks were once again thinly veiled references to Fitzgerald, whom Hemingway said hated "country" (*Selected Letters* 165) and was fascinated by the comings and goings of his social set. And while this letter confirms Hemingway's intention to write a serious work—"A greater *Gatsby*," rather than a *Torrents*-like "hollow" satire—his acknowledgment of satirical elements may help explain his reluctance to show Fitzgerald early drafts of the novel, something which, that fall of 1925, greatly upset the latter (*Moveable Feast* 184).

If Hemingway had initial parodic inclinations, having Fitzgerald looking over his shoulder would have been awkward. No wonder Fitzgerald (when he finally saw the manuscript) complained about "the elephantine facetiousness" and could not "imagine how [Hemingway] could have done these first 20 pps. so casually" (Svoboda 139). Fitzgerald may have sensed the satire-in-progress, for he observed in his ten-page critique penned on the French Riviera that some sections didn't even have Hemingway's rhythm, adding "I think that there are about 24 sneers, superiorities and nose-thumbings-at-nothing that mar the whole narrative up to p. 29 where (after a false start on the introduction of Cohn) it really gets going" (Svoboda 138). Fitzgerald further commented on Hemingway's attempt at humor, admonishing "I find in you the same tendency to envelope [*sic*] or (as it turns out) to *embalm* in mere wordiness an anecdote or joke thats [*sic*] casually appealed to you, that I find in myself in trying to preserve a piece of 'fine writing'" (Svoboda 138).

Curiously, some of the things Fitzgerald pointed to as elements of "condescending *casualness*" are those which allude to and seem to poke fun at the opening of *Gatsby*. Consider the first paragraph of the final typescript, including a line which was cut [shown here crossed out]:

> This is a novel about a lady. ~~She does not appear for about twenty pages. Originally the book started off with~~ Her name is Lady Ashley and when the story begins she is living in Paris and it is Spring. That should be a good setting for a romantic but highly moral story. As every one knows Paris is a very romantic place. Spring in Paris is a very happy and romantic time. Autumn in Paris, although very beautiful, might give a note of sadness or melancholy that we shall try to keep out of this story. (Svoboda 100)

Never before had Hemingway employed such combined self-consciousness and direct address in his fiction. The line he cut is obviously tongue-in-cheek and referential, for there could be no other purpose for including it. Perhaps not coincidentally, in *Gatsby*, a book Seldes praised for its structure, the hero doesn't appear for twenty-one pages. Hemingway's emphatic repetition of "romantic" is likewise an indicator of ironic intent, one which, given *Gatsby*'s opening emphasis on the hero's "extraordinary gift for hope, a romantic readiness such as [Nick has] never found in any other person" (18), seems to have been directed at Fitzgerald. Then there is Hemingway's naming of Lady Duff "*Ash*- ley," which seems too close to the Valley of the Ashes to be coincidental—and ironic, if one considers that Jake's "dream girl" is a denizen of the societal ash heaps, as is the prostitute the reader first meets, one Jake picks up for the evening "because of a vague sentimental idea" (16). Such deliberate references to base impulses or sexual longings are repeated later in the novel when Mike tells an enraged and love-struck Robert Cohn that the object of his grand passion is with the bull-fighter Romero: "They're on their honeymoon" (190).

   Given Nick Carraway's extensive opening monologue on judgment and criticizing, as well as his closing appraisal of Gatsby as being "worth the whole damn bunch of them put together" (*Gatsby* 132), Hemingway's reference in the excised section to a "highly moral story" with a narrator who has "highly moral urges" (Svoboda 131, 134) is so tongue-in-cheek that it seems to waggle again directly at *Gatsby*. Nick begins his *Gatsby* narrative by quoting advice from his father: "Whenever you feel like criticizing anyone . . . just remember that all the people in this world haven't had the advantages that you've had," adding that he's "inclined to reserve all judgments" (17). Nick, of course, judges throughout the novel, but the notion of an unreliable narrator used for ironic effect seems to have escaped Hemingway, who apparently felt *Gatsby*'s essen-tial weakness was rooted in Fitzgerald's own wide-eyed fascination with the rich, as reflected through the narrative eyes of Nick Carraway. In a section cut from Chapter Sixteen in an earlier draft, Jake, sounding like a more realistic and flawed Nick, thinks to himself, "In life you tried to go along with out criticising the actions of other people but sometimes they offended you in spite of yourself" (Svoboda 20). An even greater coincidence of narrative occurs at approximately the same space in the final versions of each novel, with Nick and Jake pausing to contemplate what they've written: Nick, "Reading over what I have written . . ." (*Sun* 57) and Jake considering "Somehow I feel I have not shown Robert Cohn clearly" (45).

   More than a few critics have noticed contrasts between the narrative personae of the novels or argued their reliability. But while Lauter cautions that "Hemingway's narrator . . . does not simply provide a clear glass through which we view distinctly the people of the book" and that readers "must always take into consideration Jake's distortions, born of conflict with the others" (341), a reading of Hemingway's novel as a partial parody of Fitzgerald's turns up this interesting contrast: Nick confesses that "Every one suspects himself of at least one of the cardinal virtues, and this is mine: I am one of the few honest people that I have ever known" (*Gatsby* 59); Jake, early in the novel (as if in alluding rebuttal), proclaims, "I mistrust all frank and simple people" (*Sun* 4). More telling, while Nick watches taxicabs bound for the theater district feeling "a sinking" in his heart and fantasizes, imagining that he too "was hurrying toward gayety and sharing their excitement" (58), Jake knows what goes on inside taxicabs bound for nightclubs. In fact, *The Sun Also Rises* is framed by two taxicab journeys wherein Brett and Jake ride and confide. Nick is a social outsider by demeanor rather than by choice, and, so emotionally wistful, provides an echo of Gatsby's larger-scale idealism of one denied; Jake, by contrast, is not quite the outsider that critics have claimed. He's a passenger inside those taxicabs which seem to be going to places of excitement—though, of course, in Hemingway's version there *are* no places of excitement, and nothing much happens inside the taxi.

When Jake declaims in an excised section that "I did not want to be in love with any woman. And I did not want to have any grand passion that I could never do anything about" (Svoboda 21), he is clearly speaking of his own reluctance to allow himself to be trapped by emotion. But once again, echoes of *Gatsby* are unmistakable. Gatsby, the idealist, pursued Daisy with "colossal vitality," throwing himself into it "with creative passion" (*Gatsby* 88). At his arranged meeting with Daisy, Gatsby was so consumed by his passion that Nick observes that they had forgotten he was in the room. In Gatsby's dazed state, Nick writes, he "didn't know me now at all" (88). Once, when Nick watched him from afar, he saw Gatsby visually fixated on the green light of Daisy's dock as he "stretched out his arms toward the dark water in a curious way, and, far as I was from him, I could have sworn he was trembling" (31). This Moses-like Red Sea image is reflected in language Hemingway uses to describe Robert Cohn's first longing for Brett: "He looked a great deal as his compatriot must have looked when he saw the promised land" (22).

In the omitted section, Jake talks about how, when he was in love, the world seemed "one dimensional and flat and there was nothing but Brett and wanting Brett" (Svoboda 21). However, while Gatsby suffered for his love of the dream girl, Jake in this section—cut perhaps because it was too strong—"killed her" off in his mind by deliberately thinking of her with Lord Ashley or Robert. That, it would seem, was another dig at Fitzgerald's hero, who was not content to receive Daisy's love and would not settle for anything less than the assurance that she never loved someone else—a romantic but impossibly unrealistic position.

Unlike Nick, who writes that "reserving judgments is a matter of infinite hope" (*Gatsby* 17), Jake in the excised section does in fact pass judgment, pronouncing Brett "vulgar" (Svoboda 20). Hemingway addresses the issue of judgment even more ironically at the beginning of Chapter Two in the galleys and apparently takes another swipe at Seldes's praise of *Gatsby*'s passion:

> I did not want to tell this story in the first person but I find that I must. I wanted to stay well outside of the story so that I would not be touched by it in any way, and handle all the people in it with that irony and pity that are so essential to good writing. I even thought I might be amused by all the things that are going to happen to Lady Brett Ashley and Mr. Robert Cohn and Michael Campbell, Esq., and Mr. Jake Barnes, but I made the unfortunate mistake, for a writer, of first having been Mr. Jake Barnes. So it is not going to be splendid and cool and detached after all. "What a pity!" as Brett used to say.
>
> "What a pity!" was a little joke we all had. (Svoboda 133-34)

Fitzgerald's narrator takes great pains to convince the reader that he is going to be objective. Hemingway's, meanwhile, confesses to the impossibility of such a task, if one also happens to "live in the process"—a criticism of not only Nick but Fitzgerald as well. An additional "pity" can be found in this excised section, where Hemingway, like Bill Gorton, won't let go. One paragraph later Brett is painted by a portrait painter who, upon hearing that she will lose her title when she marries Mike Campbell, exclaims, "What a pity" twice (134).

In another section not included in the published novel, Hemingway wrote,

> There were about . . . twenty five more pages like that which ~~now~~ have been cut out of this novel which now opens with Robert Cohn who ~~will~~ may be a great disappointment to the reader who has just been promised Lady Ashley. But if the reader will stay around Lady Ashley will come into the story again in a little while and will stay in until the end. A large amount of material about the author has also been cut out in the twenty five pages that have been eliminated and I feel sure that this will compensate the reader for any loss he may feel about Lady Ashley. (Svoboda 104)

This last section, Svoboda reports, was added after Hemingway decided to "cut to the middle of the second Chapter" as Fitzgerald suggested, "beginning with Robert Cohn" (Svoboda 104). While this section offers a not-so-subtle jab at Nick's digressive narrative of self, the opening that it replaced provided a comic exaggeration of the first chapter of *The Great Gatsby*, for after the discussion of Jake's confessed lack of objectivity or withholding judgment—an echo of Nick's long-winded monologue—Jake, like Nick, gave a lengthy summary of his past (Svoboda 134).

In this "false start" of Hemingway's (Svoboda 138), gossip and suspicions of marital infidelities—key elements Fitzgerald establishes at the beginning of *Gatsby*—surface, for we're told that

> Robert Cohn had lived with a lady who lived on gossip, and so he had lived in an atmosphere of abortions and rumors of abortions, doubts and speculations as to past and prospective infidelities of friends, dirty rumors, dirtier reports and dirtier suspicions, and a constant fear and dread by his lady companion that he was seeing other women and was on the point of leaving her. (Svoboda 135)

Like Daisy, whose "voice is full of money" (*Gatsby* 106), Brett in this excised section is declared "much too expensive" for her first husband (Svoboda 131). Her second husband, Hemingway writes, "was a dipsomaniac" (Svoboda 131). That reference, along with long sections devoted to a description of the stages of drunkenness through which Brett and fianceé Mike Campbell progress, amounts to a near-pedantic treatise on their inability to handle alcohol—an inability Hemingway detested in Fitzgerald and detailed in *A Moveable Feast*.

There are a good many "uns" or negations in this aborted beginning, which also suggests that it was written as a response to Fitzgerald's novel. Brett's second husband, like the lieutenant from Daisy's past, is a "sailor," but one who "died of some very *un*romantic form of dysentery" (Svoboda 131; emphasis added). Even more referential is Hemingway's echo of Tom Buchanan's preoccupation with the "Nordic race" (20), where Cohn is "eager to learn and with an un-Nordic willingness to accept useful criticism" (Svoboda 136).

If Hemingway's first impulse in writing *The Sun Also Rises* was, as I'm suggesting, parodic, such apparently half-critical/half-playful allusions to *Gatsby* may help to explain some of the more bizarre details that occur in the published version of the novel—like the elk tooth that Count

Mippipopolous wears on his watch chain, a physical reminder of the human-molar cuff links worn by Meyer Wolfshiem (73). What James Hinkle termed "the fractured English of Count Mippipopolous" (133) is also remarkably like the butchered English of Wolfshiem and his "gonnegtions" (71)—a characteristic reflected in the count when Brett exclaims, "Oh, you always have some one in the trade" (56).

As Gatsby was an "Oggsford" man, Hemingway made Cohn, the romantic who had read *The Purple Land* too late in life, a graduate of Princeton—Fitzgerald's alma mater—an Ivy Leaguer, echoed in Tom Buchanan's Yale background. Instead of talk about the butler's nose in the first chapter of *Gatsby*, talk in *Sun* centers on Cohn's altered boxing nose. It's emphasized as well that Cohn, like Fitzgerald, was dominated by a woman who "evidently led him quite a life" (*Sun* 7).

Another curious scene from *Sun* occurs when Bill and Jake get drunk while they're fishing. Their discussion of who went to what college or who comes from what background has a vaudevillian "Who's on First?" quality:

> "Do you know what you are?" Bill looked at the bottle affectionately.
>
> "No," I said.
>
> "You're in the pay of the Anti-Saloon League."
>
> "I went to Notre Dame with Wayne B. Wheeler."
>
> "It's a lie," said Bill. "I went to Austin Business College with Wayne B. Wheeler. He was class president." (123)

If we recall the first party at Gatsby's mansion, where the conversation centers on rumors of Gatsby being a bootlegger or an Oxford man (61, 52), rumors that are quickly challenged or negated by others, this section becomes not just inanely funny but pointedly so.

And while it might be reaching a bit, what about the otherwise unexplainable scene where a drunken Bill and Jake wander the boulevard and Bill suddenly begins chattering about wanting to buy a stuffed dog at the taxidermist's? (*Sun* 72-73). Out of all possible animals one could purchase at a taxidermist—a trade which normally deals in wild, not domesticated, animals—why a *dog*? Unless, of course, Hemingway was poking gentle fun at another of Fitzgerald's memorable scenes from *Gatsby*, where Myrtle is equally insistent about buying a dog for her New York apartment (36). It's evident that Tom Buchanan knows he's being used but still submits when he tells the peddler, "Here's your money. Go and buy ten more dogs with it"

(36). Given this exchange, Bill's echo of Jake's credo—getting one's money's worth—takes on additional significance: a "Simple exchange of values. You give them money. They give you a stuffed dog" (72).

Finally, there is Jake's trip to San Sebastian, taken after the true action in *The Sun Also Rises* has ended—a scene which seems less tacked on if one considers the ending of *The Great Gatsby*. Just as Nick goes on his last night to the beach by Gatsby's house, where he "sprawled out on the sand" (152), Jake goes to the beach where he swims out and, "floating," sees "only the sky" and feels "the drop and lift of the swells" (237). But whereas Nick's inactive reverie is unbroken, allowing his thoughts to expand from speculation on Gatsby's dream to the even grander notion of the American dream, Jake is quickly returned to uncomfortable reality by a telegram which sends him back to Brett. In the final paragraphs, which find Jake and Brett riding once more in a taxicab, the dialogue and description are much too deliberately juxtaposed to be mere Freudian inferences:

> "Oh, Jake," Brett said, "we could have had such a damned good time together."
>
> Ahead was a mounted policeman in khaki directing traffic. He raised his baton. The car slowed suddenly pressing Brett against me.
>
> "Yes." I said. "Isn't it pretty to think so?" (*Sun* 247)

That last line echoes one uttered in their first taxi ride, in which Jake says to Brett, "Isn't there anything we can do about it?" followed by a quick, "And there's not a damn thing we could do" (26). Both taxi lines reflect an understated and more hard-boiled condensation of Nick's final poetic monologue, where, still on the beach and sounding as romantic as Gatsby, he watches the "glow of a ferryboat across the Sound," sounding ever so hopeful as he builds to an emotional pitch: "Gatsby believed in the green light, the orgiastic future that year by year recedes before us. It eluded us then, but that's no matter—tomorrow we will run faster, stretch out our arms farther" (*Gatsby* 152)—an echo, of course, of the pitiful picture of Gatsby's outstretched and trembling arms extended toward Daisy's green light (31).

For Jake, there is no reaching beyond the realities of his situation. There is only a bit of wistful thinking as he, pulled away from his seaside contemplation, can only speculate about possibilites, as I do now. What if Hemingway's novel was, in fact, begun in parody, but later allowed to take on a life of its own, its theme partially deriving from his criticism of Fitzgerald's view of the world—acceptance of the real versus hope for an ideal? What if Hemingway wasn't joking when he proposed *The Sun Also Rises* as a greater Gatsby?

WORKS CITED

Balassi, William. "The Trail to *The Sun Also Rises*: The First Week of Writing." *Hemingway: Essays of Reassessment.* Frank Scafella, ed. New York: Oxford UP, 1991. 33-51.

Bruccoli, Matthew J. *Fitzgerald and Hemingway: A Dangerous Friendship.* New York: Carroll and Graf, 1994.

———. "Oh, Give Them Irony and Give Them Pity." *Fitzgerald/ Hemingway Annual 1970:* 236.

Fitzgerald, F. Scott. *The Great Gatsby.* 1925. The Authorized Text. New York: Scribners, 1992.

———. *The Letters of F. Scott Fitzgerald.* Ed. Andrew Turnbull. New York: Scribners, 1963.

Hemingway, Ernest. *Ernest Hemingway: Selected Letters, 1917-1961.* Ed. Carlos Baker. New York: Scribners, 1981.

———. *A Moveable Feast.* New York: Scribners, 1964.

———. *The Sun Also Rises.* 1926. New York: Scribners, 1954.

Hinkle, James. "What's Funny in *The Sun Also Rises*?" *Ernest Hemingway's "The Sun Also Rises": Modern Critical Interpretations.* Ed. Harold Bloom. New York: Chelsea House, 1987. 133-49.

Joost, Nicholas. *Scofield Thayer and "The Dial," An Illustrated History.* Carbondale: Southern Illinois UP, 1964.

Lauter, Paul. "Plato's Stepchildren, Gatsby and Cohn." *Modern Fiction Studies* 9 (1963-64): 338-46.

Mizener, Arthur. *The Far Side of Paradise.* 1951. New York: Vintage, 1959.

Meyers, Jeffrey. *Hemingway: A Biography.* New York: Harper & Row, 1985.

Reynolds, Michael. *Hemingway: The Paris Years.* Cambridge, MA: Blackwell, 1989.

Seldes, Gilbert. "Spring Flight." *The Dial* 79 (1925): 162-64.

Stark, Bruce. "Ernest Hemingway: Writer, Man and Myth." *Clockwatch Review* 3.2 (1986): 25-30.

Stern, Milton R. *The Golden Moment: The Novels of F. Scott Fitzgerald.* Urbana: U of Illinois P, 1971.

Svoboda, Frederic Joseph. *Hemingway and "The Sun Also Rises": The Crafting of a Style.* Lawrence: UP of Kansas, 1983.

Turnbull, Andrew. *Scott Fitzgerald.* New York: Scribners, 1962.

Vance, William L. "Implications of Form in *The Sun Also Rises.*" *Ernest Hemingway's "The Sun Also Rises": Modern Critical Interpretations.* Ed. Harold Bloom. New York: Chelsea House, 1987. 39-49.

MADWOMEN ON THE RIVIERA

THE FITZGERALDS, HEMINGWAY, AND THE MATTER OF MODERNISM

N A N C Y R . C O M L E Y

In Ernest Hemingway's post-1945 work, one is struck by the working and reworking of certain material, specifically in texts that were unfinished at his death. The most "finished" text of that period, *A Moveable Feast*, contains much of the matter that Hemingway was reworking, most of it centered on memories of the years of his first marriage, his early career, and his divorce. Another major text of the late period, *The Garden of Eden*, also is set in the early to mid-1920s,[1] and while some of this fiction has autobiographical resonance, *Garden*, with its Riviera setting and its introduction of feminine madness in the characters of Catherine Bourne and Barbara Sheldon, also suggests a strong link with F. Scott Fitzgerald's *Tender Is the Night*. The substantial number of pages in *A Moveable Feast* devoted to F. Scott and Zelda Fitzgerald would seem to support this claim. Moreover, there is another text which figures in this intertextual network, perhaps perversely, because it was initially rejected in its original and in its revised forms by Fitzgerald and Hemingway respectively: Zelda Fitzgerald's *Save Me the Waltz*. Zelda's story provides the counterpoint to the male writers' versions of the problems of the creative male with a crazy wife. This textual network locates the

French Riviera of the 1920s as a key scene of modernism. Of particular interest is Hemingway's deployment of two madwomen in *Garden*, for it raises the question of what madness represents in modernist texts, especially when it is linked to women.

Substantial parts of *The Garden of Eden*, *Tender Is the Night*, and *Save Me the Waltz*, as well as Zelda Fitzgerald's unfinished novel, "Caesar's Things," are set on the Riviera. As a scene of writing, its function is one of origination; its promise is Edenic. In *A Moveable Feast*, Hemingway presents F. Scott Fitzgerald, unable to write in Paris, "the town best organized for a writer to write in," as always thinking that "there would be someplace where he and Zelda could have a good life together again. He thought of the Riviera, as it was then before it had all been built up." Fitzgerald touts the Riviera to Hemingway as an inexpensive place where "we would both work hard every day and swim and lie on the beach and be brown" (182). In short, an ideal scenario; and for Fitzgerald, the possible fulfillment of a nostalgia for an imagined *locus amoenus*. Perhaps Hemingway is remembering not Fitzgerald's words but rather Nicole Diver's stream-of-consciousness in *Tender Is the Night* where her similar thoughts are addressed to her husband: "You're bored with Zurich and you can't find time for writing here. . . . We'll live near a warm beach where we can be brown and young together. . . . No one comes to the Riviera in summer, so we expect to have a few guests and to work" (160).

In letters and texts generated from the Riviera experience, the area is frequently described in Edenic terms. In Zelda Fitzgerald's *Save Me the Waltz*, painter David Knight exclaims upon entering their newly rented villa, "We are now in Paradise—as nearly as we'll ever get." There is irony here, generated by the decor of this Paradise: "Pastel cupids frolicked amidst the morning glories and roses in garlands swelled like goiters or some malignant disease" (*Collected Writings* 78). Certainly such description suggests a decadent, fallen Eden. In Zelda's novel, there are moments like this of acute sensory awareness; in this instance, the locale generates them: "The Riviera is a seductive place. The blare of the beaten blue and those white palaces shimmering under the heat accentuates things" (87). In that intensely felt atmosphere, with her husband David at work in his studio painting, Alabama finds that reading Dickens, Edith Wharton, and Henry James "in the long afternoons" becomes monotonous. She wonders, "What can I do with myself?" (87). With the Eve of this Eden experiencing unfulfilled desire, the stage is set for a deepening of her attraction to a new acquaintance, Jacques Chevre-Feuille, dashing French aviator.

The Riviera was the site of Zelda's romantic affair with French aviator Edouard Jozan, whose white duck uniform also appears on Tommy Barban, with whom Nicole Diver has a sexual affair in *Tender Is the Night*. Zelda presented her own fictional version of her brief romance in *Save Me the Waltz*, but in the unfinished "Caesar's Things" she renders it with greater intensity. Though Zelda's Riviera chapter begins: "Now this was paradise" (thus echoing David Knight's words in *Save Me the Waltz*), it is an inverted paradise, a "parching world" where "the beach was as attenuate as a Chirico backdrop" (VII: 7). The villa Janno and Jacob rent is a "secret house" set in a pine thicket whose garden is a confusion of "pebbled walks," "truncated vistas," and "secret places": "good places for the heart to die or the world be hid." It would appear that the Garden of Eden has evolved into a darkened *hortus conclusus*. Although Janno (the protagonist) blames destiny for what happens, she kisses Jacques on the neck, predicting for herself the consequences of "tragedy and death: ruin is a relative matter" (VII: 4). Though Zelda's affair with Edouard Jozan was apparently not sexually consummated,[2] her double rendering of this event suggests that she was deeply affected by her desire, however brief, for another man. Certainly Fitzgerald felt their marriage had been damaged by his wife's affair and also by his own affair in 1927-1928 with a Hollywood starlet, Lois Moran, who was thirteen years his junior. (Rosemary Hoyt, star of the movie *Daddy's Girl* in *Tender Is the Night*, presumably represents Moran.)

Tender Is the Night opens near the end of the Edenic phase of the Riviera with a small horde of Americans (and Britons) at play on the beach. "One could get away with more on the summer Riviera. . . . Pretty much of anything went at Antibes," Fitzgerald wrote in "Echoes of the Jazz Age" (1931). And "by 1929, at the most gorgeous paradise for swimmers on the Mediterranean no one swam anymore, save for a short hang-over dip at noon" (Wilson 19). Sara Murphy set the date of the tourist invasion at 1927, as did *Vanity Fair* magazine, which described Antibes in 1927 as "Broadway's most popular outpost" and noted, "By this past summer, the migration [of 'a herd of Americans'] had become such a mass movement that old Antibes devotees knew they themselves would have to pack up and move on. The crowd had discovered their retreat and they must find another or be trampled to death" (Amory and Bradlee 124). The decline and fall of Dick Diver in *Tender Is the Night* coincides with the spoliation of the simpler natural pleasures of the Riviera, a decline reflected in the contrast between the "fine man in a jockey cap and red-striped tights" (4) of the first chapter (a Dick modeled on Gerald Murphy) and the flabbier man who fails at a silly aquaplane stunt five years later. The older Dick sees his beach "perverted now to the tastes of the tasteless" where "few people swam any more in that blue paradise" (278-79).

Of the texts under consideration here, *Save Me the Waltz* was the first to use the Riviera in print. Zelda Fitzgerald wrote her novel in the first two months of 1932 while at the Phipps Clinic in Baltimore and sent it off to Maxwell Perkins at Scribners without showing it to her husband. When the latter did see it, he was furious, in part, no doubt, because he had been laboring on *Tender Is the Night* for so long. Fitzgerald wrote immediately to his wife's psychiatrist, Mildred Squires:

> turning up in a novel signed by my wife as a somewhat anemic portrait painter with a few ideas lifted from Clive Bell, Leger, ect. [sic] puts me in an absurd and Zelda in a ridiculous position. . . . this mixture of fact and fiction is simply calculated to ruin us both, . . . and I can't let it stand. . . . My God, my books made her a legend and her single intention in this somewhat thin portrait is to make me a non-entity.(*Life in Letters* 207)

Zelda, after hearing from Dr. Squires about Fitzgerald's displeasure, probably guessed the real reason for it, because she wrote in a conciliatory letter that one reason she hadn't let him see the manuscript first was that *"I was also afraid we might have touched the same material"* (*Correspondence* 289; this sentence in Zelda's letter was probably underlined by Fitzgerald). Following her husband's suggestions, Zelda revised the novel until he found it good—or so he said to Perkins. Zelda apologized to Fitzgerald in one letter, but in another, she said:

> *However, I would like you to thoroughly understand that my revisions will be made on an aesthetic basis: that the other material which I will elect is nevertheless legitimate stuff which has cost me a pretty emotional penny* to amass and which I intend to use when I can get the tranquility of spirit necessary to write the story of myself versus myself. That is the book I really want to write. (*Collected Writings* 468; emphasis in original, "possibly underlined by Fitzgerald")

In March of 1934, she wrote to her husband about the second novel she wanted to write—but only if he approved: *"Please say what you want done,* as I really do not know. As you know, my work is mostly a pleasure for me, but if it is better for me to take up something quite foreign to my temperament, I will" (*Collected Writings* 470-71; emphasis in original probably Zelda Fitzgerald's).

In 1932 Fitzgerald had reminded his wife of her unreasonable desire to dance and the "long desperate heart-destroying" training that had come to naught. He assured her that she had "'value' as a personality," but found the use of her phrase "expressing oneself" to have become "an athema [sic] in my ears." He told her:

It simply doesn't exist. What one expresses in a work of art is the dark tragic destiny of being an instrument of something uncomprehended, incomprehensible, unknown—you came to the threshold of that discovery and then decided in the face of all logic you would crash the gate. You succeeded merely in crashing yourself, almost me, and Scotty, if I hadn't interposed. (Milford 306-7)

Fitzgerald's deepest disapproval at this time was of his wife's expressing herself in writing. Certainly the fact that both of them considered their lives together as material for their writing was bound to cause friction. Fitzgerald could at times praise Zelda's writing, and of course, he had published some of her writing under his own name.[3] But after the publication of *Save Me the Waltz*, he perceived her writing as threatening to his own and to himself. Finally, in a meeting in April 1933 with Zelda and her psychiatrist, after pronouncing Zelda's talents as "third-rate," her husband delivered his ultimatum, directed at Zelda's latest project, that she was not to write about their lives: "If you write a play, it cannot be a play about psychiatry and it cannot be a play laid in Switzerland, and whatever the idea is, it will have to be submitted to me" (Donaldson 84, 85). Zelda then concentrated on painting for a while, and only after her husband's death did she return to the writing of their lives. "Caesar's Things" is to some degree a rewriting of *Save Me the Waltz*, but its surreality and disjointedness mark it as a chronicle of madness as well. Perhaps it is Zelda's attempt to write "the story of myself versus myself" (*Collected Writings* 468), the book she had said she really wanted to write.

When Fitzgerald completed his version of the "Riviera" story in *Tender Is the Night*, Nicole Diver would not be granted any creative means of expression, though in her reverie, thinking of a life of working and sunbathing on the Riviera, her desire is to "look over the whole field of knowledge and pick out something and really know about it, so I'll have it to hang on to if I go to pieces again" (160). In *Save Me the Waltz*, the most powerful section is that which tells of Zelda/Alabama's desire to dance, both as a means of expression and as a means of developing control over her body. Alabama feels that if she succeeds as a dancer, "she would drive the devils that had driven her—that, in proving herself, she would achieve that peace which she imagined went only in surety of one's self" (*Collected Writings* 118). Drive herself she does: "By springtime, she was gladly, savagely proud of the strength of her Negroid hips, convex as boats in a wood carving. The complete control of her body freed her from all fetid consciousness of it" (127). Yet her awareness of the physical presence of women dancers' bodies is evident throughout this section, as the rigor of the female world of ballet practice is described with particular emphasis on the teacher, Madame Egorova, who drives her, and to whom Alabama is devoted. Alabama does not like David and his friends to intrude into her studio life any more than David cares for her intrusion into his. Nancy Milford is quite right to say that Alabama's "quest for identity" is "her first concern" in this text (278).

As it was published, the novel is certainly much more *her* story than *their* story. Alabama's dancing ends with an injury to her foot, necessitating an operation that precludes her ever dancing again. Zelda's dancing career concluded with a mental breakdown. The novel ends with Alabama and David returning to Alabama's home for the final illness and death of her father. The "Daddy" business that would inhabit *Tender Is the Night* is an important frame in *Save Me the Waltz*, for the novel begins and ends with Judge Beggs. He is likened in the beginning to a castle, "his towers and chapels . . . builded of intellectual conceptions" (9), and as unapproachable. He is so strong that his children neglect to build their own repositories of strength. On the Riviera, Alabama, bored with her life, recalls the "slow uneventful sequence" of her childhood days as one meted out by the Judge "curtailing the excitement she considered was her due." Because David plays the authoritarian, judgmental role, Alabama blames him "for the monotony" (87). But now Alabama returns to the Judge, hoping for an answer to the reason for, or meaning of, her painful life. She returns to the issue of her body and its control: "I thought you could tell me if our bodies are given to us as counterirritants to the soul. I thought you'd know why when our bodies ought to bring surcease from our tortured minds, they fail and collapse; and why, when we are tormented in our bodies, does our soul desert us as a refuge?" (185). However, her father can only reply "Ask me something easy," before drifting back into sleep. No one would have an answer for Alabama/Zelda, whose schizophrenia ("myself versus myself") bore with it the problem of the body as other.[4]

Zelda Fitzgerald was heavily dependent on her husband for emotional support, but at one point she made it clear that she did not want him to play Doctor Diver to her Nicole; rather, she was seeking non-patriarchal nurturing: "I think we're all agreed that your role is *not to be that of doctor* and in my present condition you have to mother me" (Milford 307; emphasis in original). Believing that her mother was responsible for spoiling Zelda, Fitzgerald was not inclined to follow such advice. He was of course deeply involved in Zelda's illness; after all, he did love her, and he was footing the bills. In his letters to her doctors, he tried to analyze Zelda's background.

He seemed to believe in the inheritance of mental instability, the growth of which in Zelda's case he believed was encouraged by her being spoiled as the baby of the family. He wanted her doctors to teach Zelda to *behave*.

His perception of Zelda as an unruly child is right in line with the theory promoted by the leading authority on schizophrenia, Paul Eugen Bleuler, who had been called in by Zelda's doctor, Oscar Forel, when she was at the Swiss sanitarium, Les Rives de Prangins. Bleuler, following Freud, viewed schizophrenia as "a profound regression to the most primitive stage of 'infantile autoeroticism'" (Sass 20). Labeled as a "primitive" illness, its treatment reflected "the rather condescending assumption that schizophrenics need to be brought up or socialized and that a therapist should play the role of a benign or wise parent who gives the patient a second chance to be nurtured toward maturity" (Sass 21). That Fitzgerald firmly believed in this authoritarian doctrine is further revealed in a letter he wrote to Zelda's psychiatrist at the Phipps Clinic, Adolf Meyer, a follower of Bleuler:

> All I ever meant by asking authority over her was the power of an ordinary nurse in any continental country over a child; to be able to say "If you don't do this I shall punish you." All I have ever had has been the power of the nurse-girl in America who can only say, "I'll tell your Mama." . . .
>
> *Will Doctor Meyer give me the authority to ask Zelda when she is persistently refactory to pack her bag and spend a week under people who can take care of her, such as in the clinic?*

He would like Meyer to "impose . . . ideas of morality upon" Zelda, approving of Forel's "strictly teutonic idea of marriage" and (implicitly) disapproving of Meyers's *"benevolent neutrality"* in such moral issues as "mutual duty" (*Correspondence* 307, 309; emphasis in original).

Fitzgerald's fictional treatment of Nicole Diver's madness follows a similar pattern; Nicole is ordered more than once by her doctor husband to "Control yourself!" Practically speaking, such an edict is about as useful as telling a person with multiple personality disorder to "Pull yourself together!" Putting such words into Doctor Diver's mouth reveals Fitzgerald's lack of understanding of Zelda's illness. As his outline for the novel shows, Fitzgerald was aware of his "basic ignorance of psychiatric and medical training" (Bruccoli 80). More to the point, I think, is some understanding of Fitzgerald's concept of mental illness, especially in women. Like Bleuler and Forel, Fitzgerald had a patriarchal conception of "female psychology": namely, that for a woman to be considered healthy, she must adjust to the behavioral norms for her sex. Phyllis Chesler has pointed out in *Women and Madness* that "The *sine qua non* of 'feminine' identity in patriarchal society is the violation of the incest taboo, i. e., the initial and continued preference for Daddy, followed by the approved falling in love [with] and/or marrying of powerful father figures" (138). In *Tender Is the Night*, Nicole's madness is said to stem from her forced violation of the incest taboo. But by falling in love with and marrying a double Daddy, a doctor-Daddy, she repeats the scene of incest, and thus her "cure" consists in her eventually seeking revenge.[5] She casts off the waning Dick for a more heroic Daddy, Tommy Barban, a well-muscled soldier-of-fortune type, who is not much given to sustained thought. Nicole, whose ego is now blooming "like a great rich rose," has come to hate the beach, resenting "the places where she had played planet to Dick's sun" (287). She is relieved to have in Tommy a man "who did not try to understand her" (293).

Dick Diver fades out of the picture, a failure, presumably spoiled by Nicole's money, which has helped to undermine his professional drive. To some degree, Fitzgerald may have been writing his own story; and in that story, a dislike of women is a major feature. In the evolution of the novel that became *Tender Is the Night*, destructive women are consistently present, along with the dislike, or even fear, of them. The novel's inception was in matricide, featuring quick-tempered Francis Melarky, who murders his domineering mother in a fit of rage; this plot was followed by one featuring a homicidal woman. She evolved into a "heroine" who, in Fitzgerald's outline, is described as a young woman whose transference to her doctor "saves her— when it is not working she reverts to homicidal mania and tries to kill men" (Bruccoli 80). Nicole Diver is a modified version, a more subtly destructive schizophrenic wife, who, like a vampire, grows stronger as she feeds on her husband, who declines in strength and will, and thus becomes undesirable and indeed unnecessary. Nicole's cure is aided by the power of her money; her sister, Baby Warren, is quite open about Dick's having been bought for Nicole as a live-in doctor. In Nicole's reverie, buying a house as a place to keep Dick in is important to her: "I'm tired of apartments and waiting for you" (*Tender* 160-61). In this case, the house on the Riviera becomes a *hortus conclusus* for the male, until far fallen into abjection, he is in effect ordered out of the garden. Baby and her sister have no regrets about hastening Diver's departure, for their view is a material one: The doctor is perceived as a commodity which has been used up, or outlived its need, and should now be discarded. In his weakened condition, abdicated from his paternal role, he constitutes an embarrassment.

Ernest Hemingway's first reaction to *Tender Is the Night* was "I liked it and I didn't like it," taking Fitzgerald to task for using real people—Sara and Gerald Murphy—and making them do things "they would not do." As a result, he went on, Fitzgerald "produced not people but damned marvelously faked case histories" (*Selected Letters* 407). As for Fitzgerald's "personal tragedy," Hemingway advised him to "use it—don't cheat with it." Fitzgerald's "tragedy" was, of course, Zelda. Hemingway was convinced that Zelda was responsible for Fitzgerald's problems with writing: "Of all people on earth you needed discipline in your work and instead you marry someone who is jealous of your work, wants to compete with you and ruins you. It's not as simple as that and I thought Zelda was crazy the first time I met her . . . and, of course you're a rummy" (*Selected Letters* 408). Five years later Hemingway reread *Tender Is the Night* and wrote to Maxwell Perkins, "It's amazing how *excellent* much of it is" (483). In 1941, after Fitzgerald's death, he wrote again to Perkins that *Tender* was "The best book he ever wrote. . . . it has all the realization of tragedy that Scott ever found. Wonderful atmosphere and magical descriptions" (527).

In this same letter, which was written just after the publication of *The Last Tycoon*, Hemingway felt that novel had "a deadness that is unbelievable from Scott." But Hemingway also felt that "Scott died inside himself at around the age of thirty to thirty-five" and that "His heart died in him in France" (527, 528). A few years later, Hemingway returned to the scene of Fitzgerald's death of the heart when he began writing *The Garden of Eden*. In turning to the matter of the Riviera, Hemingway would rewrite the story of the talented writer with the beautiful but crazy wife, and it would be sad, like the Fitzgeralds' story, but not so tragic, for Hemingway's writer would survive his wife's literal destruction of his writing. While *Garden* is not autobiography, it is written with a good deal of personal investment as a reexamination of the past through the distancing lens of fiction.

For Hemingway, a return to the Riviera meant a return to the death of his first marriage, which was hastened by events of the Riviera summer of 1926. The charming ambiance emanating from Sara and Gerald Murphy's Villa America was frequently disrupted by the drunken and otherwise erratic behavior of the Fitzgeralds, and the promise of an idyllic summer on the Riviera was aborted by the Hemingways' problems of the heart. Initially, Hadley, who was supposed to accompany her husband to Spain, was instead quarantined at Antibes alone with Bumby, their son, who had whooping cough. Hemingway was in Spain, moody without female companionship, and when he returned to the Riviera, there also was Pauline Pfeiffer, who, immune to whooping cough, had invited herself. Pauline joined the Hemingways for breakfast in bed, and when the Hemingways moved to the Hotel de la Pinède in Juan-les-Pins, Pauline followed. They all swam in a private cove, and at least once the women sunbathed in the nude, with Hadley getting badly sunburned as a result. At the end of the summer, the Hemingways announced they were splitting up. Gioia Diliberto cites a letter from John Dos Passos to Hemingway expressing his dismay at their breakup as a possible source for the title of *The Garden of Eden*: "Aren't we all expatriates from the Garden of Eden?" (224, 225).

While these events of the summer of 1926 undoubtedly contributed to the germination of *Garden*, the Riviera that Hemingway creates in that novel is the one that existed just before the Americans and the international set made it fashionable in the summer. One can drive into Cannes for stylish haircuts and lunches, but back at the little Eden "in the pines on the Estérel side of La Napoule" (75), David and Catherine Bourne are the only guests at the small establishment. This is the La Napoule described by Captain Leslie Richardson in *Things Seen on the Riviera* (1924): "At the eastern end of the red littoral, where the hills dip down to the valley near Cannes, La Napoule provides the landscape with a note of medieval romance, for here a feudal castle was built on the ruins of a Roman victualling garden" (55).

The Bournes have chosen La Napoule because there "is no one there" in summer; no one on the beaches where they swim and sunbathe in the nude. In its published form, *The Garden of Eden* is an altogether sparsely populated novel—almost as sparsely populated, one might say, as the original Eden. In *Garden*, echoes of paternal authoritarianism can be heard in Catherine Bourne's promises to be a "good girl" for David, the Papa figure in their paradise. (To enhance this image, there is probably about the same age difference—ten years—between Catherine and David as there is between Nicole and Dick.) The type of madness that Catherine reveals is destructive, like Zelda's; that is, as Hemingway read Zelda. In *A Moveable Feast*, he reasserts what he wrote to Fitzgerald in 1934: that he believed from the beginning of his friendship with the Fitzgeralds that Zelda was crazy. Hemingway could not forgive Zelda for what he read as her jealousy of her husband's work: "He would start to work and as soon as he was working well Zelda would begin complaining about how bored she was and get him off on another drunken party" (180-81).

This is Hemingway's Zelda, one of the texts that creates the Zelda we know. In her own time, she was already textualized; recall Fitzgerald's remark to her psychiatrist: "my books made her a legend." However, as Nicole Diver, she would oversee her husband's failure. Fitzgerald not only used his experience of his wife's breakdown as the model for Nicole Diver, but he also paraphrased or quoted directly from Zelda's own letters in Nicole's letters to Dick Diver. This version of herself as someone "awful" who "ruined" her husband's life upset Zelda (Milford 342); aware that this might be the case, Fitzgerald warned her against rereading the novel. Hemingway appropriated the Fitzgeralds' story of the talented writer with the crazy wife, but he would adapt it to a character like himself as writer. Zelda, as his model for madness, spoke not only in his memory, and through Fitzgerald's texts, but also through her own.

To Maxwell Perkins, who had sent Hemingway a copy of *Save Me the Waltz*, Hemingway wrote, "Zelda I found to be completely and absolutely unreadable. I tried to read it but I never could" (*Selected Letters* 376-77). We should note the conflation here of Zelda and her novel: having considered Zelda "crazy" from his first meeting with her, Hemingway suggests that she, as well as her novel, are texts he either cannot or does not wish to read. How much or how little of Zelda's novel Hemingway actually read is not an issue; it's very likely he didn't finish reading it, for Zelda herself and Zelda's text were too closely wedded for Hemingway to read comfortably. In noting the conflation of Zelda and her novel, I wish to suggest that the two conjoined provided the discourse of madness that Hemingway would draw on in creating the Catherines of *The Garden of Eden*.

As a source of Catherine's madness, Hemingway adopts a belief similar to Fitzgerald's that madness is inherited, as is apparent in Colonel Boyle's remarks regarding Catherine's family and his warning to David that "The get's no good" (65). In *Garden*, Catherine Bourne, like Zelda, is jealous of her husband David's work, unless he is engaged in writing their narrative, the story of their marriage, for in that text she can see herself reflected. When David stops writing the narrative and switches to material emerging from his adolescent years in Africa and his strained relations with his father, Catherine feels herself shut out of his textual world, which, in the African material, is essentially a patriarchal one. She detests David's African stories, considering them bestial and cruel, and one day she burns them. David considers this a consummate act of madness. However, while it is suggested that the source of Catherine's madness is an inherited one, it is also suggested that her sexual changings, which are considered transgressive in this text, can lead to madness. Indeed, Marita, who becomes the third in this Riviera ménage à trois, chortles to herself that she can exercise control over her sexual changes and Catherine, in her opinion, can't. Marita rejects the concept of transgression: "It's not perversion. It's variety," she says (Comley and Scholes 62-62, 99-102).

In Madrid, after a night of changes, Catherine is greeted by David as "Devil," his term of endearment for her and an acknowledgment of her powers of seduction. Their nocturnal activities leave David with a feeling of remorse, but Catherine refuses to accept that there is anything to be remorseful about. She asks him to watch her change, there in the outdoor café, and then asks if he likes her as a girl.[6] To his "Yes," she responds, "I'm glad someone likes it because it's a god damned bore," launching into a little litany of everything that's wrong with being female: "Scenes, hysteria, false accusations, temperament" (*Garden* 70)—not to mention menstruation, the present sign of what Catherine feels is her failure to conceive, though David nobly offers, "That could be my fault" (71). Finding an outlet for her creative urges is as much a problem for Catherine as it was for Zelda (or Alabama, or Nicole). In *The Garden of Eden,* Catherine is denied the right to write by her creator, but her creativity is exercised in two ways: first, through her desire for metamorphosis, manifested not only in the sexual changes of the dark but also in outward and visible signs such as bleached hair and a darkly tanned body, the latter signaling a desire for racial change. Second, though Catherine does not write, she has been granted the power of telling; indeed, much of the power of this novel resides in its dialogue, and particularly in the sharp wit Catherine is endowed with by her creator.

Catherine's sexuality attracts both sexes, further complicating her erotic life. In Fitzgerald's novel, Nicole's madness and destructiveness are demonstrated at certain points but diminish as her cure develops. In Hemingway's novel—at least in its manuscript version—feminine madness is more strongly asserted because it is doubled. *The Garden of Eden* was originally conceived as the book of the two Catherines: Catherine Bourne and Catherine (later Barbara) Sheldon. It might be worth mentioning that in Hemingway's limited repertoire of names, Catherine has pride of place as "the most pleasant name," probably because it was linked to Hadley Hemingway.[7] There is also Catherine Barkley of *A Farewell to Arms,* who loves well and dies miserably, and who is initially perceived by Frederic Henry as a bit crazy. Both Catherines in Hemingway's *Garden* are mentally unstable. Barbara Sheldon, who is a bit older than Catherine Bourne, is attracted to her, but she perceives Catherine as destructive and herself as "destroy material" (Comley and Scholes 64).[8]

Lesbian relationships rank high among acts considered transgressive in this text, and Barbara feels that such an engagement would drive her into madness. Catherine herself does experiment with a sapphic engagement with Marita, who has just emerged from one lesbian relationship and has been attracted to Catherine. Catherine responds to her as if compelled to do so, telling David "I'm going to do it until I'm through with it and I'm over it" (*Garden* 114). She finds it a deadening experience and feels a sense of loss in being "unfaithful" to David. David, who finds lesbianism repugnant, terms it "perversion," while the initiator of the tryst, Marita, lightly says, "It's only something girls do because they have nothing better" (120).

As she is constructed, Marita is an amalgam of mixed codes, representative of her creator's ambivalence toward her: She blushes, and she is a virgin (signs of innocence); yet she is given a slightly exotic name, is experienced in lesbian relationships, and, labeled by David as a "street arab," she feels she can do anything Catherine can do better. She has blithely offered to Catherine, "I can be your girl, if you ever want one, and David's too" (105). But Marita is soon cured of any lingering sapphic tendencies through some good healthy hetero sex with David. Marita's advantage over Catherine is that she can engage in sexual role-playing without guilt or any other psychic repercussions. As Catherine notes of Marita, "You're a girl and a boy both and you really are. You don't have to change and it doesn't kill you and I'm not. And now I'm nothing. All I wanted was for David and you to be happy. Everything else I invent" (192). Her major invention, she says, is David and Marita as a couple.

Catherine's compulsion to try lesbian sex has a price: Because sapphism has been labeled as a perversion by David, who represents the law of the father in this Garden, penance must be done, psychic dues be paid. Catherine's compulsions lead her toward madness, and Barbara Sheldon sees for herself a similar danger in her attraction to Catherine, which she terms an "obsession," joking edgily about pleasure turning to vice. She recognizes Catherine as a very "wild girl," and though Barbara is attracted to her, she tells David, "I know I'm strange. But I'm not a queer or I never was. Crazy if you like and with special things or one thing that I wanted and got it or have it or had it." She feels now that she "had a good head once and that's all gone" (Comley and Scholes 64). She has given up painting because though she painted "well enough for a woman," it was not, she felt, good enough to interest her. And in any case, she feels her work to be inferior to her husband's. Yet Nick admires Barbara's talent: "She's not afraid of all the things I'm afraid of." He notes that in her landscape painting, she filters out the picturesque and leaves "only the geometry." With this assessment of aesthetic control, Nick's appraisal suggests that Barbara has learned from Cézanne, but a contradictory assessment is made by Andy, another writer who is engaged in the Sheldons' story: "Her painting worried me and I think it worried her too. It was very close to the edge and that shows clearer in painting than in almost anything else" (Comley and Scholes 63).

While Andy's reaction is reminiscent of Fitzgerald's apprehensions about his wife's work, the contradictory views of Barbara's painting raise the issue of the readable and the unreadable and, of course, the issue of who is doing the reading. It would also be fair to say that the contradictions here are a signal of the author's ambivalence and of the unresolved problems that left *The Garden of Eden* an unfinished text. Barbara is unable to have a baby, another sign of thwarted feminine creativity in this text. Andy, who has declined Barbara's offer to form a ménage à trois with the Sheldons, does at her urging make love with her, and while this tryst is taking place, Nick is killed, his bike struck by a car. Barbara breaks down, and Andy takes care of her. (And his writing, like David's after Catherine's purge, strengthens during this bad time.) Though Barbara seems to improve while on a trip to Venice, she commits suicide in the (appropriately named) Old Luna Hotel with an overdose of sleeping pills. (The manuscript shows Hemingway wavering between this method and a drowning at high tide—when the waters of Venice are cleaner.) Barbara leaves a note saying that they had certainly built the castle, referring to the sand castle they'd actually never built at the beach, and to a monograph that Andy is supposed to be writing about the Sheldons which would contain illustrations of them in a sand castle they keep trying to build, but that always gets washed away in the high tide.

The sand castle, which is the title of a subsection in a short outline that Hemingway made for *The Garden of Eden*, was washed away by Scribners along with the Sheldons and Andy and much else. This is a shame, because the sand castle is a useful metaphor, with its echoes of innocence and ephemerality and its suggestion of innocent pursuits on Riviera beaches in a prelapsarian time more imagined than real. The sand castle may also serve as a metaphor for Hemingway's first marriage, which has acquired the mythical status of a loving union of innocents as memorialized in *A Moveable Feast.* For the Sheldons are another representation of that poor young sensitive couple, living on love and honest work in Paris, until the rich folk discovered them and corrupted them and their marriage was washed away. The sand castle may be considered a work of art as well, but it is a form of performance art that can never reach formal completion. Late in the manuscript version of the novel, after Catherine has burned David's manuscripts and gone away, David jokes bitterly with Marita: "Crazy woman burned out the Bournes," he says, deciding "I'll write in the sand. . . . That's my new medium. I'm going to be a sand writer" (Spilka 358, n. 12). What he writes in the sand is their name, "the Bournes," as affirmation for a supposedly forthcoming marriage, but this would be washed away, for as the manuscript shows, Hemingway could not write this conclusion. However, the burned stories return to David Bourne, with the father in the stories now stronger, having "more dimensions than he had in the story before," and "there was no sign that any of it would ever cease returning to him intact" (*Garden* 247), which suggests that Catherine's fire may be considered a refining one.

In writing *The Garden of Eden*, Hemingway seemed to be taking the advice he gave Fitzgerald in 1934, just after he'd read *Tender Is the Night* regarding his "personal tragedy" (Zelda): "when you get the damned hurt use it—don't cheat with it" (*Selected Letters* 408). Working with the Fitzgeralds' lives and texts as well as his own proved to be a challenge of great complexity, for it involved a struggle between masculine and feminine discourses. On one hand, Hemingway's Catherine Bourne is destructive: She burns David's stories of the father, writing she characterizes as masturbatory, calling it "the solitary vice" (Burwell 119), writing which has cut off the marriage narrative, in which she has a creative investment as well. Along with Zelda Fitzgerald's destructive tendencies, then, Hemingway has also imported her desire to create. On the other hand, the bisexual adventures that Catherine has initiated, and in which David has been a willing partner, have stimulated him creatively; at one point he muses: "so far as you corrupt or change, [your ability to write] grows and strengthens" (Burwell 119). The other woman, Marita, who has no creative urges, is merely the handmaiden of David's masculine texts.

Yet in the end—the provisional end, to be sure—Catherine has succeeded in having David write their narrative: We have just read it (assuming we have read the entire manuscript of *The Garden of Eden*). In the provisional ending, Catherine has returned to David from a stay in a sanitarium. She recalls her prideful desire to make everything in her own image until this desire for changing made her crazy. She knows she is not fully recovered and that if there is a next time, it will be worse. As her words suggest—and I have had to paraphrase them here—she believes she tried to play God and her hubristic attempts at creation have nearly destroyed her. Should her madness return, she will not go back to what she probably sees as a death-in-life in a Swiss sanitarium but would choose suicide, and David promises to join her. They are left on the beach, moving into the lengthening shadows and out of the sun that neither can tolerate as well now, staring at the sea in which they may—or may not—drown themselves. Catherine has paid a hefty price to reclaim the narrative she had felt threatened to be permanently interrupted by David's own. Her somewhat fragile and repentant condition suggests that she is unlikely to try to "express herself" again.

Certainly the Fitzgeralds' novels and Hemingway's *Garden of Eden* have in common struggles over narrative rights. In *Garden,* they are played out in the text; with the Fitzgeralds, the struggle that underlies *Save Me the Waltz* and *Tender Is the Night* raised this question: When a couple's life together is considered by both as narrative material, does only one of them have the rights to it? F. Scott Fitzgerald seemed to think so, but for Zelda, there was more than one story to be written from that material. Fitzgerald need not have worried so about damage to his image, because if Hemingway found Zelda's novel "unreadable," most didn't even try to read it. In effect, Fitzgerald won the struggle, but as the story plays itself out in *Tender Is the Night,* his would seem to be a Pyrrhic victory: The price of the wife's cure in *Tender* is the (figurative) death of the husband/author.

In returning to the matter of the Riviera, Hemingway may very well have been confronting a present anxiety: the waning of his creative powers, his loss of potency as a writer. In *The Garden of Eden* he was, in a sense, writing against the Fitzgeralds' texts. As Rose Marie Burwell has pointed out, Hemingway, who obsessively compared himself with Fitzgerald, invested Zelda Fitzgerald with an archetypal power as a succubus (169; 232, n. 36), the very role Nicole Diver plays in *Tender Is the Night.* In constructing David Bourne, in whom he has a substantial self-investment, it was imperative for Hemingway that his writer resist the self-destructive tendencies that distinguish Fitzgerald's Dick Diver (and, some would say, that distinguished Hemingway himself). Hemingway's crazy women would differ from Nicole/Zelda as well, in part because they share characteristics belonging to Hadley Hemingway, whom Hemingway had loved deeply and later regretted losing. As a result, Catherine Bourne's distinctive complexity and craziness make her a sympathetic character. The deployment of crazy women also enabled the playing-out of bisexual fantasies, in that madness allows (can be an excuse for) going beyond the moral boundaries—the laws of the father—that are implicit in this text. Yet it is the women who pay the price of madness for transgression, and as we have seen, transgression consists not only of sexual acts but also of the women's attempts at creativity. To try to compete with the male (or to play God and create in one's image, as Catherine puts it in what can only be described as her confession) is to trespass. A woman had to be crazy to do it—like Zelda—or, if one tried to create, one's incipient madness surfaced, as with Catherine, or like Barbara Sheldon, madness led to suicide.

Hemingway, in having the last word in the Riviera story, reasserted the primacy of the male writer and, symbolically, of masculine discourse, which in his text rises phoenix-like from the flames with renewed strength.

However, this (oedipal) African narrative is located within a larger narrative, a narrative that testifies to the complexity of sexuality and to the necessary role of the feminine in a man's act of creation.

NOTES

1. Other unfinished texts that use the matter of the 1920s are "Philip Haines was a writer . . ." and "For two weeks James Allen . . . ," which draw on the period between Hemingway's leaving Hadley and marrying Pauline, when he was living by himself in Paris. *Islands in the Stream* contains sequences of memories of this period, as well as the brief return of a beautiful blond movie-star wife (perhaps the fictional realization of Robert Jordan's erotic movie-star fantasies in *For Whom the Bell Tolls*).

2. In an interview with Nancy Milford some years later, Edouard Jozan insisted that "Zelda's infidelity was imaginary" (*Zelda* 145).

3. In a ledger in which Scott Fitzgerald listed earnings from writing, twenty stories and articles written by Zelda are listed under "Zelda's Earnings" (*Ledger* 54, 143). Seven of these pieces were published under Zelda Fitzgerald's name; nine were published jointly; four were published under Fitzgerald's name only. Publication information may be found in Zelda Fitzgerald's *Collected Writings*. Of five stories written by Zelda but published jointly in *College Humor*, Fitzgerald noted to his agent Harold Ober that they "have been pretty strong draughts on Zelda's and my common store of material" (Milford 186).

4. As described by Gilles Deleuze:

> The schizophrenic body appears as a kind of bodysieve. Freud emphasized this schizophrenic aptitude for perceiving the surface and the skin as if each were pierced by an infinite number of little holes. As a result, the body is nothing but depth; it snatches and carries off all things in this gaping depth, which represents a fundamental involution. Everything is body and corporeal. . . . Bodysieve, fragmented body, and dissociated body—they give evidence of the general breakdown of surfaces. (286, 287)

> R. D. Laing, who discusses the self/body split at length in *The*

Divided Self, summarizes the schizophrenic's dilemma:

> The divorce of the self from the body is both something that is painful to be borne, and which the sufferer desperately longs for someone to help mend, but it is also utilized as the basic means of defence. This in fact defines the essential dilemma. The self wishes to be wedded and embodied in the body, yet is constantly afraid to lodge in the body for fear of there being subject to attacks and dangers from which it cannot escape. (161)

5. Dick Diver does everything Freud says not to do in his essay "Observations on Transference Love" (1915): "If the patient's advances were returned it would be a great triumph for her, but a complete defeat for the treatment. She would have succeeded in acting out, in repeating in real life, what she ought only to have remembered, to have produced as psychical material and to have kept within the sphere of psychical events. . . . The love-relationship in fact destroys the patient's susceptibility to influence from analytic treatment. A combination of the two would be an impossibility. It is, therefore, just as disastrous for an analysis if the patient's craving for love is gratified as if it is suppressed" (383).

6. Bisexuality has been linked to schizophrenia. In a 1968 study cited by Phyllis Chesler, female schizophrenics were observed to be more likely than males to exhibit "a total or partial rejection of one's sex-role stereotype" and to be "more overtly concerned with sexual or bisexual pleasure, than are female 'depressives'" (56, 50). This question then arises: Is such role reversal "what is labeled 'crazy,' or is [it], partly, what the disease is about"? Chesler cites a study of role-playing in which female schizophrenics "chose 'male' roles in imaginary plays: they preferred being 'devils' to 'witches'" (53).

7. "Catherine" and its diminutives "Cat" and "Kit" or "Kid" were nicknames Hemingway used for Hadley.

8. Because quoting from unpublished Hemingway manuscripts is at this time a litigious affair, quotations used here from *The Garden of Eden* manuscript will show as their source one of three texts in which the material was previously published with permission: Burwell, Comley and Scholes, and Spilka.

WORKS CITED

Amory, Cleveland, and Frederic Bradlee, eds. *"Vanity Fair": A Cavalcade of the 1920s and 1930s.* New York: Viking, 1960.

Bruccoli, Matthew. *The Composition of "Tender Is the Night": A Study of the Manuscripts.* Pittsburgh: U of Pittsburgh P, 1963.

Burwell, Rose Marie. *Hemingway: The Postwar Years and the Posthumous Novels.* New York: Cambridge UP, 1996.

Chesler, Phyllis. *Women and Madness.* Garden City, NY: Doubleday, 1972.

Comley, Nancy R., and Robert Scholes. *Hemingway's Genders.* New Haven, CT: Yale UP, 1994.

Deleuze, Gilles. "The Schizophrenic and Language: Surface and Depth in Lewis Carroll and Antonin Artaud." *Textual Strategies.* Ed. Josue V. Harari. Ithaca, NY: Cornell UP, 1979. 277-95.

Diliberto, Gioia. *Hadley.* New York: Ticknor and Fields, 1992.

Donaldson, Scott. *Fool for Love: A Biography of F. Scott Fitzgerald.* New York: Dell, 1983.

Felman, Shoshana. *What Does a Woman Want?* Baltimore, MD: Johns Hopkins UP, 1993.

Fitzgerald, F. Scott. *The Correspondence of F. Scott Fitzgerald.* Ed. Matthew J. Bruccoli and Margaret M. Duggan. New York: Random House, 1980.

———. *F. Scott Fitzgerald's Ledger: A Facsimile.* Ed. Matthew J. Bruccoli. Washington, DC: NCR/Microcard Editions, 1972.

———. *The Letters of F Scott Fitzgerald.* Ed. Andrew Turnbull. London: The Bodley Head, 1963.

———. *A Life in Letters.* Ed. Matthew J. Bruccoli, with the assistance of Judith S. Baughman. New York: Scribners, 1994.

———. *Tender Is the Night.* 1934. New York: Collier Macmillan, 1986.

Fitzgerald, Zelda. "Caesar's Things." Unpublished. Zelda Fitzgerald Papers. Princeton University Library, Princeton, NJ.

———. *The Collected Writings.* Ed. Matthew J. Bruccoli. New York: Collier Macmillan, 1991.

Freud, Sigmund. "Observations on Transference Love." *The Freud Reader.* Ed. Peter Gay. New York: Norton, 1989. 378-87.

Hemingway, Ernest. *Complete Poems.* Ed. Nicholas Gerogiannis. Lincoln: U of Nebraska P, 1979.

———. *Ernest Hemingway: Selected Letters, 1917-1961.* Ed. Carlos Baker. New York: Scribners, 1981.

————. "For two weeks James Allen. . . ." Unpublished. Item 648b. Hemingway Collection. John F. Kennedy Library, Boston.

————. *The Garden of Eden*. New York: Scribners, 1986.

————. *Islands in the Stream*. New York: Scribners, 1970.

————. *A Moveable Feast*. New York: Scribners, 1964.

————. "Philip Haines was a writer. . . ." Unpublished. Item 648a. Hemingway Collection. John F. Kennedy Library, Boston.

Kert, Bernice. *The Hemingway Women: Those Who Loved Him—The Wives and Others*. New York: Norton, 1983.

Laing, R. D. *The Divided Self*. 1959. Baltimore: Penguin, 1965.

Milford, Nancy. *Zelda*. New York: Avon, 1970.

Richardson, Leslie. *Things Seen on the Riviera*. London: Seeley, Service, 1924.

Sass, Louis A. *Madness and Modernism*. Cambridge, MA: Harvard UP, 1994.

Spilka, Mark. *Hemingway's Quarrel with Androgyny*. Lincoln: U of Nebraska P, 1990.

Wilson, Edmund, ed. *The Crack-up*. 1945. New York: New Directions, 1956.

THE METAMORPHOSIS OF FITZGERALD'S DICK DIVER AND ITS HEMINGWAY ANALOGS

R O B E R T E . G A J D U S E K

F. Scott Fitzgerald's *Tender Is the Night* was born after a nine-year gestation period, during which it went through several elaborate metaphoric stages. It seemed to resist its realization—perhaps because the author was embroiled during these troubled years with the desperate personal circumstances which found their fictive expression in the novel. In *Tender*, Fitzgerald was dealing with his own alcoholism and moral disequilibrium, his wife's mental illness, and the complex lives and situations of Sara and Gerald Murphy and other friends who appear thinly veiled in the fiction. Set against the background of the Paris, Switzerland, and Riviera settings of the 1920s and 1930s, the characters were painfully close to Fitzgerald's own tragedy. Indeed, it was this "closeness" of the material to the fiction that troubled Hemingway, and he so told Fitzgerald (*Selected Letters* 407-9).

In Hemingway's career, one of his last great works, *The Garden of Eden*, also underwent an equally extended series of metamorphoses and a difficult birth process, consuming—as did *Tender* for Fitzgerald—many creative years. Remarkably, it was focused on a writer and his wife living on the Riviera during this same time and in about the same location as Fitzgerald's characters. Hemingway's couple, David and Catherine, bear a remarkable resemblance to Fitzgerald, the then-successful writer, and his bored and unfulfilled wife, Zelda, whose competitive sense, like Catherine's, attacks the creative process of the artist-husband. Indeed, the Catherine of *Garden* has many traits Hemingway had observed in Zelda—even the tales of lesbian interludes and the facts of mental disease are shared—and although unquestionably Hemingway's heroine was based, as closely as was Fitzgerald's Nicole, on his own wife and other loves, Zelda's imago lurks behind Catherine just as completely as does Fitzgerald's own image behind his fictionalized Gerald Murphy. It is fascinating to note that in Zelda's account, *Save Me the Waltz* (1932), which used, as Fitzgerald affirmed, the same and "his" material—covering as it did the same period and many of the same incidents as Fitzgerald had with his Nicole and Dick Diver—her self-projection as her heroine, Alabama, is married to her thinly veiled portrait of her husband, David. Hemingway's choice of David for his protagonist's name undoubtedly suggests an additional level of allusive sophistication in his work.

It is not an arbitrary relationship between the two novels that I define here but one essential to an understanding of the deeper levels of meaning within the texts. As Fitzgerald leans his characters heavily on their real perceptible historical analogs, he seems almost to be crying out for a reader's understanding that the biographies and lives so transparently overlaid should imaginatively be brought to bear as another level of meaning to be added to the fate of his characters. It is really almost impossible for a literate reader to avoid Sara and Gerald Murphy who are concomitantly F. Scott and Zelda Fitzgerald as they all inhabit the fates of Nicole and Dick Diver, but in fact Fitzgerald wished to be Gerald even as he wished his wife to be Sara. André Le Vot, one of Fitzgerald's finer biographers, readily saw this and wrote of them in his *F. Scott Fitzgerald*: "Gerald-Scott, Sara-Zelda, Scott-Sara in juxtaposition, permutation, fascination with themselves and each other" (208). Le Vot saw that the "subject" of *Tender Is the Night* was really the "degradation of the Murphys in Fitzgerald" and that their relations were "an impossible romance in which the beloved's face was sometimes Gerald's, sometimes Sara's, seen in shifting moods of admiration and despite and defiance." Le Vot recognized that Gerald thoroughly understood "that process of symbiosis that would form the composite character of the Divers in *Tender Is the Night*" (208-9). Murphy described the four of them in a letter to the Fitzgeralds of September 19, 1925: "Currents run between us regardless: Scott will uncover for me values in Sara, just as Sara has known them in Zelda through her affection for Scott" (Miller 19). Fitzgerald's novel at last would be his exposition of this, his process of transformation and metamorphosis.

Hemingway seems to make a similar demand, calling up to the sophisticated reader the ménage à trois of his first wife, Hadley, his second wife, Pauline, and himself, while simultaneously almost insisting on applying over these an imagery taken from the Fitzgeralds' lives as well as other allusions to his own. He had very early found the advantages of this style for myth-making, so that his persona looms large and inescapable behind and within his fictive scenarios and scenes. Of course, a concomitant liability of this process was for Hemingway the participation of his texts in the creation of the Hemingway persona which has enveloped his fiction and obsessively drawn to itself the criticism and attention that should have been focused on the texts and their casts of characters.

I am here suggesting, however, that these particular novels do not merely use personal experience as the base of their fiction—as all writers do—but instead use it deliberately so that history, biography, and myth may play against and together with the fictive details to establish a more complex genre elucidating a more complex myth. What both novels (and the other works of both men) ask us to perceive in their alluded-to lives as well as in their fictions is a composite in which the two are intricately and inextricably interwoven, so that the mysteries of role and sex inversion in the lives and concerns of both authors can be more profoundly and finely explored. It is these metamorphic transformations that will here be explored.

Fitzgerald's novel, showing the effect of a new historical consciousness and of his early excitement for Spengler's *Decline of the West* (published sequentially in two volumes in 1918 and 1922 and in one volume in 1932),[1] is, like his earlier *Great Gatsby* (1925), aiming at greater range than mere psychological portraiture: It attempts to study the great subject of the great books of its time—Joyce's *Ulysses* (1922), Hemingway's *In Our Time* (1925), Ford's tetralogy *Parade's End* (published as four novels sequentially in 1924, 1925, 1926, and 1928),[2] Eliot's *The Waste Land* (1922), and D. H. Lawrence's *Women in Love* (1920)—the decline and fall of the patriarchal tradition. As Dick Diver has softened and as the women about him have concomitantly hardened or seized male prerogatives and even costume, a historical change is being studied, especially in the declining powers of its spoiled "high priest." When Dick says his own farewell over his father's grave, "Good-by, my father—good-by, all my fathers" (*Tender* 205), the larger sense of a farewell to a lost male-centered world is inescapably there, for the speech echoes against his reflections over other graves, when, earlier in the novel, near Amiens, in the falling rain over the indistinguishable fallen heroes, he had historically considered the end of an age.

Diver, however, has long ago abandoned the old virtues of this fallen world, and he has laid down his weapons: His own "spear had been blunted," he had "let himself be "swallowed up like a gigolo" and "permitted his arsenal to be locked up in the Warren safety-deposit vaults" (201). Going on about him in his world is an acknowledged "obscure yielding up of swords" (298). Such almost obscenely clear Freudian imagery belongs to a novel where a psychiatrist, unable to maintain the detachment of a surrogate father—indeed, the detachment upon which the Western patriarchal tradition is based—has in incestuous self-projection overthrown the guardian father in himself for the indulgent lover and by the indulgence lost whatever paternal authority he might have had. Therefore the simplistic Freudian symbolism is itself a statement about complexity reduced to simplicity and about clichés and sentimentalities that have replaced the sophistications upon which real cultural authority rests. Fitzgerald accents this: " . . . the cloudy waters of unfamiliar ports, the lost girl on the shore, the moon of popular songs. . . . A part of Dick's mind was made up of the tawdry souvenirs of his boyhood" (196). This imagery also, however, expresses with this disempowerment a setting aside of male attributes. When Maria Wallis kills a man in the Gare St. Lazare, we are told he can scarcely be identified because she had neatly "shot him through his identification card" (84): In the act she is described as, like a warrior, having a "helmet" of hair, while his ineffectual cardboard identity is her target.

The protagonists of both *Tender Is the Night* and *The Garden of Eden*, however autobiographically based, intriguingly illustrate at once their unique individual fates and also exemplify the historical fate of their age, as it is examined and understood by their authors; and both writers demand a shared group of symbols elucidating a common threat to their protagonists that they believe is unique *in our time*—therefore, a word about historical transformations.

Fitzgerald's perceptions in *Tender* grew out of the situation he observed in the world about him. The Paris that both he and Hemingway shared in the 1920s strongly exhibited the situations he fictively defines. That Paris not only gave a stage to and flaunted the mannerisms of the homosexual world so vividly portrayed at the Bal Musette in Hemingway's *The Sun Also Rises*, and in the scene in the "house hewn from the frame of Cardinal Retz's palace in the Rue Monsieur" (71) in Fitzgerald's *Tender*, but also in multiple ways brought women into masculine roles while stripping men of their prewar authoritative posture. These were basic social transformations, taking place everywhere in the postwar world, but more actively and readily and visibly in Paris, which did not attempt to hide the process or its mode. Dress, as flauntingly displayed in the Bal des Quatre Arts or in Natalie Barney's Ecole des Amazons, flagrantly displayed cross-dressing; and the styles of Dolly Wilde or Romaine Brooks and others exhibited on the street the sexual shifts being explored. "Women like these women I have never seen before" (306), exclaims old Gausse, the hotel owner in *Tender Is the Night;* and Hemingway's audience could just as well have said that about the Brett of his first novel and the Catherine of his last.

That postwar world was forced to acknowledge transfers of power from the patriarchs to their wives and daughters. The leisures of the American educational scene provided the children of the robber barons—who themselves were too preoccupied by their practical affairs and businesses to be so distracted—with the seductions of history and culture which were European based. Millionaires like Cunard and Ellerman, Loeb and Guggenheim, Singer, Cross, and J. P. Morgan were able to underwrite the salons and presses and Paris experiences and power of the Princess de Polignacs (Winaretta Singer), the Natalie Barneys, the Nancy Cunards, and the Caresse Crosbys of Paris. And the apparently self-sufficient authorities of Gertrude Stein's salon and Sylvia Beach's Shakespeare and Company owed themselves to money sent from lesser fortunes to sustain such daughters and inheriting women. Even Robert McAlmon's Contact Publishing Company was an alimony "spin-off" from Bryher's fortune, amassed by her father, Sir John Ellerman, "the heaviest taxpayer in England"; and Harold Loeb's magazine *Broom* owed itself to the Loeb/Guggenheim fortune just as much as Harry and Caresse Crosby's Black Sun Press owed itself to Harry's uncle J. P. Morgan, Jr. The profits of American entrepreneurial genius, exercised by men too consumed by business, or too aged or too ill, or ill-equipped by temperament (or too dead) to be gallivanting about Europe, frequently passed into the hands of the active, energetic, and adventuring and inheriting wives and daughters. Fitzgerald throughout his novel records the phenomenon: "The hostess—she was another tall rich American girl, promenading insouciantly upon the national prosperity" (*Tender* 73).

This usurpation of power or transfer of it from men to women Fitzgerald studied, and developed his observations in his work through the metaphoric or actual masculinization of women and an attendant effeminization of men. Both Nicole and Baby Warren of *Tender Is the Night* are classical portraits of the process, in which the women not only finally break ties to the sources of their power, pretending self-sufficiency, but also often break the spirits of the men they submit to their wealth and subdue with its power. "We own you, and you'll admit it sooner or later. It is absurd to keep up the pretense of independence" (177) is Baby Warren's unspoken thought. Fitzgerald, pronouncing on Nicole, writes that she, "wanting to own him, wanting him to stand still forever, encouraged any slackness on his part, and in multiplying ways he was constantly inundated by a trickling of goods and money" (170). The danger to the male of this power shift was also a theme of Hemingway's work—well illustrated in "The Snows of Kilimanjaro," but earlier studied in Robert Cohn of *The Sun Also Rises* (1926), a man dependent upon money given by his mother.

The dominant undercurrent of the surface action of *Tender Is the Night* is a state of undeclared war. Newly equipped and armored women were everywhere about Hemingway and Fitzgerald in Paris, and as they often "hardened" to the practicalities and necessities of the work they had assumed, their more inert, less engaged men, no longer in the lists of financial combat, were often, in being deprived of their usual weapons, unmanned, made impotent or essentially castrated. Lovely, still dewy-eyed Rosemary Hoyt is nonetheless a warrior: "It was good to be hard, then; all nice people were hard on themselves"(55), Rosemary reasons, already well trained for combat by her mother. As noted earlier, Maria Wallis, shooting a man in the Gare St. Lazare, is a woman with hair "like a helmet" who hits "her target" (83). Dick "scented battle from afar" with Nicole and has been "hardening and arming himself" for that encounter (100), yet earlier, when he is being defeated by Baby Warren in a preliminary skirmish, Fitzgerald reflects, "It would be hundreds of years before any emergent Amazons would ever grasp the fact that a man is vulnerable only in his pride, but delicate as Humpty-Dumpty once that is meddled with" (177).[3] This sense that the battles are those of masculinized women defying an established patriarchate is voiced by one of Dick's patients, who cries out in her suffering, "I'm sharing the fate of the women of my time who challenged men to battle." Trying to ease her pain, he urges that "many women suffered before they mistook themselves for men" (184).

The great fact of the matter was that a major cataclysmic event had stripped from the French a generation of its men, for whom there was no replacement. The multiple deaths of fathers that Fitzgerald records in his novel were historical facts as well as symbols. Fathers themselves, whether indicted for causing the war or through not surviving it, left the future to undiscerned unknown inheritors, and a cynicism as deep as their seldom-visited or unknown graves suggested that whatever forms a new world might take, whatever transformations of old styles to new there might be, they would not be borrowed from the old patriarchal past. The postwar revulsion against the dealing of death extended itself—as it did after World War II—to the weapons that sustained it, and the putting aside of guns and male symbols of power in the postwar world was to be expected. Put aside with them was the temper and philosophy and the skills that had shaped them and used them, the attitudes that had trained generations in their use—a general loss of male equipment for male lists of honor. In Dick's own encounters, Nicole is described as "disarming" him (188). The "blunted" spears, the "yielded up" swords, the "locked up" arsenals spell out a belatedly recognized lack of male preparation for battle.

In Fitzgerald's novel, the personal and historical situation, which records in multiple ways the mode of overthrow of phallic and paternal power—as surely as does Jake's missing phallus in *The Sun Also Rises*—is answered by an equivalent symbolism (which runs throughout *Tender Is the Night*) of the inversion-effeminization of Dick Diver. This occurs simultaneously with the inversion-masculinization of such women as Nicole and Baby Warren, Mrs. Speers (Rosemary's mother), Lady Caroline, and Mary North. Even as Mrs. Speers in her name bears the missing male weapons, so Dick's spear is "blunted"[4] and Dick Diver in his name drowns his masculinity in the feminine depths and waters he explores but from which, as the novel ends, he cannot emerge. These waters are characterized in the novel, like the moon and cycle—from which "cycling" takes its metaphoric meaning: on the last page of the book, Dick's fate is described as one in which he is cycling "a lot"—as essentially feminine.

What is especially fascinating to study in Fitzgerald's novel is the actual and metaphoric sexual metamorphosis of Dick Diver. After Fitzgerald chose the title of his novel from Keats's "Ode to a Nightingale," he carefully omitted two of the vital lines of that poem from his epigraph:

> And haply the Queen Moon is on her throne
> Cluster'd about by all her starry fays

Fitzgerald was well aware of the effeminate overtones of "fay" or fairy, and these omitted lines, as in most Hemingway works where the omitted part is crucial or the point of it all, establish the major concern: Who is enthroned and who has taken power and just what are the conditions of "her" servitors? That Fitzgerald's first version of the novel was a tale of matricide suggests the enormous mythic distance the book came as its author realized that the more interesting story lay not in recording the attempt to hold off the Great

Mother but rather in visualizing the mode and stages by which her enthrone-ment was inevitably achieved and at what cost. An elaborate symbolic system throughout the novel elevates the action to a divine cosmological level, where gods and goddesses battle for power. Early in the book, its setting in the Villa Diana and events "managed" by the Moon are but indications of this overlay. Although at one moment Nicole declares "I am Pallas Athene" (*Tender* 160), her consistent profane identification is with "the night from which she had come" and the dark woods from which she emerged "into clear moonlight" when "The unknown yielded her up" (135). The sense of her witchery and Dick's early controlling divinity are sternly there in the novel, though Dick is at the beginning given to the reader as a godlike figure with his consort and is only later seen as a god captive and destroyed. Mrs. Speers, intent upon sharpening her daughter into a mascu-linized competitor in what is still a man's world, and knowing her daughter's need to use both masculine and feminine weapons to win advantage in that world, is a typical Great Mother.

As the novel begins, Dick Diver is centered as a principle of belief for all those who "believe in" (29) his world: he is adored (31, 112), he is listened to with "wild worship" (112) by Rosemary who sees him as "something fixed and godlike" (104); he makes an "apostolic gesture" (27) while Nicole brings "everything to his feet, gifts of sacrificed ambrosia, of worshipping myrtle" (137). Tommy Barban defends the Divers against those like Mrs. McKisco who can ask, "Are they so sacred?" (43). Indeed, they are, in the mythos of the novel, where Dick is described as one who "evaporated before their eyes" (28), as appearing and disappearing in an instant (35). At one moment Rosemary advises her mother they "really are divine" (95). The reader is told that, like a god in the mind of a believer, "so long as [everyone] subscribed to [his world] completely," it existed within its "intensely calculated perfec-tion," but "at the first flicker of a doubt . . . he evaporated before their eyes" (28). Early, as the children sing "Ouvre-moi ta porte Pour l'amour de Dieu," the gate to Dick's garden tinkles open to admit the "body" of the other guests (29). Rosemary, who has been "in adoration" and "believed in him," feels the cloth of Dick's coat "like a chasuble" and is "about to fall to her knees before him" (38). In the prison where he has gone to help Mary North and Lady Caroline, he is described as "like a priest in the confessional" (304). At the end of the novel, before he leaves, though already proven a "spoiled priest," he nevertheless appears "with a papal blessing" "blessing the beach"; and Nicole, even at that moment raised by him—she gets "to her knees": "I'm going to him" (314)—is pulled down by Tommy Barban. But if this is the Nicole to whom Dick earlier has "devoted" himself—that profane believer who had later "crossed herself reverently with Chanel Sixteen" (291)—part of Dick's metamorphosis is from a godlike principle of belief into the priest who finally cannot sustain devotion or compel belief.

The world of *Tender Is the Night* is also a world where the gold star "muzzers" come to "mourn for their dead" sons (101), where the graves of heroes cannot be found, where Dick's father's death seems the death of all fathers. It is a world where a father whips and punishes his son to drive him toward "manliness," and another, trying to protect his "nervous brood," succeeds "merely in preventing them from developing powers of adjustment to life's inevitable surprises" (186)—parental failures both. Focused on parental incest, the supreme cultural paternal abdication, and set in a milieu where the need for fathers is the primary fact, the novel belabors the patriarchal failures of the time. Fitzgerald himself, who had been embarrassed by his own father's failures and weaknesses, was constantly attentive to and advising or offering his daughter lists and strategies for development and success, obviously trying to avoid such parental failure.

"Death By Water," a theme that T. S. Eliot had enunciated in *The Waste Land* (1922), is the studied patriarchal fate. Nicole's father's death, when he can take on "nothing except liquids" (247), will be, the reader is told, "a sinking" (*Tender* 248). This seems natural for what is throughout carefully described as a world drowning in enveloping waters, with "lavish liquidations taking place under the aegis of American splendor" (133). Rosemary, who embraces these waters and wallows in them (5) where they reach up for her and pull her down into them (5), and who seems in alliance and league with them, yearns "to surround [Dick] and engulf him" (66). The "entirely liquid" (73) Abe North's dying, it is predicted, will seem like "the wreck of a galleon" (82) as voices that come to say farewell to him mimic "the cadence of water" (83). It is a world "already undergoing a sea-change" (83): "Full fathom five my father lies" is the unquoted but heard new condition in which life is lived. It is on a "watery day" that, near Amiens, Dick and those who listen to his lecture on the meaning of history face the "dissolutions" of soldiers under the rain (59).

These are the carefully defined feminine waters that will surround and engulf Dick, until, with "the ethics of his profession dissolving" (256), his life "inundated by a trickling of goods" (170), he will at last be unable to aquaplane, to walk on the water, but rather will lie floating exhausted on those very waters he cannot master and above which he can no longer redemptively raise another (285). Nicole's schizophrenia has its own hydrodynamics: Considering her madness, Dick reflects that "the versatility of madness is akin to the resourcefulness of water seeping through" (191). The irony is that it is Dick who takes on this water from Nicole and that as he consequently declines, her fortunes rise. Fitzgerald has earlier in the novel made the point about the funicular, that for one car to rise the other must take on water and consequently, inevitably, by natural law descend.

As Dick downplays the danger of his son possibly being exposed to dirty infected water, he can no longer serve as a protective father, for to that son he has become the betraying father. The point is made that, in having failed the office, he has forfeited a father's rights and privileges. This is certainly true with Rosemary, the fatherless girl he met on the beach and with whom he had metaphorically assumed the role of father and teacher— and genuine fathers subsequently flee him, while more forthright men, like Earl Brady, refuse "the fatherly office" Dick has assumed and then betrayed (31). The dissolutions and drownings define another transformation in the Fitzgerald male: Becoming the victim of waters that he once dominated, fluidity and its attendant flaccidities and macerations replace the fixity and firmness of the earlier heroic world.

The subtitle of the novel might well have been "The Cycling of Dick Diver": Engulfed and encircled, Dick predictably ends up as the victimized *cyclist*. Fitzgerald openly tells the reader that Rosemary wanted to "devour him . . . to surround and engulf him" (66). Turning "round and round" (5) in the water, her advice to McKisko is to "roll." "Round and round in a corkscrew" (149) goes the funicular that brings Dick and Nicole together. When Dick early meets Nicole, it is under the moon with his bicycle. Again she meets him coming from a wood into the moonlight on "a rolling night" (135). When she plays a revolving record for him, it is "Lay a silver dollar / On the ground / And watch it roll / Because it's round" (136). Later Dick watches as she "curved into the half-moon entrance" of the Palace Hotel in a "Rolls" while "the air around him was loud with the circlings of all the goblins on the Gross-Münster"(145). Significantly, when Dick meets her again, it is when he is cycling into Montreux.

Married to her at last, having shifted his devotion to this cyclical moon-endorsed principle, he has metamorphosed from a dominating sun god—the reader is explicitly told that Nicole "had played planet to Dick's sun"(289)—to an attendant to the moon. Fitzgerald elevates his analysis to a historical dimension as he tells the reader that from where Dick meets Nicole, on the slopes above Lake Geneva, one confronts the "cyclorama" that reveals "the true center of the Western world" (147). He admits to Franz that "We're beginning to turn in a circle" (179), and he describes the mentally disturbed as those "beginning . . . another ceaseless round of ratiocination, not in a line as with normal people but in the same circle. Round, round, and round. Around forever" (182). Nicole is similarly described in her madness as "like one condemned to endless parades around the circumference of a medal" (277). Out of control in Italy, Dick's world "reels" (226). It is at the Agiri Fair—which they approach through "mammoth steam rollers"—that mad Nicole flees from him; and then, in desperate pursuit of her, Dick "wheels" and, leaving the children with a woman beside the lottery wheel, then circles the merry-go-round to find Nicole atop a revolving Ferris wheel (189). Retrieved, Nicole, with her mad hand clutching the steering wheel, nearly kills them all (192). No wonder that at the end, as the legend of the upstate New York cyclist, Dick can arbitrarily be found "in one town or another": Once the principle of firmness and absoluteness, he has had his solar fixity stripped from him forever.

The alteration in Dick, from hard to soft, from firm to fluid, and from fixed and straight to cyclical, whose first name suggests his phallic potential and whose last describes his envelopment by and commitment to the very principle of his dissolution, can best be studied in his transformation as he relates to Rosemary and especially to her mother. To Rosemary, Dick, to whom she prays, is "perfect"—but to her, her mother is "forever perfect," too, and "Mother is perfect, she prayed" (37). Rosemary's mother has assumed the father's role of guardian and teacher, and she is now the enlightener who advises Rosemary in the ways of the world. At last she casts Rosemary adrift to be self-sufficient, even as Dick will seem to cast Nicole adrift to be self-sufficient and cured. Rosemary intones to Dick, "I think you're the most wonderful person I ever met—except my mother" (38), and in one breath she recites, "I love mother and I love you" (65). Even as Rosemary is Mrs. Speers's child, so to Dick, Rosemary is "child" and "baby." In one chapter Dick is "with her in her heart" while her mother is "with her in her heart." Redundantly she declares, "You like to help everybody . . ." and "Mother likes to help everybody" (84). After her quarrel with Dick, she says, "I feel as if I'd quarreled with mother" (219). This enforced linkage of the mother and Dick, even as he is himself overthrowing his paternal role, receives its obvious inevitable summation as Nicole becomes afraid "of what the stricken man . . . would feed on while she must still continue her dry suckling at his lean chest" (279). When Nicole finally leaves Dick, she has "cut the cord forever" (302). Such specific maternal imagery, associated with Dick and emerging from Nicole as Dick is inverted into the unsatisfactory nurturing breast, finally comes from Dick himself when he is "uneasy about what he had to give to the ever-climbing, ever-clinging, breast-searching young" (311).

Dick is moved from phallocentric man to ineffectual breast nurturer. As the whores' step-ins are inverted to become the flag— "Oh say can you see the tender color of remembered flesh"(297)—that inversion imagery speaks of a lost heroic world based on principle, now seduced by sensation: Feminine sexuality imaged in the lower-centered step-ins now dominates the sky. Mary North and Lady Caroline in male costume trying to pick up two girls authorize the sexual inversion, one that is studied on another level in the transfer of financial power from Devereux Warren to Baby Warren. Devereux's incest with Nicole merely prepares for Dick's multiple incestuous inversions, and incest itself in this novel is the uroboric overthrow of the basis of civilization, time made eternally to cycle about a past center, no longer capable of linear historical progression.[5] That is what incest means: stopped unprogressive time. It is, therefore, metaphorically appropriate that Dick, yielding the world to its inheriting masculinized women, should accept his metaphoric effemi-nized death by water, while becoming the cyclist.

What of the Fitzgerald behind this portrait? Evidence suggests his excessive castration anxiety, his ready fear of being stripped of his masculine authority and power. He fled repeatedly from the feminine in himself—which undoubtedly supported his genius—feeling threatened and intimidated by its emergence; he coevally, however, played with those very feminine attributes which caused his embarrassment. If Zelda's desire for creative success as a writer threatened her husband, the latter was equally painfully susceptible and vulnerable to her suggestions of his unmanliness, masculine deficiency, or his femininity. Nancy Milford, in *Zelda*, records Fitzgerald's confession to his wife's physician, Dr. Rennie, in later years—"In the last analysis she is a stronger person than I am. I have creative fire, but I am a weak individual. She knows this and really looks upon me as a woman" (261)—and André Le Vot repeats Sheilah Graham's comment that Zelda "tried to emasculate Scott" (237). Zelda terrorized her husband by implying or stating that she believed he and Hemingway were in a homosexual relationship, and Fitzgerald chal-lenged her in a long letter, "Written with Zelda gone to the Clinique," reprinted in Milford: "The nearest I ever came to leaving you was when you told me you [thought] I was a fairy" (181). John Kuehl and Jackson Bryer, in *Dear Scott/Dear Max*, publish Fitzgerald's letter to Maxwell Perkins of November 15, 1929, in which he reveals how tortured he was by knowing McAlmon had "assured Ernest I was a fairy" (159). That there was a basis for Fitzgerald's fear of Hemingway's perception can be seen in the latter's portrait in *A Moveable Feast* of the Fitzgerald he met in Paris:

> Scott was a man then who looked like a boy with a face between handsome and pretty. He had very fair wavy hair, a high forehead, excited and friendly eyes and a delicate long-lipped Irish mouth that,

on a girl, would have been the mouth of a beauty. His chin was well built and he had good ears and a handsome, almost beautiful, unmarked nose. This should not have added up to a pretty face, but that came from the coloring, the very fair hair and the mouth. The mouth worried you until you knew him and then it worried you more. (149)

Fitzgerald himself developed the basis of his own fear by projecting feminine attributes and mannerisms on his self-projections in his work. As the reader meets Dick Diver on the beach near Cannes in the first book of the novel, he appears for a moment "clad in transparent black lace drawers. Close inspection revealed that they were lined with flesh-colored cloth. 'Well, if that isn't a pansy's trick!' exclaimed Mr. McKisco contemptuously" (*Tender* 21).

Fitzgerald's fears allowed him readier access than most of his contemporaries (except perhaps Hemingway) to signs of the effeminization of the Western psyche. Ernest Hemingway spent his childhood in a home governed by his masterful and castrating mother—see the biographies and the autobiographical revelations of "Now I Lay Me" (*Short Stories* 363-71)—who was only gradually uncovered by her son in her long-standing possibly lesbian liaison with one of the maids in the Hemingway household, Ruth Arnold. As a result, he had been made extraordinarily susceptible to role reversals and gifted with an unconscious sympathetic understanding of the lesbian world. Lesbians were among Hemingway's closest friends throughout his life, and in Paris they gravitated to him—Gertrude Stein, Janet Flanner, Sylvia Beach, Jane Heap, and Margaret Anderson among others. We also know they were occasionally among his staunchest supporters (Sylvia Beach) and that he was attracted to them: Gertrude Stein, Margaret Anderson, and Djuna Barnes.

In Hemingway's works, gender inversion has been well studied, from the masculinized image of Brett in *The Sun Also Rises* (1926) as "one of the chaps," to Pilar of *For Whom the Bell Tolls* (1940) as stirring spoon/baton wielder of power in the cave once Pablo has been "cowed," and on to *The Garden of Eden*, where such inversion is overt and central to the novel. What has not been adequately noted is that the sex-role inversions in Hemingway's works link up in a consistent pattern, one that reveals a need for therapeutic sexual role inversions: male to female and female to male. Indeed, *Across the River and Into the Trees* (1950) is an extended essay on the historical necessity for such inversion, while *The Garden of Eden* is an example of it.

In *The Sun Also Rises*—where we are told "Caffeine puts a man on her horse and a woman in his grave" (115), that Abraham Lincoln ("A faggot") "was in love with General Grant" and that "The Colonel's Lady and Judy

O'Grady are Lesbians under their skin" (116), and where the order of drumstick and egg is reversed—readers should be well prepared for mysteries of sexual inversion. It is no accident that the women in the novel all bear suggestively masculine names: Brett, Edna, Jo, Frances, and Georgette. Brett, in her hairstyle, her manner of speaking, and her aggressive behavior, flaunts a masculinized image and seized power, but the reader must be equally alert to Jake's inversion: His inability to make love to Brett is due not only to his lacking male equipment but to his having been physically remade into an unsatisfactory image of a woman, a man bearing a wound where he might wear his potency. In an early scene in the novel in Jake's apartment Hemingway is careful to let it seem that he passively lets Brett make love *to him*— this is the "getting something for nothing"(148) that he alludes to later. His inadequacy as customer to the prostitute Georgette leads him to jest about *her* buying him *his* dinner, a jest that throws him into the female role, a role he takes upon himself. Later, at Burguete, it will be Bill who tries to marry irony and pity to the tune of "The Bells are Ringing for Me and my Gal" (114), casting Jake as the bride—this, shortly after Jake has been diligently searching for worms and urging Bill into "getting up," in a chapter subsequently rich with sexual inversions where men without women, as in other Hemingway works—"The Three-Day Blow" and "A Simple Enquiry," for example—enter into elaborate sex-role reversal play. Such metamorphosis into feminine identity has been with Hemingway from the start. Many of the boys and men of *In Our Time* assume what had earlier been considered femininely passive positions—in "Cat in the Rain" and "The Doctor and the Doctor's Wife"—and in "The End of Something," "Soldier's Home," and "Mr. and Mrs. Elliot," power and authority shift to the woman.

Jake's alteration is mimicked in *A Farewell to Arms* (1929) in Frederic Henry's metaphoric assumption of pregnancy and morning sickness. In *Across the River and Into the Trees*, as Colonel Cantwell permits Renata to slip into *his* "pocket" *her* matrilineally inherited green emeralds, coded as the feminine family jewels, and also as he momentarily tastes the blood in his mouth with pleasure immediately after Renata declares her sexual dysfunction due to menstruation, he *also* puts on feminine identity. For him, before the novel ends, the "shooting is over," the guns put down. Such metamorphic movement away from male identity, as I have tried to indicate, begins well before this. In *To Have and Have Not* (1937), scores of characters lack a patronymic, and even allusions to public figures—those like Sylvia *Sidney*, Ginger *Rogers*, Gracie *Allen*, or Babe *Ruth*—refer to a world of lost fathers, for all of these discard surnames or patronymics and bear only what seem to be doubled "given" names. This stripping away of paternal authority is true throughout Hemingway's work, whether we note the names of the "heroes" of the major novels or stories—Nick Adams, Jake Barnes, Frederic Henry, Henry Morgan, Robert Jordan, Thomas Hudson—or simply note the dephallused hero of *The Sun Also Rises*.

In *The Garden of Eden*, Hemingway's last novel, sodomy is the metaphor for Catherine's assumption of masculine identity and David's assumption of feminine identity. This fact may retrospectively say something about the real source of Jake's aversion to and dislike of the "superiority" of the homosexuals, to whom he is joined by virtue of his "wound" in Hemingway's first novel, *The Sun Also Rises*. That Catherine in *The Garden of Eden* seems to get little satisfaction from "opening up the mail [male]," finally doing it "like someone shelling peas," suggests that the described gender inversion, however desired, may be no more satisfying for Catherine than it was for David. The "opening up of the [male]," however—when it is meant as Hemingway meant it, the breaking down of the protective barriers of the male ego which insularly refuses to risk itself in exposure to what lies beyond itself—is something Hemingway has been about since the beginning: It can stand as metaphor for his texts.

The return of Pablo, in *For Whom the Bell Tolls*, has been described as the turning point of that novel. Indeed, many have speculated that his return, based as it is on Saint Paul's revelation on the road to Damascus, which led him to reverse his direction, is the "miracle" that changes everything—the future of mankind. That reversal, related to such a fine and seemingly incidental act as the blowing of a bridge, can indeed alter everything.[6] Pablo's patriarchal mode, supporting laissez-faire economics, individualism and private property as well as proprietary sexuality, is under pressure to change, and Hemingway labors the point that everything may hinge upon Pablo's willingness and ability "to change": "Forced to a change, he will be smart in the change" (95). Jordan's reconciliation with the returned and altered Pablo is described by Pilar as a homosexual encounter: "What are you two doing? Becoming *maricones*? . . . cut thy goodbyes short before this one steals the rest of thy explosive" (404). The necessity for Pablo's "change" is given by Hemingway as due to the fact "the river is rising" (95). This rising of the waters, which in Fitzgerald is a concomitant of the overthrow of patriarchal power and the emergence of matriarchal power, can be seen as a metaphor related to the effeminization of the masculine that Fitzgerald and Hemingway shared.

As the river is high and the moon is full in *The Sun Also Rises*, Brett, the feminine vortex about which men dance, makes her successful appeal to her acolyte Jake to help her capture Romero, who, as *torero*, is, in the mythos of the bullfight, solar hero. In *For Whom the Bell Tolls*, as "the river" rises, Pablo's change is forced upon him; in *A Farewell to Arms*, it is as the river has risen almost to the bridge that Frederic Henry commits himself to those waters in a carefully structured rebirth/transformation rite of escape from which he emerges no longer a warrior but a significantly altered dependent man. In "The End of Something," with the moon rising over the waters of the lake, Marjorie is revealed as the competition and threat Nick fears. When in "The Three-Day Blow" he and Bill on a wet day attempt regression to an insular masculine world where the threat of the feminine is excluded, Hemingway carefully codes the feminine world as allied with the cycles and the waters from which they contraceptively and carefully guard themselves as they turn instead to fire and spirits. In the last story of *In Our Time*, "Big Two-Hearted River," Nick Adams finally knows that the days are coming when he will be able to fish the swamp, where the fishing is tragic and the waters rise dangerously against you. Harry Morgan's, Santiago's and Thomas Hudson's transformative encounters were dangerous and fatal sea journeys, but that way lay their manhood. Only as Harry Morgan, dying, not only accepts but also yields himself to and takes the "roll" of the moon-driven sea, does he come to terms with, and accept an alliance with, the feminine powers of the world: "No matter how a man alone ain't got no bloody fucking chance" (225) is his dying wisdom. It is, however, only in his last published work, *The Garden of Eden*, that Hemingway intricately explains in sexual metaphor and psychic shift the inner dynamics he has advocated throughout his career: the crossover inversion into the territory of the other sex that is necessary for the full individuated wholeness of a human being.

The Garden of Eden begins with David fishing in the canal on the Mediterranean, and in its penultimate chapter David goes to the sea on the Riviera and high dives into the "circle of milling water . . . making a boil in the water that a porpoise might have made reentering slickly into the hole that he had made in rising" (241). Joining together his diving and his rising, the sea and the sky, he places his salty mouth against Marita's and says, *"Elle est bonne, la mer. . . .Toi aussi,"* then he kisses the tip of her left breast and then the right. Such reconciliations of opposites, pairings and integrations that bring masculine and feminine, male and female into new creative combinations are everywhere in the novel. In one instance, David studies the nipple of the female breast as masculine in its erectile response while being circular and maternally milk-providing. As David, at the novel's end, reconciles Marita's two breasts, he is accepting and reconciling the dualities hidden in gender. This reconciliation of opposites, this joining of the sea and the woman, this acceptance of the dark depths of the sea and the bright heights of the sun-struck air, and of the dualisms hidden within a single sex—a strategy similarly used by Jake Barnes at San Sebastian in *The Sun Also Rises* to bring himself to wholeness—is Hemingway's strategy here for victory over the very watery conditions that drowned and cycled Dick Diver. I do not think it fanciful to assume that Hemingway structured *his* David's successful diving scene to echo against Fitzgerald's failed Diver, and made his David's mode of masculine and feminine integrative reconciliation a reproof for Fitzgerald's Diver who had not learned how to master his necessary immersions in and commitments to the feminine fluid medium in which he was metaphorically cycled and drowned.

What conclusions can be drawn from this brief overview of symbolism germane to gender inversion in the work of both writers? I think we can see gender inversion at the very heart of Hemingway's and Fitzgerald's shared perception of the altering nature of the West. Both writers saw clearly the role inversion and effeminization of the masculine psyche taking place in their time, and both clearly saw the end of the patriarchate. Hemingway's *Across the River and Into the Trees* is his major analysis of the dynamics of this psychic crossover, and Fitzgerald's *Tender Is the Night* is his historical recognition of the situation in which we find ourselves. Dick Diver's "Good-by my father—good-by, all my fathers" finds its literary mythic equivalent in Colonel Cantwell's "The shooting is over." What is especially interesting is the shared nature of their special language, its imagery and symbolism. Both use water in its relation to cycles and the moon and the feminine with its classical burden of associations, but both additionally emphasize its association with matriarchal threats to the male world. Both recognize as well the dangers of male submission to rolling, cycling, submersion, and immersion in fluid process—such are portents of and agents of masculine death. This imagery itself readily explains that this fear is a fear of regression to the womb, to the undifferentiated fetal state from which the male ego had been extricated and risen to consciousness. The aptness of the incestuous basis of Fitzgerald's novel is immediately apparent as one reflects that incest usually culturally identifies such regression. Yet each author takes a remarkably different stance with respect to this knowledge: Fitzgerald studies uxory in action and the overthrow of or damage to the male in his encounters with women, waters, the moon, and cycling; while Hemingway consistently throughout his work—though he as fully as Fitzgerald recognizes the risks and dangers—nonetheless advocates male mastery through submission to these forces as the only way to acceptable or full or worthy manhood.

Throughout Fitzgerald's works is lament, whether for Gatsby or Diver, whose uxorious dependencies leave them both fatally floating on waters that *master* them. His summary attitude can be well seen as Dick leaves the field to victorious Baby Warren: "the American Woman, aroused, stood over him: the clean-sweeping irrational temper that had broken the back of a race and made a nursery out of a continent, was too much for him" (*Tender* 232).

Increasingly, throughout Hemingway's texts, there is an acceptance of an inevitable new dynamics for a reconstituted male identity achieved by healing immersion in the experience of feminine identity. One of the signs of this is the command "Roll!" that repetitively occurs throughout his texts. We find it as early as *A Farewell to Arms*. In that novel, however, it is ambivalently understood: Frederic and Catherine flee for safety and their luxurious idyll out of war to Switzerland, where, they are told, there are "no rolls" (265). It is a weak pun, to translate croissants as cycles, but the continuing novel exists to prove that biological "rolls" are inescapable—Catherine dies in her ninth-month roll on the inescapable wheel of her pregnancy, and Frederic, walking off at the very end "in the rain" (314), walks in "the permanent rain" (4). If rolls, the cycles implicit in rain and birth, are indeed the concomitants of tragedy, it is increasingly in the Hemingway text the man who yields to them, who runs the risk of feared death together with his feared feminine side—like Cantwell, Harry Morgan, and the Frances Macomber who has gone over to the "rolling" other side to accept and acknowledge the feared "other"—who is worthy at last of our respect and his own true manliness.

Fitzgerald's Dick Diver dissolves in or becomes a cycled victim of waters he cannot master; the effeminization he well understands yet fears is his undoing. Gatsby lies dead, floating at last on the waters destined to claim him. In Hemingway's works, the rains are indeed coming—see *Green Hills of Africa*—and although he knows as well as Fitzgerald what that means mythically, culturally, and psychically, his strategies of survival in a time of the rising of the waters include accommodation and male transformation.

NOTES

1. Oswald Spengler's *Decline of the West* was introduced to Fitzgerald early by his famous Princeton professor Christian Gauss, but throughout his life he returned to the work, citing it, quoting from it—obviously still strongly influenced by it (Le Vot 37).

2. *Parade's End* is a name given to the Christopher Tietjen novels, which make up the four-volume tetralogy of Ford Madox Ford (Hueffer). The

novels were published singly and in succession as: *Some Do Not* (1924), *No More Parades* (1925), *A Man Could Stand Up* (1926), and *The Last Post* (1928).

3. The identification of the male Humpty Dumpty with the egg is a fascinating sexual confusion that hides the rhyme and reason of the fairy tale, as, I suspect, it here hides the feminization of Dick Diver. The insensitive manipulation of male pride can well be seen elsewhere as Mrs. Speers advises her daughter, "Wound yourself or him— whatever happens it can't spoil you because economically you're a boy, not a girl" (40). Dick later well perceives how callously Mrs. Speers has used him to promote her daughter's sexual education, even as he well sees how Baby Warren has similarly discarded consideration of him in her concern for her sister.

4. Hemingway also often deliberately and flagrantly played sexual jokes. His story of sexual challenge, "The Doctor and the Doctor's Wife," where Dick Boulton demonstrates his phallic contempt for the impotent father, begins with the name of the powerful Indian "Dick," who later will taunt the doctor father: "'Don't go off at half cock, Doc,' Dick said" (*Short Stories* 100).

5. See Neumann and my article "Death, Incest, and the Triple Bond in the Later Plays of William Shakespeare," where I conclude:

> Incest seems to be itself a metaphor for the dissolution of consciousness, the breakdown and yielding of the ego to the primal material from which it once emerged. Incest is the fundamental pan humanistic metaphor for regression to the original state of undifferentiated unconsciousness in uroboric introversion in the womb of the Great Mother. The incest taboo is the transcultural device, the alarm, imbedded in the psyche of man to alert him to the dangers of the loss of ego, of selfhood, of consciousness itself, once it has been seized or rescued as the original light breaking in upon the great and primal darkness. (158)

6. Aborted, blown, incomplete, and destroyed or crossed bridges determine the significant action in most Hemingway works—see my essay "Bridges, Their Creation and Destruction in the Works of Ernest Hemingway." I ask the reader to acknowledge Jake's missing phallus the blown bridge of that first novel. Were he intact, the space could

be crossed, a crossover would be possible, into the other and inner terrain of the "other."

WORKS CITED

Fitzgerald, F. Scott. *Correspondence of F. Scott Fitzgerald*. Ed. Matthew J. Bruccoli and Margaret Duggan. New York: Random House, 1980.

———. *The Letters of F. Scott Fitzgerald*. Ed. Andrew Turnbull. New York: Scribners, 1963.

———. *Tender Is the Night*. 1934. New York: Scribners, 1983.

Fitzgerald, Zelda. *Save Me the Waltz*. 1932. New York: New American Library, 1968.

Gajdusek, Robert E. "Bridges, Their Creation and Destruction in the Works of Ernest Hemingway." *Up in Michigan: Proceedings of the First National Conference of the Hemingway Society*. Ed. Joseph J. Waldmeir and Kenneth Marek. Traverse City: Michigan State, 1983. 75-81.

———. "Death, Incest, and the Triple Bond in the Later Plays of William Shakespeare." *American Imago* 31.2 (1974): 109-58.

Hemingway, Ernest. *Across the River and Into the Trees*. 1950. New York: Scribners, 1970.

———. *Ernest Hemingway: Selected Letters, 1917-1961*. Ed. Carlos Baker. New York: Scribners, 1981.

———. *A Farewell to Arms*. 1929. New York: Scribners, 1957.

———. *For Whom the Bell Tolls*. New York: Scribners, 1940.

———. *The Garden of Eden*. New York: Scribners, 1986.

———. *A Moveable Feast*. New York: Scribners, 1964.

———. *The Short Stories of Ernest Hemingway*. 1938. New York: Scribners, 1966.

———. *The Sun Also Rises*. 1926. New York: Scribners, 1954.

———. *To Have and Have Not*. 1937. New York: Scribners, 1965.

Kuehl, John, and Jackson R. Bryer, eds. *Dear Scott/Dear Max: The Fitzgerald-Perkins Correspondence*. New York: Scribners, 1971.

Le Vot, André. *F. Scott Fitzgerald*. Tr. William Byron. 1979. New York: Warner Books, 1984.

Milford, Nancy. *Zelda: A Biography*. New York: Harper and Row, 1970.

Miller, Linda Patterson, ed. *Letters From the Lost Generation: Gerald and Sara Murphy and Friends*. New Brunswick, NJ: Rutgers UP, 1991.

Neumann, Erich. *Art and the Creative Unconscious*. New York: Harper & Row, 1959.

FIGURING THE DAMAGE

FITZGERALD'S "BABYLON REVISITED" AND HEMINGWAY'S "THE SNOWS OF KILIMANJARO"

J . G E R A L D   K E N N E D Y

During the pastoral interlude in *The Sun Also Rises* between the "fiesta-ing" in Paris and Pamplona, a sodden Bill Gorton harangues his fishing companion, Jake Barnes, about the destructive consequences of living abroad: "You're an expatriate. You've lost touch with the soil. Fake European standards have ruined you. You drink yourself to death. You become obsessed by sex. You spend all your time talking, not working. You are an expatriate, see? You hang around cafés" (119). The hypocrisy of his tirade hints at its satirical purpose. As a parody of Gertrude Stein's famous remark, "You are all a lost generation" (one of the novel's two epigraphs), Bill's indictment elicits from Jake a sarcastic retort—"It sounds like a swell life"— that insinuates Hemingway's mockery of Stein and his need to repudiate her authority.[1] Ironically, however, many of Bill's charges seem applicable to Jake, who in Book I spends far more time talking in Left Bank cafés than working in his office, who has developed "a rotten habit of picturing the bedroom scenes of [his] friends" (13), and who makes a fair effort, especially in Pamplona, to drink himself into oblivion. Presumably, Hemingway's growing ambivalence toward expatriate life, as reflected in his correspondence, gives the passage its doubly ironic rancor.[2]

Bill's blathering charge—which also smacks of 1920s Puritanism— nevertheless scants those aspects of literary exile in France that enabled so many American writers to develop new voices and to launch important careers. In *A Moveable Feast*, Hemingway idealized Paris as "the town best organized for a writer to write in that there is" (182), and so the city must have appeared to scores of writers eager to escape oppressive influences back home. Repeated studies generally have celebrated expatriate life in Paris as liberating, productive, and transformative (Benstock, Carpenter, Ford, Kennedy, Pizer, and Wickes). But such perspectives privilege textual achievement, celebrate the public literary persona, and discount the personal calamities that occasionally attended the life caricatured by Bill Gorton. Although disasters can occur anywhere, and although geography seems at first glance irrelevant to the conduct of life, Paris nevertheless affected many American exiles (as Malcolm Cowley observed) like "a great machine for stimulating the nerves and sharpening the senses" (135). The escape from U. S. Prohibition; the greater range, availability, and acceptance of pleasures licit and illicit; and the practical advantage of a soaring exchange rate all combined with the wild exuberance of the 1920s (called in France *les années folles*) to encourage expatriate recklessness and risk-taking. Both Hemingway and his literary cohort, F. Scott Fitzgerald, later had occasion to assess the damage incurred during their years in France, and in memorable narratives written in the 1930s, each composed patently autobiographical meditations on loss and failure, on the costly profligacies associated with life abroad. Although Fitzgerald's "Babylon Revisited" and Hemingway's "Snows of Kilimanjaro" emerged from vastly different personal circumstances, both tend to deromanticize the antics of the Lost Generation by portraying scenes of self-confrontation and remorse. In each case, the protagonist's crisis leads to a reconsideration of the expatriate's "swell life" and raises unsettling questions about the ultimate influence of Paris, inscribed in both stories as a landscape of desire.

1.

The biographical context of "Babylon Revisited" possesses obvious relevance to the narrative itself. In March 1929, seven months before the great Wall Street Crash of 1929, the Fitzgeralds embarked on their last, catastrophic visit to France, and in April 1930, six months after Black Tuesday, Zelda Fitzgerald suffered an acute mental breakdown in Paris. After a period of observation and sedation at a facility in Malmaison, she decamped in angry defiance of her physician but shortly thereafter experienced the suicidal depression that led to her subsequent confinement at a Swiss psychiatric clinic (Bruccoli, *Epic Grandeur* 285). While Fitzgerald waited anxiously for news of his wife's treatment at Les Rives de Prangins in Nyon, he composed "Babylon" in December at a nearby hotel. The story appeared in the *Saturday Evening Post* two months later and belongs to a set of magazine stories (including "The Swimmers," "The Hotel Child," and "One Trip Abroad") issuing from that last trip to Europe and culminating in the publication of *Tender Is the Night* (1934). Like many a post-Romantic writer, Fitzgerald transformed private sorrows into public fables of loss, inventing tales about enervated American expatriates like himself, beset by failing marriages and complicated parental responsibilities. Discouraged by his wife's collapse, their long-strained marital relationship, and his inability to complete the new novel, Fitzgerald produced a handful of short stories that variously mirror the brokenness of his own life. As he dramatized his own sense of disintegration, he often placed his magazine characters in international dilemmas, torn between the seductiveness and moral laxity of postwar European cosmopolitanism and the quaint pieties of an earlier American way of life. Fitzgerald understood fiction as social mimesis and typically portrayed the breakdown of his jaded exiles as reflective of the broader historical and cultural shifts that marked the era of high modernism—the loss of certainty, the fading of traditional morality, and the rise of cultural relativism and skepticism.

Arguably, "Babylon" stands closest to *Tender* in its evocation of a profoundly tragic view of life, a point suggested by Fitzgerald's recycling of two key passages from the story in the longer work. As scholars and editors have often observed, the early description of Charlie Wales's melancholy taxi ride "through the tranquil rain" ("Babylon" 617), as well as his late, despairing realization that "he wasn't young any more, with a lot of nice thoughts and dreams to have by himself" (633), reappear in *Tender* to confirm the patent connection between Charlie's fall and that of Dick Diver, Fitzgerald's dashing yet ultimately defeated psychoanalyst-hero.[3] In both narratives, the writer implies an analogy between personal, domestic crisis and the stock market disaster of 1929.[4] Like Dick, Charlie yearns for the moral certainty of nineteenth-century America and wants "to jump back a whole generation" to "trust in character again as the eternally valuable element" ("Babylon Revisited" 619). Yet (again like Dick) he discovers the antithesis of that morally upright world in the alluring spectacle of Paris.

For Fitzgerald, as for his fictional American businessman, the city represented a scene of previous triumph. Writing to his wife in 1930, the author recalled his arrival five years earlier, shortly after the appearance of *The Great Gatsby*: "Then we came to Paris and suddenly I realized that it hadn't all been in vain. I was a success—the biggest man in my profession every-body admired me and I was proud I'd done such a good thing" (*Life in Letters* 187). In 1925 he lived with his family at 14, rue Tilsitt, literally within the lengthened shadow of the Arc de Triomphe, a location that perhaps suited his momentary sense of literary conquest. Gertrude Stein hailed him and young Ernest Hemingway envied him, soliciting his editorial advice about unpublished work. With a handsome income from stories published by the *Saturday Evening Post*, Fitzgerald lived like a rajah on the Right Bank. Similarly, Charlie Wales recalls with pleasure the economic power (born of advanta-geous exchange rates) enjoyed by expatriate Americans in Paris during the 1920s: "We were a sort of royalty, almost infallible, with a sort of magic around us" ("Babylon" 619). Americans unmistakably controlled the Ritz bar and seemed to own the city itself, as many a famous café underwent renovation to become a *"bar américain."* Money made things happen: Charlie recalls "thousand-franc notes given to an orchestra for playing a single number, hundred-franc notes tossed to a doorman for calling a cab" (620). Fitzgerald himself had known that sense of power in which Paris figured as the symbolic reward for Yankee cleverness, an artificial paradise that, according to a new mythology of American exceptionalism, yielded its pleasures to the moneyed expatriate.[5]

Yet by 1930 Fitzgerald also regarded Paris as a place of debauchery and ruin. After the notorious summer of 1925, which in his addled memory consisted of "1000 parties and no work" (*Ledger* 179), his new friend Hem-ingway advised him: "Paris is poisonous for you" (*Selected Letters* 182). Fitzger-ald nevertheless returned for extended, riotous visits in 1928 and again in 1929; he was living in the rue Pergolèse near the Porte Maillot, literally and figuratively on the far side of Triumph's Arch, when his wife collapsed from mental and physical exhaustion. During the months that followed, he left his nine-year-old daughter Scottie with a French governess while he lan-guished in Switzerland reading Freud, writing stories, and waiting for reports from the psychiatric clinic. In that season of regret, Gay Paree may have seemed the very source and image of his misfortune. Suggestively Charlie Wales recalls the dissipation that marked his Paris years, especially the "terrible February night" that began with a scene at the Hotel Florida and ended when he locked his wife outside in a snowstorm. He realizes that he "lost everything [he] wanted" during the crazy years when too much easy money created a sense of fantasy, and men "locked their wives out in the snow, because the snow of twenty-nine wasn't real snow. If you didn't want it to be snow, you just paid some money" ("Babylon" 633). For Charlie, Paris is preeminently a scene of personal debacle, a locus of "utter irresponsibility"

(629), and the central irony of his situation is that he must return to this "Babylon" to retrieve his nine-year-old daughter, Honoria, and whatever honor she may represent.

As Carlos Baker observed some years ago, Fitzgerald structures the action of the story around two opposed motifs—the "luxury and wickedness" of Babylon and the "quiet and decent home life" Charlie yearns to establish with his daughter (182). The genius of the story lies, however, in Fitzgerald's ability to insert these themes into a specific and suggestive cartography. From the outset, Paris itself embodies and reflects the contradictions that propel the hero back and forth between the Right Bank and the Left, between the Ritz bar and the Peters's apartment on the rue Palatine, as Fitzgerald charts a crucial topographical distinction. Charlie's negotiation of the city's geography—his movement within a symbolic landscape—suggests rather precisely the unfolding of an inner conflict that seems, in the final analysis, far more compelling than the custody battle with his sister-in-law, Marion Peters. At issue are three questions that suggest the uncertainty of his private situation. The most obvious of these concerns the extent of Charlie's recovery: Has he become a new man freed from his susceptibility to drink, or is he the old Charlie, still vulnerable to temptation, still parentally irresponsible? This is, of course, Marion's insistent suspicion, but the unflattering light in which she appears diminishes the apparent validity of her concern. Charlie moreover reassures her (and himself) that he has recovered, signaling this newfound self-control by the single, daily drink that demonstrates his sobriety. He thinks of the drink somewhat equivocally as the "spoonful of medicine" ("Babylon" 630) that preserves his emotional equilibrium, and throughout the story he adheres to this conscious regimen. Yet even as Fitzgerald insists on the self-discipline of his hero, he puts that recovery in question, and never more pointedly than when, during a tense scene at the Peters's, the narrator notes that "for the first time in a year Charlie wanted a drink" (626).

Fitzgerald elsewhere manipulates the geography of the story to suggest the insistence of Charlie's latent yearning for alcohol. Significantly, the narrative begins and ends at the Ritz bar (a place frequented by Dick Diver in *Tender* and habitually, in real life, by Fitzgerald himself), with Charlie taking his mandatory drink; the bar constitutes his refuge in Paris, the point of reference from which he gets his bearings. In the Ritz bar, significantly, he makes the Freudian slip that ultimately thwarts his effort to recover Honoria: A few lines into the story he asks the barman to give Lincoln Peters's address to Duncan Schaeffer, his old drinking pal, who at the wrong moment arrives drunkenly and unexpectedly on the rue Palatine with

Lorraine Quarrles to derail the custody negotiations. Although Charlie pointedly declines to give Duncan and Lorraine the address when he encounters them in the second section of the story, still his "conscious volition"—the wish to avoid trouble—cannot finally protect him from the consequences of his initial parapraxis (Twitchell 156-60). A profoundly conflicted character, Charlie betrays the perverse, unresolved tension between conscious will and unconscious desire in his attraction to the Ritz. If his daily, self-consciously consumed drink "proves" his sobriety, the hastily scribbled address he leaves for Schaeffer betrays his irrepressible urge to reconnect himself with those lost years of bibulous gaiety.

A second, more complex question thus grows out of the first and concerns Charlie's relationship to the recent past: Does he at bottom regard "those crazy years" ("Babylon" 629) as an epoch of disastrous irresponsibility or as a period of freedom when "a sort of magic" and an ample bank account afforded him a charmed life? Charlie's insistent expressions of remorse seem to resolve the question, but his geographical movements betray conflicting attitudes. His wanderings around Montmartre at the end of the first section neatly reveal this divided sensibility, conveying the simultaneous attraction and repulsion that mark his relation to the past. After dining with the Peters family and Honoria on the Left Bank, Charlie decides "not to go home" but rather to revisit scenes of prior folly: "He was curious to see Paris by night with clearer and more judicious eyes than those of other days." His soirée includes a stop at the Casino de Paris (16, rue de Clichy) to watch Josephine Baker "go through her chocolate arabesques" (619) and a walking tour past Bricktop's, Zelli's, the Café of Heaven, and the Café of Hell. As the two Dantesque names suggest, his journey seems an exercise in self-reproach, evoking disgust: "So much for the effort and ingenuity of Montmartre. All the catering to vice and waste was on an utterly childish scale, and he suddenly realized the meaning of the word 'dissipate'—to dissipate into thin air; to make nothing out of something" (620). The nocturnal spectacle finally assumes a frightening, surreal quality, as Charlie discovers a Montmartre previously concealed by his own delusions of power and indestructibility. His perambulations invite us to consider the impulse that has lured him to the *quartier* of the place Blanche and that draws him back repeatedly to the Right Bank in this story of turning and returning.

The significance of this pattern lies in the contrast between the Right Bank, with its multiple associations of past hilarity, and the so-called provincial quality of the Left Bank, which in "Babylon Revisited" has nothing to do, curiously, with the expatriate hub of Montparnasse. Instead, Fitzgerald restricts his Left Bank to the rue Palatine—and by extension to the dour, ecclesiastical quarter that surrounds the Eglise St. Sulpice. Situated in the same neighborhood where the Fitzgeralds lived in 1928 and again in 1929, the address of the apartment refers explicitly to the Palatine Hills of Rome, linking the Peters to St. Peter and the Roman Catholic Church, an institution the lapsed Catholic Fitzgerald habitually associated with repression and guilt. All apartments on the short rue Palatine face the south facade of St. Sulpice—a circumstance that perhaps helps to explain the "fear of life" attributed to Marion Peters.

But as Carlos Baker has noted (271), an equally important association links the rue Palatine address with an earlier, pre-exilic home life. When Charlie enters the Peters's apartment, Fitzgerald notes: "The room was warm and comfortably American" ("Babylon" 618). Marion Peters has once possessed "a fresh American loveliness," and in her presence Charlie immediately comments on the scarcity of their compatriots in Paris: "It seems very funny to see so few Americans around" (619). At the Peters's, Charlie has an instinctive sense of connection with his own national origins, with the familiar values of hearth and home, family and faith. But his antipathy for Marion perhaps also betrays a converse expatriate scorn for conventional American values, leaving him uncomfortable in this "provincial" space. Significantly, after each of his three visits to the Peters's apartment, he departs immediately for the Right Bank: On the first occasion, as discussed earlier, he wanders Montmartre; on the second, he strolls back to his Right Bank hotel, feeling "exultant" as he crosses the Seine; and on the third, he goes "directly to the Ritz bar" (632). Thus, despite the moral outrage and shame evoked by Right Bank scenes that recall a scandalous past, Charlie seems compelled to return to those settings in which his life once seemed enchanted.

Fitzgerald shows the grip of this repetition mechanism in the story's second section, when Charlie takes Honoria out for lunch and entertainment. Throughout this scene, the action hovers between conscious banter and unconscious desire, the father-daughter dialogue implying a flirtation that dimly prefigures the incest theme in *Tender Is the Night*. Charlie has chosen their dining place because it was "the only restaurant he could think of not reminiscent of champagne dinners and long luncheons that began at two and ended in a blurred and vague twilight" (620-21). But even as he tries to escape the memory of his wild years, his choice of the elegant Grand Vatel (275, rue du Faubourg St. Honoré) brings him back ineluctably to the Right Bank, where—significantly—he encounters "sudden ghosts out of the past" (622) in the persons of Duncan Schaeffer and Lorraine Quarrles. Although Charlie refuses, in a gesture of will, to disclose the name of his hotel, he does announce his next destination, the Empire music hall (41 avenue de Wagram), a showplace also located on the Right Bank and comparable to the Casino de Paris, which he had revisited earlier.[6] History repeats itself even as Charlie tries to escape its influence. When Duncan and Lorraine show up at the Empire, embodying the persistence and presence of the past, he agrees to have a drink with them. In a symbolic sense he thus renews his connections with the "crazy years" through a seemingly innocent excursion to two Right Bank locations.

Fitzgerald sharpens the contrast between those opposing spheres of meaning and experience, the Right Bank and the Left, in the fourth section of the story with the arrival of the *pneumatique* from Lorraine that evokes the remembrance of prior frivolity. The letter arrives at Charlie's hotel, having been "redirected from the Ritz bar where Charlie had left his address for the purpose of finding a certain man" (629). Fitzgerald pointedly refers to the mistake at the Ritz, yet his coyness here seems intriguing: By suppressing the name of Duncan Schaeffer, the narrator seems to participate in the hero's own psychic denial. The past that Charlie had unconsciously hoped to find has now found him, and Lorraine's note recalls a zany episode in which Charlie has pedaled a stolen tricycle "all over the Etoile"—that is, around the Arc de Triomphe—in the hours just before dawn. His recollection of the incident brings, however, no accompanying sense of triumph: "In retrospect it was a nightmare" (629).

Rejecting the invitation to meet Lorraine "in the sweat-shop at the Ritz"—at the geosymbolic nexus of the orgiastic past—Charlie thus proceeds to the Peters's apartment to conclude his custody talks with Marion. But in a brilliant scene that figures the intrusion of the "crazy years" into the present moment and the penetration of Right Bank revelry into the Catholic, provincial milieu of the place St. Sulpice, Fitzgerald stages the unexpected arrival of Duncan and Lorraine in the rue Palatine: "They were gay, they were hilarious, they were roaring with laughter. For a moment Charlie was astounded; unable to understand how they ferreted out the Peters' address" (631). In yet another allusion to his Freudian slip, he later tells Marion that Duncan and Lorraine "must have wormed [her] name out of somebody" (632). They know the address, of course, because Charlie has left it, perhaps subconsciously hoping to be rescued from cozy domesticity by his former companions in mirth. When Duncan makes the drunken suggestion that "all this shishi, cagy business 'bout your address got to stop" (631), he alludes to the crucial problem of place—to the question of where and how Charlie will situate himself within the city's symbolic landscape. Caught between the luxury and excess of the Right Bank and the provincial severity of the place

St. Sulpice, simultaneously attracted to and repelled by both, Charlie finds himself now displaced within the paradise of exile.

This predicament seems linked to the third question Fitzgerald poses: Does Charlie repent his wayward past and accept responsibility for the losses he has suffered? The story's title here assumes particular significance, for the name "Babylon" recalls the seventy-year Babylonian captivity of the Israelites and the city's infamous association with international debauchery and decline: "Babylon was a golden cup in the Lord's hand, making all the earth drunken; the nations drank of her wine, and so the nations went mad" (Jeremiah 51:7). The great city which had once been an emblem of power and glory became through its own corruption "an object of horror among the nations" (Jeremiah 51:41). In the prophet Jeremiah's account, God causes Jerusalem to fall to King Nebuchadnezzar and subjects the Israelites to exile as punishment for their faithlessness and disobedience; God thus redeems the captives, paradoxically, by subjecting them to the greater wickedness of Babylon. By evoking the biblical city of sin that occasioned spiritual testing and penitence, Fitzgerald implicitly raises the question of whether Charlie himself performs penance and receives symbolic forgiveness or whether he remains an unrepentant exile.

Unmistakably the visit to Montmartre resembles a penitential journey, as when Charlie pauses before the Café of Hell and meditates on the word "dissipate," realizing that he has made "nothing out of something." He has "squandered" his money to forget "the things most worth remembering, the things that now he would always remember—his child taken from his control, his wife escaped to a grave in Vermont" (620). Later, at dinner at the Peters's, he assumes "the chastened attitude of the reformed sinner" but he does so, Fitzgerald notes, merely to "win his point" (625) with Marion. And he recoils defensively when she recalls the morning Helen arrived "soaked to the skin and shivering" (625) after Charlie had locked her out. Marion poses the central moral problem succinctly when she remarks: "How much you were responsible for Helen's death, I don't know. It's something you'll have to square with your own conscience" (627). Precisely so; Charlie's return to Paris produces an incessant struggle with conscience, projected symbolically upon the geography of the city. When he recalls "that terrible February night" that began on the Right Bank with a scene at the Hotel Florida (12, Boulevard Malesherbes) and ended with his locking out Helen, he implicitly denies responsibility: "How could he know she would arrive an hour later alone, that there would be a snowstorm in which she wandered about in slippers, too confused to find a taxi?" (628). Yet Lorraine's *pneumatique*, with its reference to the tricycle incident, awakens both memory and guilt: "How many weeks or months of dissipation to arrive at that condition of utter irresponsibility?" (629).

Charlie's struggle with penitence culminates in the final scene at the Ritz bar, when he confesses to the bartender that he has "lost everything [he] wanted in the boom" by "selling short" (633)—by sacrificing for the sake of momentary gratification what he should have treasured and husbanded. Yet Fitzgerald's famous formulation—"the snow of twenty-nine wasn't real snow" (633)—captures the radical ambiguity of the confession: Does Charlie blame himself for his actions, or does he attribute them to the unreal Zeitgeist of the 1920s? His subsequent self-pitying remark ("they couldn't make him pay forever" [633]) implies that he sees himself as more oppressed than culpable. He returns to Paris but fails to recover his daughter because he cannot elude Duncan and Lorraine, those personifications of recklessness; although he recognizes his general "irresponsibility," he never accepts blame for Helen's "escaping pneumonia by a miracle, and all the attendant horror" (628). Failing to acknowledge responsibility for Helen's decline—or the need for contrition obliquely represented by the rue Palatine and the implied presence of the Eglise St. Sulpice—Charlie thus remains unrepentant and unabsolved. His visit to Paris forces him to confront the results of his carelessness, but unlike the Israelites he remains too deeply enamored of the pleasures of Babylon to recover his Honor(ia) or to escape the condition of spiritual exile. In a moment of brief moral insight, Charlie realizes: "I spoiled this city for myself" (618). He must therefore return to Prague to endure the captivity imposed by his own recalcitrance.

Whatever autobiographical freight the story finally carries, we must not, however, impute to Fitzgerald the moral obtuseness that afflicts Charlie Wales. Indeed, the author's subtle, recurrent reminders of his hero's fatal parapraxis comprise a lacerating self-indictment for the havoc Fitzgerald inflicted upon himself and his wife in Paris. Juxtaposed against the scene of inadvertent self-betrayal with which the story begins, that lame final paragraph, so suffused with self-pity and denial, offers the definitive expression of Charlie's blindness, his ultimate refusal to own up to his inner conflicts and his inevitable agency in the damage he has sustained. Fitzgerald enables us to see, through the geography of the narrative, the persistence of "that condition of utter irresponsibility" which is the essence of Charlie's problem. Belatedly Fitzgerald understood how he and Zelda had managed in Paris and elsewhere "to make nothing out of something." In 1930 he used that insight to reverse the process, miraculously extracting something wise and brilliant from the emotional debris of the 1920s. But the end of "Babylon" also prefigured, with ironic prescience, the loneliness and disappointment that would darken his final decade.

2.

As Hemingway revised "The Snows of Kilimanjaro" in early 1936, he found himself brooding upon the evidence of Fitzgerald's decline. With disgust he had read in *Esquire* a series of confessional essays by Fitzgerald (later published collectively in *The Crack-up* [1945]), and he began to imagine his former expatriate crony as the epitome of the broken writer he meant to portray in "Snows." His story even included a biting reference to "poor Scott Fitzgerald"—later changed to "poor Julian"—and his naive idealization of the rich: "He thought they were a special glamourous race and when he found they weren't it wrecked him just as much as any other thing that wrecked him" (53). Always the moralist despite himself, Hemingway composed "Snows" as an analysis of wreckage and self-ruin; privately he excoriated the "miserable" *Esquire* pieces and Fitzgerald's willingness to "whine in public," and while he conceded that it was "rotten to speak against Scott after all he had to go through," Hemingway complained that he had seen "the first part of it and it was all so avoidable and self imposed" (*Selected Letters* 437-38). He *had* seen "the first part of it" in Paris and Antibes, but what lay beneath Hemingway's angry fixation with Fitzgerald's dissolution was, of course, his own intense yet unacknowledged identification with his friend's "avoidable and self imposed" destruction. As "Snows" eloquently suggests, Hemingway already suspected that, like the pathetic writer in his story, "he had traded away what remained of his old life" (46). Within the African story about a dying writer's reflections, he embedded a secret narrative of deception and betrayal to explain—albeit obliquely—how he started down the path to self-ruin and lost "*the Paris that he cared about*" ("Snows" 52; unless otherwise indicated, emphasis in original).

In the six years since abandoning his Left Bank apartment in January 1930, Hemingway had bought a home in Key West, become an aficionado of big-game fishing, gone on safari in Africa, and published three new books, all of which drew criticism for their cynical self-indulgence.[7] His relationship with Pauline Pfeiffer—the romance that brought an end to "the first part of Paris" in 1926—had, apart from interludes of edgy domesticity, settled into a routine of evasion and deceit: Hemingway went off fishing for weeks at a time on the *Pilar* (ironically, his pet nickname for Pauline), and since 1932 he had been involved intermittently in a dalliance with a wealthy socialite named Jane Mason. The hardworking, winsome young man who achieved literary fame in Paris in the 1920s had become (in Jeffrey Meyers's formulation) the "swaggering hero" of the 1930s, swiftly evolving into the "drunken braggart" of the 1940s. Meyers suggestively remarks that "in the mid-1930s Hemingway ironically and irrationally began to blame Pauline, as Harry blamed Helen in 'The Snows of Kilimanjaro,' for the corrupting influence of her wealth" (70, 290). Hemingway perhaps felt the same sense of depletion he ascribed to the dying Harry: "He had had his life and it was over and then he went on living it again with different people and more money, with the best of the same places, and some new ones" ("Snows" 44). The appearance of Fitzgerald's *Crack-up* pieces only intensified the latent self-judgment that fueled "Snows." After seven years in Key West, Hemingway worried that, like Fitzgerald and like his own dying writer-hero, he had "destroyed his talent by not using it" (45). His new story, arguably the most daring he ever composed, probed his blackest anxieties to reckon the extent of his own dissolution. The story looked back, ruefully yet elliptically, to a turning point in his apprenticeship as an expatriate writer.

Hemingway inscribed the secret narrative of that epoch in the italicized flashbacks that represent Harry's *recherche du temps perdu*. These reconstructed moments or episodes comprise "the things that he had saved to write" (41), the stored materials that, as a result of the writer's gangrene and septicemia, would never become the stuff of literature except insofar as the metatextuality of "Snows" preserves them. The flashbacks unfold a panorama of scenes from places where Harry (and Hemingway himself) had lived or traveled—Turkey, the Austrian Vorarlberg, the Black Forest, a ranch in Wyoming. Taken together, they sketch the story of Harry's experiences in World War I and his glimpses of the ensuing conflict between the Greeks and the Turks; they tell of later skiing vacations, fishing trips, and cattle drives. They incorporate haunting images of the dead or the dying: Williamson, the officer disemboweled by a stick bomb and begging to be shot (53); the dead soldiers in Turkey wearing *"white ballet skirts and upturned shoes with pompons on them"* (48); the frozen, gnawed body of the old man killed by the *"half-wit chore boy"* (52) at the ranch. And the flashbacks return insistently, as critics have observed, to the enigmatic image of the snow, presaging the story's final, mystical turn toward the summit of Kilimanjaro (Oldsey 69-73). But embedded within the italicized passages lies a covert, fragmentary account of Harry's self-ruin, composed of glancing allusions to his formative experiences in Paris.

Hemingway suggests the geosymbolic importance of Paris early in "Snows" when Helen remarks about Harry's infected scratch: "You never would have gotten anything like this in Paris. You always said you loved Paris. We could have stayed in Paris or gone anywhere" ("Snows" 41). Putatively a beloved place in the geography of Harry's life, Paris represents safety and comfort, a refuge from misfortune and mortality. Inexplicably, however, Harry's own effort to recollect the city leads to an explosion of self-contempt:

> "Where did we stay in Paris?" he asked the woman who was sitting by him in a canvas chair, now, in Africa.
>
> "At the Crillon. You know that."
>
> "Why do I know that?"
>
> "That's where we always stayed."
>
> "No. Not always."
>
> "There and at the Pavillion [sic] Henri-Quatre in St. Germain. You said you loved it there."
>
> "Love is a dunghill," said Harry. "And I'm the cock that gets on it to crow." (43)

This cryptic exchange offers several clues to the secret story of Harry's relation to Paris. It resonates with other accusations about the corrupting effect of Helen's wealth by identifying two luxury hotels—one on the place de la Concorde and one in the suburb of St. Germain-en-Laye—as places where the couple "always stayed" in Paris. The flicker of disagreement ("No. Not always.") moreover hints at the discrepancy between Helen's carefully idealized remembrance of the recent past and Harry's troubled recollection of his early days in Paris. Her reference to the Pavillon Henri-Quatre elicits a sudden virulence, apparently because the hotel evokes for Harry not luxurious pleasure but degraded desire, associated with waste and possible transgression. His repugnant metaphor exposes a scornful self-contempt, rooted in his unmistakable disgust with love, the "dunghill," and sexual conquest, figured by the crowing cock—the latter reference slyly linking France itself (through its insignia, le coq gaulois) with phallic hubris.

The notion that Harry associates Paris with duplicity as well as desire becomes more apparent as he reflects on his various *amours*. He admits that lies have made him "more successful with women than when he had told them the truth" (44), and he wonders acerbically why "when[ever] he fell in love with another woman, that woman should always have more money than the last one?" (45). Contemplating his liaison with Helen within a history of fractious relationships, he thinks to himself, "He had never quarrelled much with this woman, while with the women that he loved he had quarrelled so much they had finally, always, with the corrosion of the quarrelling, killed what they had together. He had loved too much, demanded too much, and he wore it all out" (48). This chain of reflection leads, with psychic inevitability, to the flashback that constitutes the crux of his covert narrative. Here Harry uncovers a primal scene of desire significantly associated with Paris, the scene to which all of his other conquests have a secondary, mimetic relationship:

> He thought about alone in Constantinople that time, having quarrelled in Paris before he had gone out. He had whored the whole time and then, when that was over, and he had failed to kill his loneliness, but only made it worse, he had written her, the first one, the one who left him, a letter telling her how he had never been able to kill it. . . . How when he thought he saw her outside the Regence one time it made him go all faint and sick inside, and that he would follow a woman who looked like her in some way, along the Boulevard, afraid to see it was not she, afraid to lose the feeling it gave him. How every one he had slept with had only made him miss her more. How what she had done could never matter since he knew he could not cure himself of loving her. He wrote this letter at the Club, cold sober, and mailed it to New York asking her to write him at the office in Paris. (48)

In this complex remembrance, the writer dying in Africa recalls his visit to Constantinople (during the 1922 Greek-Turkish War) and the fateful letter that he composed back in Paris "at the Club." Reconstructing the epistolary moment, he remembers the phantasmic, unnamed "first one," standing outside the Café-Restaurant de la Régence (161, rue du Faubourg St. Honoré). His imperishable yet uncertain glimpse—"he thought he saw her" (emphasis added)—makes him feel "all faint and sick inside"; distance and separation define his momentary gaze, for now, presumably, she is someone else's lover. Using the Proustian mode of habitual past action Harry recalls a bleak period in Paris when "he would follow a woman who looked like her along the Boulevard," in a pattern of obsession confirming that the object of desire is always obscure, always displaced from its apparent incarnation, always quite literally disembodied. These other women are not the beloved but evoke by physical resemblance the "feeling" associated with her, the longing that ultimately has no proper object or embodiment. The unnamed first love occupies a totemic place in the writer's unconscious precisely because she was "the one who left him," and who thereby remains an irrecoverable absence. Harry perceives the emotional and symbolic linkage between the original beloved and his subsequent liaisons ("*every one he had slept with had only made him miss her more*"). The loss of his first love has shaped the economy of desire: The more desperate his efforts to recover her symbolically on the plane of the erotic, the more intensely he experiences his own emptiness and loneliness. For Harry, love is figuratively a dunghill.

The remembered glimpse of the beloved "*outside the Regence*" thus triggers a crucial revelation about the pattern of emotional wreckage in Harry's life. This recollection of a primal scene of desire on the rue du Faubourg St. Honoré folds into Harry's memory of another epoch in Paris and his symbolic reciprocation of the abandonment he has experienced. For Harry frames the remembrance of "*the first one*" and "*what she had done*" with an oblique reference to her successor, the wife with whom he "*quarrelled in Paris before he had gone out.*" He has "*whored the whole time*" in Turkey in 1922 ostensibly because of their quarrels but actually—as we learn—because he has never been able to "*kill his loneliness,*" the sense of solitude rooted in his originary rejection by the nameless beloved. Thus in Constantinople he picks up "*a girl,*" has dinner with her, and then abandons her for "*a hot Armenian slut,*" a "*smooth-bellied, big-breasted*" woman who needs "*no pillow under her buttocks*" (48). That is, he acts out his own rejection by picking up one woman and then leaving her to bed another, all the while betraying a third woman back in Paris—his wife, the unknowing object of his sexual revenge—to "*kill*" the feelings of rejection inflicted by a fourth woman, his first love.

This pattern of betrayal recurs when Harry returns to Paris and (from the masculine sanctuary of his "Club") writes a supplicating letter to his first love. He performs this act, significantly, in the context of his reunion with "*his wife that now he loved again, the quarrel all over, the madness all over*" (49). Feeling "*glad to be home*" from Constantinople and "*back at the apartment*"—apparently the apartment near the place Contrescarpe mentioned later—he receives a shock when a letter from his first love arrives "*on a platter one morning*" (49) among some mail from the office. Hemingway here stages a brief but profoundly revealing moment as Harry tries to cover his symbolic betrayal with an act of deception: "*When he saw the handwriting he went cold all over and tried to slip the letter underneath another. But his wife said, 'Who is that letter from, dear?' and that was the end of the beginning of that*" (49). Vaguely reminiscent of another Parisian scene of unsuccessful dissembling in Poe's "Purloined Letter," Hemingway likewise emphasizes the repetition compulsion inherent in an effort to conceal the sign of secret desire. For although Harry tries to slide the telltale letter from "*the first one*" under another envelope, he cannot repress or conceal his longing for her, nor can he apparently escape the repetition mechanism that causes him to reenact his initial abandonment by betraying the beloved's successor. Indeed, the purely symbolic infidelity enacted here seems finally a trope for later acts of deception, including (presumably) the relationship with Helen associated with the Crillon and the Pavillon Henri-Quatre. Harry's terse final comment, *"that was the end of the beginning of that,"* seems to signal the impending breakup of the marriage, as if the letter, the sign of a hitherto hidden and obsessive relation, had inevitably set in motion a chain of subsequent betrayals. And in a sense it has. But the reversal of the anticipated word order—we expect him to say "that was the beginning of the end" of their marriage—carries another implication, one having to do as much with the beginning of Harry's relationship to Paris as with his abandonment of the wife he *"loved again"* back in the apartment near the place Contrescarpe.

In the convoluted unfolding of Harry's secret story, his narrative of self-ruin, the next flashback culminates in a significant four-paragraph reconstruction of his memories of the working-class neighborhood on the Left Bank near the Panthéon. Sweat, poverty, and drunkenness typify the *quartier* around the Café des Amateurs, an area that stands in marked contrast to the milieu of luxury that Harry and Helen have subsequently inhabited. Hemingway remarks that Harry *"knew his neighbors in that quarter then because they all were poor"* (51). Oddly, however, the remembrance avoids any reference to the "wife" associated with the events of 1922. Instead, she disappears into the pronoun *"they,"* as when the flashback mentions *"the Bal Musette they lived above."* But in two oblique ways Hemingway suggests Harry's subliminal remorse about the way he destroyed his marriage. First, the flashback betrays an insistent interest in relations between husbands and wives, with Harry recalling *"the locataire across the hall whose husband was a bicycle racer,"* *"the husband of the woman who ran the Bal Musette"* (51), and finally Marie, the *femme de ménage* who explains that her husband's shorter working days will mean more drinking: *"It is the wife of the working man who suffers from this shortening of hours"* (52).

Another reflection of Harry's repressed feelings about his former wife inheres in the sense of loss evoked by the old neighborhood. With palpable regret, Harry recognizes that *"he had never written about Paris. Not the Paris that he cared about"* (52). The Paris that he cherishes is precisely the shabby place Contrescarpe *quartier* of 1922, linked explicitly to the origin of his literary career and tacitly to the wife whom he loved despite the quarrels. In effect he projects his attachment to her into the particulars of place:

> *And in that poverty, and in that quarter across the street from a Boucherie Chevaline and a wine co-operative he had written the start of all he was to do. There never was another part of Paris that he loved like that, the sprawling trees, the old white plastered houses*

*painted brown below, the long green of the autobus in that round square, the purple flower
dye upon the paving, the sudden drop down the hill of the rue Cardinal Lemoine to the
River, and the other way the narrow crowded world of the rue Mouffetard.* (51)

Noting that *"there were only two rooms in the apartments where they lived,"* Harry again
avoids mentioning his wife. Through an act of desperation, signaled by the
arrival of the letter, he has betrayed her; now, perhaps to avoid the pain of
remorse, he denies her very place in that world, figuring her only as a
shadowy absence, a pronominal trace. By metonymic substitution, however,
the old neighborhood becomes the site and symbol of Harry's longing for
the irrecoverable: for youth, for his literary beginnings, for the self that he
once was, and for the spouse whom he loved. His comment about locale—
"there never was another part of Paris that he loved like that"—implicitly distinguishes
his wife from the other lovers he has known there. Hemingway suggests that
Paris has been the essential scene of Harry's erotic life; it has witnessed the
various stages of his metamorphosis from wounded lover, to unfaithful
husband, to cynical rake. From the experience of loss on the rue du Faubourg
St. Honoré to the dunghill of desire at the Pavillion Henri-Quatre, the dying
Harry now understands the phases of his life in relation to the city he has
loved, the place where he has *"written the start of all he was to do."* Yet that
implicitly epochal event—the arrival of the letter—has marked *"the end of the
beginning"* (49) of his career and of his relation to the Paris he loves. He has
forfeited that best of all possible worlds because he *"loved too much, demanded
too much,"* because he could not surmount the pain of losing *"the first one"* (48).
To relieve his *"hollow sick"* loneliness, he has cast off his wife and inflicted
upon himself a perverse self-punishment: He falls prey to Helen, to the
charms of wealth and indolence, and thereby destroys his marriage, his
connections with working-class Paris, and eventually his discipline as a
writer. Only belatedly, as a dying man on an African plain performing the
final audit of his earthly account, does he recognize the damage he has done
and the irretrievability of all that he has lost.

By 1936 Hemingway had achieved enough distance from his Paris
years to survey the personal wreckage caused by his own destructive decisions and impulsive *liaisons dangereuses*. Although he rose from obscurity to
renown and fashioned (in Archibald MacLeish's phrase) "a style for his time"
on the Left Bank, the city's sensual, epicurean value system affected him
profoundly, fostering a brooding awareness that "nothing was simple there"
(*Feast* 58). Virtually from his arrival, Hemingway experienced moral ambivalence: He jeered at the "inmates" frequenting the Café Rotonde, then
himself became a confirmed Bohemian who (in Bill Gorton's phrase) liked

to "hang around cafés"; he learned to write "true sentences" from mentors like Anderson and Stein and then brusquely repudiated them, denying their influence; and in letters he flaunted his conjugal bliss with Hadley while becoming increasingly obsessed with unconventional sexual practices (Reynolds 24-25, 34). In the same neighborhood recollected by the dying writer in "Snows," he watched prostitutes plying their trade at the dance hall they lived above, and he discovered at the nearby Bal de la Montagne Sainte-Geneviève the spectacle of same-sex dancing and cross-dressing. At the cafés he met gay and lesbian couples (such as Jane Heap and Margaret Anderson), encountered intriguing bisexuals like Djuna Barnes, followed the semipublic affairs of Ezra Pound and Ford Madox Ford, and heard about the Montparnasse fad of group sex "sandwiching."

Although Hemingway went to Paris partly to escape the straight-laced moralism personified by his mother, Grace Hall Hemingway, he remained decidedly conventional—"ninety per cent Rotarian," as Stein calculated—at least until early 1924, when he and Hadley (possibly in reaction to recent parenthood) decided to plunge into the new hedonism of the postwar era: "We lived like savages and kept our own tribal rules and had our own customs and our own standards, secrets, taboos, and delights" ("As long as I . . ." 4).[8] The couple cultivated same-sex hairstyles, wore matching clothing, and fantasized about switching genders. The innocuous sexual game-playing hinted, however, at problems in their relationship. Hemingway's increasing restlessness led in 1925 to a tantalizing flirtation with Duff Twysden (the prototype of Brett Ashley) and soon thereafter to a steamy romance with Pauline Pfeiffer, an affair intermittently conducted (as *A Moveable Feast* implies) as a virtual ménage à trois. The break with Hadley, which occurred in 1926, marked the definitive end of an epoch—"the early days when we were very poor and very happy" (*Moveable Feast* 211). As his memoir suggests, nothing would ever seem simple or innocent again.

Why a writer so guarded as Hemingway saw fit to reconstruct his private history in "Snows" is an intriguing question. Transparently, Harry's tortured recollection of *"the first one"* and the arrival of the incriminating letter amounts to a veiled rationalization for the breakup of Hemingway's first marriage. The biographical subtext becomes more profoundly suggestive when we note that Hemingway exchanged letters in late 1922—more than a year after his marriage to Hadley—with Agnes von Kurowsky, the Red Cross nurse with whom he fell in love in Italy in 1918. His urge to contact her suggests that he had not entirely recovered from the emotional wound inflicted in March 1919 by the "dear John" letter describing her engagement to an Italian officer. Possibly, like his fictional protagonist, he wrote to Agnes

from the Anglo-American Press Club just after his return from Constantinople—a junket that had occasioned a bitter quarrel with Hadley. The reply
from Agnes reached him, however, not in Paris but in Chamby, Switzerland,
where Hemingway was skiing with his wife in early 1923 during the holiday
season. While there is no evidence that the young reporter had a heartbreak-
ing glimpse of Agnes on the streets of Paris, her December 1922 letter may
provide the origin of that imaginary scene:

> ... sometimes I get lonesome, and then ... I dream of Paris—that dear
> old place, where I had so much time on my hands, and roamed about
> in so many funny places. If I could only stand just now—at early
> twilight—at the Place de la Concorde, and see the little taxis spinning
> around those corners, & the soft lights, & the Tuileries fountain—oh,
> my, I'm homesick for the smell of chestnuts on a grey, damp Fall day—
> for Pruniers, the Savoia (Noel Peters) and my pet little restaurant
> behind the Madelaine [sic]—Bernard's, where I ate crème chocolate
> every night. Maybe I'd better stop, or the paper will get soft & blurry
> out of sympathy for my sorrows. (von Kurowsky 166-67)

Between Red Cross service missions, Agnes had spent four months in Paris
from October 1920 until February 1921. Depicting herself provocatively
with "so much time on [her] hands," Agnes mentions being most recently
in the city "a year ago this Nov."—barely a month prior to the arrival of
the newlyweds, Ernest and Hadley, in December 1921. By a few weeks,
that is, Hemingway had missed a chance reunion with Agnes at Prunier's,
or the Savoia (also known as Noël Peters's) or Bernard's—restaurants all
located roughly in the same Right Bank *quartier* where he installed himself
in early 1922 as a regular at the Anglo-American Press Club. The thought
of that missed encounter with his first love must have tormented him: Soon
thereafter he wrote "A Very Short Story," the first literary evidence of the
persistent fantasizing about Agnes that culminated in *A Farewell to Arms*.
Harry's recollection in "Snows" of the letter to his lost love extends that
preoccupation into the mid-1930s, and the imagined glimpse of *"the first
one"* outside the Régence marks a revealing excavation from the writerly
unconscious: Hemingway apparently reached back almost fifteen years to
resurrect—*from a letter he still preserved*—the image of Agnes von Kurowsky
emerging from a Right Bank restaurant "on a grey, damp Fall day" in
November 1921.

　　If so, Hemingway's own remembrance of things past—as figured in
"Snows"—contains an important insight into the fate of his first marriage.

It implies his realization that the end of his marriage began in 1922 with an act of infidelity: Not the "whoring" in Constantinople that Hemingway later confessed was his only sexual betrayal of Hadley until the affair with Pauline (Kert 125), but rather the letter to Agnes that implicitly indicated his fixation with her. Although Hemingway had told Hadley about his wartime romance and somewhat perversely visited with her the Italian settings associated with that relationship, the unexpected arrival of the letter from Agnes in response to his own may have heightened the marital tensions provoked by Hadley's loss of Hemingway's manuscripts a few weeks earlier.[9] Despite its decorous, friendly tone, the communication from Agnes would have exposed the hitherto secret letter from Ernest, allowing Hadley to glimpse both his continuing obsession with Agnes and his propensity for duplicity. And indeed Hemingway's fictional reference to an awkward scene of discovery—shifted from Chamby to Paris—hints that Hadley did see the letter. The author figures the moment as the incipient yet irreversible breakdown of marital trust, the prelude to an unspecified later episode in Harry's amatory career that brought actual separation and divorce. Yet the coded narrative in "Snows" may also be seen as a disguised (and equivocal) apology to Hadley. By representing Harry's betrayal as a symptom of compulsive desire, his inability to "kill the loneliness" inflicted by his first love's rejection, Hemingway was implicitly rationalizing his abandonment of Hadley, even as he intimated his residual feelings for her in Harry's plangent remembrance of the old apartment and "the Paris he cared about."

By ridiculing the *Crack-up* essays and the "shamelessness of defeat" epitomized by Fitzgerald, Hemingway attempted in 1936 to displace his own sense of failure and wasted opportunity. But the embedded story in "Snows" conveys an unsparing indictment of himself for damage inflicted upon Hadley—and ultimately upon himself as a writer—during the "nightmare winter" of 1925-1926 and the "murderous summer that was to follow" (*Moveable Feast* 207). The need to recover and celebrate the "magic" life destroyed during that period of upheaval haunted Hemingway to the end of his days. Among other tasks, *A Moveable Feast* makes restitution to Hadley by idealizing her and restoring her to that "cheerful, gay flat" near the place Contrescarpe. It reconstructs in all of its luminous particularity "the first part of Paris" whose traumatic loss he had figured in the cryptic story concealed two decades earlier in "Snows." Hemingway's repositioning of Hadley within the memoir of those early years reverses the narrative gesture by which he repressed her presence in the African story of 1936.

3.

"Babylon Revisited" and "The Snows of Kilimanjaro" thus reflect on each author's missteps in Paris during the Jazz Age. From the more somber Zeitgeist of the 1930s, Fitzgerald and Hemingway produced fictions calculated, on one level, to evoke sympathy for the male protagonists with whom they so obviously identified. But in a move that reveals their maturation since the "crazy years," both ultimately resisted the impulse to self-pity and subjected their fictional doubles to unsparing scrutiny, dramatizing the remorse and self-questioning—the deepening of moral insight—that represents perhaps the most significant literary consequence of the personal wreckage they sustained abroad. Their determination to revisit the ruins of their own youthful marriages and early careers, to contemplate again (admittedly, with minor evasions and equivocations) the heedless acts and bad decisions of the 1920s, corroborates Faulkner's famous declaration that "the problems of the human heart in conflict with itself . . . alone can make good writing because only that is worth writing about" (3). "Babylon" and "Snows" each bear witness to a lacerating conflict between an older, authorial self and a younger, experiential self—between a judgmental and thus patently American self and an insouciant, expatriate self.

Although their paths subsequently diverged, Fitzgerald and Hemingway shared the life of literary exile and—somewhat to their mutual chagrin—discovered themselves linked in the public mind (thanks to Stein's quip) as leaders of the "lost generation." The uneasy friendship that began in the Dingo Bar in 1925 underwent numerous reversals, permutations, and estrangements during the fifteen years that it endured. After the summer of 1929—the last season of their expatriate camaraderie in Paris—Fitzgerald felt that he could no longer assume with Hemingway a relationship of literary equality and common respect. Writing in his Notebooks, he remarked: "I talk with the authority of failure—Ernest with the authority of success. We could never sit across the same table again" (Wilson 181).

For Fitzgerald, the past was prologue to an even more difficult decade. When he returned from Europe in 1931, facing the nightmare of Zelda's illness and the ordeal of completing Tender Is the Night, he gave up the fantasy of recovering a glamorous expatriate life. Though he contemplated a transatlantic journey in the summer of 1932, the plan never materialized, and over the next few years Fitzgerald's own reduced circumstances made European travel increasingly unthinkable. Like Dick Diver, Fitzgerald had suffered a "lesion of vitality" in Europe, and he struggled unsuccessfully during the last nine years of his life to recover the imaginative facility of his pre-exilic years. Although he managed to finish his novel (remaining tormented, to the end, by its imperfections), the chaos of his personal life before and after the "crack-up" of 1935 greatly debilitated him as a writer. In the mid-1930s he conjured up a series of lame, romantic tales about a medieval French knight named Philippe, thus perhaps assuaging his memory of expatriate disasters with a dream of Gallic heroism, projected onto a character curiously reminiscent of Hemingway. Fitzgerald's work in Hollywood in the late 1930s led to a film script based on "Babylon Revisited," but in that screenplay, entitled "Cosmopolitan," Paris represents little more than a flimsy backdrop for the drastically revised, melodramatic action. In producing that treatment—as Matthew J. Bruccoli notes—Fitzgerald "removed the *revisited* theme" (*Babylon Revisited: The Screenplay* 189). There was no going back: even the Paris of memory had become irrecoverable.

Hemingway likewise returned from Europe deeply changed, though the nature of his transformation was less apparent. In the 1930s he demonstrated a deepening cynicism (flaunted in "A Natural History of the Dead"), a greater callousness in personal relationships, and a new preoccupation with self-indulgent travel journalism. After the earlier achievement of *The Sun Also Rises* (1926) and *A Farewell to Arms* (1929), his only novel of the decade, *To Have and To Have Not* (1937), reflected a palpable decline in creative power, and his stories of the period were notoriously uneven in quality (Lynn 409-10). His sense of decline as an author may underlie the crisis—not to say the "crack-up"—that he suffered in August 1936 (the same month that "Snows" appeared in *Esquire*), when he confessed to Marjorie Kinnan Rawlings, "Lately I have felt I was going to die in a short time" (*Selected Letters* 449). The same month he jested with Archibald MacLeish: "Me I like life very much. So much it will be a big disgust when [I] have to shoot myself" (*Selected Letters* 453). Hemingway postponed his fatal disgust another twenty-five years, however, outliving Fitzgerald and returning repeatedly to Paris. He sojourned there several times during the 1930s and helped to liberate "Paname" from Nazi occupation in 1944; he embarked in the postwar years on a trilogy of ultimately posthumous works (*Islands in the Stream, The Garden of Eden,* and *A Moveable Feast*) testifying to the deep and lasting influence of the early years that he spent in France. In *A Moveable Feast* Hemingway's fetishizing of certain elements of his life there—the old apartment, his dinners with Hadley, the Luxembourg gardens, Sylvia Beach's bookstore, the racetracks and the velodrome—reflects more than nostalgia; it betrays a complex, tragic awareness that what he had gained and lost then had been elemental, essential, and irreplaceable.

Reckoning the effects of the Paris years in "Babylon" and "Snows," Fitzgerald and Hemingway implicitly raised intricate questions about the city's influence on their own lives and writings. As noted earlier, their shared emphasis on emotional wreckage implicitly challenges extant studies celebrating exile in France unproblematically as boon and privilege. It would be reductive, of course, to attribute each writer's problems during the 1930s to the excesses of expatriate life in the 1920s, for many other factors affected their personal and professional vicissitudes. But it would be equally naive to assume that the consequences of living abroad had been uniformly propitious.

Decades ago, Malcolm Cowley discussed the "deracination" of his generation, the way that it had been "wrenched away from [an] attachment to any region or tradition" (9, 27-48). Fitzgerald and Hemingway initially reveled in their uprooting. Freed from American mores and family influences, inhabiting a culture more tolerant of vice and pleasure than our own, *both* writers indulged in "secrets, taboos, and delights," revolted against middle-class conventions, and managed to smash apart their personal lives. With palpable regret, both belatedly recognized (and dramatized in fiction) the results of their recklessness. Far from their native shores, released from any attachment to "region or tradition," they explored in Paris the beguiling possibilities of an expatriate life predicated on the desire—the ineluctable "hunger" metaphorized in Hemingway's memoir—that always culminates in the present moment.

But in that foreign place, neither writer could escape the weight of time, the inevitability of consequence, or the burden of memory. The retrospective vision of "Babylon" and "Snows" imposes a sense of fate and history upon the geography of exile. Facing different kinds of adversity in the 1930s, Fitzgerald and Hemingway reached similar conclusions about their experiences in France. Those passionate years had seemed truly "magic," and Paris, the site of the Modern and the source of the New, the place (in Stein's phrase) "where the twentieth century was," seemed a locus of unconstrained pleasure and creativity. But as Hemingway later perceived, Paris was also "a very old city" where everything was "more complicated" than it first appeared (*Moveable Feast* 119), and where young American writers hell-bent on fame could succumb to their own illusions of greatness and indestructibility, make irreversible mistakes, and lose the very things they cared about most. Eventually, however, the disasters of the 1920s produced moral insight: Not until they had fallen, failed, and experienced irrevocable losses could Fitzgerald and Hemingway confront the potential delusions of literary exile and write the enduring stories of the 1930s that calculated the possible personal costs of the expatriate's "swell life."

NOTES

1. Writing to Maxwell Perkins about a review of *The Sun Also Rises*,
    Hemingway observed: "It was refreshing to see someone have some
    doubts that I took the Gertrude Stein thing very seriously—I meant
    to play off against that splendid bombast (Gertrude's assumption of
    prophetic roles)" (*Selected Letters* 229). Matthew J. Bruccoli counts Stein
    among several literary friends with whom Hemingway eventually
    broke, noting that he had "a compulsion to declare his independence
    from, or non-indebtedness to, writers who could be said to have
    helped or influenced him" (*Fitzgerald and Hemingway* 4).
2. Though he mocked Stein's characterization of his generation, Hem-
    ingway acknowledged in a letter to his mother that he meant to
    portray the expatriates as "burned out, hollow and smashed" (*Selected
    Letters* 243). Hemingway's explanations to his mother should not be
    accepted uncritically, but there is corroborating evidence in his
    comments to Maxwell Perkins that he felt "a great deal of fondness
    and admiration for the [abiding] earth *and not a hell of a lot for my
    generation*" (*Selected Letters* 229; emphasis added). About his waning
    enthusiasm for life on the Left Bank, Hemingway remarked in a letter
    to Jane Heap in August, 1925: "Paris is getting shot to hell. Not like
    the old days."
3. Fitzgerald's account of the taxi ride, as published, will perplex anyone
    familiar with the geography of Paris: en route to the Peters's residence,
    Charlie crosses the Seine into the Left Bank, then recrosses the river
    to the avenue de l'Opéra on the Right Bank before finally returning to
    the Left Bank. As Garry N. Murphy and William C. Slattery have
    shown, Fitzgerald intended to delete the paragraph referring to the
    Boulevard des Capucines and the place de la Concorde.
4. Fitzgerald made this connection even more apparent in his revision of
    "Babylon" as the screenplay "Cosmopolitan" in 1940. His hero, Charles
    Wales, has just decided to give up a fabulous career as a Wall Street
    trader when the action begins; en route to Europe, while Charles is
    negotiating a deal in the ship's Brokerage Office, his wife commits
    suicide by jumping into the ocean. See *Babylon Revisited: The Screenplay*.
5. This is very nearly the imagery used by Malcolm Cowley in *Exile's
    Return*, one of the earliest and best accounts of the American expatriate
    movement of the twenties. For Cowley, France was the "Holy Land"
    where literary gods like Flaubert might be propitiated (102-3).

6. The Empire and the Casino de Paris are listed together under "Music Halls" in the Baedeker guide, *Paris and Its Environs* (34). It is worth noting that the music hall listed just ahead of the Empire was the Olympia (28, boulevard des Capucines), where Zelda took ballet lessons in an upstairs apartment in 1929.

7. Both *Death in the Afternoon* (1932) and *Green Hills of Africa* (1934) contained potshots at literary contemporaries as well as at irritating critics. *Winner Take Nothing* (1933) included some great stories (like "A Way You'll Never Be," "A Clean, Well-Lighted Place," and "Hills Like White Elephants") but also some of Hemingway's laziest work. Kenneth S. Lynn remarks, "Nothing that Fitzgerald ever peddled to a slick-paper publication was shoddier than 'One Reader Writes' or 'A Day's Wait'" (410).

8. In *Imagining Paris* (134-39) I discuss this tantalizing fragment in detail.

9. This well-known episode—recounted memorably in *A Moveable Feast* (73-75) and fictionalized in *The Garden of Eden* as well as the narrative published as "The Strange Country"—apparently contributed to the "friction" that developed between Ernest and Hadley from late 1922 on.

WORKS CITED

Baedeker, Karl. *Paris and Its Environs: With Routes From London to Paris—Handbook for Travellers*. 19th rev. ed. Leipzig: Karl Baedeker, 1924.

Baker, Carlos. "When the Story Ends: 'Babylon Revisited.'" *The Short Stories of F. Scott Fitzgerald: New Approaches in Criticism*. Ed. Jackson R. Bryer. Madison: U of Wisconsin P, 1982. 269-77.

Benstock, Shari. *Women of the Left Bank: Paris, 1900-1940*. Austin: U of Texas P, 1986.

Bruccoli, Matthew J. *Fitzgerald and Hemingway: A Dangerous Friendship*. New York: Carroll & Graf, 1994.

———. *Some Sort of Epic Grandeur: The Life of F. Scott Fitzgerald*. San Diego: Harcourt Brace Jovanovich, 1981.

Carpenter, Humphrey. *Geniuses Together: American Writers in Paris in the 1920s*. Boston: Houghton Mifflin, 1988.

Cowley, Malcolm. *Exile's Return: A Literary Odyssey of the 1920s*. 1932. New York: Penguin, 1976.

Faulkner, William. "Nobel Prize Address." *The Faulkner Reader*. New York: Modern Library, 1961. 3-4.

Fitzgerald, F. Scott. "Babylon Revisited." *The Short Stories of F. Scott Fitzgerald: A New Collection.* Ed. Matthew J. Bruccoli. New York: Scribners, 1989. 616-33.

———. *Babylon Revisited: The Screenplay.* Intro. Budd Schulberg. New York: Carroll and Graf, 1993.

———. *F. Scott Fitzgerald's Ledger: A Facsimile.* Washington, DC: NCR/Microcard Editions, 1972.

———. *The Letters of F. Scott Fitzgerald.* Ed. Andrew Turnbull. New York: Scribners, 1963.

———. *A Life in Letters.* Ed. Matthew J. Bruccoli, with the assistance of Judith S. Baughman. New York: Scribners, 1994.

———. *Tender Is the Night.* New York: Scribners, 1934.

Ford, Hugh. *Published in Paris: American and British Writers, Printers, and Publishers in Paris, 1920-39.* Yonkers, NY: Pushcart P, 1975.

Hemingway, Ernest. "As long as I did newspaper work. . . ." Unpublished. Item 526. Hemingway Collection. John F. Kennedy Library, Boston.

———. *Ernest Hemingway: Selected Letters, 1917-1961.* Ed. Carlos Baker. New York: Scribners, 1981.

———. Letter to Jane Heap, ca. August 25, 1925. Unpublished. *Little Review* Collection. University of Wisconsin-Milwaukee Library, Milwaukee, WI.

———. *A Moveable Feast.* New York: Scribners, 1964.

———. "The Snows of Kilimanjaro." *The Complete Short Stories of Ernest Hemingway.* New York: Scribners, 1987. 39-56.

———. *The Sun Also Rises.* New York: Scribners, 1926.

Kennedy, J. Gerald. *Imagining Paris: Exile, Writing, and American Identity.* New Haven CT: Yale UP, 1993.

Kert, Bernice. *The Hemingway Women: Those Who Loved Him—The Wives and Others.* New York: Norton, 1983.

Lynn, Kenneth S. *Hemingway.* New York: Simon and Schuster, 1987.

Meyers, Jeffrey. *Hemingway: A Biography.* New York: Harper & Row, 1985.

Murphy, Garry N., and William C. Slattery. "The Flawed Text of 'Babylon Revisited': A Challenge to Editors, a Warning to Readers." *Studies in Short Fiction* 18 (1981): 315-18.

Oldsey, Bern. "The Snows of Ernest Hemingway." *Ernest Hemingway: A Collection of Criticism.* Ed. Arthur Waldhorn. New York: McGraw-Hill, 1973. 56-82.

Pizer, Donald. *American Expatriate Writing and the Paris Moment: Modernism and Place.* Baton Rouge: Louisiana State UP, 1995.

Reynolds, Michael. *Hemingway: The Paris Years.* Cambridge, MA: Blackwell, 1989.

Twitchell, James B. "'Babylon Revisited': Chronology and Characters." *Fitzgerald/Hemingway Annual 1978:* 155-60.

von Kurowsky, Agnes. *Hemingway in Love and War: The Lost Diary of Agnes Von Kurowsky, Her Letters and the Correspondence of Ernest Hemingway.* Ed. Henry Serrano Villard and James Nagel. Boston: Northeastern UP, 1989.

Wickes, George. *Americans in Paris.* 1969. New York: Da Capo, 1980.

Wilson, Edmund, ed. *The Crack-up.* New York: New Directions, 1945.

NOTES ON CONTRIBUTORS

JACQUELINE VAUGHT BROGAN is Professor of English at the University of Notre Dame and the author of *Stevens and Simile: A Theory of Language* and *Part of the Climate: American Cubist Poetry*, as well as editor of the forthcoming *Women Poets of the Americas*.

JACKSON R. BRYER is Professor of English at the University of Maryland and cofounder and President of the F. Scott Fitzgerald Society. He is the author of *The Critical Reputation of F. Scott Fitzgerald*, editor of *New Essays on F. Scott Fitzgerald's Neglected Stories*, *The Short Stories of F. Scott Fitzgerald: New Approaches in Criticism*, and *F. Scott Fitzgerald: The Critical Reception*, and coeditor of *The Basil and Josephine Stories*, *F. Scott Fitzgerald in His Own Time: A Miscellany*, and *Dear Scott/Dear Max: The Fitzgerald-Perkins Correspondence*.

JOHN F. CALLAHAN is Morgan S. Odell Professor of Humanities at Lewis and Clark College. He has been a fellow at the Woodrow Wilson Center for International Scholars at the Smithsonian Institution. He is the author of *The Illusions of a Nation: Myth and History in the Novels of F. Scott Fitzgerald* and *In the Afro-American Grain: The Pursuit of Voice in 20th Century Black Fiction*, a second edition of which appeared under the title *Call-and-Response in 20th Century Black Fiction*. His editions of *The Collected Essays of Ralph Ellison* and Ellison's *Flying Home and Other Stories* have recently been published.

CLAUDE CASWELL is an Adjunct Assistant Professor in the Liberal Arts Department of the Maine College of Art. He is also on the faculty of the University System of New Hampshire's College for Lifelong Learning, where he won the Distinguished Faculty Award for 1995.

NANCY R. COMLEY is Professor of English at Queens College of the City University of New York. She is coauthor with Robert Scholes of *Hemingway's Genders* and of several articles on Hemingway.

KIRK CURNUTT is Assistant Professor of English at Troy State University, Montgomery. His essays have appeared in the *Hemingway Review*, the *Journal of the Short Story in English*, *Style*, and *College English*. His book, *The Critical Response to Gertrude Stein*, is forthcoming. He is at work on a book about American literature and twentieth-century youth culture.

SCOTT DONALDSON retired in 1992 as G. T. Cooley Professor of English at the College of William and Mary. He is the author of biographies of Winfield T. Scott, Ernest Hemingway, F. Scott Fitzgerald, John Cheever, and Archibald MacLeish, and is the editor of *Critical Essays on F. Scott Fitzgerald's "The Great Gatsby," Conversations with John Cheever, New Essays on "A Farewell to Arms,"* and *The Cambridge Companion to Hemingway*.

ROBERT E. GAJDUSEK is Professor Emeritus of English at San Francisco State University, where he was named Outstanding Professor of Humanities. He is the author of *Hemingway's Paris* and *Joyce: A Study in Debt and Payment*. He has published many articles on Hemingway, Lawrence, Shakespeare, film, and aesthetics, and his poetry has been published as *A Voyager's Notebook: Selected Poems of Robin Gajdusek*. He has recently published a memoir of his war experiences, *Resurrection*, and is now writing another volume of reminiscences.

J. GERALD KENNEDY is Professor of English at Louisiana State University. He is the author of *Imagining Paris: Exile, Writing, and American Identity* and has published two books on Poe, as well as a recent collection of essays, *Modern American Short Story Sequences*. He directed the 1994 Hemingway/Fitzgerald International Conference in Paris and is currently co-editing a volume on Poe and race.

ROBERT A. MARTIN recently retired as Professor of English and American Literature at Michigan State University, after teaching for a number of years at the University of Michigan. He is the editor of *The Theater Essays of Arthur Miller, Arthur Miller: New Perspectives, The Writer's Craft,* and *Critical Essays on Tennessee Williams,* and coeditor of *Rewriting the Good Fight*. He has published essays on Fitzgerald, Hemingway, Faulkner, Wharton, Heller, Vonnegut, Plath, and Gaddis, among others, in numerous journals and collections.

JAMES PLATH is Associate Professor of English at Illinois Wesleyan University and was Director of the annual Hemingway Days Writers' Workshop and Conference in Key West, Florida. He is the editor of *Conversations with John Updike* and of a forthcoming collection of critical essays on Raymond Carver.

RUTH PRIGOZY is Professor of English at Hofstra University. She is a cofounder and Executive Director of the F. Scott Fitzgerald Society. She is the editor or coeditor of *Short Stories: A Critical Anthology,* the special Fitzgerald issue of *Twentieth Century Literature, The Modern Detective in Fiction and Film,* and of the forthcoming *F. Scott Fitzgerald: New Perspectives* and *The Cambridge Companion to F. Scott Fitzgerald,* as well as of the Oxford University Press World's Classics edition of *The Great Gatsby.* Her book on F. Scott Fitzgerald and popular culture will be published by University Press of Mississippi.

FELIPE SMITH is Associate Professor of English at Tulane University and has published articles on Alice Walker, Toni Morrison, and African-American poetry, as well as on Fitzgerald. He is the author of *American Body Politics: Race, Gender, and Black Literary Renaissance.*

H. R. STONEBACK is Professor of English and Director of Graduate Studies at the State University of New York at New Paltz. He is the author of *Cartographers of the Deus Loci,* a book of poetry, and of more than one hundred published articles on American, British, Chinese, and French literature, including more than thirty essays on Hemingway.

JACQUELINE TAVERNIER-COURBIN is Professor of English at the University of Ottawa and editor of the scholarly journal *Thalia: Studies in Literary Humor.* She is the author of *Ernest Hemingway: l'éducation européene de Nick Adams, The Making of Myth: Ernest Hemingway's "A Moveable Feast,"* and *"The Call of the Wild": A Naturalistic Romance,* and editor of *Critical Essays on Jack London.*

WELFORD DUNAWAY TAYLOR holds the James A. Bostwick Chair of English at the University of Richmond. His work on Sherwood Anderson includes a critical study, numerous articles, and an edition of the *Buck Fever Papers.* He is the author of *Robert Frost and J. J. Lankes: Riders on Pegasus;* his biography, *The Woodcut Art of J. J. Lankes,* studies the artist whose designs embellished the works of Anderson, Frost, and others.

WILLIAM BRAASCH WATSON is Associate Professor of Modern European History at the Massachusetts Institute of Technology. His primary interest in Hemingway has focused on the author's involvement in the Spanish Civil War. In 1988, he edited Hemingway's Spanish Civil War dispatches for the *Hemingway Review.*

GEORGE WICKES recently retired as Professor of English at the University of Oregon. His books include *Americans in Paris, The Amazon of Letters, The Memoirs of Frederic Mistral,* and most recently, *Henry Miller & James Laughlin, Selected Letters.* He has taught in Germany, Italy, England, and France (three times as a Fulbright lecturer) and has received fellowships from the Center for Twentieth-Century Studies at the University of Wisconsin-Milwaukee, the National Endowment for the Arts, and the Camargo Foundation.

INDEX

"Accents in Alsace" (Stein), 124
Anderson, Margaret, 8, 82, 334
Anderson, Sherwood, viii, xiii, 4, 101,125-
26, 266; influence on EH, 101-16; Parisian sojourn of, 102; response to *The
Torrents of Spring*, 111-12
"Art of the Short Story, The" (EH), 16, 17,
28, 117
Atlantic Monthly, 18, 105, 131
"Autobiography of Alice B. Hemingway,
The" (EH), 131; conciliatory tone of,
133
Autobiography of Alice B. Toklas, The (Stein),
xiii, 130, 131, 134
"Babylon Revisited" (FSF), xv, 4, 5, 10-12,
161, 163, 180; and *Tender Is the Night*,
319; as analysis of self-ruin, 318-27,
337-39; biographical context of, 318-
19; persistence of past in, 323-24; question of responsibility in, 325-26; Right/
Left Bank contrasts in, 321-24; Ritz bar
in, 321, 326; symbolic geography of,
321, 324-25; title of, 325
Baker, Josephine, 143, 200, 201, 322
Barnes, Djuna, 309, 334
Barney, Natalie, 99, 199, 300, 301
Beach, Sylvia, viii, xiii, 6, 9, 17, 103, 107,
112, 116, 301, 338
Beautiful and Damned, The (FSF), 210
Bird, William, 8, 239
"Black Ass at the Cross Roads" (EH), 41
Boni & Liveright, 15, 102
Brassaï (Gyula Halasz), 76, 98; description
of prostitution by, 89-91
Bricktop, 9-10, 184, 201, 211n, 322
"Butterfly and the Tank, The" (EH), 150-52
Callaghan, Morley, x, 11, 55, 102, 116, 210
"Canary for One, A" (EH), 41
Cézanne, Paul, 5, 76, 220, 289
"Chauffeurs of Madrid, The" (EH), 142,
146-48
"Che Ti Dice La Patria?" (EH), 42, 45
Church, Ralph, 112-13
Collier's, 8, 18
Communist Party, 144, 154, 155
"Composition as Explanation" (Stein), 126,
129, 132
Conrad, Joseph, 7, 190, 236, 250n

Cosmopolitan, 17
"Cosmopolitan" (FSF), 338
Cowley, Malcolm, 318, 340n; and deracination, 339
Crack-up, The (FSF), 327
"Crack-up, The" (FSF), xi, 177
"Crime and Punishment" (EH), 77
Dark Laughter (Anderson), 101, 104, 107,
108, 110, 114, 125; as target of *The Torrents of Spring*, 107; deficiencies of, 105;
Parisian flashbacks in, 109
Decline of the West (Spengler), 205, 299, 314n
"Denunciation, The" (EH), 149
"Diagnosis" (FSF), 170
Dial, The, 8, 103, 258
"Divine Gesture, A" (EH), 117
Dos Passos, John, 109, 116, 125, 130, 144,
149; disillusionment with EH, 150
Eastman, Max, 130
"Echoes of the Jazz Age" (FSF), 10, 169,
178, 199, 205, 206; cultural decline in,
194-96
Eliot, T.S., 43, 190, 299, 305
Esquire, xi, 38, 131, 134, 135, 144, 327
Farewell to Arms, A (EH), x, 27, 79, 89-91,
338; and Agnes von Kurowsky, 335
"Fathers and Sons" (EH), 42, 85
Fathers and Sons (Turgenev): influence on *The
Sun Also Rises*, 106
Fifth Column, The (EH), 150
"Fifty Grand" (EH), 15, 16-18, 23
"Fight, The" (Anderson), 117
Finnegans Wake (Joyce), 6, 7
Fitzgerald, F. Scott, 94, 109, 116, 125, 129;
and American sexual mores, 194; and
decline of "Aryan man," 205-6; and
decline of white, male authority, 195;
and EH's "Fifty Grand," 16-18; and
expatriate hedonism, 202-3; and expatriate life, 10; and modern women, 198,
204; anti-Semitism of, 205; critique of
The Sun Also Rises, 22-24; Emersonian
vision of, 165, 170; impressions of
Paris, 193; influence on EH, vii, 15-29;
racial anxieties of, 190-91, 193;
response to France, 173-86; response to
Paris, ix, xii, 4, 319-20; sense of place
in, 183; tourist vision of, 165; view of

Americans abroad, 167, 169; view of EH as French knight, 40, 53, 338; view of France, 190-91; "world elsewhere" of, 164-65

Fitzgerald, Zelda, viii-xi, xv, 165, 174, 184, 192, 193, 204, 262; and *Save Me the Waltz*, 15, 278-82, 298; belief that FSF was homosexual, 308; dalliance with Edouard Jozan, 184, 230, 278-79; EH's view of, 285-87; lesbian tendencies of, 199; mental illness of, 11, 176, 192, 282-83, 318, 337

Flanner, Janet, 95, 130

For Whom the Bell Tolls (EH), xi, xiii, 89, 141, 156, 309, 311-12

Ford, Ford Madox, 8, 22, 334; influence on Hemingway, 7-8

France: as wasteland, 51-52; Clemenceau as personification of, 35; exile in, 339; "intelligence and good manners of," ix; of EH, 34-54; of FSF, 173-85; persistence of, 176; Tour de, 50; travel to, 167-68

"Franco-German Situation, The" (EH), 37

"Freeze-Out, A" (FSF), 164

Friendship of Fitzgerald and Hemingway, vii-xi, 11, 22, 28, 189, 191, 257, 308, 337

Galantière, Lewis, 103, 112, 117

Garden of Eden, The (EH), xi, xiv, 34, 37, 52-53, 235-50, 277, 286-93, 297-98, 311-12, 338; "African Story" in, 236-37; Catherine's madness, 287-88; David's writing, 249; lesbianism in, 288-89; money in, 238, 242-44, 248; sexual reversal in, 246, 291, 312; veiled allusions to Zelda and FSF, 286-87, 290, 298, 313

Gellhorn, Martha, 154

Geography and Plays (Stein), 124

Gide, André, 102, 215

Gingrich, Arnold, 131, 144

Great Gatsby, The (FSF), vii, xiv, 10-11, 20, 67, 164, 177, 184, 190, 204, 210; and *The Sun Also Rises*, 257-74

Green Hills of Africa (EH), 28, 122, 133

Heap, Jane, 8, 82, 264, 309, 334

Hemingway, Ernest: admiration for Anderson, 102; and expatriation, 3; and integrity of the writer, 152; and liberation of France, 39, 41, 53-54; and moral corruption, 86; and myth of sexual prowess, 93-94; and Paris, viii-ix, 5, 43-44;

and prostitution, 75-99; and Spanish Civil War, 141-57; and voyeurism, 95; anxiety of influence in, 106, 115, 122-24; as French knight, 54, 56; Chicote's Bar stories of, 148, 149; criticism of Anderson, 103; denial of Anderson's influence, 104, 113; denial of Stein's influence, 122, 123; downplays help of FSF, 15, 18; editorial advice of FSF, 19, 28; in the 1930s, 327; on death and dying, 153, 154; on expatriation, 4, 317; prostitution metaphor in, 77; purported influence on Stein, 122; rationale for *The Torrents of Spring*, 112; rediscovery of vocation, 142; relationship to Stein, 121; relation to France, xii, 34-54; response to Paris, ix, xii, 5, 12, 44, 75, 87; review of Anderson, 103; review of Stein, 124, 126; rivalry with FSF, 244, 249, 257-74; satire of *The Great Gatsby*, 20, 257-74; scorn for Anderson, 113; symbolic geography of, 34, 40; unpublished manuscripts of, 35, 36-37, 123, 127, 133; view of FSF, 193; waning support of Spanish Civil War, 155; writing as lovemaking in, 97

Hemingway, Grace Hall, 334; comparison of EH to Anderson, 105

Hemingway, Gregory, 40

Hemingway, Hadley (Richardson), viii, 19, 20, 38, 99, 103, 110, 116, 123, 334; in *A Moveable Feast*, 336; loss of EH's manuscripts, 336

Hemingway, John Hadley Nicanor, 19, 20

Hemingway, Mary (Welsh), 39, 55, 92

Hemingway, Pauline (Pfeiffer), x, 39, 86, 110, 129, 328, 334; praise of *The Torrents of Spring*, 111

"I'm A Fool" (Anderson), 104, 113

In Our Time (EH), 17, 24, 79, 101-4, 111, 125, 239, 310, 312; Anderson's influence on, 104

in our time (EH), 9, 15

"Intimate Strangers, The" (FSF), 169

Islands in the Stream (EH), xi, 85, 338

It Was the Nightingale (Ford), 8

Ivens, Joris, 145, 150

"I Want to Know Why" (Anderson), 104

James, Henry, 7, 25-27

Joyce, James, viii, 6, 7, 95, 103, 174

Kansas City Star, 76

Keats, John, 174, 183

Kiki, (Alice Prin), 87, 95

"Killers, The" (EH), 117
"Landscape with Figures" (EH), 142, 153
"Last of the Belles, The" (FSF), 170
LeBlanc, Georgette, 82
Lewis, Wyndham, 113, 130
"Light of the World, The" (EH), 85
Little Review, 8, 117, 264
Liveright, Horace, 104, 111, 116
Loeb, Harold, xiv, 87, 95, 235, 238-41, 244-45, 260, 301
Lost generation, 19, 25, 62, 114, 128, 190, 317, 318, 337
"Love in the Night" (FSF), 163, 169-70
Lucy Church Amiably (Stein), 122
MacLeish, Archibald, 39, 105, 106, 144, 338
Making of Americans, The (Stein), 7, 122
Many Marriages (Anderson), 104, 105
Maupassant, Guy de, 89, 106
McAlmon, Robert, 7, 8, 72n, 98, 202, 239, 301, 308
McCall's Magazine, 19
Miller, Henry, 87, 162
Miró, Joan: "The Farm," 131
"Monologue to the Maestro" (EH), 134
Moveable Feast, A (EH), xi, xiii, xiv, 6, 7, 9, 11, 12, 22, 28, 52, 86, 96-97, 114, 122, 123, 128, 135, 211, 334, 338; and loss, 338; and Stein, 123, 135; and writing in Paris, 318; idealization of Hadley in, 336; money in, 245; Paris reading by EH, 107; portrait of FSF in, 18, 192; 257, 262, 264, 277, 278, 308; relationship with Pauline in, 86, 334; view of Zelda, 286
Münzenberg, Willi, 144, 145
Murphy, Gerald, 116, 182; as model for Dick Diver, 192
Murphy, Gerald and Sara, viii, 10, 19, 21, 184, 189, 192
"My Lost City" (FSF), 193
"My Old Man" (EH), 41; influence of Anderson on, 103-4
"My Own Life" (EH), 123, 128, 129
"Mysticism of Money, The" (Loeb), 238-41; and new American writing, 240
"Natural History of the Dead, A" (EH), 338
"New Leaf, A" (FSF), 169
New Negro, The (Locke), 199
"News of Paris—Fifteen Years Ago" (FSF), 162
Nigger Heaven (Van Vechten), 199
"Night Before Battle" (EH), 152-53

"Nobody Ever Dies" (EH), 142, 154-55
No More Parades (Ford), 7, 315n
"Not in the Guidebook" (FSF), 161, 167, 169
Novel of Thank You, A (Stein), 122
"Ode to a Nightingale" (Keats), 174, 183
"Old Man at the Bridge" (EH), 142, 147, 148
"One Trip Abroad" (FSF), 165
Parade's End (Ford), 7, 299, 315n
Paris: and prostitution, 88-90; as hedonistic paradise, 209; bordellos in, 90; images in film, 168; images in songs and musicals, 167-68; influence on American expatriate writers, 190, 339; in the 1920s, 143; in the 1930s, 142, 143; open sexuality of, 204; sexual ambiguity of, 76
"Paris 1922" (EH), 96
"Penny Spent, A" (FSF), 165
Perkins, Maxwell, 9, 15, 16, 18, 21, 24-27, 113, 129, 130, 133
Portrait of the Artist as a Young Man (Joyce), 6
Pound, Ezra, viii, 38, 94, 103, 117, 125, 126, 128, 334; influence on Hemingway, 6
Prohibition, 4, 42, 166, 318
prostitute: as symbol of modernity, 76
popular aliases of, 79-80
prostitution, 75-79; in Paris, 98
Putnam, Samuel, 87, 98
Ray, Man, 95
"Rich Boy, The" (FSF), 10
Rising Tide of Color, The (Stoddard), 211
Robles, José, 149, 150
Saturday Evening Post, 8, 10, 18, 167
Save Me the Waltz, (Zelda Fitzgerald), xiv, 277-82, 298
Scribner, Charles, 122
Scribner's Magazine, 16, 17
Scribners (publishers), 15, 18, 21, 25, 102, 111
"Sea Change, The" (EH), 41
Shakespeare and Company (bookstore), viii, 9, 17, 126, 301
"Snows of Kilimanjaro, The" (EH), xi, xv, 28, 86; allusion to FSF in, 327; as analysis of self-ruin, 327, 328-36, 337-39; autobiographical implications of, 333, 334; composition of, 327; Paris in, 328, 329, 332, 333; primal scene of desire in, 330, 331; prostitution of Harry in, 85;

secret, embedded narrative in, 328, 332, 336; symbolic geography of, 328

"Soldier's Home" (EH), 125; allusion to Stein in, 124

Spanish Civil War, xiii, 141-57

Spanish Earth, The (film by Joris Ivens), xi, 145, 153

Spengler, Oswald, 205

Sportsman's Sketches, A (Turgenev), 107

Stearns, Harold, 117n, 245

Stein, Gertrude, viii, x, xiii, 5, 12, 95, 103, 109, 114, 116, 117, 174, 190, 198, 339; influence on EH, 5; on Paris, 3; reaction to The Torrents of Spring, 112, 113; relationship to EH, 121; satire of EH, 130; trademark style of, 122

Story Teller's Story, A (Anderson), 103

Sun Also Rises, The (EH), x, xii-xiv, 4, 5, 7, 8, 15, 61-71, 111, 122, 125, 126, 129, 190, 257-74, 338; American identity of Jake, 67, 70; American values in, 61, 63, 69; and artistic development of EH, 106; and Jake's code, 49-50; as response to Gatsby, 257-74; attitudes toward Paris, 62; Bill Gorton in, 64-66; Brett and Duff Twysden, 87; bullfighting in, 70, 83; deleted opening section 21-24; discarded references to FSF, 19; effects of World War I in, 82; expatriate status of Jake Barnes, 66, 68; France/Spain contrast in, 43-50; Georgette as prostitute in, 78-83; "lost generation" in, 62; meals in, 46-48; Paris and France in, 43-52; pilgrimage structure in, 51; prostitution metaphor in, 78, 83-84; revisions of, 24-26; rivalry with FSF, 257-74; Robert Cohn in, 62-66, 80; taxi scenes in, 78-79

"Swimmers, The" (FSF), 192

Tender Is the Night (FSF), vii, xiii-xiv, xv, 10, 162, 163, 167, 169, 187-210, 337; American history in, 176-77; "being here" of France, 175; blacks in Melarky drafts of, 199-202; breakdown of color line in, 188, 201, 207; composition of, 184; Dick's dissociation from places in, 183; Dick's loss of discipline, 179; difference between France and Switzerland in, 180; evocation of place in, 174; homosexuality in Melarky drafts, 197, 202; image of France in, 173-86, 173; influence of EH in Melarky drafts of, 202; Melarky drafts of, 196-210; murder of Jules Peterson in, 187-210; Parisian setting in, 189

This Quarter, 8

This Side of Paradise (FSF), 22

Three Stories and Ten Poems (EH), 103

To Have and Have Not (EH), 141, 338

Toklas, Alice B., 103, 112, 122

Tolstoi, Leo, 106, 107

Toronto Star, viii, 23, 37, 102, 117

Torrents of Spring, The (EH), xiii, 23, 264, 266; as response to Dark Laughter, 105; as satire of Anderson, 101-17, 101, 125; autobiographical details in, 110; influence of Turgenev, 107; Parisian references in, 109, 110; scheme to break publishing contract, 102, 111; suppressed preface of, 108

Torrents of Spring, The (Turgenev), 108, 110, 116

tourism of 1920s, 166

transatlantic review, ix, 7, 9

transition, 7

Turgenev, Ivan, xiii; influence on EH, 106-8

Twain, Mark, 165

Twysden, Duff, 86-88, 334

Ulysses (Joyce), 6, 109, 299

"Under the Ridge" (EH), 155

"Valentine for Sherwood Anderson" (Stein), 103

Van Vechten, Carl, 199

"Very Short Story, A" (EH), 79, 335

von Kurowsky, Agnes, 79, 334; letter to EH (1922), 335-36

Walsh, Ernest, 8

Waste Land, The (Eliot), 42, 45, 295, 305

Wilson, Edmund, viii, ix, 22, 103, 104, 114, 122, 141, 190, 191

"Wine of Wyoming" (EH), 42

Winesburg, Ohio (Anderson), 104, 105

Winner Take Nothing (EH), 42

World War I, 77, 82